THE PAPERS OF
BENJAMIN FRANKLIN

SPONSORED BY

The American Philosophical Society
and Yale University

Jonathan Shipley

THE PAPERS OF

Benjamin Franklin

VOLUME 18 *January 1 through December 31, 1771*

WILLIAM B. WILLCOX, *Editor*

Dorothy W. Bridgwater, Mary L. Hart, Claude A. Lopez, C. A. Myrans, Catherine M. Prelinger, and G. B. Warden, Assistant Editors

New Haven and London YALE UNIVERSITY PRESS, 1974

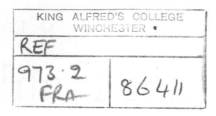
Library of Congress catalog card number: 59–12697
International standard book number: 0–300–01685–9

Designed by Alvin Eisenman and Walter Howe,
and printed by Cambridge University Press.

Published in Great Britain, Europe, and Africa by
Yale University Press, Ltd., London.
Distributed in Latin America by Kaiman & Polon,
Inc., New York City; in Australasia and Southeast
Asia by John Wiley & Sons Australasia Pty. Ltd.,
Sydney; in India by UBS Publishers' Distributors Pvt.,
Ltd., Dehli; in Japan by John Weatherhill, Inc., Tokyo.

Administrative Board

Thomas C. Cochran, University of Pennsylvania, *Chairman*
Whitfield J. Bell, Jr., American Philosophical Society Library
Carl Bridenbaugh, American Philosophical Society
Chester Kerr, Yale University Press
Edmund S. Morgan, Yale University
Walter M. Whitehill, Boston Athenaeum
William B. Willcox, Yale University, *Secretary*

Advisory Committee

Thomas Boylston Adams
Samuel F. Bemis
Charles Braibant
Prince Louis de Broglie
Lyman H. Butterfield
Julien Cain
I. Bernard Cohen
Gaylord Donnelley
Morris Duane
Sir Frank C. Francis

Andrew Heiskell
Wilmarth S. Lewis
David C. Mearns
Sir Owen Morshead
Howard H. Peckham
John E. Pomfret
Clifford K. Shipton
Robert E. Spiller
S. K. Stevens

Since the appearance of the previous volume the Advisory Committee has been reduced, to our deep regret, by the deaths of two members, Mr. Bromwell Ault and Mr. Bernhard Knollenberg. Mr. Ault was a devoted Yale alumnus who made the initial suggestion that led to the editing of the Franklin Papers, and was thus the godfather of the whole project; Dr. Knollenberg, after several other distinguished careers, became the elder statesman par excellence among scholars of the Revolution. Both will be greatly missed.

Contents

CONTENTS

CONTENTS

CONTENTS

List of Illustrations

Contributors to Volume 18

The ownership of each manuscript, or the location of the particular copy used by the editors of each rare contemporary pamphlet or similar printed work, is indicated where the document appears in the text. The sponsors and editors are deeply grateful to the following institutions and individuals for permission to print or otherwise use in the text of the present volume manuscripts or other materials which they own.

INSTITUTIONS

American Philosophical Society
British Museum
Harvard University Library
Haverford College Library
Historical Society of
    Pennsylvania
Huntington Library
Library of Congress
Lilly Library, University of
    Indiana
Maine Historical Society
Massachusetts Historical Society
National Society of the Daughters
    of the American Revolution

New-York Historical Society
Pennsylvania Hospital
University of Pennsylvania
    Library
Philadelphia Recorder of Deeds,
    Department of Records
Pierpont Morgan Library
Princeton University Library
Public Record Office
The Royal Society
University of Virginia
    Library
Yale University Library

INDIVIDUAL

Mrs. T. V. Phillips, Westtown,
    Pa.

Method of Textual Reproduction

An extended statement of the principles of selection, arrangement, form of presentation, and method of textual reproduction observed in this edition appears in the Introduction to the first volume, pp. xxiv–xlvii. What follows is a condensation and revision of part of it.

Printed Material:

Those of Franklin's writings that were printed under his direction presumably appeared as he wanted them to, and should therefore be reproduced with no changes except what modern typography requires. In some cases, however, printers carelessly or willfully altered his text without his consent; or the journeymen who set it had different notions from his—and from each other's—of capitalization, spelling, and punctuation. Such of his letters as survive only in nineteenth-century printings, furthermore, have often been vigorously edited by William Temple Franklin, Duane, or Sparks. In all these cases the original has suffered some degree of distortion, which the modern editor may guess at but, in the absence of the manuscript, cannot remedy. We therefore follow the printed texts as we find them, and note only obvious misreadings.

We observe the following rules in reproducing printed materials:

1. The place and date of composition of letters are set at the top, regardless of their location in the original printing.

2. Proper nouns, including personal names, which were often printed in italics, are set in roman except when the original was italicized for emphasis.

3. Prefaces and other long passages, though italicized in the original, are set in roman. Long italicized quotations are set in roman within quotation marks.

4. Words in full capitals are set in small capitals, with initial letters in full capitals if required by Franklin's normal usage.

5. All signatures are set in capitals and small capitals.

6. We silently correct obvious typographical errors, such as the omission of a single parenthesis or quotation mark.

7. We close a sentence by supplying, when needed, a period or question mark.

Manuscript Material:

a. *Letters* are presented in the following form:
   1. The place and date of composition are set at the top, regardless of their location in the original.
   2. The complimentary close is set continuously with the text.
   3. Addresses, endorsements, and docketing are so labelled and printed at the end of the letter.

b. *Spelling* of the original we retain. When it is so abnormal as to obscure the meaning, we supply the correct form in brackets or a footnote, as "yf [wife]."

c. *Capitalization* we retain as written, except that every sentence is made to begin with a capital. When we cannot decide whether a letter is a capital, we follow modern usage.

d. Words underlined once in the manuscript are printed in italics; words underlined twice or written in large letters or full capitals are printed in small capitals.

e. *Punctuation* has been retained as in the original, except:
   1. We close a sentence by supplying, when needed, a period or question mark. When it is unclear where the sentence ends, we retain the original punctuation or lack of it.
   2. Dashes used in place of commas, semicolons, colons, or periods are replaced by the appropriate marks; when a sentence ends with both a dash and a period, the dash is omitted.
   3. Commas scattered meaninglessly through a manuscript are eliminated.
   4. When a mark of punctuation is not clear or can be read as one of two marks, we follow modern usage.[1]
   5. Some documents, especially legal ones, have no punctuation; others have so little as to obscure the meaning. In such cases we silently supply the minimum needed for clarity.

[1] The typescripts from which these papers are printed have been made from photocopies of the manuscripts; marks of punctuation are sometimes blurred or lost in photography, and it has often been impossible to consult the original.

f. *Contractions and abbreviations* in general are retained. The ampersand is rendered as "and," except in the names of business firms, in the form "&c.," and in a few other cases. Letters represented by the thorn or tilde are printed. The tailed "p" is spelled out as per, pre, or pro. Symbols of weights, measures and monetary values follow modern usage, as: £34. Superscript letters are lowered.

g. *Omitted or illegible words or letters* are treated as follows:

1. If not more than four letters are missing, we supply them silently when we have no doubt what they should be.

2. If more than four letters are missing, we supply them conjecturally in brackets, with or without a question mark depending on our confidence in the conjecture.

3. Other omissions are shown as follows: [*illegible*], [*torn*], [*remainder missing*], or the like.

4. Missing or illegible digits are indicated by suspension points in brackets, the number of points corresponding to the estimated number of missing figures.

h. *Author's additions and corrections.*

1. Interlineations and brief marginal notes are incorporated in the text without comment, and longer notes with the notation [*in the margin*] unless they were clearly intended as footnotes, in which case they are normally printed with our notes but with a bracketed indication of the source.

2. Canceled words and phrases are in general omitted without notice; if significant, they are printed in footnotes.

3. When alternative words and phrases have been inserted in a manuscript but the original remains uncanceled, the alternatives are given in brackets, preceded by explanatory words in italics, as: "it is [*written above:* may be] true."

4. Variant readings of several versions are noted if important.

Abbreviations and Short Titles

Acts Privy Coun., Col.	W. L. Grant and James Munro, eds., *Acts of the Privy Council of England, Colonial Series, 1613–1783* (6 vols., London, 1908–12).
AD	Autograph document.[1]
ADS	Autograph document signed.
AL	Autograph letter.
ALS	Autograph letter signed.
Alvord and Carter, eds., *Trade and Politics*	Clarence W. Alvord and Clarence E. Carter, eds., *Trade and Politics 1767–1769* (Illinois State Historical Library *Collections*, XVI; Springfield, Ill., 1921).
Amer.	American.
APS	American Philosophical Society.
Autobiog.	Leonard W. Labaree, Ralph L. Ketcham, Helen C. Boatfield, and Helene H. Fineman, eds., *The Autobiography of Benjamin Franklin* (New Haven, 1964).
BF	Benjamin Franklin.
Bigelow, *Works*	John Bigelow, ed., *The Complete Works of Benjamin Franklin . . .* (10 vols., N.Y., 1887–88).
Board of Trade Jour.	*Journal of the Commissioners for Trade and Plantations . . . April 1704 to . . . May 1782* (14 vols., London, 1920–38).
Butterfield, ed., *John Adams Diary*	Lyman H. Butterfield *et al.*, eds., *Diary and Autobiography of John Adams* (4 vols., Cambridge, Mass., 1961).
Candler, ed., *Ga. Col. Recs.*	Allen D. Candler, ed., *The Colonial Records of the State of Georgia . . .* (26 vols., Atlanta, 1904–16).
Carter, ed., *Gage Correspondence*	Clarence E. Carter, ed., *The Correspondence of General Thomas Gage . . .* (2

1. For definitions of types of manuscripts, see above, 1, xliv–xlvii.

vols., New Haven and London, 1931–33).

Chron. — Chronicle.

Cobbett, *Parliamentary History* — William Cobbett and Thomas C. Hansard, eds., *The Parliamentary History of England from the Earliest Period to 1803* (36 vols., London, 1806–20).

Coll. — Collections.

Crane, *Letters to the Press* — Verner W. Crane, ed., *Benjamin Franklin's Letters to the Press, 1758–1775* (Chapel Hill, N.C., [1950]).

Cushing, ed., *Writings of Samuel Adams* — Harry Alonzo Cushing, ed., *The Writings of Samuel Adams . . .* (4 vols., New York, 1904–08).

DAB — Dictionary of American Biography.

DF — Deborah Franklin.

Dictionnaire de biographie — *Dictionnaire de biographie française . . .* (11 vols. to date, Paris, 1933–67).

DNB — Dictionary of National Biography.

DS — Document signed.

Duane, *Works* — William Duane, ed., *The Works of Dr. Benjamin Franklin . . .* (6 vols., Philadelphia, 1808–18). Title varies in the several volumes.

Exper. and Obser. — *Experiments and Observations on Electricity, made at Philadelphia in America, by Mr. Benjamin Franklin . . .* (London, 1751). Revised and enlarged editions were published in 1754, 1760, 1769, and 1774 with slightly varying titles. In each case the edition cited will be indicated, e.g., *Exper. and Obser.* (1751).

Gaz. — Gazette.

Geneal. — Genealogical.

Gent. Mag. — *The Gentleman's Magazine, and Historical Chronicle.*

Gipson, *British Empire* — Lawrence H. Gipson, *The British Empire before the American Revolution* (15 vols., New York, 1939–70; I–III, revised ed., N.Y., 1958–60).

Hinshaw, *Amer. Quaker Genealogy*	William W. Hinshaw, *Encyclopedia of American Quaker Genealogy* (6 vols., Ann Arbor, Mich., 1936–50).
Hist.	Historical.
Hutchinson, *History*	Thomas Hutchinson, *The History of the Colony and Province of Massachusetts-Bay...* (Lawrence S. Mayo, ed.; 3 vols., Cambridge, Mass., 1936).
Jour.	*Journal.* The citation "Jour." is of Franklin's MS account book described above, XI, 518–20.
Kammen, *Rope of Sand*	Michael G. Kammen, *A Rope of Sand: the Colonial Agents, British Politics, and the American Revolution* (Ithaca, N.Y., [1968]).
Ledger	The Franklin MS described above, XI, 518–20.
Lewis, *Indiana Co.*	George E. Lewis, *The Indiana Company, 1763–1798: a Study in Eighteenth Century Frontier Land Speculation and Business Venture* (Glendale, Cal., 1941).
LS	Letter signed.
Mag.	*Magazine.*
Mass. Acts and Resolves	Abner C. Goodell *et al.*, eds., *The Acts and Resolves, Public and Private, of the Province of Massachusetts Bay* (21 vols., Boston, 1869–1922).
Mass. Arch.	Massachusetts Archives, State House, Boston.
Mass. House Jour.	*A Journal of the Honourable House of Representatives of His Majesty's Province of the Massachusetts Bay...* (Boston, 1715[–85]). The title varies, and each session is designated by date. The Massachusetts Historical Society is republishing the volumes (Boston, 1919–) and has reached 1765; for later years we cite by session and date the original edition, which is most readily available in microprint

	in Clifford K. Shipton, ed., *Early American Imprints, 1639–1800*.
MS, MSS	Manuscript, manuscripts.
Namier and Brooke, *House of Commons*	Sir Lewis Namier and John Brooke, *The History of Parliament. The House of Commons 1754–1790* (3 vols., London and N.Y., 1964).
N.J. Arch.	William A. Whitehead *et al.*, eds., *Archives of the State of New Jersey* (2 series, Newark and elsewhere, 1880–). Editors, subtitles, and places of publication vary.
Nolan, *Franklin in Scotland and Ireland*	J. Bennett Nolan, *Benjamin Franklin in Scotland and Ireland, 1759 and 1771* (Philadelphia and London, 1938).
N.Y. Col. Docs.	E. B. O'Callaghan, ed., *Documents relative to the Colonial History of the State of New York* (15 vols., Albany, 1853–87).
Pa. Arch.	Samuel Hazard *et al.*, eds., *Pennsylvania Archives* (9 series, Philadelphia and Harrisburg, 1852–1935).
Pa. Col. Recs.	*Minutes of the Provincial Council of Pennsylvania*... (16 vols., Harrisburg, 1851–53). Volumes I–III are reprints published in Philadelphia, 1852. Title changes with Volume XI to *Supreme Executive Council*.
Phil. Trans.	The Royal Society, *Philosophical Transactions*.
PMHB	*Pennsylvania Magazine of History and Biography*.
Priestley, *History*	Joseph Priestley, *The History and Present State of Electricity, with Original Experiments*...(3rd ed.; 2 vols., London, 1775).
Proc.	*Proceedings*.
Pub.	*Publications*.
Rev.	*Review*.
Sabine, *Loyalists*	Lorenzo Sabine, *Biographical Sketches of Loyalists of the American Revolution*... (2 vols., Boston, 1864).

Schofield, *Scientific Autobiography* — Robert E. Schofield, ed., *A Scientific Autobiography of Joseph Priestley...* (Cambridge, Mass., and London, [1966]).

Sibley's Harvard Graduates — John L. Sibley, *Biographical Sketches of Graduates of Harvard University* (Cambridge, Mass., 1873–). Continued from Volume IV by Clifford K. Shipton.

Smyth, *Writings* — Albert H. Smyth, ed., *The Writings of Benjamin Franklin...* (10 vols., N.Y., 1905–07).

Soc. — Society.

Sparks, *Works* — Jared Sparks, ed., *The Works of Benjamin Franklin...* (10 vols., Boston, 1836–40).

Trans. — *Transactions.*

Van Doren, *Franklin* — Carl Van Doren, *Benjamin Franklin* (N.Y., 1938).

Van Doren, *Franklin—Mecom* — Carl Van Doren, ed., *The Letters of Benjamin Franklin & Jane Mecom* (American Philosophical Society *Memoirs*, XXVII, Princeton, 1950).

Votes, N.J. — *Votes and Proceedings of the General Assembly of the Province of New-Jersey...* (New York, Woodbridge, etc., 1711–). A separate volume was published for each session and is so designated, e.g., *Votes, N.J.* (Oct.–Dec., 1771).

W&MQ — *William and Mary Quarterly*, third series.

WF — William Franklin.

Wroth and Zobel, *John Adams Legal Papers* — L. Kinvin Wroth and Hiller B. Zobel, eds., *Legal Papers of John Adams* (3 vols., Cambridge, Mass., 1965).

WTF, *Memoirs* — William Temple Franklin, ed., *Memoirs of the Life and Writings of Benjamin Franklin, LL.D., F.R.S., &c....* (3 vols., 4to, London, 1817–18).

Introduction

The year 1771 appears at first sight to have been a lull between storms. The controversy over the Townshend Acts had faded away after their partial repeal, and the nonimportation agreements were only a memory. Parliament took no action that the colonists considered a grievance; instead the House of Commons blundered into a domestic confrontation with that *imperium in imperio,* the City of London.[1] The whole American question was seemingly in abeyance. But new winds and even whirlwinds were in the offing, and signs of them were there for the reading. Neither side had retreated from its principles, and on some issues the controversy was sharpening.

One such issue, in which Franklin was involved at the beginning of the year, was the status of the colonial agents. In January he presented his credentials from the Massachusetts House of Representatives to Hillsborough, who angrily denied that his appointment was valid. Franklin, for all his professed surprise at this denial, must have recognized it as part of the Secretary's ongoing effort to establish—or, from the administration's viewpoint, reestablish—the principle that an agent was chosen by an act of the governor and both houses of the legislature.[2] The point at issue was significant: if Hillsborough's view prevailed, the governor and council would regain their former position as a counterweight to the popularly elected house; if the choice rested entirely with the latter, the agent might be, and in the case of Massachusetts almost surely would be, the spokesman of radicalism. Hillsborough was determined to prevent this by restoring the traditional balanced representation of the various interests in each colony. Having disposed, as he thought, of Franklin in Massachusetts, he went on to attack him in New Jersey, where again the lower house alone had long chosen the agent. Here the Minister won a technical victory when Franklin, thanks to his son's persuasive powers as

1. See the second paragraph of BF to Galloway below, April 20.
2. See the headnote on BF's interview with Hillsborough below, Jan. 16.

governor, was reappointed by a formal legislative act.[3] This assertion of earlier constitutional practice was a paper triumph, which doubtless gratified the bureaucratic love of tidiness.

New Jersey was a relative backwater; Massachusetts was the crucible of new ideas, to which Franklin was now fully exposed. As the year wore on, his relationship with the leaders in Boston, regardless of Whitehall's disapproval, stimulated his own thinking in order to keep up with theirs. They distrusted him, he knew, as a placeman and the father of a placeman and, perhaps partly in consequence, turned a deaf ear to his appeal for faith in the King. But they were now going beyond such negativism to develop positive claims that struck at the essence of the crown's prerogative powers as well as Parliamentary authority. The claims, although they often arose from what seemed to conservatives and even moderates to be trifling causes, had implications that were far from trifling. A case in point was the provincial taxes levied on the customs commissioners' salaries: when in July Governor Hutchinson, acting on instructions, vetoed the bills that provided for such taxation, the House replied by denying not only the right of Parliament to create the commission in the first place, but also the right of the crown to order a veto.[4] The prerogative as exercised through instructions was simultaneously under challenge in other matters, such as the Governor's transferring the General Court to Cambridge and refusing, again on orders from London, to accept a salary from it. The leadership of the House was setting its face not only against the legislative authority of Parliament but also against the executive authority of the crown.

Franklin had long been moving toward an open denial of the first, but denying the second was another matter. Although he clearly sympathized with complaints against the misuse of the prerogative, denying it on principle struck at his whole newborn concept of the empire as a league of coequal states with a common sovereign.[5] Remove that sovereignty, and what was left of the league? He did not face the question in those terms, but it was

3. See the headnote on the formal appointment of BF by the New Jersey legislature below, Dec. 11–20.
4. See the headnote on the Committee of the Mass. House to BF below, July 13.
5. See above, XVII, 160–1.

there; and it may have accounted for some of the ambiguity in his letters to his Boston friends. On the one hand he shared their resentment of official policy, sometimes to the point of encouraging their phobic sense of a conspiracy against them; on the other hand he continued to urge a blend of firmness and patience. His appetite for a crisis was no greater than ever, yet he embraced the grievances that might at any moment bring on a crisis—which is merely to say that he was in the dilemma of any perceptive moderate when battle lines are being drawn.

The other aspects of his public life during the year were much less significant than his relations with Massachusetts. Georgia, New Jersey, and Pennsylvania presented him with little more than routine problems, and the affairs of the Walpole Company continued in their usual inactive state as government departments mused in silence on the requested land grant. Franklin for once had ample leisure. He employed it in buying books, corresponding on scientific subjects, and seeing and visiting friends; during the summer he was twice a house guest at Bishop Shipley's country estate near Winchester, and on the second occasion he began writing what was to be his most famous work, the *Autobiography*.

He also took time for more extensive traveling than he had done for years. In May he and three friends toured the industrial north, inspected its marvels of machinery, and for contrast looked over the palaces of Wentworth Woodhouse and Chatsworth.[6] At the end of August he left, with Richard Jackson, for his first introduction to Ireland, where to his delight he was received in Parliament and, to anything but his delight, was entertained by Lord Hillsborough at his country seat.[7] Franklin then crossed to Scotland, a return visit after twelve years; there he joined forces with a new friend, Henry Marchant of Rhode Island, and renewed many old acquaintances. His tour closed with the Baches at Preston, Lancashire, where he met his son-in-law for the first time and returned with him to London in late November. The year ended quietly, untroubled by the approaching storms.

6. See the résumé of Jonathan Williams' Journal below, May 28.

7. See below, BF to Cushing, Jan. 13, and to WF, Jan. 30, 1772. He saw more than high society: the condition of the Irish peasantry shocked him, as did that of the Scottish soon afterward; see BF to Babcock below, Jan. 13, 1772.

Chronology of 1771

January 16: BF's stormy interview with Lord Hillsborough virtually severs diplomatic relations between them.

February 8: The House of Commons begins action against printers who publish its debates.

February 13: In a final Parliamentary debate the Falkland Islands crisis is laid to rest.

March 14: Lieutenant Governor Thomas Hutchinson succeeds Sir Francis Bernard as governor of Massachusetts.

March 25–27: The House of Commons acts to commit an alderman and the Lord Mayor of London to the Tower.

April 26: Polly Hewson's first child is born, William, Jr., BF's godson.

May 18–June 1?: BF, John Canton, Dr. Ingenhousz, and Jonathan Williams, Jr., are on a tour of northern England. They explore the Duke of Bridgewater's canal (May 21), call on Dr. Priestley at Leeds (May 23), and visit Boulton's Soho ironworks (May 28).

June 24?: BF ends his first visit to Bishop Shipley at Twyford.

July 30?–August 13: BF visits Twyford the second time, and begins work on his *Autobiography*.

August 19: Henry Marchant arrives from America, bringing letters to BF from John Winthrop and Speaker Cushing.

August 23: BF umpires the dispute between William Hewson and Dr. Hunter.

August 25: BF and Richard Jackson leave London for their Irish tour.

September 5–October 14: The two are in Dublin, where they attend the opening of the Irish Parliament (October 8) and are received by the House of Commons (October 10).

October 16–20: They visit the American Secretary at Hillsborough House.

October 24?: BF leaves for Scotland.

October 26–November 6: BF in Edinburgh; lodges with David Hume.

November 6–12: BF and Henry Marchant visit Lord Kames at Blair-Drummond.

November 12–15: BF and Marchant in Glasgow.

November 15–21: They visit the Carron ironworks (November 15–17), and then return to Edinburgh.

November 23–25: BF visits the Baches in Preston, and meets his son-in-law for the first time.

November 30?: BF and Richard Bache return to London.

December 11–20: BF appointed agent of the province of New Jersey, not of the Assembly alone.

THE PAPERS OF
BENJAMIN FRANKLIN

VOLUME 18

January 1 through December 31, 1771

From Samuel Cooper

ALS (draft): British Museum

Dear Sir,   Boston, 1 Jany.—71

In my last of Novr [15] I mention'd the Uses I had made of the Sentiments you were pleas'd to communicate to me,[1] and the Effect they had upon the leading Men of our House of Commons. I did this with much Caution as that no Disadvantage can acrue to you from any Quarter. The same Caution I shall ever use respecting my Friends on your Side the Water who are so good as to write to me with Freedom in these troublesom Times. I the rather mention this because it has been industriously reported here that you and G[overnor] Pownall have been question'd on your Letters to America.

You will hear before this reaches you of the Acquittal of Capt. Preston, and the soldiers concern'd in the Action of 5 March instead of meeting with any unfair or harsh Treatment had ev'ry Advantage that could possibly be given them in a Course of Justice—in the Disposition of Judges, in the Appointment of the Jury, in the Zeal and Ability of Lawyers in the Examination of Witnesses, and in the Length of the Trials, unexampled I believe both in Britain and the Colonies, in a capital Case, by which the accused had the fairest opportunity several days after the Evidence for the Crown had been given in, of producing and arranging their own. These Trials must, one would think, wipe off the Imputation of our being so violent and blood thirsty a People as not to permit Law and Justice to take place on the side of unpopular men;[2] and I hope our Friends will make this kind Improvement of them; tho they have not, as far as my Observation reaches, at all alter'd the Opinion of the People in General, of that tragical Scene.

There seems now to be a Pause in Politics. The agreement of the Merchants is broken.[3] Administration has a fair Opportunity of adopting the mildest and most prudent Measures respecting the

1. In BF to Cooper above, XVII, 162–4.
2. For a modern account of the trials see Hiller B. Zobel, *The Boston Massacre* (New York, [1970]), chaps. 18 and 19.
3. The Boston merchants had voted unanimously on Oct. 11, 1770, to abandon nonimportation except as applied to tea. See Charles M. Andrews, *The Boston Merchants and the Non-Importation Movement* (New York, [1968]), pp. 96–7.

Colonies without the Appearance of being threatned or drove; The Circumstances of Europe lead to such measures,[4] and are sufficient to shew the Propriety of securing the Affections as well as the Submission of the Colonies. I doubt not of your Ability and Readiness to improve these, and many more Arguments than I can pretend to hint at, in your Negotiations for us; and should Government be so temperate and just as to place us on the old Ground on which we stood before the Stamp Act, there is no Danger of our rising in our Demands. I send this by the only Son of our Friend Mr. Bowdoin a young Gentleman of a sweet Disposition, and whose good Qualities have rais'd the most agreable Hopes in his Friends.[5] He leaves the College, and takes this Voyage chiefly on Account of his Health, and is follow'd with the warmest good Wishes of all who are acquainted with him. I am Sir, with the greatest Esteem and most faithful Attachment Your obedient Humble Servant   S. COOPER

To Doctor Franklin

Copy.

Endorsed: To Dr Franklin. 1. Jany.—71.

To Deborah Franklin   ALS: American Philosophical Society

My dear Child,   London, Jan. 2. 1771
    This is just to acknowledge the Receipt of your kind Letter of Nov. 25. which came to hand last Night, per Capt. Sparks. I had before received those per Capt. Falconer,[6] by whom I shall write fully to you and all my Friends that correspond with me. I am, Thanks to God, as well as ever. My Love to our Children and the Kingbird, as you call him.[7] In haste, I am, Your affectionate Husband   B FRANKLIN

Addressed (torn in half vertically): Franklin / Philadelphia

4. A reference to the threat, by this time virtually ended, of an Anglo-Spanish war over the Falkland Islands.
    5. See James Bowdoin to BF below, Jan. 2.
    6. The letter of Nov. 25 has not been found. Falconer had brought four notes of introduction and a letter from DF: above, XVII, 244–6, 250–5.
    7. Their grandson, Benjamin Franklin Bache, who was approaching one and a half.

4

From James Bowdoin[8]   ALS: Massachusetts Historical Society

Dear Sir   Boston January 2 1771.

I take this opportunity by my Son to express my own Pleasure, and the general Satisfaction at your appointment as Agent for the House of Representatives. The Council have recommended to their Agent Mr. Bollan to consult and cooperate with you for the best interest of the Province: which as it has distinguished itself in the great cause of American Liberty is now become the Principal Object of ministerial resentment. But it is hoped your Endeavours in concurrence with the other friends of America will dissipate the Cloud that seems ready to discharge upon it. My Son's health being precarious I have been lately advised to let him try the Effect of a Voyage, which it is apprehended may be beneficial to him. This occasions his going to England sooner than I intended. Permit me to recommend him to your Friendship, as I also do his Uncle Mr. Stewart, who does me the favor to take him under his Care.[9] Your Advice to him, particularly with regard to his Conduct, and the means of improvement I shall esteem a singular favor. I am with the greatest regard Dear Sir Your most Obedient and very humble Servant   JAMES BOWDOIN.

[*In the margin:*] My Son will deliver you a Pamphlet containing Proceedings of the Council,[1] which you already have had in manuscript.

Dr. Benjn. Franklin

8. For a biographical note on BF's old acquaintance see above, IV, 69 n.

9. James Bowdoin, Jr. (1752–1811), his father's only son, was eighteen at the time; his health remained precarious throughout his life. He studied at Oxford, traveled in Europe, and returned home after the outbreak of the Revolution. *DAB*. His maternal uncle, Duncan Stewart (d. 1793), was customs collector at New London; he subsequently became a Loyalist and moved to England. Sabine, *Loyalists*, II, 331.

1. The furor in the Council over Andrew Oliver, for which see above, XVII, 283 n.

From John Hawkesworth[2]   ALS: American Philosophical Society

My dear Sir   Bromley Kent 5th Jan 1771

The Bearer, Mr. Ackland, is a Candidate for the Afternoon Preacher-ship at the Foundling Hospital:[3] and I earnestly recommend him to your Assistance; in this I am not only countenanced by your Friendship, but prompted by Duty. Mr. Ackland is a worthy and ingenious Man, and a most excellent Preacher, and to serve him in his profession is to promote rational Christianity, favour Merit, and do credit to the Institution to which, if this Application succeeds, he will belong. I know not if you are a Governor, but I am sure you know many who are, and I am sure that with all who know you, the same Qualities for which I love and honour you, give you a powerfull Interest.

If I thought this Letter required an apology I would not have written it. I shall only add that any favour conferred on Mr. Ackland will be considered as an Obligation upon Dear Sir Your ever faithfull affectionate   JNO HAWKESWORTH

P.S. If you should give Mr. Ackland a Letter for Dr. Moreton, do not mention me, because I was examined to prove the Sanity of his wife's Mother, Mrs. Pratt, whose will it was much his Interest to set aside.[4] I hope the End of the Month will bring us together.

Dr Franklyn

Addressed: To / Benja. Franklin Esqr / at Mrs Stevenson's Craven Street / Charing Cross

Endorsed: Dr Hawkesworth

2. BF's friend, the essayist, editor, and playwright; see above, IX, 265 n, and subsequent volumes.

3. He was probably the Rev. Thomas Ackland (1743–1808), who had been ordained only three years before. John A. Venn, *Alumni Cantabrigienses*... (10 vols., Cambridge, 1922–54), pt. 2, I, 5. For the Hospital for the Maintenance and Education of Exposed and Deserted Young Children, known as the Foundling Hospital, see above, VIII, 286 n.

4. For Dr. Morton, the physician at the Foundling Hospital, see above, X, 71 n. He had married a widow, Lady Savile; she was the daughter of Honoretta Pratt, the wife of John Pratt of Dublin. Mrs. Pratt had died in September, 1769. [Thomas Wotton,] *The Baronetage of England*...(Edward Kimber and Richard Johnson, eds; 3 vols., London, 1771), I, 71; *London Chron.*, Sept. 26–28, 1769. The *DNB*, under Morton, mistakes the date of his marriage.

6

From John Foxcroft[5]

ALS: American Philosophical Society

My Dear Friend   Philadelphia Janry: 14th 1771

Yours of Novr. 7th. I have just receiv'd for which you have my sincere thanks. This will be Deliver'd to you by my Brother whom I beg you will take most cordially by the hand as I do assure you that you will find on being well acquainted with him that he'll merit every Act of Friendship which you will please to conferr upon him, this sudden Voyage is owing to Letters receiv'd by this last packet concerning my Brothers affairs, not one half penny of the Debts due to him having been collected since I left London.[6] His stay will be but for two or three Months no body knows of his Voyage, as there are so many hungary harpies always ready I thought it would be rather dangerous as some of them might have seized on his place during his absence. If you should determine on coming over next Summer he would be extremely happy in taking his passage in the same Ship and I believe he will be able to afford you some small amusement at that Noble game of Chess, which you so deservedly prefer before all others.

I notice what you say about the payment made to Mr. Trevor and will give you Credit accordingly as well as for the £500 which I had off you before I left London.[7] By the first Ship that Sails from this Port for London I will send you the two Barrells of Flour as you desire the best that can be procured; I Am quite happy in what you write me that there seems a disposition to be favourable to this Country for I think nay am sure that nothing can be done on your side of the Water to distress this growing Country but what will fall doubley on themselves at last. Trade is again begining to hold up her head and if not check'd by some Act of the present Parliament I verily believe will return into it's old Channel and flourish as it did before these late unhappy times, an

5. He and his wife, the former Judith Osgood, had sailed for America almost immediately after their wedding in early August, 1770; they had arrived in Philadelphia in late October. *Pa. Gaz.*, Nov. 1, 1770.

6. Thomas Foxcroft had been postmaster of Philadelphia since 1766; see above, XII, 77 n. The debts were presumably due him from the Post Office.

7. For Robert Trevor, the receiver general of the Post Office, see above, X, 222 n. BF's loan to Foxcroft in the previous August is recorded in his Jour., p. 25.

Act at this time to Encourage and Extend the trade of this Country would be an Act of Grace indeed and worthy of the British Senate, as it would banish even the least Appearance of discontent from this happy Climate, and bury every disagreable thing that's past in oblivion. And why should it not take place, for surely no sensible Man will attempt to deny that what is of Advantage to America, must be certain gain to the Mother Country for in spight of every resolution to the Contrary it will settle there at last.

I thank you for your very Friendly Answer to Mr. Todd on his communicating what he had heard concerning me, you did not tell him too much, you might safely have answer'd for me, I dare my Accusers (tho' I imagine they will never appear). Mr. Todd heard from me more than any other Man besides yourself whiles't in England let my private opinion have been what it would I never committed it to paper, having too many recent Instances before me of what others had suffer'd by A misplaced confidence;[8] I think I know the Quarter from whence the Information came, you may Recollect that I told you of a conversation which happen'd at Messrs. Batson & Co. Bankers between me and one Mr. Blackburn who was formerly Anthony Bacons Clerk but now a New York Merchant[9] who receiv'd the first Account of the New Yorkers breaking through the agreement; the conversation happen'd in consequence of that, when I thought He made rather too free with your Name saying that He had got ample proofs of your being the grand Incendery between the two Countrys and that if it had not been for what you and some others had wrote over no disturbances whatever had happen'd, that their Names were all come over and that probably some of them who held places under

8. He had also suffered himself, by committing to paper what he later tried to disown: above, XVI, 36–7. For Anthony Todd, secretary of the Post Office, see above, X, 217 n.

9. The scene of the conversation was the office of Batson, Stephenson & Hoggart in Lombard St.; for the firm see *Kent's Directory*... (London, 1770), p. 15; F. G. Hilton Price, *A Handbook of London Bankers*... (London, 1876), p. 117. Foxcroft's interlocutor was undoubtedly the John Blackburn mentioned above, XVI, 42 n; he was not a New Yorker but a merchant trading with New York. His former employer had been for a time a Maryland storekeeper, and had then become a London merchant and M.P.; see Lewis B. Namier, "Anthony Bacon, M.P., an Eighteenth-Century Merchant," *Jour. of Economic and Business History*, II (1929–30), 20–70.

the Government would be haul'd over the Coals.[1] I thought He look'd at me as if he would have the Company believe that I was one of the Number, I told Him that I dared to say whatever Letters you had wrote, you would not disown when they made their appearance, and that I imagined it was no more than what every American then in England had done, this Spoke with some warmth Occasion'd Mr. Batson the Banker to say I hope you don't look upon yourself as an American. I told him yes I did and Gloried in the Name, for that I look'd upon a Good Englishman and a good American to be synonimous terms it being impossible to be one without being the other also; here ended the discourse which I think not impossible may have given rise to the other. Mrs. Foxcroft joins me in Sincere Compliments to yourself and Friends I am as ever your Friend and obliged humble Servant

JOHN FOXCROFT

Franklin's Account of His Audience with Hillsborough

AD:[2] American Philosophical Society

Almost exactly three years earlier, on January 20, 1768, Lord Hillsborough had become Secretary of State for the American Colonies. Franklin's initial attitude toward the new office and the man who filled it had been favorable, but disillusionment had soon set in.[3] Hillsborough had ordered troops to Boston, had opposed total repeal of the Townshend Acts, and until his volte-face at the end of 1769 had blocked the ambitions of the Walpole Company.[4] Although his personal relations

1. New York abandoned nonimportation on July 9, 1770. The news was published in the *London Chron.* on Aug. 25–28, and Blackburn, even though he was the first to hear it, could not have heard long before that. Hence mid-August is the earliest possible date for this conversation, and it had no bearing on BF's appeal to Lord Le Despencer on July 26 (above, XVII, 199–201) against being "haul'd over the Coals" by losing his position in the Post Office.

2. In his letter to Cooper below, Feb. 5, BF enclosed a copy in another hand, which is now in the British Museum; it has only two variations of consequence, and they are noted below.

3. See above, XV, 17–19, 189.

4. For the volte-face see above, XVII, 8; Peter Marshall, "Lord Hillsborough, Samuel Wharton, and the Ohio Grant, 1769–1775," *English Hist. Rev.*, LXXX (1965), 717–39; Gipson, *British Empire*, XI, 464–76.

with Franklin remained at least polite until the interview described below, the two men were poles apart. When the American called to present his credentials as agent of the Massachusetts House, politeness disappeared.

Franklin's account of the scene between them does not clarify the Secretary's position. Hillsborough had been concerned ever since coming to office with regularizing colonial administration, and one of the outstanding irregularities was the agencies. The traditional view of them in Whitehall was clear enough. Although a branch of the legislature, such as the Massachusetts House, might appoint an agent to act for it in a specific matter within its bailiwick, the general rule until recently had been, despite some exceptions, that an agent who acted for the colony at large was appointed by both houses and the governor.[5] This rule had been largely disregarded since 1765, and Hillsborough was attempting to revive it. Dennys DeBerdt, Franklin's predecessor for Massachusetts, had had his status questioned: he had been chosen to represent the House in working for repeal of the Stamp Act, Hillsborough had suggested, and had no standing once that objective had been achieved.[6] Although DeBerdt had nevertheless been tolerated, Franklin might have guessed that whoever succeeded him on the same basis would not be welcomed with open arms at the American Department.

Massachusetts was rapidly becoming a thorn in the side of administration, and so was Franklin. His letters to America in 1770, favoring nonimportation, had recently appeared in England;[7] and their thinly veiled references to the incompetence of the ministry could scarcely

5. Within a fortnight of taking office Hillsborough had attempted to have the rule enforced in Massachusetts; see *Board of Trade Jour.*, 1768–75, p. 10; *Acts Privy Coun., Col.*, v, 264. Whitehall considered the regular agent to be an officer of the colony, who as such was an appointee of the governor and both houses, but occasionally countenanced in practice the *ad hoc* agent of one legislative branch. Our conclusions in this murky area are based on the following sources: Hutchinson's letters in Mass. Arch., XXVII, 52–5, 93–4; and his *History*, II, 139–40; III, 176 n, 229; George Chalmers, ed., *Opinions of Eminent Lawyers*... (2 vols., London, 1814), I, 262; 6 Mass. Hist. Soc. *Coll.*, IX (1897), 253–5, 266–7, 274–5, 316–17; Conn. Hist. Soc. *Coll.*, XVI (1916), 516–17. See also A. Berriedale Keith, *Constitutional History of the First British Empire* (Oxford, 1930), pp. 284–6; Jack M. Sosin, *Agents and Merchants: British Colonial Policy and the Origins of the American Revolution, 1763–1775* (Lincoln, Neb., 1965), pp. 144–6; Mass. Arch., XXII, 585-7; Kammen, *Rope of Sand*, pp. 67, 233-5.
6. See above, XV, 198 n, and Mass. House to BF below, June 29, n. 7.
7. BF to Cooper below, Feb. 5; Hutchinson, *History*, III, 227–9.

have endeared their author to the minister chiefly concerned. Hillsborough also, whatever he might say, was no friend to the Walpole Company, of which Franklin was a leading promoter; the Earl's opposition to its schemes was what forced him from office in 1772. He probably did not welcome any development that increased Franklin's influence, and least of all one that gave the American a claim to be what he said he was, "an Agent for the *People*" of the most explosive British colony.[8]

Franklin's account of the interview leaves much unexplained, not only about Hillsborough's conduct but also about his own. Why did he take the unusual step of presenting his credentials to the Secretary of State, rather than to the secretary of the Board of Trade? Had he really convinced himself that those credentials were valid enough to secure his official acceptance as agent? If so, he showed much less awareness of the governmental position than he had on other occasions. If not, he chose the one method that virtually ensured a confrontation, and so precluded a working relationship based on the kind of unofficial recognition that DeBerdt had had. Neither Franklin nor his constituents in Massachusetts stood to gain, it would seem, from a complete breach; yet he took the initiative in seeking an interview that achieved precisely that. Hillsborough refused to see him again, except for one extraordinary outburst of hospitality in Ireland.[9] A principal channel of communication with the government was consequently closed, and remained so for a year and a half.

All we know about the course of the interview is what Franklin tells us. Hillsborough, he says, received him graciously and even cordially. At the mention of Massachusetts, however, the Earl's well known courtly manners suddenly evaporated; he turned waspish and showed himself to be a mixture of ignorance, arrogance, and insecurity. The agent's mild attempts to pacify stopped as his own anger mounted; on leaving he said in effect that the Secretary himself was the barrier to any reconciliation with the colonies. This is the dialogue as Franklin recorded it. He may well have been accurate, or he may not have been. He had a constituency in Massachusetts, it is worth remembering, that had been divided about selecting him because his loyalty to the American cause was suspect; and his account of the interview was intended for that constituency. His situation may have influenced him, consciously or unconsciously, to retouch the picture he was drawing, in

8. As BF soon realized, the nominations of Lee and himself "have not been at all agreeable to his Lordship." To Cushing below, Feb. 5.

9. See Kammen, *op. cit.*, pp. 256–8, and for the visit to Hillsborough in Ireland BF to WF below, Jan. 30, 1772.

order to portray himself as the champion of colonial rights and the Minister as their inveterate enemy.

Wednesday, Jan. 16. '71

At the earnest Instance and Request of Mr. Strahan[1] I went this Morning to wait on Lord Hillsborough. The Porter at first deny'd his Lordship, on which I left my Name, and drove off. But before the Coach got out of the Square, the Coachman heard a Call, turn'd, and went back to the Door, when the Porter came and said, His Lordship will see you, Sir. I was shown into the Levee Room, where I found Governor Barnard, who I understand attends there constantly. Several other Gentlemen were there attending, with whom I sat down a few Minutes. When Secretary Pownall came out to us, and said his Lordship desired I would come in.[2]

I was pleas'd with this ready Admission, and Preference, (having sometimes waited 3 or 4 Hours for my Turn) and being pleas'd, I could more easily put on the open chearful Countenance that my Friends[3] advis'd me to wear. His Lordship came towards me, and said "I was dressing in order to go to Court; but hearing that you were at the Door, who are a Man of Business, I determin'd to see you immediately." I thank'd his Lordship and said that my Business at present was not much, it was only to pay my Respects to his Lordship and to acquaint him with my Appointment by the House of Representatives of the Province of Massachusetts Bay, to be their Agent here, in which Station if I could be of any Service—I was going on to say, to the Publick I should be very happy; but his Lordship whose Countenance chang'd at my naming that Province cut me short, by saying, with something between a Smile and a Sneer,

L H.　　I must set you right there, Mr. Franklin, you are not Agent.

B F.　　Why; my Lord?

1. The phrase appears to be lightly deleted, and the copy omits it.
2. Gov. Bernard was thought to be behind much of the Secretary's American policy; see Cooper to BF below, July 10. John Pownall, who was both secretary of the Board of Trade and Undersecretary of the American Department, unquestionably had influence over Hillsborough and even more over his successor, Lord Dartmouth; see Franklin B. Wickwire, *British Subministers and Colonial America, 1763–1783* (Princeton, 1966), pp. 73–6.
3. BF originally wrote "Mr. Strahan."

L.H.　You are not appointed.

B.F　I do not understand your Lordship. I have the Appointment in my Pocket.

L.H.　You are mistaken. I have later and better Advices. I have a Letter from Governor Hutchinson. He would not give his Assent to the Bill.

B.F.　There was no Bill, my Lord; it is a Vote of the House.

L.H.　There was a Bill presented to the Governor, for the Purpose of appointing you, and another, one Dr. Lee, I think he is call'd,[4] to which the Governor refus'd his Assent.

B.F.　I cannot understand this, my Lord. I think There must be some Mistake in it. Is your Lordship quite sure that you have such a Letter?

L H.　I will convince you of it directly. *Rings the Bell.* Mr. Pownall will come in and satisfy you.

B.F.　It is not necessary that I should now detain your Lordship from Dressing. You are going to Court. I will wait on your Lordship another time.

L.H.　No, stay, He will come in immediately. *To the Servant.* Tell Mr. Pownall I want him. *Mr. Pownall comes in.*

L.H.　Have not you at hand Govr. Hutchinson's Letter mentioning his Refusing his Assent to the Bill for appointing Dr. Franklin Agent?

SEC. P.　My Lord?

L H.　Is there not such a Letter?

SEC. P.　No, my Lord. There is a Letter relating to some Bill for payment of Salary to Mr. DeBerdt and I think to some other Agent, to which the Governor had refus'd his Assent.[5]

L H.　And is there nothing in that Letter to the purpose I mention?

SEC. P.　No, my Lord.

4. Arthur Lee, the physician in process of becoming a lawyer, had been named BF's alternate as agent of the House; see above, XVII, 257–8.

5. In 1770 Hutchinson had vetoed a bill for DeBerdt's and Bollan's salary on the ground that the appointment of separate agents, although current practice in several other colonies, was contrary to the imperial constitution; he had then written home for instructions on this point. DeBerdt's salary had long been a bone of contention; see the Mass. House to BF below, June 29, n. 7.

13

B F.   I thought it could not well be, my Lord, as my Letters are by the last Ships and mention no such Thing. Here is an authentic Copy of the Vote of the House appointing me, in which there is no Mention of any Act intended. Will your Lordship please to look at it? (*With some seeming Unwillingness he takes it, but does not look into it*).

L H.   An Information of this kind is not properly brought to me as Secretary of State. The Board of Trade is the proper Place.[6]

B.F.   I will leave the Paper then with Mr. Pownall, to be—

L.H.   (*Hastily*) To what End would you leave it with him?

B F.   To be entred on the Minutes of that Board, as usual.

L.H.   (*Angrily*) It shall not be entred there. No such Paper shall be entred there while I have any thing to do with the Business of that Board. The House of Representatives has no Right to appoint an Agent. We shall take no Notice of any Agents but such as are appointed by Acts of Assembly to which the Governor gives his Assent. We have had Confusion enough already. Here is one Agent appointed by the Council, another by the House of Representatives; Which of these is Agent for the Province? Who are we to hear on Provincial Affairs? An Agent appointed by Act of Assembly we can understand. No other will be attended to for the future, I can assure you.

B.F.   I cannot conceive, my Lord, why the Consent of the *Governor* should be thought necessary to the Appointment of an Agent for the *People*. It seems to me, that—

L H.   (*With a mix'd Look of Anger and Contempt*) I shall not enter into a Dispute with YOU, Sir, upon this Subject.

B F.   I beg your Lordship's Pardon. I do not presume to dispute with your Lordship: I would only say, that it seems to me, that every Body of Men, who cannot appear in Person where Business relating to them may be transacted, should have a Right to appear by an Agent; The Concurrence of the Governor does not seem to me necessary. It is the

6. This may seem to be a quibble, when Hillsborough was both Secretary of State and President of the Board of Trade. But usual procedure would have been, as mentioned in the headnote, to present credentials to Pownall as secretary of the Board.

14

	Business of the People that is to be done, he is not one of them, he is himself an Agent.
L H.	Whose Agent is he? (*Hastily*).
B F.	The King's, my Lord.
L H.	No such Matter. He is one of the Corporation, by the Province Charter. No Agent can be appointed but by an Act, nor any Act pass without his Assent. Besides, This Proceeding is directly contrary to express Instructions.
B.F.	I did not know there had been such Instructions,[7] I am not concern'd in any Offence against them, and—
L H.	Yes, your Offering such a Paper to be entred is an Offence against them. (*Folding it up again, without having read a Word of it.*) No such Appointment shall be entred. When I came into the Administration of American Affairs, I found them in great Disorder; By *my Firmness* they are now something mended; and while I have the Honour to hold the Seals, I shall continue the same Conduct, the same *Firmness*. I think My Duty to the Master I serve and to the Government of this Nation require it of me. If that Conduct is not approved, They may take my Office from me when they please. I shall make 'em a Bow, and thank 'em. I shall resign with Pleasure. That Gentleman knows it. (*Pointing to Mr. Pownall.*) But while I continue in it, I shall resolutely persevere in the same FIRMNESS. (*Spoken with great Warmth, and turning pale in his Discourse, as if he was angry at something or somebody besides the Agent; and of more Importance*) Consequence to himself.[8]
B.F.	(*Reaching out his Hand for the Paper, which his Lordship returned to him*) I beg your Lordship's Pardon for taking up so much of your time. It is I believe of no great Import-ance whether the Appointment is acknowledged or not, for I have not the least Conception that an Agent can *at*

7. The new instructions to Hutchinson, as successor to Gov. Bernard, were being drawn up at the time; BF was naturally in ignorance of them. See *Acts Privy Coun., Col.*, v, 264, and for the particular article on the agency Leonard W. Labaree, ed., *Royal Instructions to British Colonial Governors, 1670–1776* (2 vols., New York and London, [1935]), i, 387.

8. The phrase in roman is in another hand. BF originally wrote "the poor Agent"; the copy omits the adjective and "Importance."

present be of any Use, to any of the Colonies. I shall therefore give your Lordship no farther Trouble. *Withdrew*.9

From Jonathan Williams, Sr.

ALS: American Philosophical Society

Honoured Sir   Boston Janry 19th. 1771
I received your kind favour of the 7 and 9 Novr by Which We
are [*torn*] happy to find our Sons and Brother Safe arival and of the
kind Reception thay have from you and Good Mrs. Stevensons
kind offer of Service to Whom our Respects.1
By the next post I Shall Send to Mr. Pease for the Bond you
mention and Shall Recover the money as Soon as Possible then
Shall Consult in What Way it may be Improv'd per account to
advantage. We Shall take pleasure to Incourage your Benevolent
Schem2 the Ship Sails this Day have not time to ad; I have answard
your Litters in Regard to the Lottery in Which I Concluded to
Risque the two Ticketts3 and Gave your Account Current Credit
for the Balance you Directd. In hast I am Your Dutifull Nephew
and Humble Servant   JONA WILLIAMS
PS I have not yet been able to Let your House and Believe Shall
not untill Spring.4

Addressed: To / Benjamin Franklin Esqr / at Mrs Stevensons in
Craven street / London / per

9. A marginal note in another hand, which looks like James Bowdoin's,
describes the document as "a singular Conversation."
1. His two sons were Josiah and Jonathan, Jr.; his brother was John
Williams the customs inspector. Mrs. Stevenson had taken them in as lodgers.
See above, XVII, 212–13, 284–5.
2. The bond was from Samuel Hall, a Salem printer and BF's nephew by
marriage; a year later it was still unpaid. Van Doren, *Franklin–Mecom*, p. 133;
Williams to BF below, Sept. 19, 1771, and BF to Williams, Jan. 13, 1772. The
benevolent scheme was to assign the proceeds to Jane Mecom.
3. For the long affair of the lottery tickets see above, XVII, 137, 156.
4. The house in Unity Street which BF had repaired and rented for the
support of Jane's mad son Peter. Whenever there was no tenant, BF paid Jane
what she was not receiving in rent. See above, X, 355–7; Van Doren, *Franklin–Mecom*, pp. 24–5, 78–9; and BF's reply to this letter below, March 5.

From [Thomas] Life[5]

ALS: American Philosophical Society

⟨Basinghall St., Jan. 24, 1771. Talked with Mr. Jackson on the 21st about the Georgia acts,[6] and agreed to wait on him with Franklin on the 30th. Wants to talk with Franklin first, and if convenient will call on him at noon on Saturday next, the 26th; if inconvenient, please set any time except the 28th.⟩

From a Committee of the Library Company of Philadelphia

LS: American Philosophical Society

Sir   Philadelphia Jany. 25. 1771

We are appointed by the Directors of the Library Company of Philadelphia, to inform you that your Favour of the 7th July 1769 was received and laid before them by Mr. Charles Thomson, but the Confusion, which necessarily arose from the Union of the several Libraries, gave them so much Employ as to put it out of their Power to answer your Letter, so soon as the great Respect they bear to any Thing coming from you, induced them to wish.[7] They concur with you in Opinion of the Propriety of having in some of our Public Libraries all the Transactions of every Philosophical Society in Europe, but before they would venture to send for so expensive a Collection they apprehend it proper to take the Sentiments of the Company upon the Occasion and in order thereto they would be much obliged to you to favour them with The Price of each Set and also of the French Encyclopedia. We have taken the Liberty to send you a Catalogue of Books and to request you would be kind enough to procure them for us and furnish us with your Account, we have not remitted any further Sum, but whenever we are acquainted with the Ballance, it will be sent by the earliest Opportunity.[8] If there are any late publications not

5. For the London solicitor see above, x, 369 n.

6. See above, XVII, 293–4.

7. The Library Co. had absorbed the other city libraries in 1769; see above, XVI, 125. Hence BF's letter (above, XVI, 171–2) had gone unanswered for a year and a half. Its contents explain what follows.

8. The minutes of the Library Co. indicate that the committee was ap-

mentioned in our List, which you think proper for our Library, we shall be glad you would send them. The Directors are very thankful for the Trouble you have taken in their Service, but are fearful your many other Engagements, will render their further Applications inconvenient, if that should in the least be the Case, they beg you would recommend some Person who will supply the Company in future with Books on the most advantageous Terms. We are with much Respect your obedient humble Servants

ML. HILLEGAS
NICHOLAS WALN
R. STRETTELL JONES[9]

Addressed: To / Doct: Benjamin Franklin / London per

To William Knox   ALS (draft): Historical Society of Pennsylvania

⟨Craven St., Jan. 26, 1771. Is directed by the Georgia Assembly Committee of Correspondence to request the plan of the lands in that province claimed by the estate of Sir William Baker.[10] Please deliver the plan to the bearer, Thomas Life.⟩

From [Thomas] Fitzmaurice[1]

AL: Historical Society of Pennsylvania

⟨Pall Mall, Saturday evening, Jan. 26, 1771, a note in the third person. If Franklin is disengaged tomorrow, should be glad of his company in Pall Mall for dinner and the evening, where he will meet a friend or two. Had hoped to deliver the invitation in person this morning, but was prevented.⟩

---

pointed on Oct. 29, 1770, and that this letter from it was approved on Jan. 7, 1771, but do not include the list of books ordered.

9. For Hillegas and Waln see above, respectively, XVI, 8 n; XII, 311 n. Jones (1745–92) was a secretary of the APS, a director of the Library Co., and a manager of the Pennsylvania Hospital. He later moved to New Jersey, where he served in the legislature. Charles P. Keith, *The Provincial Councillors of Pennsylvania*... (Philadelphia, 1883), pt. 2, p. 199.

10. See above, XVII, 139 n. Knox's reply is below, Jan. 29.

1. For the younger brother of Lord Shelburne see above, X, 348 n, and for his recent correspondence with BF XVII, 218–19, 246–8.

From William Henly

ALS: American Philosophical Society

Sir: Tuesday Morn Jan. 29—71[2]

I think myself highly honour'd by your very obliging favour, and return you my sincerest thanks for your improvement of my Electrometer. I shall take the first opportunity to make that addition to my Apparatus,[3] and am well satisfied 'twill remove the objection at once.

I will now beg leave to assure you Sir that if I have been able to produce any Experiments in Electricity, which Dr. Franklin can vouchsafe to bestow the epithet *curious*[4] upon, my highest ambition, and vanity in that Science is satisfied, and fully so.

Since I wrote last, I have insulated my Jar laying under the bottom of it a pretty long pointed wire, this while the Jar is charging positively, continues to throw off a fine diverging pencil of Rays. When I charge it negatively I place a pointed bent wire in a Cork stuck in the Knob of the Jar wire, which during the charge continues to throw off the pencil in the manner before described. These apperances oblige me when I speak of the Theory of the Leiden phyal, to lay aside the Terms Dr. Franklins Hypothesis &c and always to mention its phenomena as agreeable &c to Dr. Franklins *Laws* of the Leiden phyal.[5] I beg leave to present the phyal I mention'd, and am Worthy Sir most sincerely yours

W Henly

2. The date, penciled in another hand, may be that when the letter arrived; see the endorsement.

3. For Henly's electrometer see above, XVII, 259–61. His surviving correspondence with BF gives no clue to the improvement that the latter suggested.

4. Presumably in the now obsolete sense of skillful or expert in contrivance.

5. For BF's epoch-making work on the Leyden jar see in particular above, III, 157–64, 352–65; IV, 9–34, 65–7. For a helpful discussion of the use of the terms hypothesis and law in eighteenth-century science see I. Bernard Cohen, *Franklin and Newton*... (Philadelphia, 1956), pp. 575–89; we are most grateful to Professor Cohen for criticizing our annotation of this and subsequent documents relating to electricity. Henly's experiment, one of many that he devised during the next few years to vindicate the single-fluid theory, was based largely on BF's second observation above, III, 157–8, and was published in a more sophisticated form in *Phil. Trans.,* LXIV (1774), 400 I. Henly was demonstrating visually BF's hypothesis that a jar, like all bodies, contains an unvarying amount of "natural" electricity, and therefore that if a positive charge is applied to one surface it will drive to earth from

Addressed: To | Dr. Franklin | with a phyal

Endorsed: Recd. Tuesday Jan. 29—71

From William Knox

ALS: American Philosophical Society

Sir   New Street Hanover Square 29 Jany 1771

   Inclosed I send you the Plan of the Lands in Georgia claimed by Sir Wm. Bakers Representatives which you desired in your Letter which was delivered to me yesterday.[6] I also inclose the several Papers which came with it to my hands as I imagine they may contain some information which you may think useful. I have kept no Copies of them, neither would I give you the trouble of making any, for the originals never can be of any use to me, and Copies would be a still more unnecessary incumbrance. I am Sir your very obedient humble Servant   WILL: KNOX

Endorsed: Letter to W Knox Esqr   In Answer

---

the opposite surface an equivalent positive charge, leaving a "bound" negative charge equal in magnitude to what was lost. In Henly's sketch, when the interior surface of the insulated jar on the left is charged positively, positive electricity is seen to escape from the exterior surface in the form of sparks or rays to the experimenter's hand; when the exterior of the jar on the right is charged, the electricity escapes from the interior.

   6. See BF to Knox above, Jan. 26.

List of Papers Relating to Georgia

AD: American Philosophical Society

⟨After Jan. 29, 1771: a list in Franklin's hand, by title only, of "Papers in this Parcel." All have to do with Georgia, and range through the decade 1761–71. They include actions by the legislature and the British government, letters to Franklin from the Speaker and the Assembly committee (many of them printed above), and documents relating to Sir William Baker's land claim. The latest paper mentioned is the preceding document.⟩

From Isaac Garrigues[7]

ALS: American Philosophical Society

Sir Jerusalum Coffee House Jany. 31t[?], 1771

I Received your Note of winsday Noon. But you may be assured I never Received your letter in Answer to mine of Sunday Morning or I should not have attemted to have given you Trouble the second time. I likewise wonder much I never received it. I thank you worthy Sir for all favours and have been very uneasy since receiveing the Note Yesterday—as you are pleased to say you are sorry I left Capt. Dalrymple. I assure you Sir I was intirely ignorat of my Station with Respect to my Duty and with all due Respect to your better judement imagine you where also deccived in it. It suits a Young man of 17 or 18 years of Age to goe in that Station when he wants to learn to be a Seaman but its by no means suitable for me for what respect could I have had to have shipt myself in that Station for [torn] Years and such a number of Officers above me indeed for one Voyage it might have done.

I hope Sir you will be so good as to forgive my Troubling you with this Letter as I only write it with a Veiw for you to understand me. I am well assured I did not disgrace your Recommendation as I beleive no Officer in the Ship was better thought of than myself as plainly appeared when I let them know my intentions of Leaving the Ship. I well know Sir that its imposible for you to supply every ones Occasion with Respect to money and you misunderstood my letter if you think it immediately imply'd for you

7. The grandson of BF's old friend James Ralph; see above, x, 186–7.

to supply me. I meant my disagreable Situation in Regard to my being out of employ And did not know if it had not been in your power to have got me a birth in another Ship.[8] I whish you Sir health. And I am with the Greatest Respect Your much Obliged and Most Obedient Servant   ISAAC GARRIGUES

Addressed: To / Dr: Benjamin Franklin / Craven Street / Strand

From Thomas Life: Bill for Services

AD: American Philosophical Society

⟨A long and chatty bill running from November, 1770, to February 2, 1771, for services in connection with BF's Georgia and Pennsylvania agencies. The principal entries for Georgia, in November, January, and February, are (1) for attending BF to consult on various papers sent him by the Assembly and on its act for governing slaves, for accompanying him in conferences with Jackson and others, for searching to find the Board of Trade's report on the act, and searching again to find that the Privy Council had approved it, £4 4s.; to Jackson for reporting the act, £5 5s.; to his clerk, 10s. 6d. (2) For obtaining true copies of the act for electing members of the Assembly, £1 1s.[9] (3) For drawing up the petition from inhabitants of Georgia to the King in Council,[1] and for various minor services, £5 1s. 2d. The total for Georgia was £16 1s. 2d.

The entry for Pennsylvania, under Feb. 2, 1771, is for attending the Board of Trade to find out what it had done with two acts of Assembly for issuing paper bills of credit, to the amount of

8. The disappearance of BF's note and earlier letter, and our failure to identify Capt. Dalrymple, make Garrigues' self-justification hard to follow. He had clearly been recommended to Dalrymple by BF, and had shipped with him long enough for the other officers to form an opinion of him. He had then, it seems, been asked to sign on for a term of years (the word that is partly missing looks like "four" or "five"), but at such a low rank that he quit. His request for BF's help, we conjecture, had been turned down with a reproach for leaving the berth he had had.

9. For these two acts see above, XVII, 145–7.

1. Against the land claims of Sir William Baker's estate, for which see *ibid.*, pp. 148–50, and BF to Jones below, July 3.

£14,000 and £6,000 respectively,[2] and for discovering that the King in Council would do nothing about the Board's report upon the acts, "by which Means they would pass of Course," 13s. 4d.

The total bill, £16 14s. 6d., was receipted as paid in full on Jan. 18, 1773.⟩

To James Bowdoin   ALS: Massachusetts Historical Society

Dear Sir,   London, Feb. 5. 1771

I am very sensible of the Honour done me by your House of Representatives, in appointing me their Agent here. It will make me extreamly happy if I can render them any valuable Service. I have had several Conferences with Mr. Bollan on their Affairs: There is a good Understanding between us, which I shall endeavour to cultivate. At present the Cloud that threatned our Charter Liberties seems to be blown over.[3] In Time I hope Harmony will be restored between the two Countries, by leaving us in the full Possession and Enjoyment of our Rights.

It will be a great Pleasure to me if I can be any way useful to your Son while he stays in England;[4] being, with the greatest Esteem and Respect for you and Mrs. Bowdoin, Dear Sir, Your most obedient and most humble Servant   B FRANKLIN

PS. Inclos'd I send you a Copy of an original Paper of some Curiosity now in my Hands. The first Part, i.e. the Queries, you will find in the Papers pertaining to the Governor's History: But not the Abstract or State given with them to Mr. Randolph.[5]

The old Spelling is preserv'd in the Copy.

2. See *Board of Trade Jour.*, 1768–75, pp. 198, 200–1, where as usual nothing is said about the purport of the Board's recommendation to the crown. We have found no mention of these acts in BF's surviving correspondence with the Assembly; one of them is referred to in 8 *Pa. Arch.*, VII, 6339, 6369.

3. For the threat to the Massachusetts charter see above, XVII, 279 n, 308, 311.

4. See Bowdoin to BF above, Jan. 2. Young Bowdoin, who carried that letter and the one from Cooper of Jan. 1, made a remarkably quick crossing.

5. BF enclosed a copy of the material that the government provided Edward Randolph on his mission to New England in 1676. This material consisted of (a) 12 queries about conditions in Massachusetts Bay; (b) a series of factual statements about New England, which Randolph might confirm or

To Samuel Cooper
ALS: British Museum

Dear Sir, London, Feb. 5. 1771

I have just received your kind Favour of Jan. 1. by Mr. Bowdoin, to whom I should be glad to render any Service here. I wrote to you some Weeks since in Answer to yours of July and November,[6] expressing my Sentiments without the least Reserve in Points that require free Discussion, as I know I can confide in your Prudence not to hurt my Usefulness here by making me more obnoxious than I must necessarily be from that known Attachment to the American Interest which my Duty as well as Inclination demand of me. In the same Confidence I send you the enclos'd Extract from my Journal, containing a late Conference between the Secretary and your Friend, in which you will see a little of his Temper:[7] It is one of the many Instances of his Behaviour and Conduct that have given me the very mean Opinion I entertain of his Abilities and Fitness for his Station. His Character is Conceit, Wrongheadedness, Obstinacy and Passion. Those who would speak most favourably of him, allow all this; they only add, that he is an honest Man, and means well. If that be true, as perhaps it may, I wish him a better Place, where only Honesty and Well-meaning are required, and where his other Qualities can do no harm. Had the War taken place,[8] I have reason to believe he would have been removed. He had, I think, some Apprehensions of it himself at the Time I was with him. I hope, however, that our Affairs will not much longer be perplex'd and embarrass'd by his perverse and senseless Management. I have since heard that his

disprove. The queries, together with Randolph's answers, are printed in the work to which BF refers, [Thomas Hutchinson], *Collection of Original Papers Relative to the History of the Colony of Massachusetts-Bay* (Boston, 1769), pp. 477–503. The factual statements about New England are printed almost *in extenso* in W. Noel Sainsbury, ed., *Calendar of State Papers, Colonial Series, America and West Indies, 1675–1676*... (London, 1893), pp. 362–3. BF was clearly interested in this material, and assumed that Bowdoin would be, because Randolph's mission contributed to the revocation of the Massachusetts charter in 1685, and revocation seemed to be again in the wind.

6. Cooper's July letter has been lost; those of November, and BF's reply, are printed above, XVII, 274–5, 285–7, 310–13.

7. See above, Jan. 16.

8. With Spain over the Falkland Islands; see above, XVII, 243 n.

Lordship took great Offence at some of my last Words, which he calls extreamly rude and abusive. He assur'd a Friend of mine, they were equivalent to telling him to his Face that the Colonies could expect neither Favour nor Justice during his Administration. I find he did not mistake me.

It is true, as you have heard, that some of my Letters to America have been echo'd back hither; (but that has not been the Case with any that were written to you). Great Umbrage was taken, but chiefly by Lord H. who was dispos'd before to be angry with me, and therefore the Inconvenience was the less; and whatever the Consequences are of his Displeasure, putting all my Offences together, I must bear them as well as I can. Not but that, if there is to be War between us, I shall do my best to defend my self and annoy my Adversary, little regarding the Story of the Earthen Pot and Brazen Pitcher.[9] One Encouragement I have, the Knowledge that he is not a Whit better lik'd by his Colleagues in the Ministry than he is by me, that he cannot probably continue where he is much longer, and that he can scarce be succeeded by anybody who will not like me the better for his having been at Variance with me.

Pray continue Writing to me as you find Opportunity. Your candid, clear, and well-written Letters, be assured, are of great Use. With the highest Esteem, I am, my dear Friend, Yours most affectionately   B FRANKLIN

Revd. Dr Cooper.

To Thomas Cushing

Reprinted from Jared Sparks, ed., *The Works of Benjamin Franklin...* (10 vols., Boston, 1836–40), VII, 501–6.

In 1770 Franklin, in a series of letters to American friends, began a commentary on various aspects of the imperial constitution.[1] The letter

9. A reference either to a proverb or its origin in the Apocrypha. "The earthen Pot must keep clear of the brass Kettle." Thomas Fuller, *Gnomologia: Adagies and Proverbs; Wise Sentences and Witty Sayings, Ancient and Modern, Foreign and British* (London, 1732), p. 192. "How agree the kettle and the earthen pot together? for if the one be smitten against the other it shall be broken." Ecclesiasticus 13: 2.

1. See above, XVII, 161–5, 307–9, 310–13.

below is part of this series. It discusses the current state of the American controversy and prospects for the future, and in the process touches incidentally, but in terms that would have startled an Englishman, on what the status of colonial agents should be—that of "public ministers" representing autonomous states. This was a logical development of the doctrine that the colonial legislatures were coequal with Parliament, but it was a far cry from the realities of 1771. Less than three weeks earlier Franklin had been told by the American Secretary that the Massachusetts House had no agent, and hence that he was legally non-existent; and he must have known that the weight of law and precedent supported this view.[2] Yet he seems to have been looking forward calmly to the day when he or his successor would be recognized as, in effect, the ambassador from Boston. Was this whistling in the dark? a play for time to keep his constituents quiet? an attempt to win over doubters among them by declaring himself as radical as they were? a hope for the immediate future, or a prescient glimpse of the Commonwealth to be? These are questions that an editor may legitimately raise, but not answer.

Sir,   London, 5 February, 1771.

Since mine of December 24th, I have been honored by the letter from the Committee, dated December 17th, which, with yours of November 6th, now lies before me.

The doctrine of the right of Parliament to lay taxes on America is now almost generally given up here, and one seldom meets in conversation with any, who continue to assert it. But there are still many, who think that the dignity and honor of Parliament, and of the nation, are so much engaged, as that no formal renunciation of the claim is ever to be expected. We ought to be contented, they say, with a forbearance of any attempt hereafter to exercise such right; and this they would have us rely on as a certainty. Hints are also given, that the duties now subsisting[3] may be gradually withdrawn, as soon as a regard to that dignity will permit it to be decently done, without subjecting government to the contempt of all Europe, as being compelled into measures by the refractoriness of the colonies. How far this may be depended on,

2. See the headnote on BF's interview with Hillsborough above, Jan. 16, and the references there cited.

3. After partial repeal of the Townshend Acts in 1770 the remaining duties were on sugar (4 Geo. III, c. 15), molasses (6 Geo. III, c. 52), and tea (10 Geo. III, c. 17).

no one can say. The presumption rather is, that if, by time, we become so accustomed to these, as to pay them without discontent, no minister will afterwards think of taking them off, but rather be encouraged to add others.[4]

Perhaps there was never an instance of a colony so much and so long persecuted with vehement and malicious abuse, as ours has been, for near two years past, by its enemies here and those who reside in it. The design apparently was, by rendering us odious, as well as contemptible, to prevent all concern for us in the friends of liberty here, when the projects of oppressing us further, and depriving us of our rights by various violent measures,[5] should be carried into execution. Of late, this abuse has abated; the sentiments of a majority of the ministers are, I think, become more favorable towards us; and I have reason to believe, that all those projects are now laid aside. The projectors themselves, too, are, I believe, somewhat diminished in their credit; and it appears not likely that any new schemes of the kind will be listened to, if fresh occasion is not administered from our side the water. It seems, however, too early yet to expect such an attention to our complaints, as would be necessary to obtain an immediate redress of our grievances. A little time is requisite; but no opportunity will be lost by your agents, of stating them where it may be of use, and inculcating the necessity of removing them, for the strength and safety of the empire. And I hope the colony Assemblies will show, by frequently repeated resolves, that they know their rights, and do not lose sight of them. Our growing importance will ere long compel an acknowledgment of them, and establish and secure them to our posterity.

In case of my leaving this country, which I may possibly do in the ensuing summer, I shall put into the hands of Dr. Lee all the papers relating to your affairs, which I have received from you, or from the son of your late agent, Mr. De Berdt. The present American secretary, Lord Hillsborough, has indeed objected to the As-

4. This sentence is surprising because it reverses the whole previous tenor of the paragraph. The presumption may have been the hidden motives that BF imputed to those who threw out the hints, or what he himself presumed would happen, or both. His point in any case was that colonial optimism was ill founded if resistance did not continue.
5. For the threats to the charter in 1769–70 see above, XVII, 279 n, 308, 311.

sembly's appointment, and insists that no agent ought to be received or attended to, by government here, who is not appointed by an act of the General Court, to which the governor has given his assent. This doctrine, if he could establish it, would in a manner give to his Lordship the power of appointing, or at least negativing any choice of the House of Representatives and Council, since it would be easy for him to instruct the governor not to assent to the appointment of such and such men, who are obnoxious to him; so that, if the appointment is annual, every agent that valued his post must consider himself as holding it by the favor of his Lordship, and of course too much obliged to him to oppose his measures, however contrary to the interest of the province.[6]

Of what use such agents would be, it is easy to judge; and, although I am assured, that, notwithstanding this fancy of his Lordship, any memorial, petition, or other address from, or in behalf of, the House of Representatives to the King in Council, or to either House of Parliament, would be received from your agent as usual, yet, on this occasion, I cannot but wish, that the public character of a colony agent was better understood and settled, as well as the political relation between the colonists and the mother country.

When they come to be considered in the light of *distinct states,* as I conceive they really are, possibly their agents may be treated with more respect, and considered more as public ministers. Under the present American administration, they are rather looked on with an evil eye, as obstructers of ministerial measures; and the Secretary would, I imagine, be well pleased to get rid of them, being, as he has sometimes intimated, of opinion that agents are unnecessary, for that, whatever is to be transacted between the assemblies of colonies and the government here, may be done through and by the governor's letters, and more properly than by any agent whatever. In truth, your late nominations, particularly of Dr. Lee and myself, have not been at all agreeable to his Lordship.

I purpose, however, to draw up a memorial, stating our rights and grievances, and, in the name and behalf of the province, pro-

6. Bostonian radicals shared this fear but carried it further, to the point of distrusting BF for being a placeman; no one should be agent, Samuel Adams believed, who held any office from the administration. Cushing, *Writings of Samuel Adams,* II, 66.

testing particularly against the late innovations in respect to the military power obtruded on the civil, as well as the other infringements of the charter; and at a proper time, if Mr. Bollan on due consideration approves of it and will join me in it, to present it to his Majesty in Council.[7] Whether speedy redress is or is not the consequence, I imagine it may be of good use to keep alive our claims, and show, that we have not given up the contested points, though we take no violent measures to obtain them.

A notion has been much inculcated here by our enemies, that any farther concession on the part of Great Britain would only serve to increase our demands. I have constantly given it as my opinion, that, if the colonies were restored to the state they were in before the Stamp Act, they would be satisfied, and contend no further. As in this I have been supposed not to know, or not to speak the sentiments of the Americans, I am glad to find the same so fully expressed in the Committee's letter. It was certainly, as I have often urged, bad policy, when they attempted to heal our differences by repealing part of the duties only; as it is bad surgery to leave splinters in a wound, which must prevent its healing, or in time occasion it to open afresh.

There is no doubt of the intention to make governors and some other officers independent of the people for their support, and that this purpose will be persisted in, if the American revenue is found sufficient to defray the salaries. Many think this so necessary a measure, that, even if there were no such revenue, the money should issue out of the treasury here. But this, I apprehend, would hardly be the case, there being so many demands at home; and the salaries of so many officers in so many colonies would amount to such an immense sum, that probably the burden would be found too great, and the providing for the expense of their own governments to be left to the colonies themselves.[8]

I shall watch every thing that may be moved to the detriment of the province, and use my best endeavours for its service.

No public notice has yet been taken of the inflammatory paper

7. The memorial, if it was ever written, seems to have disappeared. For the conflict of military and civil authority in Massachusetts see above, XVII, 162, 169–70, 277–8; Hutchinson, *History*, III, 221–4, 239.

8. See above, XVII, 281–2, 303, 312–13, and BF to Cushing below, June 10, n. 6.

mentioned by the Committee, as stuck up in Boston;[9] and I think the indiscretion of individuals is not now so likely, as it has been of late, to make general impressions to our disadvantage. With the greatest respect, &c.   B. FRANKLIN.

To John Winthrop

Reprinted from *The Columbian Centinel*, July 30, 1825.

Dear Sir   London, Feb. 5, 1771.

I duly received your favour of October 26, with 52s.[10] for the Royal Society. I lately found one of the last volumes of the Transactions among my books with your name in it. I had some doubts, whether I had not sent you mine instead of it, believing I had dispatched it long before. But recollecting that mine were gone to Philadelphia, I am made sensible of my inexcusable negligence in keeping it from you so long. To make you some amends, I have bundled up with it Meyer's Astronomical Tables and some other Astronomical Pieces, which I now send and beg your acceptance of. I send also as a present to the College Library two volumes 4to of a very learned work lately printed—Hoogevee on the Greek Particles: and two Mathematical Pieces of Mr. Masere, late Attorney General at Quebec, which I hope will be acceptable to the President and Corporation, whom I highly respect and honor. The Print you mention is with the books.[1]

I am glad you have at length got the Galilean Glasses, and that the Achromatic Telescope gives satisfaction. Mr. Maskelyne did not send me the Nautical Almanack for 1771 as he intended; That for 1772 is now published—If you choose it, I will procure and send them regularly to you as they come out.

9. See above, XVII, 303.
10. The text reads £52, clearly an error; see Winthrop's letter above, XVII, 263–5, which explains much of what BF discusses below.
1. To Winthrop BF sent Tobias Mayer, *Tabulae motuum solis et lunae, novae et correctae...* (Nevil Maskelyne, ed.; London, 1770), and to Harvard Hendrik Hoogeveen, *Doctrina particularum linguae graecae...* (2 vols., [Leyden, 1769]) and Francis Maseres, *A Dissertation on the Use of the Negative Sign in Algebra...* (London, 1758) and *Elements of Plane Trigonometry...* (London, 1760). The print was also for the College, possibly Fisher's mezzotint of the Chamberlain portrait; see the acknowledgment from Harvard below, June 24.

I spent a day and night lately with Mr. (now Dr.) Price,[2] and communicated to him your paper—you will see his sentiments in the enclosed letter, which I soon after received from him.

I am extremely sensible of the honor done me by your House of Commons in choosing me their agent here.

I shall be very happy in every opportunity of rendering my dear country any acceptable service.

I have nothing new in Astronomy or Natural Philosophy to communicate to you. Dr. Priestly is about to publish a History of the latter, in the manner of his History of Electricity—it will make several volumes in quarto.[3] Much entertainment is expected from it; and I think it will tend to the improvement of knowledge.

I communicated your observation of the Transit of Mercury to Mr. Maskelyne, who has laid it before the society, with your observation of the former Transit of Mercury, that you had sent to Mr. Short, but which was never printed.[4] Some time last November there were great crowds in the streets here gazing at the spots on the sun; *not through smoked glasses, but with the naked eye, which was enabled to bear it by the common smoke of the city.* With sincerest respect and esteem, I am, Dear Sir, your most obedient servant,

B. FRANKLIN

To Cadwalader Evans

Reprinted from Samual Hazard, ed., *Hazard's Register of Pennsylvania*, XVI, no. 5 (August 1, 1835), 92.

Franklin's efforts to promote the growing of silk in Pennsylvania were slowly bearing fruit. In 1769 he had urged Dr. Evans to seek help from the province; this suggestion had been laid before the American Philosophical Society, which had duly petitioned the Assembly for financial aid. When the legislature failed to act, the Society raised money by private subscription; the contributors elected twelve managers, Evans among them, who were all members of the Society, and who proceeded to set up the filature, hire a supervisor, and set prices for cocoons. The first reeled silk was displayed at a

2. The wording implies that the doctorate was recent, but in fact Marischal College, Aberdeen, had awarded it to Price in 1767.

3. See above, XVII, 155 n.

4. See above, XVI, 257 n.

meeting of the contributors in the autumn of 1770.[5] This sample was dispatched at once to Franklin with a covering letter from Evans, now lost, that asked for expert opinion on its quality. Franklin's reply is below.

Dear Doctor, London, Feb. 10, 1771.

I have not now before me your Letter which came with the Sample of Silk, having put it into the Hands of Mr. Walpole with the Sample, who has promised me full and particular Answers to all your Queries, after the Silk has been thoroughly examined. In the mean time he tells me, the best Sort appears to him to be worth in itself 27 or 28s. a pound; and will fetch that Price when some Imperfections in the Reeling it are remedied.[6] He tells me farther, that the best Eggs are to be had from Valentia in Spain, whence he will procure some for you against the next Year; the Worms from those Eggs being the strongest, healthiest, and producing the finest Silk of any others: And he thinks you should get some Reelers from Italy, which he would likewise undertake to do for you if desired. He is one of the most opulent and noble spirited Merchants of this Kingdom.[7] I shall write to you fully per Osborne,[8] with all the Information I can procure. In the mean time, Please to present my respects to the Gentlemen concern'd in the Affair, and assure them of my best Services. I am, my dear Friend, Yours affectionately, B. FRANKLIN.

Dr. Cadwr. Evans.

5. *Pa. Ga{.*, Nov. 1, 1770. For BF's initial suggestion see his letter to Evans above, XVI, 200–1; for subsequent developments see Brooke Hindle, *The Pursuit of Science in Revolutionary America* . . . (Chapel Hill, [1956]), pp. 201–3.

6. See BF to the Managers of the Silk Filature below, before May 10, 1772.

7. We are convinced that this was the Hon. Thomas Walpole, from whom the Walpole Co. took its name, even though we have no indication that trading in silk was among his wide commercial interests. BF's superlatives would fit few if any other merchants among his acquaintances; Thomas was the only Walpole we know of in that group, and the only one of the name listed in *Kent's Directory* . . . (London, 1770). We are therefore assuming, with no positive evidence, that he was the "great Silk Merchant" mentioned in BF's previous letter to Evans (above, XVII, 210–11). Walpole did not answer Evans' queries, but another expert did; see BF to Evans below, July 4, 18. BF's extant correspondence with Evans on silk culture continued into 1773, but Walpole's name did not reappear.

8. Peter Osborne had taken command the previous spring of Falconer's old ship, the *Pa. Packet*: *Pa. Ga{.*, June 14, 1770.

To Samuel Rhoads ALS: Historical Society of Pennsylvania

Dear Friend, London, Feb. 10. 1771.
I received your kind Favour of Nov. 9.[9] and am glad to hear of the Welfare of you and yours.

Mentioning to a Friend of mine, Mr. Wooller, an Engineer,[1] your Idea of Paint and Sand, to make Roofs durable and safer from Fire (which I hope you will try, as I think it very likely to succeed) he communicated to me an Account of a new Method of Covering, in the North, that is in some respects similar, may be as durable, but in my Opinion not so safe. Perhaps it may be of Use for Summer-Houses, Barns, Outhouses, or Buildings where no Fire comes (and therefore I send you the Account enclos'd); but I think I should not care to trust it in a Dwelling-House, in a Town, unless the under Side of the Boards was lathed and plaistered between the Rafters, which would add to the Expence: For tho' the Outside, hardened by the Air, and paved, as it were, by the Sand, Shells, &c. might not readily take fire, the Tar coming thro' the Seams or Craiks of the Boards might be readily inflamed by a Candle from the Inside, placed carelessly by Servants in a Garret.

The Flatness of this Roof, as well as of those with Copper, lessens a good deal the Areas to be covered, and of course the Expence.

I am glad to hear that you have good Workmen in the Stucco Way, and that it is likely to take place of Wainscot.

In some of the Paris Buildings the Floors are thus formed. The Joists are large and square, and laid with two of their Corners up and down, whereby their sloping Sides afford Butments for intermediate Arches of Brick. Over the whole is laid an Inch or two of Loom,[2] and on that the Tiles of the Floor, which are often six-square, and painted. The lower Corner of the Joints is cut off enough to admit of nailing to them the Laths that are to hold the Plaister of the Cieling of the Room beneath. Where there is any

9. Not found, but presumably an answer to BF's letter above, XVII, 181–3.
1. For John Wooler see above, XVII, 182 n.
2. Presumably a slip for "loam," although ordinary loam seems an unsatisfactory base for tiles. Perhaps BF had in mind some variety resembling casting-loam.

Apprehension of Walls spreading by the Weight of such Floor, they are prevented by Bars of Iron, with external SS. This kind of Floor seems safe from Fire: For the Joists in Contact with the Bricks above, and shielded by the Plaister Cieling below, are not very likely to kindle and burn. It likewise prevents in a great degree the Noise of what is doing overhead offending those below. But it is heavy, takes up more Room, requires great Strength of Timber and is I suppose more expensive than Boards. I apprehend those Arches are not generally us'd; but the Tiles are more commonly laid upon rough Boards, and the Joints clos'd with fine Mortar or some kind of Cement.

Plaster Floors are of late coming again into Use here. I know not whether we have the proper Materials in our Province; but I have been told there are Quarries of the kind in Nova Scotia near navigable Water. I send you however an Account of the Method of laying such Floors. Also some Specimens of a new-discover'd Limestone for Mortar that sets under Water, with a Written Account of the Method of managing it. All from my Friend the ingenious Mr. Wooller.

Remember me respectfully and affectionately to Mrs. Rhoads and my dear old Friend Mrs. Paschal. With sincere Esteem, I am, dear Friend Yours most affectionately   B FRANKLIN

I send you also a Pamphlet on the Subject of securing Houses from Fire, tho' the Method is perhaps impracticable with us.[3]

Saml Rhoads, Esqr

3. The pamphlet may well have been L. Dutens' translation of Félix François d'Espie, *The Manner of Securing All Sorts of Buildings from Fire. Or a Treatise upon the Construction of Arches Made with Bricks and Plaister, Called Flat-Arches, and of a Roof without Timber Called a Bricked-Roof. . .* (London, n.d.). If this was in fact what BF sent, he had good reason to question the applicability of the method in America.

From Joseph Sherwood[4] ALS: University of Pennsylvania Library

Warnford Court Throgmorton Street 12th. Feby. 1771.
Esteemed Friend

Some Years ago there was a dispute between Lord Baltimore and the Penn's Family, respecting as I understand the Boundaries of the two Provinces. I should be much obliged to thee to be Informed in what Year the Decree was made in that Cause, and the Names of the Parties, and indeed every other particular thou can inform me, relating to this Business,[5] which will oblige Thy respectful Friend JOSEPH SHERWOOD

Addressed: To / Benjn. Franklyn Esqr. / at Widow Stevenson's / in Craven Street / Strand.

From Katherine French[6] ALS: American Philosophical Society

My dear Sir   Monday 18th Febry. [1771]

Your very valuable opinion is much desired upon the Work I now send for your perusal. A particular friend has requested this

4. The Quaker lawyer, formerly agent for New Jersey and at the time for Rhode Island; see above, XIV, 217, 249–50.

5. Sherwood was asking for a lot, because the dispute went on for more than eighty years. The final decree in Chancery was not made until 1750, and the boundaries were not finally settled until the famous Mason and Dixon survey, completed in 1767. See Walter B. Scaife, "The Boundary Dispute between Maryland and Pennsylvania," *PMHB*, IX (1885), 241–71.

6. An acquaintance of BF since at least 1765. Our predecessors were unable to identify her with confidence, but suggested the remote possibility that she was the daughter of Richard Lloyd, Chief Justice of Jamaica, and the widow of Jeffrey French, M.P.; they were skeptical, however, because that lady's first name was supposedly Catherine (XII, 96 n). This must have been a misspelling. Mrs. Katherine French in her later life (she died in 1791) appeared several times in Horace Walpole's correspondence, under the sobriquet Old Brutus; by that time she had a house in Hanover Square and a villa at Hampton Court, and was an avid collector of *objets d'art*. Walpole ridiculed her taste and her collection, but bought several items from the latter when it was sold at auction. See Wilmarth S. Lewis and A. Dayle Wallace, eds., *Horace Walpole's Correspondence with Mary and Agnes Berry and Barbara Cecilia Seton* (2 vols., New Haven, 1944), I, 57 n, 220–1. We are convinced that Mrs. French's interest in art, as revealed in the letter below, clinches the identification of her as Jeffrey French's widow.

favor of me. He says, he thinks, you are not a Stranger to this performance, as it was shewed to you some time ago, in an incompleat state. By a Letter from the late Docr. Greg. Sharpe, which Letter I send you a Copy of, I conclude it must have real merit or should not have been prevailed upon to trouble you with it.[7] Am your obliged and very Humble Servant   KATH. FRENCH

Addressed: To / Docr. Franklin

To [Katherine French]   ALS: Yale University Library

Dear Madam,   Cravenstreet, Feb. 27 [26?], 1770 [1771][8]
After so full an Opinion in favour of your Friend's Work from the late learned Dr. Sharpe, my Sentiments of it seem unnecessary, as they can add no Weight. They will appear, however, by my

7. Our guess is that the particular friend was the author. The letter of endorsement came from the Rev. Dr. Gregory Sharpe (1713–71), prebendary of Salisbury, chaplain to the King, and master of the Temple, a distinguished classicist and orientalist as well as theologian, who had died the month before. *DNB.* His letter that Mrs. French copied for BF (APS) described the work in question as "singular and curious, instructive, elegant and magnificent," but added that its merit would not be obvious at first sight and it would not sell on the ordinary market; Sharpe suggested circulating a prospectus to the nobility, all members of Parliament, etc., soliciting subscriptions at two guineas a set. The price in the actual prospectus was a guinea; see the following document. The work, *The Senator's Remembrancer,* was dedicated to BF by the author, John Stewart of London; it originally consisted of thirteen copperplate prints on white satin. BF sent one set to Cushing and another to the N.J. Assembly; six years later he presented another, now containing fourteen prints, to the Pa. Council. Below, BF to Cushing, June 10, penultimate paragraph, and N.J. Assembly Committee of Correspondence to BF, Dec. 21; *Pa. Col. Recs.,* XI, 232.

One of the few extant copies of this bizarre publication is in the British Museum, and we are most grateful to Mrs. Sallie McKee Warden for examining it and describing it to us. The prints are a series of charts, showing how a statesman should break down the problems he confronts in various areas— war, legislation, revenue, etc.—in order to arrive at a maturely considered decision. The underlying premise, that problem-solving can be divided into a series of steps in abstract analysis, is reminiscent of BF's "Prudential Algebra" that he described to Priestley below, Sept. 19, 1772.

8. The day of the month is overwritten; the year is clearly an error, for BF is replying to the preceding document.

requesting that Five Sets more may be sent me, which I intend as Presents to my Friends the Speakers of so many American Assemblies or Parliaments. These added to the Set you have favour'd me with the Perusal of, will, at the alter'd Rate in the Printed Proposals, amount to Six Guineas, which shall be paid to the Bearer, by Your obliged and most obedient humble Servant[9]   B FRANKLIN

I do not recollect that any Part of the Work was shown to me before.

From Mrs. [William] Deane[1]

AL: University of Pennsylvania Library

Frith Street March the 1st. [1771–75[2]]

Mrs. Deane presents her Compliments to Dr. Franklin with many thanks to him, for the benefit she hopes, she has received, from the perusal of *Richards Maxims,* which are so *Excellent* they ought to be framed and hung up in every House.[3] Mrs. Deane is much obliged to Dr. Franklin for his kind remembrance of her, and hopes he will Consider of the other request, for the benefit of the Females of Great Britain. General Deane joins in Compliments

Addressed: To | Dr. Franklin | Craven Street | Strand

From Katherine French

ALS: American Philosophical Society

My dear Sir   Friday 1st. March. [1771]

I return you my Thanks for the unquestionable proof you have given of your approbation, of the Work I sent you. I made my

9. BF was trusting enough to provide the money in advance. On Feb. 28 he paid the six guineas (Jour., p. 31; Ledger, p. 43); Mrs. French replied (below, March 1) that she did not yet have the additional five sets.

1. The wife of General Deane, the governor of Upnor Castle. The Deanes were old acquaintances of BF; see above, VII, 321–2.

2. Deane was promoted to major general on April 30, 1770: *A List of the General and Field-Officers...for the Year 1775* (London, [1775]), p. 4. BF left for America in late March, 1775.

3. She is referring to the collection of aphorisms and maxims in *Poor Richard*, first published in 1757 and so frequently reprinted thereafter that it is impossible to tell what edition BF had given her. See above, VII, 326–40.

friend extremely happy in shewing your Letter to him. When I am in possession of the other 5 sets Will dispatch them to your House.[4] I was unwilling my friend Miss Jennings's civil acknowledgement of your kind favor, should wait a moment,[5] therefore hope you will forgive the present trouble. Am with the utmos t esteem your obliged and very humble Servant

KATH. FRENCH

Addressed: To / Doctor Franklin.

From Theodorus Swaine Drage[6]

ALS (incomplete): American Philosophical Society

In this long letter, from a man whom Franklin had sponsored for Anglican ordination almost two years before, the writer described his struggle to establish a missionary parish in the piedmont of North Carolina. The letter is in bad condition: the ink is faded, some of the pages are torn or stained, some clearly missing, so that the text as reproduced is at times conjectural and has occasional holes. Its vividness, nevertheless, compensates for its shortcomings. Although Drage was no master of English prose, he knew the neighborhood well after a year and a half in it; and it was a community in trouble and turbulence.

The root of his difficulties as a missionary of the Society for the Propagation of the Gospel was the church itself. With no bishop nearer than London to ordain clergy and remove the unfit, with no determination of where the right lay to appoint parochial rectors and no effective means of levying taxes for their salaries, the church in North Carolina languished.[7] Its position was further weakened by the great influx of dissenters from the north, which was part of the colony's sensational growth in population.[8] Drage's troubles, particularly with a vestry that refused to serve, were shared by many of his fellow clergymen; but he

4. She is responding to BF's request above, Feb. 26 or 27.
5. Miss Jennings was presumably accepting BF's offer to give her some packets of seed; see her note to him and his reply below, March 20–21.
6. See above, XVI, 70–1.
7. See Sarah McC. Lemmon, "The Genesis of the Protestant Episcopal Diocese of North Carolina, 1701–1823," *N.C. Hist. Rev.*, XXVIII (1951), 426–45; Hugh T. Lefler and Albert R. Newsome, *North Carolina: the History of a Southern State* (revised ed.; Chapel Hill, [1963]), pp. 122–5.
8. The population is estimated to have been roughly 50,000 in 1752 and 345,000 in 1775: *ibid.*, pp. 70–81.

was perhaps singularly unfortunate in his parish, which was huge, controlled by a Presbyterian oligarchy, and almost out of touch with the distant seat of authority at New Bern. The dissenters among his parishioners insisted that they were defending their religious rights, as they had their civil, against British intrusion. He insisted on upholding the position of the Anglicans, for if he failed they would, he was convinced, either emigrate to other colonies or become absorbed into the sects.[1]

He was writing at the height of the Regulator movement, which had its climax less than three months later in the Battle of Alamance.[2] The part of his letter that describes the activities of leading Regulators and their opponents is too badly damaged to be of much value, but other parts explain much of what caused the unrest —the oppressive burdens laid upon the people by a corrupt and self-perpetuating clique of local officeholders. As the battle lines formed, Drage seems to have been caught in the middle. Although he lost no love on rioters, he was acutely aware of their grievances; and he was anxious that Franklin, as a friend of liberty, should also be aware of them.[3]

The Regulator movement in the province collapsed after the Battle of Alamance, but Drage's own troubles grew worse. He apparently never did get a salary, and for another two years or so lived on the contributions of a few faithful Anglicans. Then he gave up his parish, fruitlessly petitioned the legislature for redress, and moved to South Carolina.[4] There he died in 1774.

Dear Sir   March 2d. 1771
It is not from a want of a sense of the pleasure and Honour I have had in your long acquaintance and Friendship that I have not wrote since my arival in these parts. I had nothing to tell you

1. See Drage to Gov. Tryon, March 13, 1770, William L. Saunders, ed., *The Colonial Records of North Carolina...* (10 vols., Raleigh, 1886–90), VIII, 180.
2. For the Regulators see William S. Powell, James K. Huhta, and Thomas J. Farnham, eds., *The Regulators in North Carolina: a Documentary History, 1759–1776* (Raleigh, N.C., 1971); Lefler and Newsome, *op. cit.*, pp. 173–8; John S. Bassett, "The Regulators of North Carolina," Amer. Hist. Assn., *Annual Report...for the Year 1894* (Washington, 1895), pp. 141–212; M. L. M. Kay, "An Analysis of a British Colony in Late Eighteenth Century America in the Light of Current American Historiographical Controversy," *Australian Jour. of Politics and History*, XI (1965), 170–84.
3. Some, at least, of the Regulators wanted BF to act as well as understand: those in Anson County, when petitioning the Assembly in 1769, asked that he be made agent to convey their grievances to the crown. Saunders, *op. cit.* VIII, 78.
4. See *ibid.*, IX, 507, 520, 622.

but the common Ocurrencies of a voyage, or Inland Journey of near four hundred miles to a Town called Salisbury, a village of about Thirty houses mean in its buildings, but scituated in one of the finest climates in the world, as I have since experienced, Temperate in Summer, the nights always cool, the winter cold very moderate our rains for a day, then succeeds serene fine weather. It is the County Town of Rowan, which is composed of Chiltern and vale,[5] watered with three fine Rivers, the Dan, the Yadkin, and the Catawba and plenty of Streams makes their Course into those Rivers. The Soil fertle and capable with small Industry to produce whatever desired. To what I attribute the fine climate is, there is a large ridge of mountains bounds it North and South and again East and West these mountains are cloathed with woods, and capable of producing the finest vines. This Country as the promised land was originally possessed by the Cananites. It is not my opinion, from spleen, but have the publick authority for it our Governor's speech to the Assembly in November, when the late Governor Dobbs came over here, he brought a colony from his neighbourhood in Ireland, to be here provided for, they [were] put into Posts, others were made attornies, and the rest to live like soldiers upon free Quarter,[6] you know it was an asylum for Thieves and cheats from the Northward, character was no exception against their being well received by their Countrymen and with those whom were not so there was a conformity in manners, the first setlers lived by the gun so were ferocious in their manners, many Hunters, Volunteers in the late Expeditions, Indrian Traders, and the Group is compleated by the People of Conegocheeke York and Cumberland Countys[7] being I think all arrived here of

5. Rolling country with chalky or sandy hills.

6. We have been unable to track down Governor Tryon's speech, but it must have referred to his predecessor, Arthur Dobbs, who for many years before he became governor in 1754 had encouraged, and to some extent financed, an emigration of Ulstermen to lands he owned in North Carolina. See Desmond Clarke, *Arthur Dobbs, Esquire, 1689–1765*...(Chapel Hill, [1957]), pp. 95, 104–5. William Tryon (1729–88), an army officer, had been governor since 1765, and had just been transferred to the governorship of New York; he left for his new post immediately after winning the Battle of Alamance in May. *DAB*. It is clear from his correspondence cited below, n. 9, that he was doing everything in his power to support Drage.

7. Areas in west central Pennsylvania; the Conecocheague valley was then in Cumberland County.

late years, there hath been many also more civilized People who were circumscribed in their Lands in MaryLand, Virginia, also from Pennsilvania having not room to settle their children, many Germantown Quakers, and from whom the Colony hath some share of Industry. I shall now confine myself to speak of my own Parish of St. Lukes or County of Rowan 180 miles in length and 120 in breadth, which I have visited all over and more than once, and from the variety of People I have conversed, am the best acquainted of any person whatever of the real cause of our disorders here. Mr. Dobs's Friends, and all the Scotch Irish are clanned in one Settlement together [and] had Interest enough to get the County Town adjacent, but no way a proper place, with respect to the Dimensions of the County, and not recommended by its extraordinary scituation. The Town is also full of them but they chose to have their Tribunal near as the Government of the County was intrusted to them exclusive of all others. They are Dissenters by Profession but of many various Sects, so never had a Teacher amongst them only Itinerant Preachers from the North, four or five in a year, who preach once at a place get collections made return with the money, and leave Political Instructions with the Elders. The last two years there is one setled amongst them in the lower part of the County: a church of England man is an abomination, much more a Parson, but I have got footing as their Rector. It is to be considered that these People are three hundred and odd miles from the Seat of Government, and scarce have three hundred and odd pence to carry them there any one of them. Charles Town is the market they go to[8] so cannot Support the Grievances or Abuses of any particular officers, the officers can attend and one justifies the other. If they are Innocent, the others are Rascals and their Behaviour hath been so Irregular, and inexcusable as it gives a Countenance to what their opponents say. It is not force, the Friction only increases the heat, the cause is known, remove that and the Peace of the Country will be restored and they will become a healthy thriving People. Here is a kind of Police very suitable to the Scituation of the People in these distant parts. The freeholders every Easter monday are to choose twelve

8. Because of the configuration of the river valleys the inhabitants of the piedmont had easier communication with the tidewater of South Carolina than of North; see Lefler and Newsome, *op. cit.* p. 19.

41

persons for a vestry, who are intrusted with the Care of the Church and Poor, but they take Care here, when they are chosen to evade the Law, by not Qualifieing, so starve the Parson and the Poor, by no Provision being made for them.[9] But as these should be chosen out all parts of the County, they would be as the States of the County, to whom the People could make known their Grievances, and they would be a respectable Body, whose representations in either in the Courts, or to the Governor and assembly would be of weight, and the People would be easy under these as their Patrons. This hath been continual in Virginia. Also the Magistrates should be more numerous one in every Fifteen miles, but the case is in one place there is not a Magistrate in ninety, in others [none] who act in forty or Sixty. In the Irish Settlement they are numerous, and in other parts, not but Two who are of the Church of England, and one of them, an honest worthy old man they Indicted for Extortion. The bill was found as to which there could be no Question and the Person who set a foot the Prosecution was of the Grand Jury. When it came the next Court of Assize to be tried the same person was Foreman of the Petty Jury, and there were on that Jury, three others, who had been on the Grand Jury. On a Jurymans making an observation as to these three, they were removed but the Foreman stood, and though the Judge, made it appear that there was no Extortion proved, or any intention of it. The Foreman withdrew his Jury, and returned a verdict that he was not Guilty of the Indictment as to matter and form, there was a duplicity in order to reflect on his Character, and

9. Drage amplified elsewhere the electoral procedure in St. Luke's Parish. In the previous election two lists of candidates had been proposed, one containing only dissenters and the other predominantly Anglican; the men on the former list were pledged, if elected, to avoid qualifying as vestrymen by refusing the necessary oath. Only freeholders with deeds to their land could legally vote, and the Anglican majority in Rowan County did not for the most part have deeds. The dissenters had; they promptly elected the vestry that would not serve, as they had done for years, and justified defying the law by arguing that it was unfair: it forced the election of a vestry that would tax parishioners to support an Anglican minister, whereas every taxpayer ought to be free to support the clergyman of his choice. The Anglican would-be vestrymen then asked Gov. Tryon to install Drage (which he did in July, 1770), and agreed to pay his salary by voluntary contributions. They also petitioned the legislature to recognize them as the legal vestry for the rest of the year, and to remove the requirement of a deed for voting. See Drage's

he had about eight or ten pounds costs.[1] The Governor becoming acquainted that the Dissenting magistrates only acted desired of me, as I passed thro the Parish a List of People proper for that office, who were of the Church of England for the consideration of himself and the Council. I executed my trust with care for a New Commission was made out, in which several of the formor Magistrates were left out, but this commission was either purposely left behind by Frohawk[2] and those who returned from Newbern, or concealed here, the same Magistrates sat, made up the County accounts, appointed the Jurys for the assizes, though all the Commissions for the militia officers, were carefully brought. I mention how little Governor or any the authority that is not according to their wish is to be regarded. Only for want of proper Magistrates the People executed their own Judgements, flogged those that stole, from thence took it into their heads to punish any person, whom they thought had offended, from thence they got the name of Regulators, than undertook in [poss?]ies to purge the Country of bad People. Thus from [*illegible*] than Force was necessary, otherwise these Insurgents could not be brought to Justice. Two partys were formed, both appeared in arms. But Husband's[3]

---

correspondence with Tryon and the secretary of the Society for the Propagation of the Gospel in Saunders, *op. cit.*, VIII, 179–81, 202–8, 217–18, 502–4.

1. We have not located the case, but the clique controlling local government clearly used the judicial process both to persecute its enemies and to defend its own members. In 1769 a group of Rowan County Regulators, acting on the assurance of Gov. Tryon and others that they could find redress through the courts, brought to the grand jury evidence of extortion by several officials; the jury was packed, and the charges were thrown out. *Ibid.*, pp. 68–70.

2. Probably Col. John Frohawk (d. 1772), a prominent member of the ruling clique and one of the officials whom the Regulators had charged with extortion. He had been an assemblyman for Rowan County and was a justice of the peace, judge of the county court, and colonel in the militia. Five days after this letter was written, a group of officials including the three Frohawk brothers, John, Thomas, and William, agreed to make restitution to the Regulators for money that they had taken illegally. *Ibid.*, pp. 521–2; see also Lefler and Newsome, *op. cit.*, p. 168; Jethro Rumple, *A History of Rowan County* . . . (Salisbury, N.C., 1881), pp. 70–1.

3. Hermon Husband (or Harmon Husbands; 1724–95) was a Quaker who was the leading spokesman for, though not a member of, the Regulators. He was a prosperous farmer on Sandy Creek in what was then Orange County, adjacent to Rowan. He wrote effectively in support of the people against an

scheme was to show his Perog[ative?] [*torn*] as he had got his People down, went freely [*torn*] Fear and without consulting his People [*torn*] to the most considerate amongst them [*torn*], the Governor upon their retreat sent an [*torn*] under the Stile of a conqueror, which did not [put them into a good?] humour. They observed that Fanning[4] and [*torn*] Sheriffs and Lawyers, had his Ear, whe[*torn*] in a slight manner to him with [*torn*] they found it made little impression, the [*torn*] representations of those who were the cause of [*torn*] on, by their unjust oppressions. The Governor is a gentleman [and as a] man of Honour, and veracity, judged the same of thos[e who] assumed the character of such, and was deceived. Husband [had?] engaged with a Lawyer one Nash to give him three hundred and odd pounds to manage the Regulators affairs in the Law, and when he signed the agreement said he shoud pay about a Small part of it, so did not regard the Sum. Nash after-

---

oppressive and corrupt officialdom, and had been elected and re-elected to the Assembly. He had recently been expelled and briefly imprisoned, however, on charges of inciting to sedition. In the following May, after the Battle of Alamance, he fled with a price on his head and settled in Pennsylvania, where he took a leading part in the Whiskey Rebellion years later, when he was approaching seventy; he was tried and condemned to death, but pardoned by President Washington. *DAB*. Husband's account of the Regulator movement, published in 1770, may be found in William K. Boyd, ed., *Some Eighteenth Century Tracts Concerning North Carolina* (Raleigh, N.C., 1927), pp. 254–333, and in Archibald Henderson, ed., "Hermon Husband's Continuation of the Impartial Relation," *N.C. Hist. Rev.*, XVIII (1941), 57–81. Local legend had it that Husband was some relation of BF, maintained oral communication with him through an intermediary when BF was in Philadelphia, and received pamphlets from him. E. W. Caruthers, *A Sketch of the Life and Character of the Rev. David Caldwell...* (Greensborough, N.C., 1842), pp. 119–20; Powell, Huhta, and Farnham, *op. cit.*, p. 566; Bassett, *op. cit.*, pp. 155–7. The story rests on the flimsiest of hearsay evidence and is *prima facie* implausible.

4. Edmund Fanning (1739–1818) was the man whom the Regulators hated most. After growing up in New York and graduating from Yale he settled in Hillsboro as a lawyer. In 1771 he was registrar of deeds, militia colonel, assemblyman, and judge of the superior court, and was thought to be using his many offices to indulge his rapacity. He had recently been beaten and had his house destroyed by the Regulators. He remained in high favor with Tryon, but his position was precarious. When the Governor left for New York Fanning accompanied him as private secretary, and soon acquired a new set of lucrative offices. He became a Loyalist, eventually moved to Nova Scotia and then to England, and rose to be a general in the British army. *DAB*.

wards sued him and recovered.[5] He than applied to the Regulators to pay their proportions, they said no, it was an agreement, which they were no way privy or assenting to and he must pay it himself, they were so disatisfied with their being seduced to Hilsborough, the Oath they had thro' his means prematurely engaged in, and some other Conduct, as they were going to Flog him. Thus was he sinking, and they the sensible People and who had Property seeking means to restore the general Peace, but could not persuade themselves, that their Oath was illegal and so could be dispensed with, but had come to an agreement I think generaly, for I was concerned in this Transaction, to pay the Tax for the year 1769, as it was set out what each particular was, and they only excepted to one 4*d*.[6] they [*torn*] to much, only they feared the than Sheriff Cole,[7] would [*torn*] to the Treasury, as he was expensive and hard [*torn*] houses. They had at that Time as with [*torn*] opinion of him. Things seemed now [*torn*], and as these Combinations consist [*torn*] of People, one who seeks Justice, and the others [*torn*] from it. It was on the latter only that [*torn*] chief dependance; But an Accident [*torn*] are to blaze out again, as the [*torn*] also [?] the Grand and Petty Juries for the assize [and the?] Quarter Sessions preceding, and some of the Regu[lators] were to be Indicted at that court, and Tried upon their indictments. It was represented that a Set of Justices, who were Creatures of Colonel Fanning, had taken an opertunity when the other Justices were not on the Bench to pack a Jury, if not designed, it was certainly Impolitick. This was Imediately made Known by Circular Letters, all called upon in defence of their Libertys to Hilsborough, and the consequence

5. For Abner Nash (*c*. 1740–86), an eminent lawyer and, during the War of Independence, Governor of North Carolina, see the *DAB*. When Husband was faced with four legal actions in 1768, and feared for his life, he retained Nash and another lawyer to defend him and to work for the Regulators' cause; they subsequently sued him and got a judgment of £375. Henderson, *op. cit.*, pp. 52–4.

6. Drage means that the Regulators, disillusioned with Husband, blamed him for drawing up their initial agreement, in 1768, to form an association for regulating abuses of public power. The agreement pledged them to pay no tax, except under compulsion, until they were sure that the money would be used as the law directed. See Bassett, *op. cit.*, p. 165.

7. William Temple Cole, a commissioner of the town of Salisbury and sheriff in 1771, was a signer of the agreement mentioned above, p. 43, n. 2.

was a most unjustifiable Riot at Hilsborough.[8] The Ferocious men could be no longer restrained by the advice of the others, and so became their Masters, and thus Husbands became more formidable than before, and the more sober and discreet part are now afraid for themselves if they do not follow the Lead of these Ferocious Men. What was done as to the last assembly, appears to have no effect. Col. Fanning, who cleared himself of the accusations alledged against himself in the house, hath not yet done it in the minds of the People, you have read the State of Frohock,[9] and no Peace will be restored until Fanning retires, and the other with his connections are removed from all Employments [*page missing?*] but now endeavour to Starve me out. There are nine hundred Families who profess now the Church of England, and about seven Thousand Souls, men, women, and children. They will not make Fifteen hundred, but are in Possession of their Patents, which is not the case with most of the others, so they are the Freeholders. The greatest number of the Magistrates is made out of them, for they take[?] the Qualifications sign the Test, and the members of the County are of them.[1] They soon brow beat the other Magistrates and drove them from the Bench, thus assumed the whole Power. They name the Sheriffs, they also appoint the Grand and Petit Juries for the assize courts. They levy and adjust the County Tax. The Clerk of Sessions and assize is with them, for the offices

8. On Sept. 24–25, 1770, the mob invaded the Hillsboro courthouse, maltreated Fanning, and drove the judge from the bench. Basset, *op. cit.*, pp. 190–2.

9. The Assembly, although it had expelled Husband and passed a stringent riot act, had also legislated a number of reforms that the Regulators were demanding. *Ibid.*, pp. 194–6. Legal actions against Fanning had failed, and he had recently regained a seat in the Assembly; but what accusations he had faced there we do not know. Neither can we understand the reference to Frohawk, or why BF should ever have heard of him. Col. John had been defeated for the Assembly in 1769, and thereafter seems to have been less in the limelight.

1. Drage's meaning is not, to put it mildly, pellucid. He is saying that his parish contains seven thousand Anglicans, most of whom lack title deeds and so cannot vote for the vestry; the voters are less than fifteen hundred dissenters, who have their deeds. The first part of the next sentence is no problem, but the remainder is obscure: the test, a pledge not to oppose the doctrine, discipline, and liturgy of the Church of England, was for vestrymen rather than magistrates; "members of the County" probably means of the county court.

46

are executed by two Brothers, but they in reality executed [as one?] man. From this Set have all the oppressions, and [*torn*] of the county in great part arose. They nominated to the Sherifdom Persons in low circumstance. The Sheriffs would declare the Tax to be more than it was and accordingly collect it which when discovered by the People, two Shillings a head extra, for it is Pole Tax, would tell them to come to Town themselves and bring their receipts they would pay them, forty sixty, or a hundred miles for two Shillings, by this means the Sherriff kept most of what he had. The money was permitted to lie in their hands a year or more after their Sheriffdom was expired, as they could not get in their deficiencys, than was setled by a committee of Justices. This was the Rule for the Treasurers receipt the Public Treasurer. They would yet collect Deficiencys after this, and to the Pocket. And it was observed that the Public moneys were short, yet the Sheriff who was in poor circumstances before, would become possessed of Negros and a trading man. This caused a Jealousy, and would take Dollars of the People at 6*s*. 6*d*. and pay them in at 8*s*. as to others they would spend great part of the money, and what they remitted to the Treasury would be there clipped again, the Sheriffs Securitys would conceal their own effects so it was hard [?] hearted to confine their Persons and they could swear themselves out as Insolvents. In Short, there was not [nought] omitted of oppression and vexation which their Powerful office was capable to inflict. Mr. Macullough, the present [?] Agent for this Province[2] had large tracts of land in this county and the adjoining on which People had setled [*illegible*]. Many continued on that land and came to an agreement with him, others quitted, and a great Tract is desolate [*illegible*] to him a large sum of money. This ocasion [*torn*] move and indeed took away almost the [*torn and illegible*]. His conduct also added to the [*illegible*] who[?] was[?] forced[?] to flee by night they could have an [*illegible*] I[?] declare if he ever came here again he need not give himself the trouble of thinking how he shall [*illegible*] them. The present Clerk of Session, whose name is Frohawk was his agent and Surveyor. On this scarcity of money more suits commenced amongst the People. The Lawyers

2. For Henry E. McCulloh, wealthy North Carolina planter and provincial agent, 1768–73, see Kammen, *Rope of Sand*, p. 325; Sabine, *Loyalists*, II, 55–7.

took high Fees from the Necessitous to keep off the Evil day. Those that wanted their money were liberal to get the Suit dispatched and often when the Cause was determined the Fees in Court exceeded the Suit. All the Tricks of office were playd, actions brought without the least foundation, in order to ruin People by way of Revenge, Executions retained or Issued ad libitum of the Clerk, no receipts given, and Issued tho satisfied a Second Time. Sheriffs officers furnished with blank writs, fomenting the People one against the other, went to one, told him such a one said this of you, if he would not bring an action of Scandal, returns to the other he succeeds the [*page missing?*] degree to another became more daring and committed the violencies at Hilsborough. Thus I have given you a fair State of our Grievances here, or the True cause of that confusion which prevails, which the Dissenters endeavour to avail themselves of, as the Friends of Government, but would have joined the rest of the People could they have prevailed with the People to have carried their first demands, to the Subversion of the constitution who aimed at only a Regulation as to the Public officers. And the violences committed, have been committed by the Dissenters principaly, tho represented to the assembly and Government it was by the People of the Church of England, tho they declared publickly while the assembly was Sitting, those up here, that if the Petition which was sent down to set aside the Test, was not complied with they would be worse Regulators than the others, whom they called Fools. They succeeded, and as it was merrily said the Government was become a Leakey Canoe, and they wanted to mend it with Church Leather. Every thing was granted them[3] and they were equaly condescending and formed an act under the name of a Riot act, which intirely vests a Despotick Power in the Governor, and the life of a man is not worth a Button, if they have a mind to Scheme it to take it from him. It is to last but a year, so will not be sent home,[4] and if seen at home would be an Eternal reproach to your Stand for Liberty, and the consequence is it hath only made the Regulating association the

3. This is puzzling, for the Assembly did not act on the petition to repeal the test.

4. The so-called Johnston Act, passed in the early days of 1771 when the Assembly believed that the Regulators were about to march on New Bern. See Bassett, *op. cit.*, pp. 195–6; Lefler and Newsome, *op. cit.*, pp. 175–6.

Stronger, thro fear. And when the Coroner appointed a Day, amongst the Scotch Irish to come and pay their Tax, These the principal Body of the Dissenters, not one came nigh to him. Husbands was expelled the House, and afterwards arrested and put in Jail for an impudent libel against one of the Judges. After the assembly broke up, he was still confined for want of Bail, a Large Body of People, to the amount of four hundred, with a waggon to every forty men set out, from this County to be joined by a greater number in Orange, and to march to Newburn. Those that went from hence were mostly Dissenters. They were to send Five persons down before them to bail Husbands, and if they did not meet him coming home, they were to go and break the Jail, which is in the same Town with the Governors Palace. This an Instance how little Sincerity there is in these People with respect to the Government, and of what little Efficacy the Proceedings of the late assembly have been towards restoring of the Public Peace. I must mention another anecdote. Frohawk who was Lt. Col. of Militia was to be at a muster of Four Companies of Militia, at the Moravian Town in October.[5] They had formed a design to regulate him, that is Flog him, as they had done Fanning. I heard of it, and on Inquiry found it true. Frohawk got an account of it so did not come. The officers were afraid of a Riot, they desired me to stay as they knew I could Influence the People, also many of the Leading Regulators came early to endeavour to keep Peace, but as Frohawk was not there and the Major mustered them, there was better Order and Decency kept than could possibly be expected from such a Body of People, not the least offence or disturbance, yet when he was at Newburn and the Colonel gave up his Commission, the Governor was such a Stranger to what a light he stood in with respect to the People that he made him Colonel.

This letter comes by two Germans honest Planters here they will shew you their Business[6] and should it be convenient would

5. The Rowan County militia had its annual muster in 1770 at the Moravian village of Bethabara, now Old Town, to the terror of the inhabitants: Adelaide L. Fries, ed., *Records of the Moravians in North Carolina* (7 vols., Raleigh, N.C., 1922–70), II, 62.

6 Sixty German Lutheran families were sending two emissaries, Christopher Rintleman and Christopher Layerly, to England and Germany to raise a fund for the support of a German-speaking Lutheran minister and schoolmaster. On Drage's instigation the Governor, after himself giving £5 5s. to

recommend them to the notice of your Friends. They and those
on whose part they come, have not been Regulators, tho many of
them have suffered very considerably by the publick officers.

What I have wrote, I do not consider as a Secret, and you have
leave to communicate it as you see proper. It is late a Saturday
night so must Stop my Pen, and these men go tomorrow Evening.
All I can say I am well. May God continue your health is the
Sincere wish of your Sincere Friend and oblidged Servant

THEODORUS SWAINE DRAGE
Rector of St. Lukes Parish
in the County of Rowan
in the Province of North
Carolina, at Salisbury.

A Letter by the Charles Town Packet directed to the care of Wm.
Glen & Son Merchants in Charles Town[7] will come to hand.

Endorsed: Revd Mr Swaine Drage   No. Carolina Salisbury
Mar. 2d. 71

From Noble Wimberly Jones

ALS: American Philosophical Society

Revered Sir   Savannah 4 March 1771.
I take this oportunity to acquaint you that on the 22d. of last
month our Assembly met with the same fate of that in Decr. 1768,
the principal cause seemed to be their having Committed the

the cause, recommended the two emissaries to the Bishop of London and the
Society for the Propagation of the Gospel. Both responded: the Bishop con-
tributed £6 6s. (outdoing the Archbishop of Canterbury by a guinea); the
Society took charge of the funds raised, and swelled them by a gift of £40.
Saunders, *op. cit.*, VIII, 506–7, 630–3. The minister and schoolmaster, the
Rev. Adolph Nussman and John Gottfried Arends, arrived in due course, and
spent the rest of their lives in North Carolina. Jacob L. Morgan *et al.*, eds.,
History of the Lutheran Church in North Carolina, 1803–1953 (n. p., [1953]),
pp. 20–3, 366, 375.

7. William Glen (1701–85) was a Charleston merchant and plantation-
owner, who subsequently became a Loyalist; his sons were William and John,
born respectively in 1741 and 1744. Philip M. Hamer, George C. Rogers, Jr.,
et al., eds., *The Papers of Henry Laurens* (3 vols. to date; Columbia, S.C.,
[1968–72]), I, 31 n.

deputy Secretary for refusing to give evidence to a Committee of the House on an information against the deputy surveyor general for taking double fees in his Office which the Governor (like some other of his[8] declarations) said the Assembly had no Right to do.[9] Another reason he gives is A Resolution of the House not to enter on a Tax Bill for the present year the four Southern Parishes not being Represented.[1] I receiv'd a Note from the Governor about or near 12 o Clock at noon when I waited of him, After telling me the cause of sending he recommended an Alteration in those parts of the Journals of the House and desired I would use my influence with the Members for that purpose which I refused not thinking it consistant as Speaker to be consernd in such a matter or message of any kind, and on his urging the affair of Mr. Moodie deputy Secretary I told him it would then appear (if that was struck off the Minets) that the Speaker Issued Warrant without any Authority for so doing. Some Gentlemen of the Council did mention the Governors request to several of the Members and that he would disolve the Assembly unless they did alter the Journals of that week which threat they disdaind, and the House not having any thing before them for that day adjournd to the next morning. But about 8 that evening the Governor Disolv'd us by Proclamation so that

8. Jones here inserted "arbitrary," and then lightly deleted it.
9. The Governor had dissolved the Assembly in 1768 because it had insisted on discussing the letter from Massachusetts opposing the Townshend Acts. William W. Abbot, *The Royal Governors of Georgia, 1745–1775* (Chapel Hill, [1959]), pp. 148–9. In 1771 the House, after receiving a complaint that Thomas Shruder, the deputy surveyor general, was exacting twice the legal fees, had demanded that the deputy secretary, Thomas Moodie, be questioned on oath about the matter. Moodie had refused to take the oath, claiming that it was unprecedented; the House had branded his refusal a breach of privilege, and ordered him arrested for contempt. Candler, ed., *Ga. Col. Recs.*, xv, 295–6.
1. The Governor's other reason was the real one. On Feb. 20, 1771, the Assembly had refused to consider a tax bill until the four parishes were represented. The next day Wright received permission to issue writs for those parishes; he so informed the House, through Jones as speaker, and added that Whitehall had agreed to all its requests except a three-year limitation on the length of a session. He expected that this good news would induce the legislators to pass the needed tax bill, but they fastened on the point denied them as ground for renewing their refusal of funds. The Governor then dissolved the House. *Ibid.*, pp. 153–5; for the development of the issue see Candler, *op. cit.*, xv, 153 ,155, 175, 183–4, 189, 202, 206–7, 298–9.

the whole business of the Session dropd amongst which were several ready for the Assent some of great consiquence. I trust you have receivd the Bills of Exchange before this two of which I have sent one sett by Capt. Hall which we hear has arrived[2] therefore have not sent the third set. And remain with great esteem and assurance of the late Assembly's Confidence in your inclinations and abillities Sir Your Most Obedient and Very Humble Servant

N W JONES

This comes by Mr. Ed: Telfair Member Assembly in the year 1768.[3]

Addressed: To | Benjamin Franklin Esqr. | Provincial Agent for | the Province of Georgia, | London | per favour of | Capt. T. Ash by way | Cows

To Noble Wimberly Jones

ALS: Historical Society of Pennsylvania

Sir,   London, March 5. 1771
    I duly received your several Favours of Oct. 9. and December 13. inclosing Bills of Exchange, viz.

On Greenwood & Higginson for	£100 0s. 0d.
On Campbell for - - - - - - - - -	20 0s. 0d.
	£120 0s. 0d.

which are paid and carried to the Credit of the Province Account. I am much obliged to you and the Assembly for so readily transmitting them, and it makes me very happy to understand that my Endeavours in their Service are in any degree acceptable.[4]
    Notwithstanding the ample Recommendations brought over by Mr. Winter, the Bishop of London has refused him Ordination, for two Reasons, as I understand; his mechanical Education, and

2. The bills were in payment for the mace and gowns that BF had purchased for the Commons House; see above, XVII, 242, 298. Thomas Hall was master of the *Governor Wright.*

3. Edward Telfair (*c.* 1735–1807) was a Scottish-born merchant, who had represented St. Paul's Parish in 1768. He subsequently served in the Continental Congress. *DAB.*

4. See the preceding document.

his Connection with Mr. Whitefield and the Methodists. I did not think either of these of so much Weight as to discourage me from attempting to get him ordain'd by some other Bishop, or to make so strong an Application to the Bishop of London as might overcome his Lordship's Objections. Accordingly I endeavour'd to engage in his Favour the Associates of Dr. Bray, a Society of which I have long been a Member. As it was established for Purposes similar to that of Mr. Zouberbuhler's Will, I hoped they would readily have afforded us the Weight of their Recommendation, on my laying before them a Copy of the Will, Copies of several Letters from you and Mr. Habersham, &c.[5] But the Idea of his being a Methodist, and the Imagination of his neglecting the Negroes and becoming an Itinerant Preacher, disturbing regular Congregations, &c. &c. as soon as he should obtain Ordination, I found were thought sufficient Reasons to prevent their concerning themselves in the Affair.[6] However I do not yet quite despair of it.

Mentioning Mr. Whitefield, I cannot forbear expressing the Pleasure it gave me to see in the Newspapers an Account of the Respect paid to his Memory by your Assembly.[7] I knew him intimately upwards of 30 Years: His Integrity, Disinterestedness, and indefatigable Zeal in prosecuting every good Work, I have never seen equalled, I shall never see exceeded.

The enclos'd Paper has been put into my Hand by Mr. Maudit, a principal Man among the Dissenters here. I promised him to

5. For Cornelius Winter and the bequest for missionary work among Zouberbuhler's slaves see above, XVII, 299. The Associates of Dr. Bray were particularly interested in Negro education; see above, VII, 100 n and *passim*.

6. The conservative's distrust of ordained itinerant preachers went back to the origins of Methodism in England, when Wesley and his clerical companions had gone from parish to parish carrying their gospel of repentance and salvation; they had often convulsed the congregations and antagonized the clergy. George Whitefield, who had converted Winter in the first place, was instrumental in transforming Methodism from a revival within the Church of England to a movement outside it. The idea of reversing the process, even to the extent of ordaining one of his protégés, aroused understandable opposition in the establishment.

7. The Assembly had voted money for putting Christ Church, Savannah, into mourning, for bringing Whitefield's remains from Newburyport, where he had died, to his Bethesda Orphanage in Georgia, and for erecting a monument to him there. Candler, ed., *Ga. Col. Recs.*, XV, 219–20. This action was reported in the *London Chron.*, Jan. 8–10, 1771.

communicate it to you. The Dissenters were for complaining to Government, and petitioning for Redress; but Mr. Maudit advis'd that Mr. Frink should first be written to, as possibly he might be dissuaded from persisting in such Demands. I know nothing of the Circumstances but what appears in the Paper, nor am I acquainted with your Laws; but I make no doubt you will advise what is proper and prudent to be done in the Affair.[8] The Dissenters in those Northern Colonies where they are predominant, have by Laws exempted those of the Church of England residing among them from all Rates and Payments towards the Support of the Dissenting Clergy; and methinks it would be a Pity to give them a Handle against re-enacting those Laws when they expire; for they are temporary, and their perpetual Laws tax all Sects alike. The Colonists have Adversaries enow to their common Privileges: They should endeavour to agree among themselves, and avoid every thing that may make Ill-Blood and promote Divisions, which must weaken them in their common Defence.

If the Laws of your Province are printed, I should wish to be furnished with a Copy; it must be some times of Use to me in the Management of your Business. With great Esteem and Respect, I have the Honour to be, Sir, Your most obedient humble Servant

B FRANKLIN

P.S. I shall shortly write fully to the Committee relating to the Matters referr'd to in their Letter of May 23. 70. in the meantime be so good as to inform them that the Business has not been neglected. The Hurry in our Public Councils during the first Part

8. The person who broached the affair to BF was Jasper Mauduit (1697–1772), a prominent London dissenter and former agent for Massachusetts, for whom see above, XII, 13 n. Neither BF here nor Jones in his reply (below, July 8) gives enough information to identify the paper, or the specific grievances for which the dissenters wanted redress; but both were products of a quarrel that had broken out in Savannah a year before between Presbyterians and Anglicans over burial fees, of which the Church of England claimed a monopoly. The chief protagonist on one side was John Zubly, pastor of the Independent Presbyterian Church, and on the other Samuel Frink (1735–71), rector of Christ Church. The squabble produced at least one pamphlet by Zubly, a law suit, and petitions by both clergymen to the Assembly, which considered various solutions but seems to have taken no final action. See Zubly to BF below, July 9; Candler, *op. cit.*, XV, 178–81; XVII, 560–3; *Sibley's Harvard Graduates*, XIV, 270–5; Mass. Hist. Soc. *Proc.*, VIII (1864–65), 217.

of the Winter, occasion'd by the Expectations of an immediate foreign War, and the domestic Confusions that took place after the Convention,[9] have been great Hindrances to proceeding in American Affairs.

Endorsed: B. Franklin 5th March 1771

To [Grace] Williams[1]

Reprinted from Jared Sparks, ed., *Familiar Letters and Miscellaneous Papers of Benjamin Franklin*... (London, 1833), pp. 139–40.

Dear Cousin,   London, 5 March, 1771.

I received your kind letter by your sons.[2] They are, I assure you, exceeding welcome to me; and they behave with so much prudence, that no two young men could possibly less need the advice you would have me give them. Josiah is very happily employed in his musical pursuits. And as you hinted to me, that it would be agreeable to you, if I employed Jonathan in writing, I requested him to put my accounts in order, which had been much neglected. He undertook it with the utmost cheerfulness and readiness, and executed it with the greatest diligence, making me a complete new set of books, fairly written out and settled in a mercantile manner, which is a great satisfaction to me, and a very considerable service.[3] I mention this, that you may not be in the

9. The convention was the agreement with Spain, signed in January, that concluded the Falkland Islands crisis. The domestic confusions were probably the beginning of the excitement over the printer's case, which a few months afterward brought the House of Commons into collision with the City of London; see BF to Galloway below, April 20.

1. The wife of Jonathan Williams, Sr., and BF's niece (C.5.3).

2. She and her husband both sent letters, but only his has survived (above, XVII, 212–13); it discusses the voyage of their sons and John Williams to London. See also *ibid.*, pp. 284–5.

3. For the past history of BF's accounts, and Jonathan's services in putting them in order, see above, XI, 518–20. After the young man completed the books in February, 1771, it is said there, BF seems to have kept them himself, and was able to strike another trial balance after returning to Philadelphia in 1775. We do not agree. A close examination of the handwriting indicates that most of the entries, including a trial balance struck apparently in May, 1775, are Jonathan's handiwork; they give no indication whether or not he taught BF double-entry bookkeeping. From midsummer, 1771, Williams was in

least uneasy from an apprehension of their visit being burthensome to me; it being, I assure you, quite the contrary.

It has been wonderful to me to see a young man from America, in a place so full of various amusements as London is, as attentive to business, as diligent in it, and keeping as close at home till it was finished, as if it had been for his own profit; and as if he had been at the public diversions so often, as to be tired of them.

I pray God to keep and preserve you, and give you again, in due time, a happy sight of these valuable sons; being Your affectionate uncle,   B. FRANKLIN.

To Jonathan Williams, Sr.   ALS: American Philosophical Society

Loving Cousin,   London, March 5. 1771

I suppose Jonathan has told you that the Lottery is drawn, and your two new Tickets had the same Success as the former, viz. One £20 Prize, and one Blank. Would you go on any farther?[4]

Josiah is very happy in being under the Tuition of Mr. Stanley, who very kindly undertook him at my Request tho' he had left off Teaching. Josiah goes constantly too to several Concerts, besides Operas and Oratorios; so that his Thirst for Music is in a Way of being thoroughly satiated. This is his principal Expence; for in all other Respects I never saw two young Men from America more prudent and frugal than he and his Brother are.

Jonathan seems to have an excellent Turn for Business, and to be a perfect Master of Accounts. In the latter he has been of great Use to me, having put all mine in order for me.[5] There is a Proposal from his Uncle of his going to East India as a Writer in the Company's Service which I wish may take place, as I think if he lives he cannot fail bringing home a Fortune. He had ordered a Cargo of Goods to be sent you for Cousin Wood's[6] Shop, and had

---

Boston for three years. On his return to London he presumably took over records that BF had kept in his absence, and put them in order as he had in 1770.

4. By winning only a £20 prize Williams was losing heavily; see above, XVII, 288.

5. See the preceding document.

6. A female, because Jane Mecom referred to her as "Aunt Wood": Van Doren, *Franklin–Mecom*, p. 119.

given Expectations of paying ready Money. But one of your Bills being protested, he seem'd [to see?] a Necessity of asking some Credit of the Mer[chants. I] advis'd him to take what was wanting of me, rather than fail in Punctuality to his Word; which is sacred here among all that would maintain a Character in Trade. He did so, and thereby also sav'd the Discount, without putting me to the least Inconvenience, provided the Money is replac'd in Six Months; and I was glad I had it in my Power to accommodate him.[7]

I hope you have before this time got another Tenant for the House, and at the former Rent. However, I would have you go on advancing to my Sister the Amount of it; as I am persuaded she cannot well do without it.[8] She has indeed been very unfortunate in her Children.

I am glad to hear, that as soon as the Weather permits, the Tomb will receive a thorough Repair.[9] Your kind Care in this Matter, will greatly oblige Your affectionate Uncle

B FRANKLIN

Jona Williams Esqr

Addressed: To / Jonathan Williams Esqr / Mercht / Boston

Endorsed: March 5, 1771

From Noble Wimberly Jones

ALS: American Philosophical Society

⟨March 7, 1771. Encloses two issues of the *Gazette*[1] dealing with the dissolution of the Assembly.⟩

7. In February BF lent young Jonathan £385 19s. 1d.; this and other loans, some apparently to Josiah, totaled £583 18s. 5½d., a debt that was settled in full, to judge by BF's books, before Jonathan sailed for America in midsummer: Jour., pp. 31, 34–5; Ledger, p. 49. But the father sent a final remittance on the first loan after that; see his letter to BF below, Aug. 5.

8. See the postscript of Williams to BF above, Jan. 19.

9. See above, XVII, 288.

1. Presumably the weekly *Ga. Gaz.*; no copies for 1771 appear to be extant.

From Michael Collinson
ALS: Historical Society of Pennsylvania

Dear Sir   Mancr. Bgs.[2] March 9th: 1771.

I return the Soliloquy which is indeed in too many Places but too wickedly entertaining and Pointed at the expence of the good old Gentleman, and the Allusion to 1715 &ca with the help of the Key which in Confidence you furnished Me with is palpable enough.[3] I am very happy, my dear Sir, that I have it just still in my Power to oblige myself by soliciting your Acceptance of half a dozen Copies of the Letter, and a detached Print or two;[4] of the former I have now only five Books left, three of which are engaged and of the Other a much less number than I wish, or a much larger of Both, Sir, would I am sure have been at your Service, and will ever be so if a new Edition or Impression should ever happen to take place; in the Intrim, and at all times, I rest with much deference and Esteem Dear Sir Your faithful and most humble Servant

MICHL. COLLINSON

Addressed: To | Dr. Franklin | In | Craven Street

2. Manchester Buildings, Canon Row, Westminster, where Collinson lived for some years after his father's death. William Darlington, *Memorials of John Bartram and Humphry Marshall...* (Philadelphia, 1849), pp. 446–59; Henry B. Wheatley, *London Past and Present* (3 vols., London, 1891), II, 460.

3. Collinson was returning a satire on Cadwallader Colden, Lieutenant Governor of New York, occasioned by Lord Dunmore's suit against him. The anonymous pamphlet, *A Soliloquy* ([Philadelphia?], 1770), was the work of William Livingston, the prominent lawyer who was later the first governor of the state of New Jersey. The satire does not allude to 1715 but refers indirectly (p. 14) to an episode during the Stamp Act disturbances, when the mob hanged an effigy of Colden inscribed "The Rebel Drummer in the Year 1715." *N.Y. Mercury*, Nov. 4, 1765. Colden, as a boy in Scotland, had reportedly drummed for recruits for the Jacobite rising.

4. The letter was an anonymous pamphlet written by Dr. Fothergill and revised by young Collinson, *Some Account of the Late Peter Collinson...in a Letter to a Friend*, for which see above, XVII, 65 n; the prints were extra copies of the frontispiece portrait.

From Robert Crafton[5] ALS: American Philosophical Society

Dear Sir Broad Street Buildg., Mar. 11. 1771.

I hope you (as an American) have not caught that epidemical Disorder, that infects our Senators on this Side the Atlantic: Law Makers should not be Law-Breakers! You and I, cum aliis, laid our wise Noddles together, and framed a wise Statute; that we and all other Persons under a certain Predicament therein express'd, should dine every Thursday at the Dog Tavern on Garlick Hill: But O tempora! O mo[res!] if I mistake not, you have been there but once[6] [*torn*] I shall take the Chair on Thursday, and do hereby en[join?] you, under pain of my greatest Displeasure, to [*torn*] in Person; and to bring with you some two or three or more young sucking Americans, that reside to the Westward, and do most probably attend your Levees; where indeed I should have been present more than once, but that the Defection of the Philadelphians, has chained me to the Oar for several Weeks past.[7] I am respectfully &c. &c. ROBT. CRAFTON

Addressed: Benja. Franklin Esq

From [Susannah?] Jennings[8]

AL: University of Pennsylvania Library

March 20.—71

Miss Jennings presents Her Compliments to Doctr. Franklin, she has used the permission He gave of shewing the list to Mr. Con-

5. A London merchant identified above, XIV, 120 n.

6. BF was overcommitted in his club life. The "Honest Whigs" also met on Thursday, and he doubtless preferred it to Crafton's group of merchants trading with America. See Verner W. Crane, "The Club of Honest Whigs: Friends of Science and Liberty," *W&MQ*, XXIII (1966), 213, 233 n.

7. Presumably a reference to the rush of orders following the abandonment of the nonimportation agreement.

8. The friend and companion of Lady Aylesbury, Henry Seymour Conway's wife. For what little has been known about Miss Jennings see W. S. Lewis and A. Doyle Watson, eds., *Horace Walpole's Correspondence with Mary and Agnes Berry and Barbara Cecilia Seton* (2 vols., New Haven, 1944), I, 369, and the references there cited. New evidence suggests that she was the Susannah Jennings of Shiplake (1725–1802) who is mentioned in Emily J.

way,[9] and the enclosed Abstract of Doctr. Franklins Copy is a list of those kinds which Mr. Conway and self would be glad to have, at the same time Miss Jennings hopes if this Catalogue should appear unreasonably long, that Doctr. Franklin will not scruple to abridge it so far as to make it quite convenient to Him. She returns many Thanks for this and his former favours.

Addressed: To / Doctr. Franklin / in Craven street / in the Strand

To [Susannah?] Jennings

AL (draft): American Philosophical Society

Cravenstreet March 21. [1771]
Immediately on receiving Miss Jennings' Commands,[1] Dr. F. apply'd to the Box in order to execute them: But to his Surprise found that (thro' some unaccountable Neglect) only a few of the Parcels contained in it were actually number'd, so that the Numbers in the Catalogue are not of the Use he expected, and it requires a Knowledge of the Seeds themselves to distinguish and pick them out. In this Knowledge Dr. F. is very deficient, and therefore sends the whole Box to Miss Jennings, intreating her to find the Sorts that she and Mr. Conway have chosen, (a Trouble he would have spar'd her if he could) and to take any Quantity of them she pleases. Dr. F. presents his respectful Compliments, and is happy in having any thing that may be acceptable to her and Mr. Conway.

Climenson, *The History of Shiplake, Oxon* . . . (London, 1894), pp. 347–8, 351; see the note on Henry Conway to Horace Walpole, June 5, 1779, in the forthcoming volume of their correspondence edited by W. S. Lewis, L. E. Troide, *et al.* We are grateful to Mr. Troide for this tentative identification.

9. A list of the seeds, presumably, that Humphry Marshall had sent. See Katherine French to BF above, March 1, and the document following this one.

1. See the preceding document.

From [Charles-Guillaume-Frédéric] Dumas[2]

ALS (incomplete): American Philosophical Society

La Haie 22e. Mars 1771

[*Beginning lost:*] Monsieur, que vous resterez encore quelque tems en Angleterre. Ayez donc la bonté de m'apprendre si je pourrai encore vous faire tenir cela à Londres, ou si j'en chargerai l'un ou l'autre Capitaine qui fera voile de nos Ports pour Philadelphie. Il y aura aussi un Exemplaire pour la Bibliothêque.

Je finirai, comme j'ai commencé, en parlant de moi. J'ai fini mes précédens engagemens, sans vouloir m'embarquer dans un autre, d'aussi longue haleine, que l'on m'a présenté. J'ai cependant entrepris, pour aussi longtems que cela me conviendroit, l'éducation chez moi de deux jeunes Patriciens d'Amsterdam. Ce que ceux-ci me laissent de loisir, je l'emploie à la traduction françoise d'un bon Ouvrage Anglois, mais de longue haleine, c'est l'Histoire Chronologique du Commerce par Mr. Anderson.[3] Je tâcherai de remédier dans ma traduction, autant qu'il sera possible, au stile un peu long et embarrassé, et à des répétitions, qu'il est bien plus facile de critiquer, qu'il ne devoit l'être au savant Auteur de les éviter en composant. J'y ajouterai des remarques là où je les croirai nécessaires. J'espere d'en venir à bout dans environ deux ans; et comme l'original est dédié à la Société qui travaille avec tant de succès en Angleterre à l'encouragement des Arts, des Manufactures et du Commerce, je voudrois dédier ma Traduction à la Pensilvanie, si vous l'approuvez, Monsieur, afin de pouvoir sans mentir, et sans bassesse, dire des choses agréables et utiles. J'ai l'honneur d'être avec tout l'estime et le respect qui vous sont dûs, Monsieur, Votre très humble et très obéissant serviteur   DUMAS

Lorsque vous voudrez bien, Monsieur, m'honorer d'une réponse, elle me parviendra le plus sûrement sous une enveloppe à

2. See above, xv, 178 n.
3. Adam Anderson (1692?–1765), *An Historical and Chronological Deduction of the Origin of Commerce from the Earliest Accounts to the Present Time.* . (2 vols., London, 1764). It was a work of enormous industry, ranging over the political, social, and industrial development of the civilized world; and the author expressed a number of views, on monopolies and the mercantilist system, that were in advance of his time. *DNB*.

l'adresse de Mr. Schlemm, *Agent de Sa M[ajesté] Brittannique à Rotterdam*, le même par le moyen de qui ce paquet vous sera rendu.

Peut-on avoir à Londres, Monsieur, le *Pensylvanian Gazet*, dont vous avez eu la bonté de m'envoyer quelques feuilles? En ce cas je vous serai fort obligé de m'indiquer l'adresse de la personne à Londres qui la reçoit et distribue, afin que je puisse lui faire écrire pour me la faire tenir à mesure qu'elle arrivera de là-bas. Autrement je verrai de me la procurer directement de Philadelphie par quelque Négociant de Rotterdam en correspondance avec cette Place, qui souscrive pour moi chez l'Imprimeur et le paye, pour me l'envoyer par paquets [lors]qu'il partira quelque vaisseau pour Rotterdam. C'est une lecture qui [me] feroit grand plaisir, si je pouvois l'obtenir de tems en tems.

From William and Mary Hewson

AL: University of Pennsylvania Library

⟨March 22, [1771–74[4]]: a note in the third person, in Polly Hewson's hand. Reminds Franklin that he has promised to dine with them next Thursday.⟩

From John Hope[5]

ALS: Historical Society of Pennsylvania

Sir   Edinb. 26 March 1771

As formerly you took the trouble of transmitting some letter from a Society at Edinburgh to Mr. John Bartram; I presume to beg you will have the Goodness of transmitting the inclosed.

That Society is now dissolved.[6] I have the honour to be Sir with the greatest respect Your most obedient Servant   JOHN HOPE

4. The Hewsons were married in July, 1770, and he died suddenly in May, 1774. The invitation could have been in any March between those dates, and according to our practice we are assigning it to the earliest possible year.

5. The Edinburgh physician and professor of botany; see above, x, 16 n.

6. The name of the organization seems to have been merely "A Society of Gentlemen at Edinburgh," although its members lived all over Scotland; its purpose was to import seeds of foreign trees and ornamental shrubs. William Darlington, *Memorials of John Bartram and Humphry Marshall*... (Philadelphia, 1849), pp. 405, 434. The letter to Bartram that Hope enclosed, dated

From Deborah Franklin

ALS: American Philosophical Society

My Dear Child   March the 30 1771

I have reseved yours of Jan the 2 and was much plesed to hear that you was well in helth which is a graite pleshur to me to hear. I have bin impashent to hear that Capt. Folner was Cume or Capt. Sparkes that I moute hear from you by sum bodey hough you had seen you.

I had not knone that the packit was to go tell a week longer or I had mis understood by the paper on thisday but this will servef to tell you that I am much as I have [been] for sum time paste but the wather has [been] verey unsetled and a verey uncumforte abel Spring althow a fine winter you know [I] did not yousd to complaine of wather but it hurtes me much now.

Salley come to let me know of the poste was cume Shee had bin oute with Mrs. Foxcrofte and had cote a cold which has given her a sever pain in her tempel which Shee has complaind for sum time paste the air paste has bin [heavy?]. Shee is not up but I hope Shee is better our child is up and cume in to see me as he dus everey morning and to pay his Dutey to his papah and unkill. The other day I shoed his Grandfather our grandfathers it plesed him and wold kiss it. I told him who it was. It was aboute 3 week ago he sat on his mothers lap and looked up to your pickter and sed papah sed qoted [*illegible*] round O M moley miller his maids name is *molley Miller*[7] he is verey fond of his Book and as he is walkein a long he stopes to tell the letters on the fine border I muste tell you we had a mape and he was plesd to pinte at the difrend Cullers and we shoed him some plases and it plesed him it was laid a way under the harpsicord he found it and broute it and pinted to it and

---

March 23, is printed in *ibid.*, pp. 435–6. It says nothing about the dissolution of the Society but, on the contrary, mentions its ample funds and offers Bartram a gold medal in its name.

7. This passage about the Kingbird is, even by DF's standards, singularly obscure. Was his "papah" his real one (then in Jamaica) or BF? If the latter, the boy may have paid his duty by looking at pictures of BF and WF. When DF "shoed his Grandfather," she doubtless gave him the mezzotint reproduced as the frontispiece of Vol. x. The young man's nursemaid, Molly Miller, has not appeared before and cannot be further identified; DF seems to be saying that he made some sounds resembling her name, or perhaps quoted from a song about some one of the same name.

seme much plesd with it and coles it my pees and allways pules it up him self. Capt. All cumes as constant as if he was to larne sum thing of him[8] but let me say what I will it donte tell halef. A littel garle came to see him so after sume time he shoed her your pickter and sed papah and then held up his finger and shone to the profeel and sed is more papah and semed plesd for her to look at it. I long for you to see him I muste adue at this time and am your Loveing wife   D FRANKLIN

Addressed: To / Benjamin Franklin Esqr / Craven Street / London

From [William Franklin]   AL: American Philosophical Society

Burln. Mar. 30, 1771

I wrote a few Lines to you by this Packet and enclosed a Letter to L.H.[9] I have several other Letters to write to him by this Opportunity which prevents my writing fully to you. I have just had the Pleasure of hearing from Mr. W. Logan that you were well the first of Janry. his Son having seen you at that Time.[10]

Addressed: To / Benjn. Franklin, Esqr / Depy. Postmaster General of / N. America / Craven Street / London / Via New York per Packet / On His Majesty's Service

Opened by W.F.

8. For Capt. Isaac All, BF's nephew by marriage, see above, XII, 31 n.

9. For WF's habit of writing to Hillsborough via BF see above, XVI, 36 n. The letter he enclosed, of March 15, is apparently unpublished; an incomplete copy in his hand is in the APS, and is worth attention. The Board of Trade had rebuked him in July, 1770, for having consented to a New Jersey act that contained a suspending clause. *Board of Trade Jour.*, 1768–75, pp. 203–4; 1 *N.J. Arch.*, X, 214. In the letter to Hillsborough that he sent his father, WF justified himself on a number of grounds. The interesting one was constitutional practice in the colonies: when a governor received a bill that was neither illegal nor disrespectful, he argued, and that contained a suspending clause, he ought to agree to it and send it on for the King's approval or rejection; for such bills were regarded as petitions cast in the form of laws. If WF had refused assent to this one, he continued, he would have been charged before the King of "having arbitrarily and unnecessarily stopp'd the Petitions and Applications of his Subjects in their way to the Throne."

10. For William Logan, Sr., see above, III, 456 n; XII, 97 n. His son William, who had received his M.D. from Edinburgh in 1770, died in 1772 at the age

To [Noble Wimberly Jones?]

ALS (conclusion only): National Society of the Daughters of the
American Revolution

⟨No place or date, but endorsed "B. Franklin Esq. March or Apl.
1771." Asks the recipient to accept "a few Seeds from India, that
I am told are of curious and useful Plants, and likely to thrive in
your Country."[11]⟩

From William Strahan to William Franklin

Extract[1]: American Philosophical Society

April 3d. 1771.

Your Father could not stir in this Business as he is not only on bad
Terms with Lord Hillsborough, but with the *Ministry in general*.[2]
Besides, his Temper is grown so very reserved, which adds greatly
to his *natural Inactivity*, that there is no getting him to take part in
anything.

Of this he is himself so Sensible, that I once heard him at my
House propose to Mr. Wharton to strike his name out of the List,
as it might be of prejudice to the Undertaking. *But all this to yourself*. My *Sole Motive* for writing you thus freely, is to *put you upon
your Guard*, and to induce you to be as circumspect in your Conduct as possible, as it is imagined here, that you entertain the same
political Opinions with your Father, and are actuated by the same
Motives with regard to Britain and America.[3]

---

of twenty-four. Charles P. Keith, *The Provincial Councillors of Pennsylvania...*
(Philadelphia, 1883), pt. 2, p. 16.

11. This phrase and the endorsement give grounds for supposing that
Jones may have been the recipient. BF thought he was interested in planting
(see the letter to him below, Oct. 7, 1772), and he was the only correspondent
of BF with that interest who lived in a climate where Indian seeds might
thrive. Jones's hand, furthermore, is at least similar to that of the endorsement.

1. Made by us from a longer extract.

2. "This Business" was the proposed land grant to the Grand Ohio or
Walpole Company, of which WF and Samuel Wharton were leaders; for BF's
difficulties with the ministry see above, XVII, 200, and his account of his
audience with Hillsborough, Jan. 16, 1771.

3. WF replied that there was no reason to imagine anything of the sort. His
opinions were in many respects different from those published on either side

From [Anthony] Todd   AL: Historical Society of Pennsylvania

⟨General Post Office, Thursday, April 4, 1771. An invitation, in
the third person, to dinner at four the next day with Mr. Wharton
and Major Trent.⁴ A bizarre postscript, in Todd's hand, reads
"Salt Fish and Brandy."⟩

From Joseph Galloway   ALS: Library of Congress

Sir   Philada. April 5th. 1771
    By Order of the House of Representatives of the Province of
Pennsylvania, I herewith transmit a Petition to his Majesty respecting the Duties imposed by the late Revenue Act of Parliament, which remain unrepealed.⁵ This Petition it is their Desire
that you shoud present to his Majesty in the most proper Manner.
I am Sir, with great Esteem and Regard your most obedient
Servant   JOSEPH GALLOWAY
                                                      Speaker

Benjamin Franklin Esqr.

Addressed: To / Benjamin Franklin Esquire / in / London

Endorsed: Jos. Galloway Esqr Ap. 5. 71.

Concg. Petition to the King

of the controversy, but he was keeping them to himself. Charles Henry Hart,
ed., "Letters from William Franklin to William Strahan," *PMHB*, xxxv
(1911), 448–9.
    4. Samuel Wharton and William Trent, two of the prime movers in the
Walpole Company. The dinner was presumably to discuss its affairs.
    5. For the petition, dated March 5, 1771, see 8 *Pa. Arch.*, VIII, 6658–9. The
fact that it was addressed to the King indicates that the Assembly's experience
with its petitions in 1768 against the Townshend Acts (above, XV, 210–11,
249) had shown the uselessness of appealing to Parliament. For the fate of this
petition see BF's memorandum below, under the end of January, 1772.

From Alexander Wilson[6]   ALS: American Philosophical Society

Dear Sir   College Glasgow, April 14th. 1771
   By last post we had a Letter from Mr. Kettleby in Dublin, informing us that he had had a Letter from you inquiring if he could furnish some Fonts of Printing Types for a Printing Office in America, and that in return he had mentioned us and recommended our Types.[7]
   I now use the freedom in letting you know that we have just now ready finished Several Fonts of the Smaller Letter, Such as English No. 3d the Same on which Our Friend Mr. Strahan printed Dr. Robertsons history of Charles the 5th. 1200 weight—Pica No. 1 800. hd. [?] on which Guthries history of Scotland was printed by Mr. Hamilton in Falcon Court. Of Pica No. 3d. 400 hd. every way Similar to the Pica so much used in London—Small Pica No. 3d. 800. hd. on which a Book entitled a Tour through Gr. Britain was lately done in London. Burgeois and Brevier the Same as Mr. Strahan uses in his Chronicle.[8] Of the first 400. hd. of the last 800. hd.

   6. A man of many talents, Alexander Wilson (1714–86) was both the first famous Scottish type-founder and the first professor of astronomy at Glasgow University. He originally studied medicine, but abandoned that career and established a foundry in 1742 at St. Andrews. Soon he moved to the environs of Glasgow and, when appointed to the chair of practical astronomy in 1760, to the vicinity of the college. He provided type for the Foulis brothers, printers to the University, and his most important achievement was the double pica cut in 1768 for the quarto edition of Gray's *Poems*; his Greek type, for the Foulis edition of Homer in 1756–58, was almost equally famous. *DNB*; Talbot B. Reed, *A History of the Old English Letter Foundries*... (A. F. Johnson, ed.; London, [1952]), pp. 258–62. BF and WF visited Wilson's foundry during their visit to Scotland in 1759: J. A. Cochrane, *Dr. Johnson's Printer: the Life of William Strahan* (Cambridge, Mass., 1964), p. 105.
   7. J. G. Kettilby was a maker of presses and other printer's materials; see his reply to BF's inquiry below, April 27. We cannot establish the purpose of that inquiry, and the connection between Wilson and Kettilby.
   8. The squiggles that we transcribe as "hd." are interlined and virtually illegible; we assume that they are all abbreviations for "weight." The books referred to were William Robertson, *History of the Reign of the Emperor Charles V*... (3 vols., London, 1769); William Guthrie, *A General History of Scotland, from the Earliest Accounts to the Present Time* (10 vols., London, 1767 68); and Daniel Defoe, *A Tour through the Whole Island of Great Britain*... (7th ed.; 4 vols., London, 1769), printed by J. and F. Rivington. For Archibald Hamilton and John Rivington see Henry R. Plomer *et al.*,

Also a 400. hd. of Burgeois on a Brevier body fit for News papers &c: If any larger or Smaller than these were to be needed we have them in our Collection.

I have made free in giving you this detail which on account of former Acquaintance I hope youl readily indulge me in. From the long encouragement which we have met with from some worthy friends we have in the Trade in London, we have been induced for some Years past to make considerable improvements in our Letter, and in point of Elegance as well as in the quality of the Metal, and good execution of the Types we doubt not but they would give satisfaction. There are opportunities almost every week to the different Ports in America from Clyde, and we are in the use of Sending out Fonts often; But if they were to be shiped for Liverpool as Mr. Kettleby mentions, they could easily be conveyed there by some of our Coasters.

Our Prices are as follow which on Account of the cheapness of Labour here are considerably below those in London.

Titling Letter above Double Pica	-	1s.
Double Pica. Great Primer. English		11d.
Pica - - - - - - - - -		11 1/2d.
Small Pica - - - - - - - -		1s. 1d.
Long Primer - - - - - - -		1s. 5d.
Small Burgeois - - - - - - -		1s. 9d.
Brevier - - - - - - - - -		2s. 2d.
Brevier Burgeois - - - - - -		2s.
Nonpareil - - - - - - - -		4s.9

In case the terms of this Letter be agreeable Your Orders will very much oblige us. Compliments to Our friend Mr. Small when you see him.[1] I ever am with Esteem Sir Your most Obedient Servant

ALEX WILSON

Addressed: To / Benjamin Franklin Esqr. / Craven Street / London

---

A Dictionary of the Printers and Booksellers Who Were at Work in England . . . from 1726 to 1775 (Oxford, 1932), pp. 114, 214. Strahan had been printing the *London Chron.* since 1757.

9. Almost all these sizes of type are translated into their modern equivalents above, XIII, 60 n. Nonpareil is 6 point, the smallest of them all.

1. Presumably William Small, for whom see above, XI, 480 n.

To a Committee of the Library Company of Philadelphia

ALS: Pierpont Morgan Library

Gentlemen,   London, April 16. 1771

I received yours of Jan. 25: with a Catalogue of Books to be purchased for the Library Company. The Collection is making with all possible Expedition, but I fear will scarce be ready to go with this Ship. I beg you would not imagine it giving me Trouble when you send me the Commands of the Company. If I can execute them to their Satisfaction, it will, on the contrary, be a very great Pleasure to me: For I have many Reasons to wish well to the Institution.

I hope to send you, with the Books, an Estimate of the Cost of the European Transactions and the French Cyclopedia.[2] I am, very respectfully, Gentlemen, Your most obedient humble Servant   B FRANKLIN

P.S. Inclos'd is the Lib. Company's Accompt, as it stands in my Books here.[3]

Messrs. Mich. Hillegas, Nicho. Waln, and R. Strettell Jones

From Joseph Priestley

ALS: Haverford College Library

Dear Sir   Leeds, 19 Apr. 1771

I am glad that you have received your *Comm Bonon.* safe.[4] I thank you for the use of them, and think myself [fortunate] in having an opportunity of doing you the smallest favour. I told you I either had or expect very soon to be possessed of the memoirs of all the philosophical societies, *of note*, in Europe, and the

2. He had asked for an estimate on the transactions from Priestley, whose long and detailed answer is the following document. If BF had also inquired about the famous *Encyclopédie, ou Dictionnaire raisonné des sciences, des arts et des métiers, par une société de gens de lettres* . . . (17 vols., Paris, 1751–65), Priestley did not mention it.

3. He had received £150 and laid out £62 1s. 6d. for books, leaving a credit balance of £87 18s. 6d. Ledger, p. 19.

4. Priestley had apparently borrowed BF's set of *Commentaria Bononiensia,* which is mentioned later in the letter.

following account of the price of them will, I fancy, be sufficient for your purpose.[5]

A complete edition of the memoirs of the *Royal Society at Paris* cannot, I imagine, be bought for less than £120. My Amsterdam edition at hand will cost about £30. NB The *Memoires Anciennes* are 11 Vols, and comprehend the *Ouvrages Adoptés*.

Memoires de Mathematique et de Physique 5 Vols 4to, about £5 5s. 0d. These are generally quoted by the name of *Memoires Presentées* or *Memoires de Savans Etrangers*.

Miscellania Berolinensia 3 Vols 4to £1 11s. 6d. Of the modern *Berlin Memoirs*, 23 Vols 4to have been published. The last is for the year 1767. They may perhaps cost 15s. at a medium, which is £17 5s. 0d. *Commentaria Bononiensia* 6 Vols 4to. I am told there are three or four more, and I think they will not be less than a pound a piece: £10 0s. 0d.

Miscellania Taurinensia 3 Vols 4to. £2 6s. 0d.

Of the *Acta Helvetica* I have 5 Vols 4to the last for 1762. I believe there are four or five more. They may perhaps cost half a guinea a Vol £5 5s. 0d.

The *Dantzig Society* in High Dutch, 3 Vols 4to. Mine, I think, cost me 18s. a Vol, at Hamburgh. I remember I thought them very dear: £2 12s. 0d.[6] Of The *Drontheim Society* in High Dutch 8vo. I have three volumes. I think Mr. Heydinger[7] told me there are 3 more. He charged me 5s. a Vol: £1 10s. 0d. Of the *Royal Society in Sweden* I have 17 Vols. 8vo the last for 1757 (a translation into High Dutch). I expect the remainder to the present time every day. They will then cost 5s. a Vol.: £6 15s. 0d.

The *Petersburg Memoirs* I have not yet received, but I remember I expected that they would cost me £30. *Acta Hafniensia* I have not yet got, and want much. They are 2 Vols 4to, and may perhaps be had for £1 10s. 0d.

5. BF had suggested, almost two years before, that the Library Company of Philadelphia purchase the transactions of all the European philosophical societies; see above, XVI, 171–2. The Library committee had recently asked for an estimate of the cost: Hillegas *et al.* to BF above, Jan. 25. On receiving this request BF had consulted Priestley, who is here responding.

6. Even a great scientist could make an error in arithmetic.

7. Probably C. Heydinger, a printer and bookseller in the Strand, for whom see Henry R. Plomer *et al.*, *A Dictionary of the Printers and Booksellers Who Were at Work in England...from 1726 to 1775* (Oxford, 1932), p. 124.

The *Acta Naturae Curiosorum Caesariensia* have been published, with some change of title, for I believe near a century, a Vol 4to every year. The *Acta Nova* are 4 Vols. perhaps 15[s.]. I have 9 Vols of the title preceding them, but they are not the whole, and contain very little philosophical knowledge, consisting almost wholly of Medical articles. The Acta Nova and the 12 Vols (I think there are) of the title preceding them will probably cost £12 0s. 0d.

Of the *Acta Upsaliensia* I know nothing.

Of the *Acta Chymica Holmiensia*, by Hierni, I have 2 Vols in 12mo. I believe no more are published. 6s. 0d.

Essays Physical and literary of a Society at Edinburgh, 2 Vols 8vo 12s. 0d.

Of the Philosophical and Medical Society at *Breslau* I know nothing.

Of an *Philosophical Transactions* I need not say anything.

This, Dear Sir, is all the intelligence I am able to give you concerning these Societies, and the price of their publications, omitting the *Acta Eruditorum*, or *Acta Lipsiensia, Journal des Scavans*, and several others, which are chiefly accounts of books, tho' they contain several Original Essays.

All the sums I have mentioned, you will find amount to £216 16s. 6d. Taking in the Philosophical Transactions, and those of which I have no information; and together with the old *Acta Curiosorum Caesariensia*, £300 will, perhaps, be about the sum requested for your purpose.

Commentarii Societatis Gottingensis 4 Vols quarto at 15s.: £3 0s. 0d.[8]

8. These transactions, in the order of Priestley's listing, were as follows: (1) The *Histoire* or *Mémoires* (the title varies) of the Académie royale des sciences ran to 70 vols. in the French edition (Paris, 1706–70). Priestley's Amsterdam edition, also in French, was probably of the *Histoire* in 48 vols. (1706–55) and of the *Mémoires* in 6 (1735–36); the latter contained the works "adopted" by the Academy before 1699. (2) The *Mémoires de mathématique et de physique, présentés à l'Académie royale des sciences, par divers savans...* contained 5 vols. by 1770 but eventually ran to 11 (Paris, 1750–86). (3) The *Miscellanea Berolinensia ad incrementum...scientiarum...* (7 vols., Berlin, 1710–43) were the transactions of what is now the Deutsche Akademie der Wissenschaften; the *Berlin Memoirs*, published by the same society, ran eventually to 25 vols.: *Histoire de l'Académie royale des sciences et des belles lettres...* (Berlin, 1746–71). (4) Priestley had all the volumes then published by what is now the Accademia delle Scienze dell' Istituto Bologna: *De*

71

You give me pleasure by your account of the success of my subscription. If it indemnify me for what is past I shall be very happy;
but that, I am afraid, is more than I can expect. We begin to print
this week. I expect the first proof every hour. I print a thousand.[9]

Bononiensi scientiarum et artium Instituto... commentarii (7 vols., Bologna,
1731–91). (5) The other Italian publication, by what developed into the
Reale Accademia delle Scienze, began as Miscellanea philosophico-mathematica
and was continued as Mélanges de philosophie et de mathématique (5 vols.,
Turin, 1759–76). (6) The Basel Physico-Medical Society had published by
this time 6 vols. of its wide-ranging Acta Helvetica, physico-mathematico-
anatomico-botanico-medica... (8 vols., Basel, 1751–77). (7) Priestley's expensive purchase in Hamburg was of Versuche und Abhandlungen der Natur-
forschenden Gesellschaft... (3 vols., Danzig and Leipzig, 1747–56). (8) His
German translation of the Trondhjem Society was incomplete: Der Dron-
theimschen Gesellschaft Schriften aus dem Dänischen übersetzt (4 vols., Copenhagen and Leipzig, 1765–70). (9) The transactions of the Royal Swedish
Academy were translated as Abhandlungen aus der Naturlehre, Haushaltungs-
kunst und Mechanik (41 vols., Hamburg and Leipzig, 1749–83). (10) The
Commentarii Academiae scientiarum imperialis Petropolitanae, in two series
(St. Petersburg, 1728–76), eventually came to 34 vols., of which 28 had
appeared by this time. (11) The Acta Hafniensia were the product of the
Copenhagen Society of Fine Arts, Scriptorum... (3 vols., Copenhagen,
1745–47). (12) The Imperial Leopoldine Academy had been publishing for
a century the Acta naturae curiosorum Caesariensia, in various series with
various subtitles, but not a volume a year; Priestley had all the volumes then
in print of the Nova acta physico-medica... (8 vols., Nuremberg, etc., 1758–
91), and all but one of the preceding series, the Acta physico-medica... (10
vols., Nuremberg, 1727–54). (13) The transactions with which he was un-
familiar were the Acta Societatis regiae scientiarum Upsaliensis... (5 vols.,
Uppsala, 1740–50). (14) His Acta chymica Holmiensia were the papers and
essays of Urban Hjärne or Hierne (1641–1724), edited by Johan G. Wallerius:
Urbani Hierne Actorum chemicorum Holmiensium... (2 vols., Stockholm,
1753); for this information we are indebted to Professor Henry Guerlac. (15)
The Philosophical Society of Edinburgh was just completing its Essays and
Observations, Physical and Literary... (3 vols., Edinburgh, 1754–71). (16)
We share Priestley's ignorance of the society in Breslau, but a German
translation of (2) above was published there in 1748–59. (17) Of the Phil.
Trans. we also need not say anything. (18) The Acta eruditorum..., in two
series, was published at Leipzig from 1682, and by this time came to 87 vols.
(19) The Journal des scavans... began in Paris in 1665 and continued until
1792. (20) The final entry, which appears to have been interlined in BF's
hand, was the Commentarii Societatis regiae scientiarum Gottingensis (4 vols.,
Göttingen, 1752–[55]).
  9. The work printed by subscription was The History and Present State of
Discoveries Relating to Vision, Light, and Colours (2 vols., London, 1772).

You say nothing of the patronage of the king, which you thought it possible to procure. I am, with the greatest respect, Dear Sir, yours sincerely   J PRIESTLEY

To [Jeremiah] Meyer[1]

AL (draft): Historical Society of Pennsylvania

One of the great difficulties in knowing Franklin through the written words he left behind him is that he rarely, on paper, lost his temper. He sometimes did in his marginalia, his most private comments; but in his correspondence with others he preserved a calm that was undoubtedly more Olympian than the flesh-and-blood man could maintain. This draft by a thoroughly angry Franklin, therefore, has a human value that has nothing to do with whether he sent what he had drafted, or moderated its tone to accord with his public persona.

[Before April 20, 1771[2]]
Dr. Franklin presents his Compliments to Mr. Meyer, and prays him not to detain any longer the Picture from which he was to make a Miniature, but return it by the Bearer. Hopes Mr. Meyer will not think him impatient, as he has waited full Five Years,[3] and seen many of his Acquaintance tho' applying later, serv'd before him. Wishes Mr. Meyer not to give himself the Trouble of making

Priestley's hopes for it were disappointed: it did not indemnify him for the time he had spent on it, and he abandoned his plan to go on to an inclusive history of the experimental sciences. Schofield, *Scientific Autobiography*, pp. 52, 82–3, 99, 121–4.

1. An artist famous in his day. Meyer (1735–89) was born in Tübingen, came to England as a boy, and by 1764 was enamel-painter to the King and miniature-painter to the Queen; four years later he was a founding member of the Royal Academy. It should be added, in view of the contents of BF's note, that he was widely esteemed not only as a painter but as a person. *DNB.*

2. The day when the painting that occasioned this note was sent to WF. See the final paragraph of the following document.

3. Longer than that—some eight and a half years. The picture was a portrait of WF that BF had commissioned from Benjamin Wilson (for whom see above, IV, 391 n) while his son was in London. Charles C. Sellers, *Benjamin Franklin in Portraiture* (New Haven and London, 1962), p. 409. When WF returned to America late in 1762, he left the portrait with Meyer to be copied in three miniatures set in bracelets. WF to William Strahan, Nov., 1762, Yale University Library; James A. Cochrane, *Dr. Johnson's Printer . . .* (Cambridge, Mass., 1964), p. 110.

any more Apologies or to feel the least Pain on Account of his disappointing Dr. Franklin who assures him, he never was disappointed by him but once, not having for several Years past since he has known the Character of his Veracity, had the smallest dependance upon it.

To William Franklin

AL (incomplete draft[4]): American Philosophical Society

Dear Son,   London, April 20. 1771
    It is long since I have heard from you. The last Packet brought me no Letter, and there are two Packets now due. It is supposed that the long easterly Winds have kept them back.
    We have had a severe and tedious Winter here. There is not yet the smallest Appearance of Spring. Not a Bud has push'd out, nor a Blade of Grass. The Turnips that us'd to feed the Cattle have been destroy'd by the Frost. The Hay in most Parts of the Country is gone, and the Cattle perishing for Want, the Lambs dying by Thousands, thro' Cold and scanty Nourishment. Tuesday last I went to dine at our Friend Sir Matthew Featherstone's thro' a heavy Storm of Snow. His Windows you know look into the Park. Towards Evening I observ'd the Snow still lying over all the Park, for the Ground was before too cold to thaw it, being itself frozen and Ice in the Canal. You cannot imagine a more winterlike Prospect! Sir M. and Lady F. always enquire kindly of your Welfare: As do Mr. and Mrs. Sargent.[5]
    Sir John Pringle has heard from Mr. Bowman of your Kindness to that Gentleman and desires I would present his particular Acknowledgements for the Attention you have paid to his Recommendation.[6]
    I send enclos'd my Account against you for Money advanced

4. Sparks deleted the incomplete final paragraph and added BF's signature to the previous one (*Works*, VII, 518); subsequent editors followed suit.
    5. For Sir Matthew Featherstonhaugh see above, x, 214 n, and for Mr. and Mrs. John Sargent VII, 322.
    6. Bowman was undoubtedly the young man who BF had thought was bound for Newport more than a year earlier, and whom we cannot identify. Above, XVII, 30.

and paid here since my being in England. There are two Articles, viz. May 2. 1765. Prints £12 10s. 0d.; and July 11. 1769. Books £22 17s. 6d. from which you are to make proper Deductions; as I would not have you charg'd with any Prints you might have given away to our common Friends, but only with what have been sold for your Account. And among the Books were some that I desired you to put into a Booksellers Hands to be sold for my Account.[7] The heaviest Part is the Maintenance and Education of Temple; but that his Friends will not grudge when they see him.

The Ohio Affair seems now near a Conclusion. And if the present Ministry stand a little longer, I think it will be compleated to our Satisfaction.[8] Mr. Wharton has been indefatigable, and I think scarce any one I know besides would have been equal to the Task, so difficult it is to get Business forward here, in which some Party Purpose is not to be served: But he is among them eternally, and

7. The accounts that BF sent, now lost, began an interchange between father and son. WF responded with two sets of queries, not in his hand, which BF docketed as "Remarks on B.F.'s English Acct. against W.F.—dated April 20. 1771 (N. 1)" and "A State of W.F.'s *English* Account with B.F. (1771) (N. 2)"; both contain a few marginal jottings by BF, and are among his papers in the APS. The "Remarks" make clear that the 1765 item was a payment to Mason Chamberlain for prints; WF took responsibility for one lot that had been consigned for sale, and deducted the cost of others given to himself, DF, and friends. The 1769 item also included prints, which had been similarly disposed of, and copies of a book by Theodorus Drage, presumably *The Great Probability of a Northwest Passage...* (London, 1768), that had likewise been consigned for sale; again WF claimed deductions.

8. The affair was in fact no nearer completion than ever. In the autumn of 1770 William Nelson, acting as chief executive of Virginia after Lord Botetourt's death, had written a long letter to Hillsborough opposing the plans of the Walpole or Grand Ohio Company as a violation of Virginia's prior rights; soon afterward Lord Dunmore, the new governor, joined in this opposition. Nelson's letter was shown to the Walpole group, and a reply was presented on March 5, 1771, which is now attributed to Samuel Wharton rather than BF. See Gipson, *British Empire*, XI, 469–72; *Statement of the Petitioners in the Case of the Walpole Company* [London, 1771], appendices II–III. Wharton's reply failed to convince the government or accelerate its pace: the matter was not referred back to the Board of Trade until a year later, and did not elicit a response from it until May, 1773. *Board of Trade Jour.*, 1768–75, pp. 293–4, 299–300, 336. DF must have been confident, despite the lessons of experience, that the game was already won; and he was not alone. William Strahan showed almost equal confidence in the letter of which an extract is printed above, April 3, and gave credit for success to Wharton.

leaves no Stone unturn'd. I would, however, advise you not to say any thing of our Prospect of Success, till the Event appears: for many things happen between the Cup and the Lip.

I have attended several Times this Winter upon your Acts of Assembly. The Board are not favourably dispos'd towards your Insolvent Acts, pretending to doubt whether distant Creditors, particularly such as reside in England may not sometimes be injured by them. I have had a good deal of Conversation with Mr. Jackson about them, who remarks that whatever Care the Assembly may, according to my Representation of their Practice, take in examining into the Cases to prevent Injustice, yet upon the Face of the Acts nothing of that Care appears. The Preambles only say that such and such Persons have petitioned and set forth the Hardship of their Imprisonment, but not a Word of the Assembly's having enquired into the Allegations contained in such Petitions and found them true, not a Word of the general Consent of the principal Creditors, or of any publick Notice given of the Debtor's Intention to apply for such an Act, all which he thinks should appear in the Preambles, and then those Acts would be subject to less Objection and Difficulty in getting them through the Offices here. I would have you communicate this to the Speaker of the Assembly with my best Respects. I doubt some of those Acts will be repeal'd.[9] Nothing has been done, or is now likely to be done by the Parliament in American Affairs: The House of Commons and the City of London are got into a violent Controversy, that seems at present to engross the publick Attention,[1] and the Session cannot continue much longer.

By this Ship I send the Picture that you left with Meyer.[2] He has never yet finished the Miniatures. The other Pictures I send with it are for my own House, but this you may take to yours.

In the Business I transacted here for Mr. Cha. Read, after paying the Solicitor there remained a Ballance to Mr. Read of £9 19s. 9d.

9. Both public and private acts were at issue. Ambiguities in a public act in 1769 were cleared up in another the following spring, which was disallowed; but the objections detailed by BF seem to have applied particularly to the Assembly's numerous private acts. See 1 *N.J. Arch.*, X, 234–5; XVIII, 90–2, 103, 170 n; *Board of Trade Jour.*, 1768–75, p. 248; *Acts Privy Coun., Col.*, V, 315–16.

1. See the second paragraph of the following document.

2. See the preceding document.

in my Hands, which I requested you to pay him. You never wrote me Word whether [you] had done it or not; so I could not give you Credit for it. If you paid it, so much must be added to the Credit side of your Account.[3] And as it is possible I may have omitted some Articles of Charge against you that you are acquainted with, I rely on your rectifying such Mistakes. This Account takes in nothing previous to [*remainder missing*]

To Joseph Galloway

ALS: Yale University Library

Dear Sir,   London, April 20. 1771

It is an Age since I have heard from you. But the long-continu'd Easterly Winds have kept back all Ships from the Westward, and we have now two Packets due.

Nothing has been handled in Parliament this Session relating to America; and our Friends have thought it best for us not to move any thing relating to our Affairs till a little Time should have worne off the Ill Humour that prevailed with regard to us. They have had enough to do, first with the Disputes about Falkland's Islands, and now with the City of London concerning the Power of the House to imprison for Contempts.[4] I own I am a little diverted in seeing that Power disputed; since, as you remember, Government

3. For Charles Read's legal efforts to secure office in New Jersey see above, XIV, 217 n. In the comments on BF's accounts, cited above, WF took credit for the £9 19s. 9d. in partial discharge of BF's debt to Read.

4. The principal debates over the Falkland Islands crisis had been in November, January, and February; Cobbett, *Parliamentary History*, XVI (1765–71), 1082–1124, 1336–46, 1358–1402. The other dispute, the celebrated printers' case, was on the boil when BF was writing. It was the last battle in the war to keep secret what went on in the House of Commons, which lost the fight because it chose to pit its privileges against those of the City of London. The printers were arrested in the City for publishing debates of the House, and John Wilkes and others utilized this infringement of London's judicial liberties to bring on a major struggle. During it Lord North was attacked and injured by the mob, and the Commons committed an alderman and the Lord Mayor to the Tower. They were released when the session ended in early May, and thereafter the House tacitly abandoned its prohibition on reporting debates. See Peter D. G. Thomas, "John Wilkes and the Freedom of the Press (1771)," Institute of Hist. Research *Bulletin*, XXXIII (1960), 86–98.

here would not allow it to our Assemblies.[5] All the Arguments used against the Claim and Exercise of such a Power in a Provincial Assembly, are now brought out against the House of Commons, who are in my mind full as likely to make an ill Use of it. So that agreable to the Proverb, what was then thought Sauce for the Goose, is now found to be Sauce for the Gander. The general Run of Discourse here is against the Commons; their boundless Claim of unknown Privileges begins to be laught at, and there is not one among them who does not now wish the Question had not been moved; but they know not how to retreat or advance with Honour or Safety. This is another Instance to convince the World of the Weakness of all Government that has not with it the Opinion of the People. And the general Corruption and Servility of Parliament is now so generally seen and known to all the Nation, that it is no longer respected as it used to be. Its Censures are no more regarded than Popes Bulls. It is despis'd for its Venality, and abominated for its Injustice. And yet it is not clear that the People deserve a better Parliament, since they are themselves full as corrupt and venal; witness the Sums they accept for their Votes at almost every Election.

I inclose a Copy of the List of our Acts lately presented to the King in Council by the Proprietary. [*In the margin:* This is from Memory, and I may mistake in the particular Acts.] I have frequently attended Mr. Jackson (now Counsel to the Board of Trade) upon them, who indeed is very tender of making Objections to them, the Board being always ready to catch at any thing that may countenance a Report of theirs for Repealing. But tho' I think he will generally report to the Board in favour of those Laws, he has privately mentioned to me some Remarks which I communicate for your Information. The special Acts for the Relief of insolvent Debtors the Board are very jealous of, lest they should sometimes operate to the Prejudice of the Merchants here: The Reasons and Foundations of such Acts should therefore clearly

5. A reference to the Smith–Moore case in Pennsylvania in 1758–59, which ended in a Privy Council ruling that the "inferior Assemblies in America" did not have the powers of the House of Commons. See above, VII, 385 n; VIII, 28–51, 60–3, 295–6, 403 n; Leonard W. Levy, *Legacy of Suppression: Freedom of Speech and Press in Early American History* (Cambridge, Mass., 1960), pp. 53–61.

appear in the Preambles; it seeming odd, that after a general Act
for the Relief of all Insolvent Debtors whose Debts do not exceed
such a Sum, there should be a special Act to relieve James Galbreath for no other Reason, as far as appears on the Face of the
Act, but that he was indebted beyond the Sum limited. And in that
for John Relfe, it only appears that he represented his having met
with Losses, but no Enquiry is mentioned to have been made, and
that the Allegations contain'd in his Petition had been verified.6 I
acquainted him with the usual Practice of the House to appoint a
Committee to enquire into the Facts, to hear the principal Creditors, &c. &c. and that in the Votes all this would appear: But as I
had not the Votes to show him, he said I might thence see the
Necessity of expressing all that in the Preambles. By the way, if
the Votes and Laws were always immediately sent to your Agent,
it would frequently enable him more effectually to support any
Act that is called in question. He had also some Doubts about the
Power given to Justices of the Peace to put Landlords into Possession in a summary Way, when Tenants are behind in the Payment
of Rent, apprehending that such Power might be sometimes mis-
used, by the artful Management of Persons that were in fact not
truly Landlords, but desirous of obtaining Possession under that
Colour. If this Act should pass here, and you think this Apprehension of his, of some moment; you may consider of some timely
Amendment; and therefore I mention it.7

It has been some time talked, that your present Governor is
expected over here shortly, and that his Brother Richard Penn is
appointed to succeed him.8 With the sincerest Esteem and Affec-

6. The maximum limit, by an act of 1764–65, was £150; see James T.
Mitchell *et al.*, eds., *The Statutes at Large of Pennsylvania from 1682–1809*
(17 vols., Harrisburg, etc., 1896–1915), VI, 392–3. For the private acts
relieving Galbreath and Relfe, both of which were finally approved, see *ibid.*,
VII, 317–19, 312–15.

7. For the act in question, which was approved, see *ibid.*, pp. 334–9. The
publications for which BF was asking were annual ones, the *Votes and
Proceedings* often cited in previous volumes and the texts of the acts passed in
each session of the House of Representatives.

8. John Penn, Lieutenant Governor since 1763, was returning to England
because of his father's death. His younger brother Richard, who had gone
home in 1769, was appointed to take his place; see Evans to BF below, May 4.
Richard served for only two years before John abruptly superseded him.

tion, I am, Dear Sir, Your most obedient and most humble Servant
B FRANKLIN

Jos. Galloway Esqr

From C[harles] W[illson] P[eale⁹]

ALS (letterbook draft): American Philosophical Society

[April 21, 1771¹]

In Compliance with that promise that I had the honor to make you when I was about leaving London, I now assume the Liberty of a Correspondent, in addressing this letter to you. I ever retain a grateful sense of the respect you shewed, and the notice you took of me when in England, marks of respect, of this nature make the strongest impressions on my mind, occasioned perhaps from my particular Circumstance early in life, being deprived of a Father,² not born to an affluent fortune, nor connected by family relation to the great, I have hitherto been indebted, for the small rise I have made in the world, to the unsollicited notice and respect, of a Number of Gentlemen who have honored me with their friendship, amongst whom my aspiring ambition would fondly have the

9. The noted artist (1741–1827) studied in London, 1767–69. A few months after his arrival, he recollected a half-century later, he mustered the courage to call on BF without knowing him. He found his host sitting with a young lady on his knee. Peale was cordially welcomed when he mentioned his father, whom BF well remembered, and explained that he had come unannounced because he could find no one who offered to introduce him; in almost the same breath he remarked that Benjamin West had received him very kindly. Charles C. Sellers, *Charles Willson Peale:...Early Life (1741–1790)* (Philadelphia, 1947), pp. 74–5, based on Peale's diary entry of Dec. 17, 1818; our reading of the entry, from a transcript kindly furnished us by Mr. Sellers, differs in minor details from his. The story is suspect. Peale had in fact been welcomed on arrival by West, who was the obvious person to introduce him to BF; why, then, did the young man not use this channel? If he took the social bit in his teeth, as he remembered in old age, he must have been singularly timid about imposing on West and self-confident about imposing on BF.

1. The draft, without date or address, is clearly that of the letter of April 21 to which BF referred in his reply below, July 4.

2. His father, Charles Peale, Jr., died when he was nine, after a lurid career that ended tamely with teaching school in Maryland. See Sellers, *op. cit.*, pp. 21–33.

80

honor of Ranking you. Since my return to America the encouragement and Patronage I have met with exceed my most sanguine
expectation, not only in Annapolis Maryld. which is my native
place but also in Philadelphia I have had considerable business,
for which I was very generously rewarded and my vanity much
flattered by the general approbation which my performance hath
hitherto met with. The people here have a growing taste for the
arts, and are becoming more and more fond of encouraging their
progress amongst them, I fondly flatter myself they will here find
patronage, and an Assylum, when oppression and tyranny shall
perhaps banish them from seats where they now flourish. We have
for sometime past been confused with the apprehension of a
French and Spanish war but late reports have expeled our fears,
by assuring us of matters being amicably Settled. Your condescending to make use of a vacant moment in writing to me will greatly
oblige Sir your very Humble and most Obedient Servant

C W P

To Humphry Marshall ALS: Yale University Library

Sir,   London, April 22. 1771
    I duly received your Favours of the 4th. of October and the 17th.
of November. It gave me Pleasure to hear, that tho' the Merchants
had departed from their Agreement of Non-Importation, the
Spirit of Industry and Frugality was likely to continue among the
People. I am obliged to you for your Concern on my Account.
The Letters you mention gave great Offence here; but that was
not attended with the immediate ill Consequences to my Interest
that seem to have been hoped for by those that sent Copies of
them hither.[3]
    If our Country People would well consider, that all they save in
refusing to purchase foreign Gewgaws, and in making their own
Apparel, being apply'd to the Improvement of their Plantations,
would render those more profitable, as yielding a greater Produce,
I should hope they would persist resolutely in their present commendable Industry and Frugality. And there is still a farther

3. Letters urging continuance of the nonimportation agreements. See
above, XVII, 110–19, 180 n, 200 n.

Consideration. The Colonies that produce Provisions grow very fast: But of the Countries that take off those Provisions, some do not increase at all, as the European Nations, and others, as the West India Colonies, not in the same proportion. So that tho' the Demand at present may be sufficient, it cannot long continue so. Every Manufacturer encouraged in our Country, makes part of a Market for Provisions within ourselves, and saves so much Money to the Country as must otherwise be exported to pay for the Manufactures he supplies. Here in England it is well known and understood, that wherever a Manufacture is established which employs a Number of Hands, it raises the Value of Lands in the neighbouring Country all around it; partly by the greater Demand near at hand for the Produce of the Land; and partly from the Plenty of Money drawn by the Manufacturers to that Part of the Country. It seems therefore the Interest of all our Farmers and Owners of Lands, to encourage our young Manufactures in preference to foreign ones imported among us from distant Countries.[4]

I am much obliged by your kind Present of curious Seeds. They were welcome Gifts to some of my Friends. I send you herewith some of the new Barley lately introduced into the Country, and now highly spoken of. I wish it may be found of Use with us.

I was the more pleas'd to see in your Letter the Improvement of our Paper, having had a principal Share in establishing that Manufacture among us many Years ago, by the Encouragement I gave it.[5] If in any thing I can serve you here, it will be a Pleasure to Your obliged Friend and humble Servant   B Franklin

Mr Humphry Marshall

Addressed: To / Mr Humphry Marshall / West Bradford / Chester County / per Capt. Osborne / with a brown Paper Parcel

4. BF is expanding upon the same point that he made to Marshall a year before: *ibid.*, pp. 109–10.

5. In his days as a printer BF had had much to do with paper-making, both providing rags and marketing paper; his most direct encouragement of the industry had been through his connection with William Parks' mill in Williamsburg. See Dard Hunter, *Papermaking in Pioneer America* (Philadelphia, 1952), pp. 41–5, 48–9.

From Elizabeth Empson[6] ALS: American Philosophical Society

Dear Sir   Pool April 23d 1771

I received yours by the last post—and return you a thousand thanks for the money you are so kind as to Alow me which I have Drawn on you for. I am affraid by the Manner and Shortness of your letter that you [are?] displeased with the freedom I have taken [in my writing?] to you. But alass Sir if you [were in my situation?] without friends or money you [would understand?] Me. I should never have solicited your favour for Mr. Empson unless I had thought it was in your power to do it as I know a Change is easily [made] if a person has a Supliant freind to speak [for him?]. I did hope to have fownd that friend [in you,] but tis My Misfortune that tis not in yo[ur power] to do anny thing for us. But perhaps [it] may yet be. I have made so free as [to] send a letter inclosed to you to be so good as to send it when you have an Oportunity.[7] Mr. Empson joines with me in best respects and Manny Thanks. I remain Dear Sir your most oblidged humble Servant   ELIZATH. EMPSON

Addressed: To / Benjn: Franklin Esqr. in / Craven Street on the Strand / London

From Joseph Galloway ALS: American Philosophical Society

Dear Sir   Philada. April 23. 1771

This will be deliverd to you by Mr. Nicholas Biddle, to whom I wish to render acceptable Service, not so much from a personal Acquaintance with him, as from the general Good Character and Esteem he has deservedly acquired among all those who have had any Knowledge or Experience of him. He is warmly recommended to me, as an Active, sensible, prudent, enterprizing young

6. This is the only letter in the papers to or from her. She was the daughter of the Franklins' Philadelphia neighbor, the silversmith Samuel Soumaine, and had married Thomas Empson in 1763. Above, XI, 190 n. Almost nothing is known about either of them after the marriage. They had reportedly been in Ireland in 1765 (above, XII, 63), and the letter suggests that they had then moved to England; in any case the husband had clearly fallen on bad times.

7. The enclosure was presumably to one or both of her parents.

Gentleman. The Merchants Service has hitherto engaged his Attention. But, not content in that Sphere of Action, where his Friends wou'd immediately promote him, 'tis laudable Ambition incites him to pursue some Thing more honourable. The Navy, under the present Prospect of Wars, is the first Object of his Wishes. But shoud the Peace continue his next View is to obtain a Birth in the East-India Company Service. He brings Letters from Several Gentlemen here to others in London.[8] Permit me also to recommend him to your Advice and Assistance, assuring you that I am confident he will never dishonour any Favor he may receive from your Friendship. I am Dear Sir your very Affectionate humble Servant JOS. GALLOWAY

Addressed: To / Benjamin Franklin Esquire / Deputy Post Master general / of North America / in / Craven Street / London / per Mr. / Nicholas Biddle.

From [Thomas] Life AL: American Philosophical Society

⟨Basinghall St., April 26, 1771, a note in the third person. Sorry that he has been too rushed with important business, which had to be finished that week, to call on Franklin about the Georgia affair;[9] will do so next Monday morning, if convenient, at eleven.⟩

---

8. Nicholas Biddle (1750–78), who was to become a hero of the infant U.S. Navy during the War of Independence, had been a sailor since the age of thirteen. Among the letters of introduction that he brought with him to London was one from Thomas Willing, the Philadelphia banker and judge, to Capt. Stirling, R.N., Willing's brother-in-law and commander of a sloop-of-war, who took Biddle on as a midshipman. The American served only briefly in the Royal Navy, perhaps because the "Prospect of Wars" over the Falkland Islands did not materialize. In 1773 he shipped before the mast on a polar expedition with another young man of promise, Horatio Nelson, and shortly thereafter returned to America. *DAB.*

9. In all likelihood the preparation of a memorial to the Board of Trade, requesting that the Parliamentary grant to Georgia for 1771 be turned over to BF as agent. The Board forwarded the memorial to the Treasury on May 10. *Board of Trade Jour.*, 1768–75, pp. 245–6.

From J. G. Kettilby ALS: American Philosophical Society

This letter reveals virtually all that seems to be known about the writer.[1] Yet that is enough to establish him as an innovator in printing: he had developed a type font composed not only of single characters but also of complete words. The invention would seem sure to have intrigued Franklin, for some years later a closely similar one, of the so-called logographic process, evoked his immediate and sustained interest.[2] But Kettilby's process apparently did not. Although his letter was clearly in response to some inquiry from Franklin, no further correspondence between the two has come to light, or any evidence that they met during Franklin's visit to Dublin later in the year. We are forced to let the letter stand by itself.

Honoured Sir,   Mitre Alley Dublin 27 April 71
You may depend on all that I have wrote to be fact, and all that I have said in my bill,[3] except the extra velocity which Error was owing to the adjacent Printers who inform'd me that 3 impressions in a Minute were as much as any man could do to hold it 12 hours and so that I was sure mine would take off 5 single and if double forms 8 sheets in a Minute successively and that by the agency of a Lad or Girl about 14 with incredible ease and precision. Their excellencies are cheapness durability ease and Elegancy in working. The Platen is a Cylinder or Roll and the tympan[4] stout felt which will make the finest impression to copper-Plate that can be invented. A word to the wise may suffice. I never had the least information in Printing nor any assistance in any part so that my proofs appear to a great disadvantage.
    I hope by September to alarm the whole Fraternity with real Exhibitions of Presses Matrices Moulds types singled and in

---

1. He appears occasionally in Nolan, *Franklin in Scotland and Ireland.* But one of the scraps of information about him there is erroneous, and the rest are undocumented.
    2. See George S. Eddy, "Correpondence between Dr. Benjamin Franklin and John Walter, Regarding the Logographic Process of Printing," Amer. Antiquarian Soc. *Proc.*, XXXVIII (1928), 349–63. This whole line of development in printing was soon abandoned.
    3. Doubtless a handbill advertising his process.
    4. A sheet of smooth cloth or other material between the platen and paper, for equalizing the pressure.

Words.[5] As to the extra No. of Boxes and the incommodeous extent of the Cases they are only imaginary for as 750 current words will be always ready at hand the less single types will do by near $\frac{1}{2}$ and of course the less room in the common cases which will make a deal of room for the whole words which will all stand upright and close tine by tine as the inclos'd specimen in $\frac{1}{2}$ Inch Boxes so that a little space will hold a large Quantity and prevent them from battering and make them more ready to the Compositiors hand than a Single loose-type can possibly be because he will never have the face nor foot of the type to invert as must inevitably be the case and that very frequent when the types lye in the cases promiscuously[6] &c. The herd of Compossitor will esteem me no better than the Press-men and Pressmakers. Tho' I can't but think I Shall have the pleasure to please the Master Printer after their Predjudice is once remov'd. And sure I am it must please the Bookseller and their customers Yes and the impatient and Ambitious Authors or Pirats will extol the inventor of so expeditious a method of getting their works out of the Printers hands.

If any of the printers should think I don't allow room sufficient for any new coin'd words I must let them know that I rejoice to find that the disgustful method of intermixing italics with Romans is generally discarded from the best offices and Justly prohibited by the most Polite Authors so that the Italian Cases may be remov'd to the Foundery or at least put up in a corner of the office by those who chuse to use them for Dedications Prefaces and Introductions which is the best use they can be converted to unless it be to print Lillys Syntax for those who cant distinguish a latin from an English Word.[7]

5. A matrix is a metal plate, stamped with the desired letter or character and used to form the face of a type, the body of which is made by the mold. Types "singled in Words" are fastened together to form separate words.

6. Kettilby, writing as one professional to another, is difficult for the uninitiated to understand; and we are indebted to Mr. James W. Boyden, Production Manager of the Yale University Press, for help in explaining his language. The words in solid type, he is saying, will reduce the space in the boxes needed for single characters or loose-types; the solid can be kept in better order and handled more rapidly by the compositor.

7. The "new coin'd words" are those that Kettilby expects to add to the 750 that he has already cast; space for storing them will be made by dis-

The Price of our Rom-Eng Size Matrices is 3*s*. 6*d*. per Matrice if for a founder's use But if for the use of a private Printer to cast for his own use or a noblemans use only 1*s*. per Matrice if only struck to a proper depth but if justified[8] and adjusted one and all to an equal depth and straight in the line 1*s*. 6*d*. per Matrice. In a single fount of Eng. Rom. their will be 150 different sorts and the Moulds if for a Founders use will be £2 12*s*. 6*d*. if for a Private persons use only £1 1*s*. The first founder in London has wrote me word that £5 5*s*. is the lowest price of the Moulds and 5*s*. per Matrice and 6*s*. for some. Mr. James I mean. Do you know how far Dr. Wilsons types excel the best founders in London for good Metal?[9] I think his will stand double the time of those imported here. If you like the face of his type I will engage for their durability from Sir, your oblig'd Humble Servant

J. KETTILBY

P.S. Please to put the inclos'd in the Penny Post.

As far as I know your Humble Servant is the only inventor of the 750 current words. If any Compositor should object against the multitude of Boxes You may tell him there is no more than in a complete Fount of Gr[eat] Pr[imer?] which is made easy by practice.

Addressed: To / B. Franklin Esqr. / London

carding italic type, which he thinks will soon be used in the body of books only when they are printed in two languages, as in the case of Lily's syntax. William Lily (1468?–1522) was one of the creators, with Colet and Erasmus, of what became virtually a national Latin grammar; it went through many forms and titles, of which a recent example was *Lily's Rules Construed...* (London, 1759).

8. Trimmed up, to align it with the other matrices.

9. John James (d. 1772) was one of the three remaining type-founders in England; the James foundry had by this time absorbed no less than nine others. Talbot B. Reed, *A History of the Old English Letter Foundries...* (A. F. Johnson, ed.; London, [1952]), pp. 213–15. For Alexander Wilson, the Scottish type-founder, see his letter to BF above, April 14.

Edward Hughes to Joshua Sharpe[1]

ALS: American Philosophical Society

These volumes have occasionally included documents that were not written by or to Franklin, but throw light on his character or activities. The one below is included for a quite different reason: it has been alleged to throw light, but in fact does not. A recent account of his second English mission concludes, from the sole evidence of this letter, that he was involved in some business so illegal that he was in danger of arrest.[2] If the evidence has nothing to do with him, the conclusion evaporates.

Dear Sir   Sheerness 28th: of April 1771

I was duly favour'd with your letter of the 8th: since which have not heard a Syllable from Mr. Francklin,[3] but of him, that he is taking his Measures to return to America in the Squadron of Admiral Montague; Tho' he promises not to stirr without my previous knowledge, his Conduct has the appearance of making that Notice so short as will probably be ineffectual, that I will not rely on these assurances, therefore earnestly beg the favour you will Act for me in this Affair respecting Mr. Francklin, as you woud do were it your own Case, but I must pray it may be Still and quiet as possible, not to expose him but to secure us, and to do all that is pro-

1. Capt. (later Admiral Sir Edward) Hughes (1720?–94) was at this time commander of a guardship; he later gained fame in the naval campaign off India, as the dogged if uninspired opponent of the brilliant Bailli de Suffren. For Joshua Sharpe, the solicitor for a number of colonial agencies, see above, VIII, 5 n.

2. Cecil B. Currey, *Road to Revolution: Benjamin Franklin in England, 1765–1775* (New York, 1968), pp. 276–80. The author's argument has been ably refuted by Paul H. Smith, "Benjamin Franklin: Gunrunner?," *PMHB*, XCV (1971), 526–9. We print the letter in order to include some evidence that Smith does not cite.

3. The text in Currey (*op. cit.*, p. 277) is inaccurate in many inconsequential details and, at this point, in one of great consequence: "Mr. Francklin" becomes "Docr. Franklin," and the name is again misspelled when it reappears. Hughes was unquestionably referring to Michael Francklin, Lieutenant Governor of Nova Scotia and of the newly formed government of St. John's (Prince Edward Island), who had been in London for some time because he was in trouble with the government. See above, XVII, 179 n; Hist. MSS Commission, *Fourteenth Report, Appendix, Part V* (Dartmouth MSS, I; London, 1887), p. 333; James S. Macdonald, "Memoir [of] Lieut.-Governor Michael Francklin, 1752–1782," Nova Scotia Hist. Soc. *Coll.*, XVI (1912), 27.

per without delay.[4] I think when he is arrested his friends will find such security you approve, rather than lett him be detain'd here. I intend waiting on you at Chambers next Thursday and am ever Dear Sir Your Oblig'd Humble Servant   EDWd HUGHES

Addressed: To / Mr. Joshua Sharpe / att his Chambers in / Lincoln's Inn / London

Endorsed: 28th April 1771 Lre Hughes

From John Bartram   ALS: American Philosophical Society

Dear worthy ould Friend   April the 29th 1771
    I have very little to write beside a repetition of real frendship haveing received never a line from thee since I sent thee a box of seeds and a letter last fall, wherein I desired to be acquainted whether the King Continued his bounty still to me or droped it. I Cant yet hear the least tittle concerning it except that William Young stiles him self thair Majesties Botanist.[5] I should be glad to hear how the affair stands but it astonisheth me very much that I cant have a line from any of my Correspondents this spring (all-tho 3 or 4 ships is arived here from London) and all thair last letters contained expressions of real friendship. My Daughter Elizabeth hath saved sevral thousands of eggs of silkworms which shee expects will hatch in a few days she intends to give them a fair tryal this spring.
    My eye sight fails me very much and I am going to thro all my business into my Son Johns hands except part of my Garden:[6] but

4. Rear Admiral John Montagu (1719–95) had just been appointed commander in chief on the American station. He and his squadron were bound for Halifax (*London Chron.,* June 8–11), a destination which in itself rules out BF as a possible passenger and makes Francklin a likely one; but the Lieutenant Governor actually stayed in London until the following year. He had promised not to leave without Hughes' consent: Douglas Brymner, *Report on Canadian Archives, 1894* (Ottawa, 1895), p. 304, a reference for which we are indebted to Dr. Paul Smith.
    5. See above, XVII, 290.
    6. He had many sons; William was probably his favorite, but completely lacked business ability. See Earnest Earnest, *John and William Bartram, Botanists and Explorers* (Philadelphia, 1940), pp. 11–12, 93.

still thee may be assured of the love friendship and best wishes of thy Sincear friend   JOHN BARTRAM

Addressed: To / Dr. Benjamin Franklin / London

Endorsed: J Bartram   April 1771

To Deborah Franklin   ALS: American Philosophical Society

Franklin rarely castigated his wife as overtly as in the letter below, where he shows his annoyance and disturbance at what he considers her extravagance. He was providing her a more than ample income, as he points out; and she was making him periodic remittances.[7] This time she had obviously run through the funds allotted her, so that in order to send him money she had had to borrow from a friend. He was understandably annoyed, for her spending put him in a difficult position. She had been growing vaguer since her illness in the winter of 1768–69 and, he virtually says, more irresponsible; he had put a monthly limit on her income, apparently without telling her, and she had now evaded it by borrowing. Strong words were perhaps needed to bring her back into line; but a note of compassion might have been expected in them, for she was old and failing. It is not there. Yet the tone of the letter, unattractive as it may be, helps to reveal the flesh-and-blood Franklin. If all the many sides of his character were admirable he would run the risk of being canonized, the flesh and blood embalmed in virtues; and he would scarcely have relished that fate.

My dear Child,   London, May 1. 1771

I wrote to you per Capt. Osborne, and have since received yours of Jan. 14. per Cousin Benezet, and of March 7. per the Packet.[8]

The Bill on Sir Alexander Grant for £30 which you so kindly sent me inclos'd, came safe to hand. I am obliged too to Mr. Hall for enabling you on a Pinch to buy it. But I am sorry you had so

7. For instances see above, XIII, 193, 332, 336; XIV, 5, 139–40, 161, 224; XV, 25–6, 291.

8. BF's letter may have been the brief note above, Jan. 2; neither of DF's letters has been found. Daniel Benezet (1723–97), a Philadelphia merchant and the brother of the celebrated Quaker, Anthony Benezet, had married Elizabeth North, almost unquestionably one of the daughters of John North (E.2.6) who are unidentified in the genealogy above, VIII, 141; in that case she was DF's second cousin. See George S. Brookes, *Friend Anthony Benezet* (Philadelphia, 1937), p. 18.

much Trouble about it; and the more so, as it seems to have occasioned some Disgust in you against Messrs. Foxcrofts for not supplying you with Money to pay for it.[9] That you may not be offended with your Neighbours without Cause, I must acquaint you with what it seems you did not know, that I had limited them in their Payments to you, to the Sum of Thirty Pounds per Month, for the sake of our more easily settling, and to prevent Mistakes. This making 360 Pounds a Year, I thought, as you have no House Rent to pay yourself, and receive the Rents of 7 or 8 Houses besides, might be sufficient for the Maintenance of your Family. I judged such a Limitation the more necessary, because you never have sent me any Account of your Expences, and think yourself ill-used if I desire it; and because I know you were not very attentive to Money-matters in your best Days, and I apprehend that your Memory is too much impair'd for the Management of unlimited Sums, without Danger of injuring the future Fortune of your Daughter and Grandson. If out of more than £500 a Year, you could have sav'd enough to buy those Bills it might have been well to continue purchasing them: But I do not like your going about among my Friends to borrow Money for that purpose, especially as it is not at all necessary. And therefore I once more request that you would decline buying them for the future. And I hope you will no longer take it amiss of Messrs. Foxcrofts that they did not supply you. If what you receive is really insufficient for your Support, satisfy me by Accounts that it is so, and I shall order more.

I am much pleased with the little Histories you give me of your fine Boy, which are confirm'd by all that have seen him. I hope he will be spared, and continue the same Pleasure and Comfort to you, and that I shall ere long partake with you in it. My Love to him, and to his Papa and Mama. Mrs. Stevenson too is just made very happy by her Daughter's being safely delivered of a Son: the Mother and Child both well.[1] Present my affectionate Respects

9. Grant was a West India merchant and former M.P.; see Namier and Brooke, *House of Commons*, II, 528. David Hall, BF's former partner, had lent DF the money after John and Thomas Foxcroft had refused her.

1. William Hewson, Polly Stevenson Hewson's first child, was born on April 26. See Thomas J. Pettigrew, ed., *Memoirs of the Life and Writings of the late John Coakley Lettsom . . .* (3 vols., London, 1817), I, 143 of second pagination.

to Mrs. Montgomery, with Thanks for her most obliging Present.[2]
It makes a nice Bag for my Ivory Chessmen. I am, as ever, Your
affectionate Husband   B FRANKLIN

Addressed: To / Mrs Franklin / at / Philadelphia / via N York / per
Packet / B Free FRANKLIN

From a Committee of the Managers of the Pennsylvania Hospital to Franklin, John Fothergill, and David Barclay[3]

Minutebook copy: Pennsylvania Hospital, Philadelphia

⟨Philadelphia, May 3, 1771. When the managers learned from
Fothergill that the money allotted to the Hospital from the unclaimed shares of the Pennsylvania Land Company is payable as
soon as attorneys are authorized to receive it,[4] they convened a
meeting of the contributors on April 30 last, which passed a resolution empowering them to issue a letter of attorney to Franklin,
Fothergill, and Barclay. They have done so, carefully following
the draft that Fothergill sent, so as to be sure of conforming precisely to the requirements of the Bank. The letter, which is
enclosed together with a copy of the resolution, has been witnessed by John Allen, Capt. Nathaniel Falconer, and one of his
seamen, who will be ready to attest to it.[5] The documents are in

2. For Mrs. Montgomery see above, XVII, 167. Her present was probably
something she had brought back from her Mediterranean travels.

3. For David Barclay, Jr., one of the founders of what is now Barclays
Bank, see above, IX, 190 n.

4. Fothergill headed a group of trustees who, by an act of Parliament passed
in 1760, held the unclaimed shares in the Company and deposited the divi-
dends in the Bank of England until June 24, 1770, when the remaining funds
were to be paid to the Hospital. See above, XIII, 274 n.

5. John Allen (d. 1778), the son of the Chief Justice, was going to London
to study law; he sailed with his sister and brother-in-law, Gov. John Penn.
He returned two years later, became a Loyalist during the Revolution, and
died just in time to save his estates from confiscation. Charles P. Keith, *The
Provincial Councillors of Pennsylvania...* (Philadelphia, 1883), pt. 2, p. 145;
James Allen, "Diary... 1770–1778," *PMHB*, IX (1885), 179, 181, 191, 433–
4. Capt. Falconer needs no introduction; his seaman is identified in the minutes as Isaac Lea, who may well have been the son of James Lea (1724–98):
ibid., LII (1928), 90.

a small box sent in care of Allen, who has been asked to deliver it to Barclay. The new managers, to be chosen at the annual election a few days hence, will inform them what should be done about selling the stock and transferring the funds.[6] Signed by Israel and James Pemberton, John Reynell, Thomas Wharton, and Samuel Rhoads.[7]⟩

From Samuel Rhoads   ALS: American Philosophical Society

Dear Friend   Philada: May the 3d 1771

I receiv'd thy kind Favour of Feb: 10 and am much oblig'd by the several usefull papers Pamphlets and Samples contain'd therein. Thy Friend Wooller has taken much Pains in explaining the Method of making our Houses secure from Fire—which I hope will be of great Service—we are much oblig'd to him.[8] I have given several little Bitts of the Lime Stone to some of my Acquantance in the Country in hopes it may be found here.[9] I am told they make Lyme in Berks County that will harden Under Water. I have sent for a Sample of it and will try it. We certainly have plenty of Stone very like this in appearance and I hope of the same Quality. I am the more concern'd for this discovery, as we are told it was very Usefull in the Masonry of the Works under water in the Duke of Bridgwater's Canal[1] and we expect shortly to be Canal mad, and may want it in such Works also.

The growing *Trade* of Baltimore Town in Maryland drawn principally from our Province west of Susquehana begins to alarm

6. The anxiety of the managers, apparent in this letter, about adhering precisely to legal forms grew in their successors, who did not dare to act until they had received assurance that their London agents had succeeded in getting the money. See their letter below, June 3.

7. Wharton and Rhoads have frequently appeared in recent volumes. For the Pemberton brothers see above, v, 424 n, and XIII, 260 n, and for Reynell IX, 372 n.

8. See above, XVII, 182, and the letter of Feb. 10 that Rhoads is answering.

9. See *ibid.*, the next to last paragraph.

1. The famous canal from Worsley to Manchester, the first in England that was entirely independent of a stream, was opened in 1761. Francis Egerton, Duke of Bridgewater, was constructing another to connect Manchester with Liverpool; it was completed at the end of 1772.

us with serious Apprehensions of such a Rival as may reduce us to the Situation of Burlington or New Castle on Delaware and we can devise no Means of saving our selves but by a Canal, from Susquehanna to Schullkil and amending the Navigation of all our Rivers so far as they lead towards our Capital City.[2] A great number of thy Friends are very Anxious for promoting this Work, particularly the Canal, if it is Practicable thro the Heart of the Country. And as thou wast kind enough formerly to send me several Papers relating to the Navigation of Calder River,[3] I request the favour of adding thereto the last Accounts and Instructions respecting Canals, the Construction of their Floodgates, wast Gates,[4] &ca. The Assembly have Order'd the Speaker to Procure the remainder of the Statutes, to Compleat their Sett in the State House Library[5] by which I suppose we shall have those relating to Canals, but if they are to be had singly Please to send [one] or two the most Instructive in the Rates Terms and Conditions of Carryage, passing thro Grounds &ca. and the Cost shall be paid.

I Congratulate thee on the *Prospect* we have of the sum of Money lodgd in the Bank, for the Pennsylvania Hospital being now paid, and of thy Pleasure in receiving it for that Charity which thou had so great a share in Establishing. We last Night executed a Power of Attorny to thee, to Doctr Fothergil, and David Barclay to apply to the Court of Chancery in Order to receive it—and least our Hospital Seal should not be sufficient Evidence of our Act and Deed we called three Witnesses who may be examined [by] your People on Oath respecting the due executing the Power of Attorny.[6] If any difficulty should Occur you will not fail of Ac-

2. Thomas Gilpin had advanced similar ideas to BF eighteen months before. See above, XVI, 218.

3. BF seems to have got hold of two anonymous and undated pamphlets on the Calder and the Aire, streams in the West Riding that join near Leeds. The pamphlets were apparently published in 1699, provoked by an act of Parliament in that year for improving the navigation of the two rivers. See Thomas S. Willan, *River Navigation in England, 1600–1750* (London, 1936), pp. 29, 141.

4. A floodgate controls the water level in a lock; a waste gate is for overflow.

5. Perhaps Owen Ruffhead's edition of Parliamentary statutes; by this time it included the first decade of George III.

6. See the preceding document.

quainting us with it by the first Opertunity. My Wife, Children, and thy old Friend Ann Paschal desire to be kindly remembred to thee. Thy sincere and Affectionate Friend   SAML RHOADS

Addressed: To / Benjamin Franklin Esqr. / Agent for Pennsylvania / in / London / per / Capt Falconer

Endorsed: S. Rhoads   May 3. 71   Canals

From William Smith   ALS: American Philosophical Society

Sir   Philada. May 3d. 1771

Agreeable to the Directions of our Philosophical Society, I have sent in a small Box by Faulkner, (directed to you) 11 Copies of the 1st. Vol. of the Transactions of the said Society; which they request you, as their President, to deliver as they are directed viz 1 Copy to the Royal Society; Do. Royal College of Physicians; Society of Arts &c. British Musaeum; Dr. Fothergill; the Astronomer Royal; Sir George Saville Bart. Mr. Ferguson; Mr. Nairne; and Mr. Coombe.[7] There is only one Copy for yourself; but the small Box would hold no more. You will however receive another Box with Copies for the Learned Societies abroad, amounting to more than a Dozen in Number as soon as we can draw up the Letters intended to accompany them; some of which are to be in French, and some in Latin. In that Box there will be 2 or 3 Copies for you to give such of your friends, as you may think wish well to our infant Undertaking and will not be too critically severe on these our first Essays.

I should be glad the Astronomer Royal had his assoon as convenient. I hope you will have no Difficulty in getting the Books Landed, as they are directed, and appear to be Presents and not for Sale. I am Sir Your most obedient humble Servant

WILLIAM SMITH

Dr Franklin

Addressed: To / Dr. Benjamin Franklin / in Craven Street / London

7. Provost Smith, BF's old enemy, was acting in his capacity as a secretary of the APS. The first volume of its *Trans.* had been published in early March

From Cadwalader Evans   ALS: American Philosophical Society

Dear Doctor   Philadia May 4th 1771.
I received your letter[8] by Capt. Sparks, who arrived at the Capes of Delaware, the same day Faulkner did, but by falling in with the land a little to the eastward, it was some days after, before he got into port.[9]
Your account of Mr. Walpole's, valueation of the Sample of Silk I sent you, gave us spirits; and I am ordered to desire you to thank that Gentleman, for his patriotick offer, in assisting us to procure eggs and reelers. We will gladly accept of the former to try how far they excell other eggs, in the qualities you mention. Last Summer we got Messrs. Willing & Morris, to write for some, to their correspondents in Spain and Italy.[1] The first answer was from Cadiz, wherein they were informed, no eggs were to be procured there, but that they had sent, a considerable distance, into the Country for some, and woud forward them by the first safe conveyance. They arrived in March, in a round Tin Canister, whose top was closely fitted; it was afterwards wrapp'd in paper, and thick canvass sewed tight about it. When we open'd the Canister, the eggs were putrid, and offensive to an uncommon degree. The heat of the weather coud not have occassioned it, but we suspect the heat of the Cabbin, or place where they were kept, might have hatched numbers, who died for want of food, and infected the whole mass, or perhaps, a perspiration from the eggs, being retained in that close vessel and too warm an air, might produce the same effect. I am thus particular, as some hints may be taken,

---

(*Pa. Ga*₹., March 14); it listed in the membership all the individuals mentioned except the Astronomer Royal, Nevil Maskelyne, and BF's young friend Thomas Coombe, who presumably received a copy because his father was a member. Fothergill, Maskelyne, and Nairne need no introduction; for Savile see above, XI, 480 n, and XIII, 145 n; and for James Ferguson VIII, 216 n, and XIV, 144 n.

8. Above, Feb. 10.
9. The two arrived about a week apart: *Pa. Ga*₹., April 11, 18, 1771.
1. Willing, Morris & Company, founded in 1754 by Thomas Willing (1731–1821) and Robert Morris (1734–1806), was one of the most prominent and stable mercantile firms in Philadelphia, and also conducted a general exchange and banking business. See Ellis P. Oberholtzer, *Robert Morris, Patriot and Financier* (New York, 1903), pp. 8–9.

for their preservation over, in a genial[2] state. Therefore, if Mr. Walpole, coud, without much trouble, procure us one or two pounds of Valencia eggs, I think they had better be put into wide mouth'd bottles, and several grooves cut in the sides of the corks, so as to admit a free communication with the outer air. Jarrs cover'd with Leather, and peirced with a large needle, or awl, might do as well. Another circumstance is worth attention; we think, a much lower degree of heat, will hatch the eggs in the Spring than the fall; if so, it will be best to send them in the forepart of winter, hung to some of the battens in the cabbin, rather than put in a chest, without the weather shoud be extream cold. We have hired a Languedocian to superintend the Filature next season, who says he was born and bred in the middle of a silk country; was always employed in the culture and manufacture of it, and having been in the East Indies, has some knowledge of their method and management of it also.[3]

We shall see how he makes out; if well, it will save Mr. Walpole the trouble of procuring reelers; if not, we shall have time enough, before next season, to beg the favour of his assistance. Upon the whole, the experiment takes in the country, beyond our most sanguine expectations, and as to the managers of the filature it is a hobby horse to each of them.

Dr. Smith, desired I woud mention to you, that he had put into the care of Capt. Faulkner, several Volumes of our Transactions, to be deliver'd to you.[4] One is for yourself, and the others, for several who have been chosen members of the Society. Some papers may be thought curious, some usefull, but, certainly, many of them shoud not have been published.

Imediately after hearing of his Fathers death Governor Penn, took Capt. Faulkners Cabbin. He was inform'd of this by Capt. Sparks, and also that his Brother's Commission for Governor, signed by his Uncle was coming over in the February Packet for

2. Generative.

3. Joseph Ottelenghe, who was actually a native of Piedmont, had superintended the proprietors' silk culture in Georgia until it declined; the managers of the Philadelphia filature had procured his services the previous summer. See *Pa. Gaz.*, Aug. 30, 1770, where he is not named, and Brooke Hindle, *The Pursuit of Science in Revolutionary America*... (Chapel Hill, [1956]), pp. 200, 203.

4. See the preceding document.

his approbation; but the Packet is not arrived yet. The Governors precipitate departure, is said to be, on account of settling the instructions—to wit who shall continue in office, and who come in, when a vacancy happens. He certainly leaves the Province with reluctance, and I am well assured, he says, he will return as soon as possible, purchase a seat 20 or 30 miles from town, [and] live in a quiet, private way.5 Some people who pass'd for Dick Penns friends, say he is illiterate, arbitrary and vindictive, and will be more apt to carry his party resentments into Government, than his brother; but as I think, we cannot be much worse off than we have been, it gives me little fresh concern.

Mr. Wharton has just reason to complain of me for not answering his last, long, and intelligent letter. My neglect was partly owing to the hopes of seeing him sooner than has happen'd; the same reason opperates more powerfully now, which I hope he will think of some weight, if it shoud happen otherwise. His own family are well; but his father has been an invalid all winter, and part of last summer. His present disorders are a slow fever, an inveterate cough, and a pertinacious refusal of all medicine.6 As I hope his father will yet do very well; shoud he be in England when this arrives, please to tell him his friend David Durrach, lived in our neighbourhood last summer, and I do not know that ever I saw him, which was almost every day, but I thought of the cordial friendship which seemed to subsist between them.

I intend to write to you shortly, by a Young Gentleman, who has lived with me several years, and goes over to improve himself in his proffession.7 In the meantime, and always, be assured I am Your truely Affectionate friend   C: EVANS

5. The death in February of Richard Penn, the father of the Lieutenant Governor and of his successor, Richard, Jr., was reported in the *Pa. Ga*\(\gamma\). on April 18. John Penn sailed with Falconer for England on May 4: Howard M. Jenkins, "The Family of William Penn," *PMHB*, xxII (1898), 81. John returned in August, 1773, not to private life but to his old position.

6. Samuel Wharton, still in England trying to move the affairs of the Walpole Company, needs no introduction; neither does his father Joseph, "the Duke," who lived until 1776.

7. Thomas Parke (1749–1835) had studied medicine under Evans and taken his degree from the College of Philadelphia in 1770. In May, 1771, he left to continue his studies in London and Edinburgh, and returned in 1773; Evans, shortly before his death, took him into partnership. See Whitfield J. Bell, Jr., "Thomas Parke, M.B., Physician and Friend," *W&MQ*, vi (1949), 569–95.

I send by Capt. Falconer a small snuff box, the manufacture of Lancaster, out of the root of a certain speceis of Laurel, I cannot tell which. It woud not be worth sending, but to an american, and merely on account of the wood.

Endorsed: Dr Cad. Evans. Nov. 26. 1770 May 4 1771

From A[nne Johnson] Clarke[8]

ALS: American Philosophical Society

Honoured Sir,   Barbados May 5th. 1771
    I take the liberty to acquaint you we arriv'd here the 9 of Dece-ber. last and tho it was a long passage it was not a bad one. I was very kindly receiv'd by Capt. Clarke's Mother and relations; Capt. Clarke not finding A [sea?] Man here, was oblig'd to go to Antigue in search of him in eight days after our arrival, upon which his Mother gave me a very friendly invitation, to stay with her till he return'd, and said to both of us, she shou'd look upon me and treat me in every respect as her own Daughter; I consented and have been with her ever since; Capt. Clarke was gone nine weeks, and when he return'd, was order'd immediately to Grenada and is not yet return'd; but I believe is on his passage; As a War was then so much talk'd of, both Capt. Clarke and his Friends thought it wou'd be very improper for me to go with him,[9] and beg'd if I cou'd make myself easy, I wou'd Continue with his Mother. My compliance was to oblige them, and I have no reason to repent, for by taking their advice, I have gain'd their esteem so far, as to see they are always glad when they can do any thing to contribute to my happiness. Capt. Clarke's family is one of the first in the Island, his Brother is very rich, and has Travel'd a great deal, and keeps open house, not only for his friends but, Strangers, both European and Foreigners, and is Commissioner of the Coustoms.[1]

8. For Anne Johnson's marriage to Capt. Peter Clarke, R.N., see above, XVII, 210, 288.
9. An Anglo-Spanish war, growing out of the Falkland Islands crisis, would have turned the Caribbean into a battle ground.
1. Doubtless Gedney Clarke, who was following in his father's footsteps as customs commissioner; he had been a member of the Barbados Council

I hope you enjoy your health, and Mrs. Stevenson, Mrs.Tickell and Mrs. Hewson theirs, to whome if you please to make best respects—love to Miss Franklin and Master Temple. A line from you to signify you and your Friends are well wou'd give the greatest pleasure to Dear Sir, Your much honour'd Niece

A. CLARKE

P.S. If you will favour me with a line, please to direct, for Mrs. Peter Clarke Barbados.

My Brother is well and joins with me in Duty to You.[2]

Addressed: To / Dr. Benjamin Franklin, / Craven Street / Strand / London

Endorsed: Mrs Clarke

From Matthew Maty[3]   ALS: Historical Society of Pennsylvania

⟨British Museum, May 6, 1771. Sends an enclosure that he has received for Franklin from a newly created society of sciences in Rotterdam.[4]⟩

---

and apparently continued to be until his death. See [George Frere,] *Short History of Barbados*... (London, 1768), p. 88; John Poyer, *The History of Barbados*... (London, 1808), p. 362; *Acts Privy Coun., Col.*, v, 563.

2. Samuel Johnson (C.5.7.1), whose mother had consulted BF about his future a few years before (above, XV, 126, 272); she had then expected to apprentice him. He was now about fourteen, and our guess is that he had joined the navy instead, under the wing of his brother-in-law, and gone to Barbados with the newlyweds.

3. Secretary of the Royal Society and a sublibrarian of the British Museum; see above, XIII, 451 n.

4. The Bataafsch Genootschap der Proefondervindelijke Wijsbergeerte (Batavian Society of Experimental Science). BF was made a corresponding member on April 28; the Society then inquired, in the letter Maty forwarded, whether he would accept the invitation. When it found that he would, it issued a formal announcement, dated June 11, which is among BF's papers in the APS.

From [John] Pownall   AL: American Philosophical Society

⟨Whitehall, May 7, 1771, a note in the third person. A warrant is signed appointing Mr. Coxe,[5] on Governor Franklin's recommendation, to the Council of New Jersey; wishes to know who will take charge of sending the warrant.⟩

To [John] Pownall   AL (draft[6]): American Philosophical Society

⟨Craven Street, May 8, 1771, a note in the third person. Believes that Mr. Sargent of Downing Street[7] corresponds with Mr. Coxe, and will take charge of sending the warrant. If Sargent is out of town or declines, Franklin will do it himself.⟩

To [John] Canton   ALS: Yale University Library

Sir,   Cravenstreet, May 12. 1771
Dr. Ingenhauss and myself purpose to set out on Friday next to visit Birmingham and some other manufacturing Towns, intending to be absent about 10 Days; a young Kinsman of mine accompanies us. Will you make a fourth, and so reduce our Triangle to a Square? The Dr. has just been here, and requested me to write to you immediately, as he is equally desirous with me of your good Company. We can stay for you till Sunday, if that will suit you better.[8]

5. For Daniel Coxe see above, xiv, 300 n. wf had recommended him in January on the death of the incumbent; the recommendation was endorsed by the Board of Trade in April and approved on May 1. 1 N.J. Arch., x, 225–6; Board of Trade Jour., 1768–75, pp. 244–5; Acts Privy Coun., Col., v, 569.
6. It is not in bf's hand, and is written at the foot of the preceding document.
7. For John Sargent, a former director of the Bank of England, see above, vii, 322 n; Namier and Brooke, House of Commons, iii, 404–5.
8. For Dr. Ingenhousz see above, xiv, 4 n. The young kinsman was Jonathan Williams, Jr.; a résumé of his journal of the trip appears below, May 28. Canton accepted, and the four travelers left on Saturday, the 18th; the tour lasted until the end of May. On June 1 young Williams, back in London, made out an account of the expenses (APS), which came to £69 19s. 6d. and were divided into four equal shares.

Dr. Ingenhauss is to carry me on Tuesday next, to see a Gentleman from Holland of a most inventive Genius, who has brought with him Models of some new and very curious Machine. I have leave to take any Friend with me: if it will be agreable to you, call upon me at 11 a Clock. The Bearer will wait for your Answer. I am, dear Sir, Your most obedient humble Servant

B FRANKLIN

Addressed: To | Mr Canton | at the Academy | Spital Square

To the Massachusetts House of Representatives Committee of Correspondence[9]

Reprinted from Jared Sparks, ed., *The Works of Benjamin Franklin . . .* (10 vols., Boston, 1836–40), VII, 521–3.

Gentlemen,   London, 15 May, 1771.

I have received your favor of the 27th of February, with the Journal of the House of Representatives, and copies of the late oppressive prosecutions in the Admiralty Court, which I shall, as you direct, communicate to Mr. Bolland,[1] and consult with him on the most advantageous use to be made of them for the interest of the province.

I think one may clearly see, in the system of customs to be exacted in America by act of Parliament, the seeds sown of a total disunion of the two countries, though, as yet, that event may be at a considerable distance. The course and natural progress seems to be, first, the appointment of needy men as officers, for others do not care to leave England; then, their necessities make them rapacious, their office makes them proud and insolent, their insolence and rapacity make them odious, and, being conscious that they are hated, they become malicious; their malice urges them to a con-

9. Composed of Thomas Cushing, James Otis, and Samuel Adams.

1. For William Bollan, agent for the Massachusetts Council, see above, XIII, 227 n. The reference to prosecutions is not clear, but the missing letter of Feb. 27 probably complained of the number of actions that royal officials had recently brought in the Court of Vice-Admiralty for violations of the revenue and forest laws. For a similar complaint from the House of Representatives see above, XVII, 280–1, and for a discussion of this legal activity Wroth and Zobel, *John Adams Legal Papers,* II, 101–6, 253–9.

tinual abuse of the inhabitants in their letters to administration, representing them as disaffected and rebellious, and (to encourage the use of severity) as weak, divided, timid, and cowardly. Government believes all; thinks it necessary to support and countenance its officers; their quarrelling with the people is deemed a mark and consequence of their fidelity; they are therefore more highly rewarded, and this makes their conduct still more insolent and provoking.[2]

The resentment of the people will, at times and on particular incidents, burst into outrages and violence upon such officers, and this naturally draws down severity and acts of further oppression from hence. The more the people are dissatisfied, the more rigor will be thought necessary; severe punishments will be inflicted to terrify; rights and privileges will be abolished; greater force will then be required to secure execution and submission; the expense will become enormous; it will then be thought proper, by fresh exactions, to make the people defray it; thence, the British nation and government will become odious, the subjection to it will be deemed no longer tolerable; war ensues, and the bloody struggle will end in absolute slavery to America, or ruin to Britain by the loss of her colonies; the latter most probable, from America's growing strength and magnitude.

But, as the whole empire must, in either case, be greatly weakened, I cannot but wish to see much patience and the utmost discretion in our general conduct, that the fatal period may be postponed, and that, whenever this catastrophe shall happen, it may appear to all mankind, that the fault has not been ours. And, since the collection of these duties has already cost Britain infinitely more, in the loss of commerce, than they amount to,[3] and that loss is likely to continue and increase by the encouragement given to our manufactures through resentment; and since the best pretence

2. A Bostonian could scarcely have written a stronger indictment of customs officials in America. For a defense of the most prominent, the Board of Customs Commissioners, see Gipson, *British Empire*, XI, 119–20.

3. The meaning is obscure. If it is that collection of the Townshend duties cost more than the yield from them, BF was correct; see Gipson, *British Empire*, XI, 241–2. If it is that duties were bad for commerce, he was wrong; the sterling value of British trade with North America reached a peak between 1766 and 1770: Elizabeth B. Schumpeter, *English Overseas Trade Statistics, 1697–1808* (Oxford, 1960), pp. 17–18.

for establishing and enforcing the duties is the regulation of trade for the general advantage, it seems to me, that it would be much better for Britain to give them up, on condition of the colonies undertaking to enforce and collect such, as are thought fit to be continued, by laws of their own, and officers of their own appointment, for the public uses of their respective governments. This would alone destroy those seeds of disunion, and both countries might thence much longer continue to grow great together, more secure by their united strength, and more formidable to their common enemies. But the power of appointing friends and dependents to profitable offices is too pleasing to most administrations, to be easily parted with or lessened; and therefore such a proposition, if it were made, is not very likely to meet with attention.

I do not pretend to the gift of prophecy. History shows, that, by these steps, great empires have crumbled heretofore; and the late transactions we have so much cause to complain of show, that we are in the same train, and that, without a greater share of prudence and wisdom, than we have seen both sides to be possessed of, we shall probably come to the same conclusion.

The Parliament, however, is prorogued, without having taken any of the steps we had been threatened with, relating to our charter. Their attention has been engrossed by other affairs,[4] and we have therefore longer time to operate in making such impressions, as may prevent a renewal of this particular attempt by our adversaries. With great esteem and respect, I have the honor to be, &c.   B. FRANKLIN.

From Thomas Percival[5] ALS: American Philosophical Society

Sir.   Manchester May 16. 1771.

Though I have not the honour of being known to you, I take the liberty of requesting your acceptance of the inclosed Attempt to

4. The Falkland Islands crisis (above, XVII, 243 n) and the printers' case (BF to Galloway above, April 20). For BF's fears about the charter see XVII, 308, 311.

5. A Lancashire dissenter, physician, author, and experimental scientist, who later did notable work in public health, Percival (1740–1804) was already

account for the different quantities of rain, which fall at different heights, and shall esteem myself happy if it meet with your approbation. I am conscious that my solution of this Phaenomenon is liable to many exceptions, and shou'd wish to be favoured with your better explanation of it.[6]

My friend Doctor Priestley flattered me last Summer with the prospect of seeing you at Manchester, and obligingly promised to introduce me to your acquaintance. If business or Curiosity shou'd call you into this part of England, I shall be extremely glad to render you any Civilities in My power, and shall think myself honoured by a visit from you. I am with the highest Esteem and respect Sir Your most obedient humble Servant

THO. PERCIVAL.

Addressed: To | Doctor Franklin | London.

From Isaac Smith, Jr.[7]   ALS: American Philosophical Society

Sir,   [Before May 17, 1771[8]]

I called at Mrs. Stevenson's yesterday, but was so unfortunate as to find you absent. As I am told that you design for the country in a day or two, and I may perhaps lose an opportunity of seeing you, I have used, sir, the freedom of addressing you in this manner and would beg the favour of your kind advice with regard to my intended expedition to France (on which I expect to enter in the course of next week,) in any instance where you may judge sir, a direction to be proper. And if I might presume, sir, so far on your indulgence I would also beg leave to ask your recommen-

---

on the way to establishing an international circle of friends and correspondents, many of great distinction. He had been elected an F.R.S. some years before, when he was said to have been the youngest man ever accorded that honor. *DNB.*

6. For the enclosure and BF's reply see below, end of June.

7. The son of a Boston merchant and Abigail Adams' first cousin; he had come to England the year before with an introduction to BF from Ezra Stiles: above, XVII, 287. We were mistaken in saying there that Smith stayed on until 1784. He sailed for America in December, 1771, entered the ministry, and did not return to England until May, 1775. *Sibley's Harvard Graduates,* XVI, 524–5.

8. See BF's reply below, May 17.

dation to any particular Gentlemen of the number of your friends either in France or [Holland, as?] the Gentlemen of the City, who are pleas[ed to ho]nour me with their friendship and acquaintance have probably few, if any connections in those countries, except such as are merely mercantile.

As you was pleased, sir, to mention a plan of Prof. Dr. Allamande's for the circuit of Holland,[9] and so obliging at the same time as to offer me the favour of a copy, I should now sir, be extremely glad to accept of this mark of your complaisance.

I am very sorry to give you the trouble of this note, sir, but, relying on your candor and goodness to forgive me, I am, sir, with the sincerest respect, Your obliged and humble servant

I. SMITH JR

Addressed: To / Benjn: Franklin Esq. / At Mrs. Stevenson's, / Cravenstreet / In the Strand /

To [Jean-Baptiste] LeRoy   ALS: American Philosophical Society

Dear Sir,   London, May 17. 1771

It is long since I have had the Pleasure of hearing from you. I hope your Health continues, and that your valuable Life will be long preserved.

This will be presented to you by Mr. Smith,[10] a young American Gentleman, of liberal Education and excellent Character, who is desirous of seeing your fine Country, the first in Europe, before he returns to his own. As he will be quite a Stranger, your Advice and Countenance will be of Use to him, which I therefore pray you to afford him on Occasion, and I beg Leave to recommend him to your Civilities.

I hope your good Brothers are well. Please to present my Compliments to them.

Sir John Pringle and I frequently recollect together, with Pleasure, the many agreeable Hours, we pass'd in your Company

9. Jean Nicholas Sebastien Allamand (1713–87), F.R.S., was a professor of philosophy and natural history at the University of Leyden, and particularly interested in electrical experiments. His "plan" seems to have been for a tour of Holland, but we have been unable to identify it.

10. See the preceding document.

at Paris. He has his Health much better this Year than for some Years past; and bids me whenever I write, to remember him to you most respectfully. With the greatest Esteem, I have the Honour to be, Dear Sir, Your most obedient and most humble Servant   B FRANKLIN

M. Le Roy

To Isaac Smith   ALS: American Philosophical Society

Sir   Cravenstreet May 17. 1771

Being greatly hurried in preparing for my Journey, I have bare-ly had time to write the enclos'd.[1] I cannot find M. Allamand's Paper: But you will meet with no Difficulty in Holland. A good general Rule in travelling foreign Countries, is, to avoid as much as possible all Disputes, and to be contented with such Provisions and Cookery as you meet with in the Inns, so you will have the best the Country affords in the Season, which you cannot know so as to direct, and if you attempt to direct the Cookery they will not understand or be able to follow your Orders, and whatever Difficulties you put them to they will be sure to charge you ex-travagantly for, particularly in Holland. I inclose a Card of the House at which I lodg'd in Paris. It is a good one, that I can re-commend to you. If full, Mrs. Mean, the Landlady, will advise you in the Choice of another. Wishing you and your Companion a good Journey and happy Return to your Friends, I am, Sir Your most obedient humble Servant.   B FRANKLIN

M. Dessin at the Hotel D'Angleterre at Calais, will advise you about your Journey, Baggage, &c.[2] His is a good House, and I recommend it to you as your Inn, when there.

Addressed: To / Mr Isaac Smith

1. BF left London the next day for a tour of northern England. What he enclosed for Smith was undoubtedly the preceding document.

2. Pierre Dessin's inn on the main street of Calais was already famous. He was later immortalized in Laurence Sterne's *Sentimental Journey*, and was host to a number of prominent Americans, among them John Adams and Thomas Jefferson. See Philip Thicknesse, *Useful Hints to Those Who Make the Tour of France* (London, 1768), pp. 278–81; Wilbur L. Cross, *The Life and Times of Laurence Sterne* (2 vols., New Haven, 1925), II, 66–8; Butterfield, ed., *John Adams Diary*, III, 147.

From Samuel Franklin[3]   ALS: American Philosophical Society

Sir   Boston, 17th may 1771.
I Received your kind favour of the 5 febr. and am verry Glad to hear that you and Coz. Sally Were Well and it adds to our joy the encouragement you give us of Seeing you once more in Boston. My wife and Children have thro gods goodness (Enjoyd) with myself a good Share of health which is a great Blessing.[4] I have one favour to ask of you Sir that is one more of the prints of your Self—for Mr. Bowen my minister, if you have any left.[5] I was to see your Sizter Mecom yesterday. She and her daughter are Well and was pleased to read of your intentions in my Letter.[6] My wife with my four daughters Joyns with me in Love to you and Coz Sally. Hoping these few Lines may find you both Well as they leave us Which is all at present after Wishing prosperity May Still attend you from your Loving Kinsman   SAMUEL FRANKLIN
Dr Franklin

From Giambatista Beccaria[7]

Translation[8] of the Italian text printed in Giambatista Beccaria, *Elettricismo artificiale . . .* (Turin, 1772), pp. vii–viii.

Beccaria, after almost twenty years, revised and expanded his well known *Dell' Elettricismo artificiale, e naturale libri due . . .* (Turin, 1753).[9] He

3. BF's first cousin once removed (A.5.2.7.1.1); see above, XIV, 215 n.
4. For "Coz. Sally" see above, XVII, 165 n. Samuel's second wife had borne him four daughters: above, I, lii.
5. The print, which BF had sent Samuel in 1767, was Fisher's mezzotint after Chamberlain's portrait; see above, XIV, 215. Bowen acknowledged the mezzotint in a fulsome letter to BF below, Nov. 6.
6. BF must have spoken of returning to Boston in his missing letter of Feb. 5.
7. For the professor of experimental physics at Turin see above, V, 395 n, and subsequent volumes.
8. The first translation was in the 1776 English edition of the work, but it was so faulty that we use another based on a rendering by Robert S. Lopez, Sterling Professor of History at Yale, to whom we are greatly indebted. Beccaria managed to be obscure in both his languages, Latin and Italian; where we are confident of his meaning we have brought it out by taking some liberty with the literal translation.
9. See above, V, 395, 428.

prefaced the new edition with the open letter printed below, which was a reply to the letter describing the armonica that Franklin had sent him a decade earlier.[1] The relevance of that instrument to *elettricismo artificiale* is not obvious. But Franklin's description had recently been published for the first time in English, and translated into Italian;[2] the armonica was in the public eye, and Beccaria may well have wanted to use his connection with its inventor to advertise his new edition. In any case Franklin was so much impressed with the work that he helped to promote an English translation, which eventually appeared as *A Treatise upon Artificial Electricity...* (London, 1776).[3]

Turin 20. May 1771

I thank you, most excellent Sir, for the exact description of your new and really harmonious harpsichord with glasses, which you have sent me (to you it is given to enlighten human minds with the true principles of the electric science, to reassure them by your conductors against the terrors of thunder, and to sweeten their senses with a most touching and suave music); and if I were entitled to it I would thank you, in the name of Italy, for having given the appellation of *armonica* to your agreeable instrument, in consideration of our harmonious language. So far as I am concerned, I do not know how better to show you my gratitude for the many other marks of your kindness, than by sending to you this new product of my labor, and accompanying it with the wish that it may still be in keeping with your first opinion of it, as you were pleased to express it.

As for the length of this volume, I hope it will not tire you; for, apart from the common excuse that I have not had time enough to write with more brevity, I have preferred to reply rather than to repeat myself whenever a reply would serve to make the subject more clearly understood;[4] and to tell the truth, I do not think that the quantity of the material that is assembled and simplified is disproportionate to the size of the work.

1. Above, x, 126–30.
2. Both in 1769; see *ibid.*, p. 116 and n. 5.
3. See Antonio Pace, *Benjamin Franklin and Italy* (Philadelphia, 1958), pp. 58, 328.
4. Here we are not sure enough of Beccaria's meaning to depart from a literal translation. But we believe he is trying to say that instead of reiterating what he had propounded in the first edition he was replying to subsequent criticism, perhaps by including the experiments and discoveries of the intervening years that supported his and BF's theories.

Nor will you be surprised that I conclude this book, too, with expressing the hope of having added further definitions to the theory; for you too teach well, by your example, how slowly and how little our senses proceed in the investigation of every little parcel of inexhaustible Nature. And how many refinements does not a science, however comprehensive, still lack today? We measure the paths of light, yet we do not know how it proceeds through them. We can define the order of the system of the world, yet we do not know the force which links its parts in a most divine way, etc.

But what would happen if further definitions of electrical matters produced another, different theory? The appearance of all that I have so far been able to see takes any such suspicion from my mind; still, even in such a case, the value of these works of mine, if indeed they have any, would subsist. The experimental data would remain the same; their connection and unity, far from crumbling, would improve.

I hear that you are preparing to go back to your country. Whether America or Europe possess you, preserve yourself to the world, to science, and the lovers of it. Wherever you may be, I shall always be the most devoted admirer of your great merit, etc.

From [Charles] Jackson[5]

AL: University of Pennsylvania Library

⟨General Post Office, May 20, 1771, a note in the third person. Sends a piece of elastic gum[6] with a thousand good wishes.⟩

From [Jacques Barbeu-Dubourg]

AL (incomplete): American Philosophical Society

A Paris ce 27e may 1771

Monsieur, oserois-je encore ajouter, et cher Ami?

Il y a bientôt huit mois que vous ne m'avez honoré de vos nou-

5. Identified by the handwriting and place of origin. For Jackson see above, XIV, 301 n.

6. In November BF sent Jonathan Williams, Sr., six "vessels" of elastic gum, costing £1 16s. Jour., p. 37.

velles, je cherche à me flatter que ce n'est que faute d'occasions;
mais je crains de me faire illusion à cet egard, attendu le grand
nombre d'Anglois qui viennent successivement en france. Aurois-
je eu le malheur de vous deplaire en quelque chose? Tandis qu'il
n'y a persone au monde de qui j'ambitionne davantage l'estime et
l'affection, j'avoue que de mon coté, il y a aussi 5 à 6 mois que je
ne vous ai donné le moindre signe de vie et d'attachement, mais
vous savez quelle est ma position, mon quartier écarté, et d'ailleurs
mes compatriotes voyagent beaucoup moins que les votres. Repar-
tirez vous donc pour l'Amerique sans nous dire le plus petit adieu?
Ne conserverez vous au delà des mers aucun souvenir de quel-
quun qui vous est si attaché, qui regarde comme le vrai paradis
terrestre le climat que vous choisissez pour votre sejour, ou vous
avez provigné[7] toutes les siences et toutes les vertus, et où il se
transplanteroit volontiers s'il etoit plus jeune, pour y recevoir de
vous des leçons dans tous les genres sur les rives du Skuilkil et de
la Delaware.

Les volumes des Ephemerides du citoyen longtems retardés par
les entraves ordinaires de la librairie de ce pays cy, ont reparu
près à près, et en voila 9 depuis 5 mois, dont je vous adresse à la
fois un exemplaire pour M. Rush,[8] independamment du votre ce
qui fait 18 volumes en tout. On nous fait esperer que les autres se
succederont rapidement, et j'ai renouvellé votre souscription à cet
effet.

Je comptois pouvoir vous envoyer par la même occasion mon
manuel de l'humanité que l'on m'a arreté pendant plusieurs mois,
et qui doit enfin etre actuellement imprimé a Bouillon;[9] je l'ai
etendu jusqu'a 92 articles, et j'ose me flatter que vous le trouverez

7. An old synonym for *multiplié*.

8. The *Ephémérides*, published between 1767 and 1772, was edited first by
Nicholas Badeau and the Marquis de Mirabeau and later by Pierre Samuel du
Pont de Nemours. See above, XV, 114 n, and "Letters of Barbeu-Dubourg to
Franklin," Mass. Hist. Soc. *Proc.*, LVI (1922–23), 133. Dr. Benjamin Rush
had made Barbeu-Dubourg's acquaintance during his visit to France in 1769:
George W. Corner, ed., *The Autobiography of Benjamin Rush . . .* (Princeton,
1948), p. 67.

9. A reference to his *Petit code de la raison humaine*. See above, XVII, 185 6,
291. No copy has been found of an edition printed in Bouillon, in the Austrian
Netherlands. In his later letters to BF (below, May 31, Oct. 9, 1772) Barbeu-
Dubourg refers to his failure to get permission for a French printing.

bien amelioré; j'y entame les plus grandes questions de la politique, et peutetre trouverez vous que je les envisage sous des points de vue que l'on n'avoit pas encore presentés au public, au moins puis-je vous assurer que je n'ai copié persone en cela. J'esperois egalement vous envoyer un exemplaire de mon petit ouvrage sur la pairie;[1] mais apres m'avoir longtems et tres indignement baloté à ce sujet, on m'envoya enfin hier une brochure qu'on me marquoit etre cela, et où je n'en ai reconnu qu'environ moitié, encadrée dans une espece de factum sur l'affaire personelle d'un homme en place. J'ai recriminé contre cet abus de confiance, mais je n'ai encore osé pousser de hauts cris de peur qu'apres avoir defiguré l'ouvrage on ne se porte jusqu'a en maltraiter egalement l'auteur, car sur quoi peut on compter sous un gouvernement tel que le notre?

Encore puis-je vous assurer que je redoute le changement dont ce gouvernement mêmes emble aujourd'huy menacé. Il semble à nos Robins[2] que le Roi et le peuple ne soient faits que pour eux; qu'avec des mots vagues de loix alleguées en gros et sans aucunes citations expresses, ils doivent decider souverainement de tout, et leur joug seroit bientôt devenu plus insupportable que celui du plus fier despote. Que resultera-t-il donc de tout cecy? C'est ce qu'il ne me paroit pas facile de prejuger.

Le Chancelier pousse vigoureusement les Parlementaires qui se defendent pitoyablement; mais les esprits sont si universellement indisposés que depuis les Princes du sang jusqu'aux poissardes des halles, tout devient frondeur.[3] Pendant ce tems là, la depredation des finances est à son comble, et comment le Roi se passera-t-il d'augmenter la charge publique, ou sur quoi mettra-t-il des nouveaux impôts, et que ne risqueroit-il pas dans une si grande fermentation des esprits, sur lesquels on diroit qu'un vent Britannique auroit soufflé d'un bout à l'autre du royaume? Louis 14 fit en 1667 une celebre ordonnance qui defendoit a ses parlements de faire

1. See above, XVII, 292. At some point Barbeu-Dubourg copied his work on the peerage for BF; the MS, undated, is among BF's papers in the APS.

2. The lawyers; their institutional focus was in the parlements, particularly that of Paris.

3. The Fronde had begun in 1648, when the arrest of leaders of the Parlement of Paris had precipitated an insurrection in the city; hence a *frondeur* was a rebel against royal authority and, by implication, a supporter of the parlement.

aucune remontrance sur ses loix qu'apres les avoir enregistrées,[4] et cette ordonnance fut par eux enregistrée purement simplement et sans aucune reclamation. Louis [15] par l'edit de decembre dernier permet les remontrances avec l'enregistrement, pourvu qu'il ne s'ensuive pas une resistance sans fin; les robins crient que c'est renverser toutes les loix et tout le monde le repete sur leur parole. Voila d'ou nous en sommes.[5]

Les Anglois sont-ils plus sages? J'en doute; mais j'espere pour l'honneur du genre humain que vous empecherez par votre profonde sagesse et votre heureuse influence que la contagion [*remainder missing*].

Journal of Jonathan Williams, Jr., of His Tour with Franklin and Others through Northern England

AD in two versions: Lilly Library, University of Indiana; and Yale University Library[6]

This journal contains the only evidence we have of Franklin's journey through the north with John Canton, Dr. Ingenhousz, and young

4. For the text of this ordinance see Athanase J. L. Jourdan *et al.*, eds., *Recueil général des anciennes lois françaises*... (29 vols., Paris, [1821]–33), XVIII, 103–80.

5. Barbeu-Dubourg was writing in the aftermath of a *coup d'état*. René Nicolas Charles Augustin de Maupeou (1714–92), ever since he had become chancellor in 1768, had been struggling to assert the King's supremacy over the Parlement of Paris. On Nov. 27, 1770, a royal edict precipitated the crisis by declaring the King to be sole law-giver and forbidding the parlement to communicate with those in the provinces, to delay the registration of edicts, and to cease functioning. On Dec. 7 the King, in a *lit de justice*, overrode the parlement's refusal to register the edict, which thus became law. *Ibid.*, XXII, 501–9. The parlement defied him by going on strike. On the night of Jan. 19–20, 1771, Maupeou had its members arrested, and all of them were soon exiled. The other parlements and the cour des aides were also suppressed, and a new judicial system created. It aroused such widespread resistance, particularly among the lawyers, that it never functioned effectively; and the whole experiment collapsed when the King died in 1774.

6. The Lilly MS is shorter and in a pocket-sized book; it is probably the account Williams jotted down en route, of which the Yale MS is his elaboration. The latter, however, does not begin until late in the third day of the tour. Neither journal is paginated in a way to make page citations feasible; all direct quotations, unless otherwise indicated, are from the Yale version.

Williams.[7] Proper names are never mentioned after the beginning, and
it is not clear that all the travelers saw everything that Williams did, or
shared his absorption with the details of the industrial processes that
they encountered. We have omitted or condensed most of these details,
despite their value for the economic historian, because we do not know
how much attention they received from his companions in general and
Franklin in particular. But the four clearly did their sightseeing together,
and the chief value of the journal is to establish their itinerary and thereby reveal the pattern of their interests. They had a wide-ranging
curiosity about the various developments that have since come to be
called the Industrial Revolution. The north had given it birth, and their
trip was designed to explore its wonders.

⟨[May 28, 1771.[8]] The travelers left London on May 18 at nine in
the morning, and at nine that evening they reached Northampton.
On entering the town they admired the cross erected by Edward I
to mark the route of Queen Eleanor's funeral procession. At five
the next morning they set out for Matlock Bath by way of Leices-
ter. On the 20th they traveled in leisurely fashion through Derbyshire. From Matlock Bath they went to Bakewell, and stopped to
visit a marble mill; Williams was much interested in the water-
driven saws and polishers. By that evening they were at Castleton,
where they explored the cavern then called the Devil's Arse.[9]
They went into it by water for 750 yards, some of the way by boat
(at times lying on their backs when the roof was little more than a
foot above them), and some of the way on the backs of guides. On
the 21st they arrived at Manchester early in the morning; they
walked round the town, visited a school for poor boys and admired
its old and well stocked library, and then embarked in a luxurious
horse-drawn boat[1] on the Duke of Bridgewater's canal and followed it to its end in the Duke's coal mines. "The Canal goes over
a Bridge and that Bridge over a River Navigable for Boats of 30

7. See BF to Canton above, May 12.
8. Both MSS end with the visit to the Soho Works at Birmingham, which
the Lilly MS dates as the 27th and the Yale MS as the 28th; internal evidence
makes clear that the 28th is correct. Precisely when and by what route the
travelers returned to London we do not know; but they were there by June 1,
when Williams drew up an account (APS) of their various expenses.
9. It now has the more genteel name of Peak Cavern.
1. "Much like the Trackscouts in Holland, according to what I hear of
them." Lilly MS. His informant was obviously BF; see above, XV, 116.

Tons which bring Goods from several parts of the Country to this Bridge, and then by a Crane they are hoisted into the Canal and are carried about the Country several Ways; under this Bridge by the Side of the River is a Road so that when a Boat is on the Canal, another Boat may be sailing and a Carriage going at the same Time under it." The last thousand yards to the first coal face were subterranean. The party observed the miners at work in cramped quarters, and watched the coal being brought out and loaded into a forty-ton canal boat, which a single horse then pulled to Manchester. There the canal again tunneled under a hill to a large hole, running up to the surface, through which a water-driven crane unloaded the coal.

The next morning the travelers left Manchester and reached Leeds by evening.[2] On the 23rd they visited the cloth hall at Leeds, where each subscriber had a booth for selling his wares on market days; the hall was then almost empty because of the demands of the American trade, which had raised the price by sixpence a yard. The travelers then called on Joseph Priestley, "who made some very pretty Electrical Experiments and some on the different properties of different kinds of Air." The next day they changed carriages at Wakefield, stopped for a tour of the Marquis of Rockingham's country estate,[3] and arrived that evening at Sheffield. On the morning of the 25th they went to see a factory making articles of silver-plated copper, and in the afternoon to inspect the ironworks and manufacture of tin plate at nearby Rotherham, and to visit an ironworks where they "saw them Melting the Iron Ore and casting Potts, etc., which is perform'd as in America."[4] What impressed Williams was the furnace, fired with charcoal and coal cinders, and the bellows driven by a water wheel. "It appeared particularly Odd to see a small River of liquid Iron running from the Furnace into the Recevoir and from thence carried in Ladles like hot broth. The Labourers have 14d. per Day their Work is extreme hard and in summer Time must be very disagreeable."

2. A detailed valuation of the West Riding cloth manufacture in 1769, estimated at almost a million and a half sterling, is inserted at this point in the Yale MS.
3. Wentworth Woodhouse, near Rotherham, the seat of the Wentworth family; the house had been rebuilt by Flitcroft for Rockingham's father, the first marquis.
4. Lilly MS.

The party returned to Sheffield for the night, and the next day toured the sumptuous home of the Duke of Devonshire at Chatsworth.[5] "Even the Window Frames of this House are gilt on the outside." That evening they reached Derby; the next morning they visited the china and pottery manufactures there, and a silk mill where a single wheel "produces 97,000 Motions by communication down to a little Wheel of about 4 Inches Diameter. There are nigh 63,700 Reels constantly Turning and the twist process is tended by Children of about 5 or 7 Years old and one Child does the Business of 63 persons."

The same day the group continued by way of Burton-on-Trent ("remarkable for good Ale"), Lichfield, and Sutton Coldfield to Birmingham. On the morning of the 28th they visited Matthew Boulton's Soho ironworks, which employed 700 people. Its products were extremely varied, from farthing buttons to hundred-guinea ornaments. "We went through his Works but there was so much and we staid so little While, that it is almost impossible for the strongest Memory to retain it. The Work of a Button has 5 or 6 branches in it each of which is performed in a second of Time. He likewise works plated Goods—Watch Rings and all kinds of hard ware all of which is performed by Machinery in such a Manner that Children and Women perform the greatest part of it."[6]⟩

5. "The Palace of the Peak," begun in 1687 and finished in 1706. Part of an older house also survived, where Mary Queen of Scots frequently stayed while she was in captivity; the visitors were shown her apartment, "kept in just the same situation as it was when she was there. The Hangings are very much worn and ragged the Bedstead and Chairs all tottering and quite different from the present Fashion."

6. The reputation of Matthew Boulton (1728–1809) rested on his success in improving not only the workmanship but also the artistic quality of his many wares. The problem of motive power for his machinery had long concerned him, and he was on the verge of entering into his momentous partnership with James Watt to produce a workable steam engine. *DNB*; see also above, x, 39 n. BF had met Boulton in 1758, had performed some experiments with him in Birmingham two years later, and had had some correspondence with him thereafter. Above, IX, 231 n; XII, 140; XIII, 166–8, 196–7.

From a Committee of the Managers of the Pennsylvania Hospital to Franklin, John Fothergill, and David Barclay

LS: American Philosophical Society

⟨Pennsylvania Hospital, June 3, 1771. Last year's committee sent them, a few weeks ago, a resolution of the contributors and a power of attorney to receive the funds due the Hospital from unclaimed shares of the Pennsylvania Land Company;[7] copies of both are enclosed. Although the needs of the Hospital are acute, the Managers dare not draw any of the money until they know that the legal requirements have been met and the transfer made. Franklin, Fothergill, and Barclay are therefore urged to inform them immediately whether the power of attorney was in proper form and, if so, whether the cash is in hand.[8] If it is, the Managers will promptly sell bills of exchange to meet their pressing needs. Signed by John Reynell, Samuel Rhoads, and James Pemberton.⟩

To a Committee of the Library Company of Philadelphia[9]

ALS: Maine Historical Society

Gentlemen,   London, June 5. 1771

Inclos'd is an Invoice of the Books shipp'd for the Library Company by Mr. Strahan. I happen'd to be in the Country when they were pack'd up, so had not an Opportunity of seeing them. But if you find any Mistake he will rectify it. I wish them safe to hand.

Upon Enquiry, I find that to purchase all the Transactions of the several Philosophical Societies in Europe will amount to about £300 Sterling,[1] which I imagine may be thought too great a Sum for our Company to lay out in such Books. I did not think they would have amounted to near that Sum. The French Encyclopedie probably contains Extracts of the most material Parts

7. See above, May 3, where the background of the present letter is explained.

8. Eleven months later the managers had had no answer to this request; see their letter below, May 16, 1772.

9. See BF's earlier letter to the committee above, April 16, which touches on most of what he is discussing here.

1. See Priestley to BF above, April 19.

of all of them. That Work may be had for about 60 Guineas at present: But a new and improv'd Edition is now in hand, which will be out in about two Years, and considerably cheaper, the Scarcity of the first Edition having greatly advanced the Price.[2] If you were to order the future foreign Philosophical Transactions as they come out, I believe they may readily be had, and am told they will amount to about 10, or 12 Guineas a Year. With great Regard, I am, Gentlemen, Your most obedient humble Servant

B FRANKLIN

Messrs. Michael Hillegas Richard Waln, and R. Strettel Jones.

Endorsed: B Franklin's Letter London, June 5, 1771 per Capt Williams

To Deborah Franklin ALS: American Philosophical Society

My dear Child, London, June 5. 1771

I have lately made a Journey of a Fortnight, to Birmingham, Sheffield, Leeds, and Manchester[3] and return'd only in time to be at Court on the King's Birthday, which was yesterday. The Joy was in a fair way of being doubled on the same Day, for the Queen was deliver'd early this Morning of another Prince, the eighth Child, there being now six Princes and two Princesses, all lovely Children. The Prince of Wales and the Bishop of Oszabrug appear'd yesterday for the first time in the Drawing Room, and gave great Pleasure by their sensible manly Behaviour.[4] My Journey

2. The new edition of Diderot's famous *Encyclopédie, ou Dictionnaire raisonné des sciences* . . . was the third, published in Leghorn in 17 vols., 1770–75.
3. See the résumé of Williams' journal above, under May 28.
4. The Queen eventually gave birth to fifteen children. Eight were alive at this time, but for all BF's interest in royalty he transposed a boy and a girl: the new baby had three sisters and four brothers. The birth dates and eventual titles of the eight were: George (1762), Prince of Wales, Prince Regent, and King (1820–30); Frederick (1763), Duke of York and from infancy Bishop of Osnabrück, a tiny principality at the disposition of his father as Elector of Hanover; William (1765), Duke of Clarence and King (1830–37); Charlotte (1766), Queen of Würtemberg; Edward (1767), Duke of Kent and Queen Victoria's father; Augusta (1768); Elizabeth (1770), Princess of Hesse-Homburg; and the newly born Ernest, Duke of Cumberland and King of Hanover (1837–51).

has been of use to my Health, the Air and Exercise have given me fresh Spirits, and I feel now exceeding well, Thanks to God.

I wrote to you lately, and have received no Line from you per Capt. Sparks who is arrived. I suppose you have written by Falconer, who is not yet heard of. My Love to our Children and Grand Son. I am, as ever, Your affectionate husband

B FRANKLIN

Addressed: To / Mrs Franklin / at / Philadelphia / via N York / Per Packet / B Free FRANKLIN

Extract of a Letter from London

Printed in *The Pennsylvania Gazette*, August 1, 1771

William Strahan had accused Franklin of inactivity, and Arthur Lee was accusing him of being Hillsborough's agent.[5] To balance the record, therefore, it is appropriate to publish a defense of him by an anonymous correspondent, which found its way into two Philadelphia newspapers.[6]

June 5, 1771.

I saw Dr. Franklin To-day. He is just returned from a little Excursion into the Country,[7] and is in perfect Health. I hope the Time is approaching, when our Ministry will have both Inclination and Leisure to call for, and listen to his Advice. No Man hath more studied, and more fully comprehends, the true Interests of both Countries, and has more enlarged Views of human Nature, and the general Interests of Mankind, than he has; no Man deserves better of Society; and, of course, no Man is fitter to be consulted upon the great Objects now in Contemplation, and upon the Grounds of Dispute, which still remain to be adjusted between us.

5. See Strahan to WF above, April 3, and Lee to Samuel Adams below, June 10.
6. William Goddard also printed it in the *Pa. Chron.*, July 29–Aug. 5, 1771.
7. BF's tour of northern England, for which see the résumé of Jonathan Williams' journal above, May 28.

To Thomas Cushing[8]   ALS: Public Record Office

During Franklin's correspondence with leading Bostonians over the past year, the gap between his views and theirs had been gradually narrowing;[9] but this letter shows that it had not yet closed. He deplored the exercise of the King's prerogative through instructions to governors, he denied that Parliament might bind the colonies without their consent, he believed that economic autonomy was within their reach, and he hoped that they would continue to assert their rights. At the same time he tried to calm the excitement in Boston over the issue of officials' salaries, and on the underlying issue counseled moderation. In one breath he rejected the only bases on which British authority could be exercised; in the next he advised against flouting it, beyond a point, while any hope of settlement remained. That hope was presumably more important to him than logical consistency.

Sir,   London, June 10. 1771
I received your Favour of the 30th. of April, a few Days since, with the Newspapers, &c. and am much oblig'd by the Information you as a private Person so kindly give me of the present State of Affairs in your Province. Such a confidential Correspondence between us I most willingly embrace, as I am persuaded it must be often useful in the prudent Conduct of our publick Interests, to interchange Intelligence that cannot so properly or safely appear in Publick Letters, since nothing written to or from an Assembly

8. This is the earliest of some twenty letters from BF that the British seized in Cushing's house during the siege of Boston in 1775. The seizure was in delayed response to earlier orders from Dartmouth, who was seeking proof that BF and Arthur Lee were involved in a conspiracy with the Bostonians: Carter, ed., *Gage Correspondence*, I, 364, 422–3; II, 167. The letters eventually found their way into the government archives, and at some point passed through the hands of Thomas Moffat, the Rhode Island Loyalist (above, XI, 191 n), who wrote comments on them. Charles M. Andrews, *Guide to the Materials for American History, to 1783, in the Public Record Office*. . . (2 vols., Washington, 1912), I, 129. In this case Moffat made two comments, almost identical. "A Scurrilous and very wicked Letter," one of them reads, "being highly defamatory of the Earl of Hillsborough and contains the most Criminal Insinuations and Instigations against the Authority of the British Parliament in North America. The letter intimates dangerous negotiations in the manufacturing Towns of Yorkshire by Him to raise Jealousies in both Countries."

9. See above, XVII, 161–5, 275–83, 285–7, 301–4, 307–13; BF to Bowdoin, Cooper, and Cushing, Feb. 5, 1771.

can be kept from the Knowledge of Adversaries, who may take Advantage of it, to the Prejudice of our Affairs and of the Persons concerned in the Management of them.

The continuing our General Court at Cambridge has always appear'd to me a Measure extreamly impolitic in Government here, as it can tend only to irritate the Members, offend the People in general, and create an Ill Humour that can never be for His Majesty's Service, or the Benefit of this Nation. For supposing the Province to be ever so great an Offender, this is not a Punishment sufficient to reform by its Severity; it is rather more fitted to affront and provoke.[1] You will therefore hardly understand it, if you do not well know the Character of the present American Secretary, proud, supercilious, extreamly conceited (moderate as

1. BF's first comment on this quarrel, which had been simmering for two years, is an appropriate place to sketch the issues involved. They were more serious than those of political expediency, to which BF confined himself. Opposition to the presence of the military in Boston in 1769 had led Gov. Bernard, acting on a suggestion of Lord Hillsborough, to transfer the legislature to Cambridge. Hillsborough recommended to Lieut. Gov. Hutchinson, after Bernard's departure, that he leave it there unless he saw strong reason to the contrary. Hutchinson hesitated, but finally interpreted this recommendation as an instruction; the Court remained at Cambridge. The House of Representatives, in its continued protests against the move, evolved two arguments that constituted a challenge to the King's prerogative in Massachusetts. First, in the charter the crown had surrendered to the governor the determination of when, where, and how long the Court should meet, so that any instruction limiting this freedom violated the charter. Second, exercise of the prerogative through such instructions had to be for the public good, of which the people's representatives were the best judge; the judgment of the House, therefore, implicitly limited the prerogative. Hutchinson met these arguments head on: he denied that the crown had surrendered anything of its prerogative in the charter, and he asserted that his commission, as part of the provincial constitution, subordinated his government to royal instructions and not to the will of the House. The result was an impasse that lasted until 1772. See above, XVII, 278–9, 302; Hutchinson, *History*, III, 169–70, 178–9, 202–3, 217–20, 241–2, 246–7, 377–99, 400–4; Alden Bradford, ed., *Speeches of the Governors of Massachusetts, from 1765 to 1775; and the Answers of the House of Representatives...* (Boston, 1818), pp. 166–72, 194–6, 199–202, 206–8, 210–15, 217–22, 229–33, 302–4; Mass. Arch., XXVI, 518, 523; XXVII, 195, 239, 246, 446–8, 451; Leonard W. Labaree, *Royal Government in America: a Study of the British Colonial System before 1783* (New Haven, 1930), pp. 194–8; Donald C. Lord and Robert M. Calhoun, "The Removal of the Massachusetts General Court from Boston, 1769–1772," *Jour. of Amer. History*, LV (1968–69), 735–55.

they are) of his political Knowledge and Abilities, fond of every one that can stoop to flatter him, and inimical to all that dare tell him disagreable Truths. This Man's Mandates have been treated with Disrespect in America, his Letters have been criticis'd, his Measures censur'd and despis'd; which has produc'd in him a kind of settled Malice against the Colonies, particularly ours, that would break out into greater Violence, if cooler Heads did not set some Bounds to it. I have indeed good Reason to believe that his Conduct is far from being approved by the King's other Servants, and that he himself is so generally dislik'd by them, that it is not probable he will continue much longer in his present Station, the general Wish here being to recover (saving only the Dignity of Government) the Good Will of the Colonies, which there is little reason to expect while they are under his wild Administration. Their permitting so long his Excentricities (if I may use such an Expression) is owing, I imagine, rather to the Difficulty of knowing how to dispose of or what to do with a Man of his wrongheaded bustling Industry, who, it is apprehended may be more mischievous out of Administration than in it, than to any kind of personal Regard for him.[2]

All Views or Expectations of drawing any considerable Revenue to this Country from the Colonies, are I believe generally given over, and it seems probable that nothing of that kind will ever again be attempted: But as Foreign Courts appear to have taken great Pleasure in the Prospect of our Disunion, it seems now to be thought necessary, for supporting the National Weight, and the Influence of our Court abroad, that there should be an Appearance as if all was pacified in America; and, as I said before, I think the general Wish is that it may be really so. But then there is an Apprehension, lest a too sudden yielding to all our Claims, should be deem'd the Effect of Weakness, render the British Court contemptible in the Eyes of Foreigners, make *us* more presumptuous, and promote more extravagant Demands such as could never be granted, and thence still greater Danger of a fatal Rupture. I am thus particular that you may judge whether it will not be prudent in us to indulge the Mother Country in this Concern for her own Honour, so far as may be consistent with the Preservation of our

2. Hillsborough was not forced out of office until August, 1772. For the quarrel that lay behind BF's comments on him see above, Jan. 16.

essential Rights, especially as that Honour may in some Cases be of Importance to the General Welfare:[3] And in this View, whether it will not be better gradually to wear off the assum'd Authority of Parliament over America, which we have in too many Instances given countenance to, with our indiscrete Acknowledgement of it in Publick Acts, than by a general open Denial, and Resistance to it, bring on prematurely a Contest, to which, if we are not found equal, that Authority will by the Event be more strongly establish'd; and if we should prove superior, yet by the Division the general Strength of the British Nation must be greatly diminished. I do not venture to advise in this Case, because I see, in this seemingly prudent Course, some Danger of a diminishing Attention to our Rights, instead of a persevering Endeavour to recover and establish them; but I rely a good deal on the growing Knowledge of them among the Americans, and the daily increasing Strength and Importance of that Country to this, which must give such Weight in time to our just Claims, as no selfish Spirit in this Part of the Empire will be able to resist. In the mean time, while we are declining the usurped Authority of Parliament, I wish to see a steady dutiful Attachment to the King and his Family maintained among us; and that however we may be induced for Peacesake, or from a Sense of our present Inability, to submit at present in some Instances to the Exercise of that unjust Authority, we shall continue from time to time to assert our Rights in occasional solemn Resolves and other publick Acts, never yielding them up, and avoiding even the slightest Expressions that seem confirmatory of the Claim that has been set up against them. My Opinion has long been that Parliament had originally no Right to bind us by any kind of Law whatever without our Consent. We have indeed in a manner consented to some of them, at least tacitly: But for the future methinks we should be cautious how we add to those Instances, and never adopt or acknowledge an Act of Parliament but by a formal Law of our own, as your General Assembly I think did in the case of the Act of Parliament relating to the Oaths mention'd in the first Paragraph of your Votes; tho' as it stands there, it seems as if the Act of Parliament had required those

3. The preceding sentences are interesting to compare, in tone as well as substance, with the second paragraph of BF to Cushing above, Feb. 5.

Oaths to be taken by your Members, and was acknowledg'd as of force for that purpose.[4]

I do not at present see the least likelihood of preventing the Grant of Salaries or Pensions from hence to the King's Officers in America, by any Application in Behalf of the People there. It is look'd on as a strange thing here to object to the King's paying his own Servants sent among us to do his Business; and they say we should seem to have much more Reason of Complaint if it were requir'd of us to pay them. And the more we urge the Impropriety of their not depending on us for their Support, the more Suspicion it breeds that we are desirous of influencing them to betray the Interests of their Master or of this Nation. Indeed if the Money is rais'd from us against our Wills, the Injustice becomes more evident than where it arises from hence. I do not think, however, that the Effect of these Salaries is likely to be so considerable, either in favour of Government here, or in our Prejudice, as may be generally apprehended. The Love of Money is not a Thing of certain Measure, so as that it may be easily filled and satisfied. Avarice is infinite, and where there is not good Œconomy, no Salary, however large, will prevent Necessity. He that has a fixed, and what others may think a competent Income, is often as much to be by-assed by the Expectation of more, as if he had already none at all. If the Colonies should resolve on giving handsome Presents to good Governors at or after their Departure, or to their Children after their Decease, I imagine it might produce even better Effects than our present annual Grants.[5] But the Course probably will soon be, that the Chief Governor to whom the Salary is given, will

4. Oaths of allegiance, as laid down in 1 Wm. & Mary, c. 8, were required by the Massachusetts charter of 1691; and in the following year the General Court implemented the requirement by an act of its own. *Mass. Acts and Resolves*, I, 76–8. Members of the Court, nevertheless, were still taking the oath as "required by Act of Parliament"; see for example *Mass. House Jour.*, 1st session, May–June, 1770, p. 3. BF's objection to this acknowledgement of Parliamentary sovereignty echoed the seventeenth-century contention of Massachusetts and Connecticut that statutes passed in Westminster were not law in a colony until re-enacted by its legislature. Charles M. Andrews, *The Colonial Period of American History*... (4 vols., New Haven, [1934–38]), IV, 140–1.

5. BF's proposal to reward governors for good behavior was presumably based on the method that the Pennsylvania Assembly had used to influence Gov. Denny in 1759: above, IX, 129, 136–7, 226 n.

have Leave to reside in England, a Lieutenant or Deputy will be left to do the Business and live on the Perquisites, which not being thought quite sufficient, his receiving Presents yearly will be wink'd at thro' the Interest of his Principal, and thus things will get into the old Train, only this Inconvenience remaining, that while by our Folly in consuming the Duty-Articles, the fixed Salary is raised on ourselves without our Consent, we must pay double for the same Service. However, tho' it may be a hopeless Task while the Duties continue sufficient to pay the Salaries, I shall on all proper Occasions make Representations against this new Mode; and if by the Duties falling short, the Treasury here should be call'd on to pay those Salaries, it is possible they may come to be seen in another Light than at present, and dropt as unnecessary.[6]

I was glad to see that Attention in the General Court to an Improvement of the Militia.[7] A War may happen in which Britain, like Rome of old, may find so much to do for her own Defence, as to be unable to spare Troops or Ships for the Protection of her Colonies: A Minister may arise so little our Friend as to neglect that Protection, or to permit Invasions of our Country, in order to make us cry out for Help, and thereby furnish stronger Pretence for maintaining a Standing Army among us. If we once lose our military Spirit, and supinely depend on an Army of Mercenaries for our Defence, we shall become contemptible, despis'd both by Friends and Enemies, as neither our Friendship nor our Enmity will be deem'd of any Importance. As our Country is not wealthy so as to afford much ready Plunder, the Temptation to a foreign Invasion of us is the less; and I am persuaded that the Name of a numerous well-disciplined Militia, would alone be almost sufficient to prevent any Thoughts of attempting it. And what a Glory would

6. Cushing, in his missing letter of April 30, may well have informed BF that the House had asked to see Gov. Hutchinson's instructions on his salary. The Governor had replied that he would reveal parts of them, when they arrived and if he thought proper. Hutchinson, *History*, III, 242. For the next stage in the squabble see the House to BF below, June 29.

7. In November, 1770, during the crisis in Europe over the Falkland Islands, the House had taken issue with the Governor over what it considered the poor state of the provincial militia. This precipitated one more quarrel, in which each side blamed the other for unpreparedness. See Bradford, *op. cit.* n. 1, pp. 289–90, 294, 300–1, 305.

it be for us to send, on any trying Occasion, ready and effectual Aid to our Mother Country!

I have lately been among the Clothing Towns in Yorkshire, and by conversing with the Manufacturers there, am more and more convinced of the natural Impossibility there is that, considering our Increase in America, England should be able much longer to supply us with Cloathing.[8] Necessity therefore, as well as Prudence, will soon induce us to seek Resources in our own Industry; which becoming general among the People, encourag'd by Resolutions of your Court, such as I have the Pleasure of seeing in your late Votes, will do Wonders.[9] Family Manufactures will alone amount to a vast Saving in the Year: And a steady Determination and Custom of buying only of your own Artificers wherever they can supply you, will soon make them more expert in Working, so as to dispatch more Business, while constant Employment enables them to afford their Work still cheaper. The lowness of Provisions with us, compar'd with their daily rising Price here, added to the Freight, Risque and Commissions on the Manufactures of this Country, must give great Advantage to our Workmen, and enable them in time to retain a great deal of Money in the Country, tho' still Trade enough should remain between us and Britain to render our Friendship of the greatest Importance to this Nation.

I was a Subscriber to a Set of Plates published here, entitled, *The Senator's Remembrancer*, a Work encourag'd by many Members of both Houses. Having a spare Copy, I beg your Acceptance of it as a small Mark of my Respect, and send it per Capt. Jarvis.[1]

8. BF underestimated the productivity of the cloth trade; see Phyllis Deane, "The Output of the British Woollen Industry in the Eighteenth Century," *Jour. of Economic History*, XVII (1957), 222–3.

9. In the previous November the House, following the lead of the Boston town meeting eight months before, had appointed a standing committee to make plans for encouraging commerce. *A Report of the Record Commissioners . . . Containing the Boston Town Records, 1770 through 1777* (Boston, 1887), pp. 12–13, 20; *Mass. House Jour.*, 3rd session, Sept.–Nov., 1770, p. 164.

1. For this bizarre publication see Katherine French to BF above, Feb. 18. The Captain was Edward Jarvis (1731–93), master of the *Hannah* and a prominent Boston Son of Liberty; he left London June 20 and reached Boston in early September. John G. Palfrey, "Sons of Liberty Who Dined at Dorchester," *Mass. Hist. Soc. Proc.*, XI (1869–70), 141; George G. Wolkins,

Should it afford to your already well-furnish'd Mind, no useful Hints in the Management of Publick Affairs, it may however be of Service to some young Friend, at least as Copies of fair and elegant Writing.

The Letters I have received from my Friends in Boston, have lately come to hand badly sealed, with no distinct Impression, appearing as if they had been opened, and in a very bungling way closed again. I suspect this may be done by some prying Persons that use the Coffee-house here. I therefore mention it, that you may, if you think fit, send yours under Cover to some Merchant of Character, who would forward them to me more safely. With great and sincere Respect I have the Honour of being, Sir, Your most obedient and most humble Servant,   B FRANKLIN

Honble Thos Cushing Esqr

(Private)

Endorsed: Dr Benj Franklin June 10. 1771

Arthur Lee to Samuel Adams

Extract: reprinted from Richard Henry Lee, *Life of Arthur Lee...* (2 vols., Boston, 1829), I, 216–18.

When Franklin was elected agent for the Massachusetts House of Representatives in the autumn of 1770, it was over the opposition of a faction led by James Otis and Samuel Adams. Their candidate was Arthur Lee, and they succeeded in having him named as alternate, to serve if Franklin were indisposed or came home.[2] But the older man's health remained robust, and he showed no sign of leaving; Lee's patience, what little there was of it, soon wore thin. He had a remarkable capacity for derogating others, and Franklin stood in his path. He therefore turned to attacking him in the obvious way, by fanning the distrust that had appeared in the debate the previous autumn. In writing to Adams, it might seem, Lee was merely preaching to the converted. But only a fool would have expected such a tidbit to remain confidential, and Lee was no fool. The extract printed below was almost certainly copied in Boston and sent anonymously to Speaker Cushing,[3] whence it spread among Franklin's friends as well as enemies.

"Daniel Malcom and Writs of Assistance," *ibid.*, LVIII (1924–25), 49–50; *London Chron.*, June 20–22, and *Boston Gaz.*, Sept. 2, 1771.

2. See above, XVII, 257–8.
3. See Cooper to BF below, Aug. 23.

Temple, June 10th, 1771.

I have read lately in your papers an assurance from Dr. Franklin that all designs against the charter of the colony are laid aside. This is just what I expected from him; and if it be true, the Dr. is not the dupe but the instrument of Lord Hillsborough's treachery. That Lord Hillsborough gives out this assurance is certain, but notorious as he is for ill faith and fraud, his duplicity would not impose on one possessed of half Dr. F.'s sagacity. And indeed what reason is there for this change? Is the oppressive plan against America abandoned; or is it discovered that an independent council will be less troublesome in the prosecution of it than they hitherto have been?[4] Neither the one nor the other; and though the reasons I have already mentioned[5] compelled his lordship to suspend the execution of his scheme, yet to trust that it is therefore laid aside, is a degree of credulity and infatuation which I hope will never be imposed on the assembly. The minister's aim in these assurances is manifest, not only to remove the odium which the discovery must bring upon him, without his plans being executed, but to lull to sleep that vigilance and precaution which the detection would produce on your side, and which would much embarrass if not frustrate his design. Could he thus smother your suspicions and silence all opposition from you, he would have nothing to obstruct him but the agent, from whom his apprehensions cannot be very great. The possession of a profitable office at will, the having a son in a high post at pleasure, the grand purpose of his residence here being to effect a change in the government of Pennsylvania, for which administration must be cultivated and courted, are circumstances which, joined with the temporising conduct he has always held in American affairs, preclude every rational hope that in an open contest between an oppressive administration and a free people, Dr. F. can be a faithful advocate for the latter; or oppose and expose the former with a spirit and integrity which alone can, in times like these, be of any service. By temporising I

4. For the proposals to revise the charter see above, XVII, 279 n, 308, 311, and Cooper to BF below, July 10. The specific proposal to which Lee is alluding was to abolish the role of the lower house in choosing the Council, and make it entirely appointive.

5. Earlier in the letter Lee had said that first the Falkland Islands crisis, then the quarrel with the City of London, had distracted Parliament from considering the charter.

mean consulting the inclination of ministers and acting conformable to that, not to the interests of the province. Thus when the Rockingham administration espoused the American cause no man was more zealous or active than Dr. F., since that he has been totally inactive; and his particular partizans here, the Quaker merchants, were opposed to the late measure of petitioning for the repeal of the revenue act; though the exciting the merchants and manufacturers here to petition against it was the great benefit expected from the non-importation agreements with you, which the Dr. immediately after advised the Philadelphians not to violate. The artifice of this is manifest, that advice made him popular in America, his preventing the effect of it recommended him to administration here; and in consequence we see, that though accounts of that letter were transmitted to Lord Hillsborough, the writer stands in the same place and favour as before, though it is a fixed rule of conduct with his lordship to displace all those who not only oppose, but who do not conform perfectly to his plan.[6]

I feel it not a little disagreeable to speak my sentiments of Dr. Franklin, as your generous confidence has placed me in the light of a rival to him. But I am so far from being influenced by selfish motives, that were the service of the colony ten times greater, I would perform it for nothing rather than you and America, at a time like this, should be betrayed by a man, who, it is hardly in the nature of things to suppose, can be faithful to his trust. Your house has done me the honour unsolicited and personally unknown, to testify their approbation of the manner in which I have treated the enemies of America and their particular foes.[7] Such an approbation is with me the highest incentive not only to oppose your avowed enemies, but to detect your false friends.

6. The argument here is involved. It has three parts: (a) BF advised the Philadelphians (presumably in his letter to Thomson above, XVII, 111–13) to stick to nonimportation in order to arouse British merchants to petition for repeal of the Townshend Acts; (b) Hillsborough knew that BF had done so and yet retained him in "place and favour"; (c) BF must therefore have been working secretly in London, through the Quakers, to dissuade the merchants from petitioning. The argument rests on the questionable assumption that a place in the Post Office depended on Hillsborough's favor, and ignores the fact that BF still held that place six months after his breach with the American Secretary.

7. By appointing him alternative agent.

From [John] Peter Miller[8]   ALS: American Philosophical Society

Sir!   Ephrata in Pennsylvania the 12th. of June 1771.

Being prevented by many Interruptions, the Discharge upon your worthy Letter was so long postponed. I send you hereby a Collection, which for the most part uncommon. I do not pretend, that they Word for Words hath been the Father's Tenets; for he himself would never publish any, and protested against others, which, by doing also, hath increased the Division in the Church.[9] Yet can I give Assurance, that if the Father was alive, and would read them, that he would own them. I wish, that it hath been in my Hand, to make all pallatable according to the modern Taste: but Truth hath haired Lipps, and used in its Utterance a rough Tune. I offer the whole to your Freedom, either to burn or publish the same, or to make such alterations, as you think best: for altho' I am convinc'd of the Veracity of the Substance of the whole, yet must I sue for Pardon when the Expressions are defective, for I am a Foreigner to the Idiotism of the Language, which I hope to obtain from your Clemency. I hope, the whole will be forwarded by the Care of your Lady, with which and her Family we have in your Absence cultivated the same Friendship, which was established for many Years: but I gave Mr. Christ. Marshal Liberty, to peruse said Writings, and even to copy of for his Friends, if he would, which have inquired for such Things, which I thought necessary not to conceal from you.[1]

8. The second head of the Solitary Brethren of the Community of Seventh Day Baptists at Ephrata (they were also called Dunkers) and one of the most learned of the Pennsylvania clergy; see the *DAB* and above, IX, 323 n. His letter is clearly in answer to one from BF that has been lost.

9. The Father was Johann Conrad Beissel, founder of the Ephrata Community, for whom see *ibid.* and the *DAB*. The massive enclosure, 147 pages in Miller's inimitable English, was primarily his exposition of Beissel's doctrines, followed by a translation of three Beissel tracts from the German: a discourse written in 1734 on the seven-headed beast in Revelations, "Ninety-nine Mystical Sentences" printed by BF in German in 1730, and fifty-seven apothegms from Beissel's writings. The last two are printed in Julius F. Sachse, "A Unique Manuscript by Rev. Peter Miller," Pa.-German Soc. *Proc.*, XXI (1910), 1–44. In the first page of his introduction Miller explained how Beissel created division among his followers by constantly frustrating their intentions.

1. For Christopher Marshall (1709–97), a Philadelphia pharmacist and diarist, see the *DAB*. He had helped to publish Miller's translation of a work by Beissel in 1765: Sachse, *op. cit.*, p. 4.

130

The Present, which I have added, was the Father's musical Book, wherein are contained the most part of the musical Concerts, by himself composed. It did cost three Brethren three Quarters of a Year Work to write the same: by the Imbellishment thereof it will appear, what a great Regard we had for our Superior, in the whole Book there is no musical Error. And as it was written, before the Mystery of Singing was fully discovered, therefore are not all the Keys therein mentioned. The Masters of that Angelic Art will be astonished to see, that therein a Man, destituted of all human Instruction, came therein to the highest Pitch of Perfection meerly through his own Industry. Also that, when he did set up a School in the Camp, not only the Members of the Single Station were therewith occupied for Many Years: but also the Family-Brethren were also thereby enamoured, that their naturall Affection to their Families suffered a great Loss.[2]

It is a Wonder, how the seven Notes and few half-notes can be so marvellously transposed, as to make thereby 1000 Melodies, all of 5 Tunes, and some of 6 Tunes, yea some of 7 Tunes, also that they came not one the other in the Way. In the Composition the Father had the same Way as in his Writings, viz: he suspended his considering Faculty, and putting his Spirit on the Pen, followed its Dictates strictly, also were all the Melodies flown from the Mystery of Singing, that was opened within him, therefore have they that Simplicity, which was required, to raise Edification. It is certain, that the Confusion of Languages, which began at Babel, never did affect Singing: and therefore is in the Substance of the

2. Beissel required continence of married couples at Ephrata, and music was apparently one way to divert their attention to spiritual matters. His own musical compositions were intricate to a degree; see Julius F. Sachse, "The Music of the Ephrata Cloister...," Pa.-German Soc. *Proc.*, XII (1901), 5–92. The Ephrata Codex, a long and richly illuminated MS that the Community had presented to Beissel shortly before his death, was what Miller sent to BF, who considered it "a most valuable Curiosity": to DF below, Jan. 28, 1772. Inside the cover of the MS is an unsigned note, supposedly in the hand of John Wilkes, saying that BF had lent the writer the codex just before leaving for America in 1775. Library of Congress, *Report of the Librarian of Congress...* (Washington, 1927), pp. 109–12. Wilkes is the last man who would have wanted to know about music as a way of subduing carnal desire. His brother Israel might have, but a careful examination of the handwriting convinces us that both men must be ruled out; the writer is unidentifiable.

131

Matter in the whole World but one Way of Singing; altho' in particulars there may be Differences.

As concerning our Oeconomy: it is true that it received by the Father's death a severe Shok; yet have we through the Grace of God, both Brethren and Sisters, hitherto maintained our Ground and a visible Congregation. But shall not propagate the Monastic Life upon the Posterity; since we have no Successors, and the Genius of the Americans is bound another way.

I have your kind Greeting communicated both to the Brethren and Sisters in the Camp: which all send you their humble Reciprocation, the number of Brethren being 12. and of the Ladies 26 all good old Warriours. We all wish, that God would grant you in your high Age the Spirit of Rejuvenescency, and that, when Satiated with Years, you might occupy your Lot in the Lord's Inheritance: in which humble Wishes I in particular remain Sir your obedient Servant   PETER MILLER

P.S. Please to tell Mr. Neate[3] the humble Respect from all the Camp, especially from Brother Obed and me.

To Benjamin Franklin Esquire!

To [Anthony Todd[4]]   ALS: American Philosophical Society

Dear Sir   June 15. [1771[5]]

I am just going out of Town for a Week, but shall endeavour to return in time for the great Pleasure you so kindly propose to me of meeting *chez vous*, that excellent good Man Baron Behr. In the mean while, pray advise your Neighbour Mr. Jackson, if he should be at any Loss about it, how to get soon ashore two Barrels of Flour (one of which is for your self) that are just arriv'd from

3. Doubtless William Neate, a London merchant trading with Philadelphia, for whom see above, XII, 192 n.

4. Todd lived in Walthamstow: *Gent. Mag.*, LXVIII (1798), 541. He was the only one of BF's correspondents who did.

5. Our predecessors conjectured (above, XIII, 300 n) that the date was 1770. But the letter mentions Falconer as master of the *Britannia*, which he was not until October, 1770; she cleared for London the following May. *PMHB*, XXVIII (1904), 348; *Pa. Gaz.*, May 9, 1771. BF speaks of leaving town for a week, furthermore, which he did in mid-June: BF to Shipley below, June 24.

Philadelphia in the Britannia Capt. Falconer. The Custom house Officers often make Difficulties about these Trifles, and detain them till they are half spoilt. Mr. Foxcroft, (who you know puffs everything from our Side the Water) says, "You will receive two of the most extraordinary Barrels of Flour by Falconer that ever was manufactur'd in America or perhaps in the World; they were made on purpose, &c."[6] I would not have your Expectations too highly rais'd by this. I only hope it will be got while sweet, and that I shall find a Pudding of it smoaking on the hospitable Board of Walthamstow, being ambitious if it should prove remarkably good, that the Baron too may taste the Produce of our American Hanover.[7] With the most affectionate Respect, I am, Dear Sir, Yours &c   B FRANKLIN

From Katherine French[8]   AL: Historical Society of Pennsylvania

Monday 17th. June [1771]
Mrs. French understands that Docr. Franklin dines with the Bishop of St. Asaph's to morrow[9] hopes he will do her the favor of dining with her on Wednesday or Thursday, both days will be giving her a double pleasure, she has provided chess players for each day.

6. Charles Jackson was an official in the Post Office (above, XIV, 301 n); for that reason, we assume, BF was invoking his aid in getting the barrels through customs. John Foxcroft, who gloried in the name of American, had promised BF the flour months before; see his letter above, Jan. 14.

7. Behr was the Hanoverian minister to St. James's; see above, XIII, 300 n. BF meant, we believe, that Pennsylvania was the American Hanover, because of its fertility or its many German settlers or both. He could scarcely have meant America: he would not have tried out on Todd, even in fun, his analogy between the colonies and Hanover as parts of the empire.

8. See her letter to BF above, Feb. 18.

9. BF was not merely dining with the Bishop, but visiting him for a week in his house near Winchester; see his letter to Shipley below, June 24.

From Stephen Crane[1]   ALS: American Philosophical Society

Elizabeth Town, East New Jersey in America, June 22d 1771.
Before this comes to Hand, you have probably received Information of the late Debate between the Governor and Assembly of this Province, relative to the granting Supplies for his Majesty's Troops stationed in it. This Dispute, gives great Concern to the House, and I could sincerely wish, the House could have found it consistant with their Duty not to have entred into it. As his Excellency's Administration, ever since his coming to this Province, has, and still continues to give general Satisfaction, the House therefore, with the greater Reluctance, entred into any Measure, that might have a Tendancy, either to make it unhappy to Him, or create the least Jealousy in the Minds of the People.

Notwithstanding his Excellency in the Course of that Debate, in his Zeal for his Majesty's Service, might have dropt some Expressions, intimating a Want of Duty and Loyalty in the House to his Majesty; Yet, I flatter myself the Impartial will wave viewing their Conduct in that Light, till they are made acquainted with the Reasons and Motives that weighed with the House for adopting those Measures.[2] The Assembly have heretofore most chearfully granted Money on every necessary Occasion for his Majesty's Service, and would no Doubt, have continued to do it, at this Time, did not the distressed Circumstance of this Province forbid it. This Reason may to some unacquainted with the State and Condition of this Colony, appear without Foundation, but I am sorry to say there is too much Truth in it. For it is evident to every common Observer, that the landed Property of this Province, is reduced to near one half, the Value it was, seven or eight Years past.

1. Speaker of the New Jersey House of Representatives, 1770–72. Crane (1709–80) had been sheriff of Essex County and judge of the Court of Common Pleas, and represented his county in the House, 1769–75. He subsequently served two terms in the Continental Congress and was a member of the New Jersey state legislature. See Ellery B. Crane, *Genealogy of the Crane Family* . . . (2 vols., Worcester, Mass., 1895–1900), II, 471, 473; N.J. Hist. Soc. *Proc.*, new ser., XV (1930), 87; 1 *N.J. Arch.*, X, 530; XVIII, 37 n, 107, 186, 505.

2. For the wrangle between WF and the House on this issue, and its eventual resolution, see *ibid.*, X, 238–68; N.J. Committee of Correspondence to BF below, Dec. 21, n. 9.

We now also from Year to Year, labour under a considerable Tax for sinking near £200000 granted for his Majesty's Service during the late War. Are also greatly distressed for want of circulating Cash, And what adds still to our Misfortunes, sometime past the Treasury of the Eastern Division was robbed of near £7000[3] which with the Demands that may now lawfully be made on it, will draw out all the remaining Money. To assist us under these Difficulties Laws were lately passed for striking £100000 in Bills of Credit which were by his Majesty for Reasons best known to Himself rejected.[4]

Was his Majesty truly acquainted with the State of this Colony, and the great Inability of the Inhabitants at this Time, to pay any additional Taxes, I must be perswaded, he would not from his known Goodness, and Desire for the Welfare of his People; direct them to be taxed for the Supply of the Troops. But should those Supplies still be demanded, it is to be hoped, his Majesty in his usual Goodness would permit, a Bill for striking a Paper Currency, the only Means I know of at this Time, to enable the House to comply with that Requisition. The Reason, the last Bill for striking a Paper Currency did not meet with his Majesty's Approbation, we may suppose was, because it was so worded, as to apppear to clash with the Act of Parliament, made for preventing the Colonies, from striking a Paper Currency, unless under certain Restrictions. To obviate that Objection, I would just remark the following Alteration, in that Law: Suppose the 49th Sect. to be intirely left out, or the Words in that Sect. "*shall continue to be taken &c.*" altered to the Words "*may continue to be taken &c.*" However I would leave this Hint, to your better Judgment. And any Service you can render in this Affair, I am confident, will at all Times be gratefully acknowledged. If this Bill could be obtained, there is no Doubt with me but the Troops would be supplyed as usual, all Murmuring stopt, and it would be most agreable to the Inhabitants of this Province in general. From the above Remark, I hope

3. The theft had occurred in 1768, and its repercussions eventually had a serious effect on WF's political fortunes; see Larry R. Gerlach, "Politics and Prerogatives: the Aftermath of the Robbery of the East Jersey Treasury...," *N.J. History*, XC (1972), 133–68.

4. See above, XVI, 254, and subsequent vols.; BF to Crane below, Feb. 6, 1772; Gipson, *British Empire*, XI, 261–2.

it will not be thought the House have proceeded with a View, to bring his Majesty to Terms, with Respect to a Paper Currency, far from it, for from my Observation in the House and private Conversation with the Members, I must believe the only Motive for their not granting the Supplies to be, the great Inability of the People at this Time to pay additional Taxes.

The Sincere Regard I have for his Majesty's Service, and the Peace and Welfare of this Province, the sole Motive, of my troubling a Gentleman of your Station and Character, without a personal Acquaintance, with the above Thoughts, will I hope be a sufficient Apology. And believe me to be with great Esteem your most obedient and very humble Servant   STEPN. CRANE

Addressed: To / The Honorable / Benjamin Franklin Esquire / in / London

To Jonathan Shipley   ALS: Yale University Library

This letter is the first that survives in a correspondence that continued for the rest of Franklin's life. The acquaintance had in all likelihood originated through Shipley's brother William, whom Franklin had known for more than fifteen years.[5] By 1771 it embraced the Bishop's whole family, and was thriving as the green bay tree.

Jonathan Shipley (1714–88) was that rarity among eighteenth-century prelates, a man who grew more liberal as he aged. He was educated at Reading and Oxford and ordained in 1738; he then became a tutor in the household of the Earl of Peterborough, whose niece he soon married. She was a maid of honor of Queen Caroline, and opened the road of preferment to him. He followed it: prebendary of Winchester, chaplain-general to the Duke of Cumberland in the War of the Austrian Succession, Dean of Winchester; in 1769 he was consecrated Bishop of Llandaff, and in the same year translated to the see of St. Asaph. There he remained, largely because he became almost at once an outspoken opponent of ministerial policy toward America. This change was undoubtedly accelerated by his ripening friendship with Franklin, but the Bishop had a mind of his own; his later stand on toleration for dissenters was of a piece with his attitude toward the

5. See above, VI, 186–9; Van Doren, *Franklin*, p. 413.

colonies.[6] He was, in short, a friend whom Franklin had reason to cherish.

My Lord,   London June 24. 1771.

I got home in good time, and well. But on perusing the Letters that were come for me during my Absence, and considering the Business they require of me, I find it not convenient to return so soon as I had intended. I regret my having been oblig'd to leave the pleasing Society of your Lordship and Family, and that most agreeable Retirement good Mrs. Shipley put me so kindly in possession of. I now breathe with Reluctance the Smoke of London, when I think of the sweet Air of Twyford:[7] And by the time your Races are over, or about the Middle of next Month (if it should then not be unsuitable to your Engagements or other Purposes) I promise myself the Happiness of spending another Week or two where I so pleasantly spent the last.

I have taken the Liberty of sending by the Southampton Stage, directed to your Lordship, a Parcel containing one of my Books for Miss Georgiana, which I hope she will be good enough to accept, as a small Mark of my Regard for her philosophic Genius:[8] And a Specimen of the American dry'd Apples for Mrs. Shipley, that she may judge whether it will be worth while to try the Practice. I should imagine that the sweet Summer Apples, which cannot otherwise be kept till Winter, are best to be thus preserv'd. I doubt some Dust may have got among these, as I found the Cask uncover'd; therefore it will not perhaps be amiss to rinse them a Minute or two in warm Water, and dry them quick in a Napkin. With the greatest Esteem and Respect, and many Thanks for your and Mrs. Shipley's abundant Civilities, I am, My Lord, Your Lordship's obliged and most obedient humble Servant

B FRANKLIN

6. *DNB*; see also Caroline Robbins, *The Eighteenth-Century Commonwealthman...* (Cambridge, Mass., 1959), pp. 333, 336.

7. A village on the River Itchen, just south of Winchester, where the Bishop had his country house.

8. The Shipleys' daughter was about fifteen at the time. She would have needed philosophic genius if BF was sending her, as we suspect he was, a copy of *Exper. and Obser.*; he suggested to her sister a few months later that Georgiana should marry a country gentleman who "lov'd to see an Experiment now and then." BF to Mrs. Shipley below, Aug. 13.

P.S. The Parcel is directed to be left at the Turnpike next beyond Winchester.[9]

Bp. of St. Asaph

From Harvard College

Reprinted from William C. Lane, "Harvard College and Franklin," *Publications of the Colonial Society of Massachusetts*, X (1907), 237.

At a Meeting of the President and Fellows June 24th 1771. That the Thanks of this Board be given to Dr. Franklin for his kind remembrance of Harvard College expressed in his many friendly Offices and valuable Donations to this Society, particularly in his late Present to our Library of two accurate Mathematical Treatises of Mr. Maseres; and the learned and elaborate Work of Hoogeveen de Graecis Particulis. They also thank Dr. Franklin for the Pleasure he has given them of placing his Effigies among those of their other Benefactors:[1] and Voted that Professor Winthrop do transmit a Copy of this Vote to Dr. Franklin.

From the Massachusetts House of Representatives

LS: University of Virginia Library and Harvard University Library[2]

Sir,   Province of the Massachusetts-Bay, June 25th: 1771.
At the present Session of the General Court, Application has been made to the Court by some of the Grantees of Townships to the eastward of Penobscot River, praying that further Time may

9. Probably Morestead, some two miles east of Twyford on the turnpike to Portsmouth; not until a half-century later was there a turnpike down the Itchen valley. Katherine M. Keynon, *Benjamin Franklin at Twyford* (Winchester, Hants., [1946?]), p. 10.
1. See BF to Winthrop above, Feb. 5.
2. The first two pages of the MS are in one library, the remaining three in the other. If the letter came into Arthur Lee's possession after BF left London in 1775, as seems likely, it may have been separated in the division of the Lee Papers in the nineteenth century, for which see Paul P. Hoffman, *Guide to the Microfilm Edition of the Lee Family Papers*... (Charlottesville, Va., 1966), p. 21.

be allowed them to procure the King's Approbation of the Grants that have been made to them. The General Court have divers Times already lengthned out the Time for that Purpose, and the two Houses think it reasonable that still further Time should be allowed them: but the Governor's Speech at the opening of the present Session has induced the two Houses to postpone that allowance and render the Grantees a more essential Service by writing to you on the Subject of their Grants.[3]

In March 1762 after repeated Petitions for that Purpose, the General Court granted Twelve Townships of the Contents of Six Miles square to be laid out on, and to the Eastward of Penobscot River, all of them contiguous; the Grantees to return to the said Court for further Confirmation a Plan of the same (taken by a Surveyor and Chainmen on Oath) by the last of July then next following: to hold to them, their Heirs and Assigns as Tenants in Common, subject to certain Reservations, Provisos and Conditions in the Grants mentioned. And afterwards Vizt in February 1763, the Governor, Council, and House of Representatives executed under the Province Seal to the Grantees Deeds of the said Townships, wherein among other Things it is provided, that these Grants shall be of no Force or Effect until his Majesty, his Heirs or Successors shall signify his or their Approbation of them. Now altho' according to this Proviso the Grantees could not acquire any Right in the granted Premises without such Approbation, yet from an Apprehension that their Settling the said Townships without Delay would recommend them to the Favor of his Majesty, and facilitate the obtaining his royal Approbation, they immediately proceeded to settle them accordingly; and it was not only with the Knowledge of the then Governor, Mr. Bernard that they did so, but they were encouraged thereto by his Example: who as soon as might be after the Grant of the Island of Mount Desart, made to him by the General Court, February 1762, under the same Proviso of obtaining the King's Approbation, laid out

3. For Gov. Hutchinson's speech and message to the House, which accused the applicants of being trespassers, see *Mass. House Jour.*, 1st session, May–July, 1771, pp. 9–10, 49–50, 67–8. The grants themselves, with one exception, contained the unusual provision that they would be void if not approved by the crown within eighteen months: Maine Hist. Soc., *Documentary History of the State of Maine,* . . . (24 vols., Portland, 1869–1916), XIII, 249–54, 257–64.

Land for a Settlement, built Mills &c., and thereby incurred a great Expence: which he has since urged, and successfully urged as a Reason for obtaining that Approbation.[4]

These Circumstances it is apprehended will serve to place the Grantees in a favorable Light with his Majesty; especially if it be further considered, that they have most of them laid out their whole Substance on those Lands, and been clearing and improving them for divers Years past with great Labor, whereby from a State of Nature they are coming to be a well inhabited, and valuable Part of his Majesty's Dominions: from which should the Grantees be removed, the Removal would operate, not only to the diminishing the Value of that Territory, but to the utter Ruin of a very great Number of His Majesty's Subjects.

The principal Reasons inducing the General Court to grant those Townships, were, to retain within the Province some Part of such Inhabitants, as after the Reduction of Canada, appear to have a Disposition for migrating: also, by taking effectual Possession of that Country, during the War, to drive the Indian Enemy to a greater Distance, and thereby better secure our Eastern Settlements against their future Depredations. To secure these Ends the General Court took Care to annex certain Conditions to the said Grants; some of which were, that the Grantees shall within Six Years after they shall have obtained His Majestys approbation of such Grants (unless prevented by War) settle each Township with Sixty good protestant Families, build Sixty Houses, clear and cultivate five Acres of Land on each Share fit for Tillage and mowing; build a House for the publick Worship of God; settle a Learned Protestant Minister; and make Provision for his comfortable and honorable Support &c. And if any of the Grantees or Proprietors of such Township shall neglect within the Term of Six Years, as aforesaid, to do and perform the Conditions aforesaid, as shall respect and belong to, his Share or Right, such Share or

4. In March, 1771, the Privy Council, after a long delay occasioned in part by the irregularity of a province's giving land to its governor, had approved the grant of Mount Desert Island to Bernard; the other grants were not approved before the Revolution. See William O. Sawtelle, "Sir Francis Bernard and His Grant of Mount Desert," Colonial Soc. of Mass. *Pub.*, XXIV (1920–22), 197–254; Edward Channing and Archibald C. Coolidge, eds., *The Barrington–Bernard Correspondence*... (Cambridge, Mass., 1912), pp. 57, 81, 222, 224; *Acts Privy Coun., Col.*, V, 220; VI, 484.

Right shall be intirely forfeited, and shall enure to the Use of this Province.

And as a further Security a Committee was appointed to take, and accordingly did take Bonds from the Petitioners for the faithful Performance of the said Conditions; all which will appear by the Extracts from the Records of the General Court herewith sent; by which may be observed the great Care taken by the Court, that the said Townships should be effectually settled, the good Ends aforesaid answered, and so valuable a Territory secured to his Majesty. Complaints have heretofore been made, that the Province have neglected to defend and improve this Territory, and in Consequence of them, Attempts have been made to deprive the Province of its Rights in it. This was the Case when Mr. Dunbar took Possession of it in behalf of the Crown in 1729. If Neglect to defend and improve this Country would be a good Reason for a Forfeiture of Right, the actual Defence and Improvement of it must be a good Reason for the Continuance and Confirmation of Right. That the Province had not neglected it, appears by the Proceedings that occasioned the Royal Order for Mr. Dunbars Withdraw:5 And that the Province has defended it, the Forts of Pemaquid and George's River, Fort-Western and Fort Halifax on Kennebeck River; and Fort Pownall at Penobscot sufficiently demonstrate; and with respect to Improvement, what better Improvement, and we may add, what better Defence could there be, than stocking it with Inhabitants; to effect which the General

5. Massachusetts, even though its charter of 1691 confirmed its title to eastern Maine, had only a tenuous control over the area; its claim had been challenged on the grounds that it had not been implemented and that defense had been neglected. David Dunbar, appointed Surveyor General of royal woods in America in 1728, had been authorized to make land grants in the area while reserving mast trees (white pines of the size and quality required for naval masts) and a yearly quitrent for the King. But the settlers had sued him for trespass and won a reversal by the Privy Council, which confirmed the right of Massachusetts to the land. See *ibid.*, III, 275–83; Cecil Headlam, ed., *Calendar of State Papers, Colonial Series, America and West Indies, 1728–29* (London, 1937), pp. 110–12, 371–3, 549, 554–5; Channing and Coolidge, *op. cit.*, p. 222; Robert G. Albion, *Forests and Sea Power...* (Cambridge, Mass., 1926), pp. 256–7; Wroth and Zobel, *John Adams Legal Papers*, II, 248–9. For the general background see Jack M. Sosin, *The Revolutionary Frontier, 1763–1783* (New York, etc., [1967]), pp. 20–60.

Court has done all that was in their Power to do, by granting the twelve Townships aforesaid; and by incorporating the Inhabitants of divers other Towns within the same Territory, on their applying for Acts of Incorporation. As contrary and inconsistent Reasons have at different Times been urged to create a Forfeiture of the Province Right, it induces an Apprehension, that we are not informed of the real Reason why the aforementioned Grants are not confirmed.

If there be no Design in Persons of Influence in England to procure a Part of this Country to themselves,[6] we should apprehend the Preservation of the Mast Trees growing thereon, was the principal or only Reason of the non-confirmation of the said Grants.[7] This is intimated in the Governor's Speech, where it is said, "That a longer Neglect of effectual measures, on our Part, to prevent any further Intrusions, and to remove those already made will occasion the Interposition of Parliament to maintain and preserve the Possession of this Country, or District for the Sake of His Majesty's Timber, with which it is said to abound." And it is more fully expressed in his Excellency's Message of the 19th. Instant to the House of Representatives, wherein it is declared, that "whether the Settlements there, be with or without Grants from the Court, in either Case the Settlers are alike Intruders, for none have the Royal Approbation; and that by means of such Intrusions Trespasses are easily committed without any great Danger of Discovery, let the Surveyors be ever so vigilant, and attentive to their Duty."

6. The region, rumor had it, was about to become a new royal province with Sir Francis Bernard as governor. 6 Mass. Hist. Soc. *Coll.*, IX (1897), 269. The Bostonians suspected that this design was part of a conspiracy against the province, and for once they had reason: Hutchinson and Bernard were doing their best to have the land east of the Penobscot detached from Massachusetts and either erected into a separate government or, that failing, annexed to Nova Scotia. See Hutchinson's letters to Bernard and Hillsborough, Mass. Arch., XXVII, 60–1, 100, 105, 286.

7. The Massachusetts charter restricted the crown's right to cut mast trees to lands outside established townships. The trees were of vital importance to the Admiralty, and the current Surveyor General, Gov. John Wentworth of New Hampshire, was inspecting large tracts in eastern Maine for royal preserves. Albion, *op. cit.* n. 5, pp. 268–9. This was the background of the Privy Council's failure to act, as mentioned above, on the Massachusetts grants.

The Preservation of the Mast Trees is a Matter of great Importance, which the General Court would do all in their Power to effect, if they knew the Means of doing it. The most likely Method we can Devise (unless the Parliament should interpose) is to settle that Country with Inhabitants. This was the Sense of the General Court formerly, in a similar Case, as more fully will appear by reading an Act, intitled An Act for preventing of Trespasses, made and passed in the Twelfth of George the First, which Mr. Bollan is perfectly acquainted with, and hath very much answered the Ends proposed.[8] It is certainly very difficult to detect and convict Trespassers when positive Witnesses cannot be had; and this will always be the Case when the Land has no Inhabitants; but when the same is inhabited, the Case is and will be quite otherwise. It may be further remarked that the Trees reserved by Charter, are chiefly back of said Settlements, but few within them; and that had there none of these Settlements been made, it would have been impossible to have transported them to the Water side without incurring an Expence to the Crown of perhaps ten Times the value of the Masts.

Upon the whole, with Regard to the Grantees aforesaid; as also the Grantees of a Township since granted at a Place called Mall-

8. Jurisdiction over those who cut trees illegally, which the first White Pines Act of 1711 entrusted to a single justice of the peace, was transferred in a statute of 1722 to the Vice-Admiralty courts. Massachusetts responded with the trespass act referred to, which empowered the regular provincial courts to try any one who cut trees on private property without permission: *Mass. Acts and Resolves*, II, 383–5. The effect of the act, whatever the intent, was to embolden settlers on disputed land to prosecute contractors who cut trees for the crown. The House must have known that the King's right to such trees in the wilds of Maine was wholly unenforceable; on this point see Albion, *op. cit.* n. 5, pp. 259–68; Wroth and Zobel, *John Adams Legal Papers*, II, 247–74; Joseph J. Malone, *Pine Trees and Politics . . .* (Seattle, 1964), *passim.* For more than thirty years William Bollan had been familiar with the problems involved. He had been attorney for a royal contractor in a celebrated case, and in the early 1740s had taken a leading part in trying to suppress the settlers' illegal cutting of mast trees in Massachusetts; two decades later he had helped to frustrate an attempt to annex the province's eastern lands to Nova Scotia. See Andrew M. Davis, "The Suit of Frost v. Leighton," Colonial Soc. of Mass. *Pub.*, III (1895–97), 246–64; John A. Schutz, *William Shirley, King's Governor of Massachusetts* (Chapel Hill, 1961), pp. 65–6; 6 Mass. Hist. Soc. *Coll.*, IX (1897), 269–70.

chias under the like Conditions and Restrictions,[9] you are desired, and are hereby instructed, by Memorial to his Majesty, and in any other Way you shall judge proper, to use your best Endeavors to procure for them his Majesty's Confirmation of the Grants made of the Townships aforesaid. And if any Attempts shall be made to deprive this Government of the Jurisdiction over, and Property in, the Territory within which those Townships are situated, you are also instructed to do your Utmost to frustrate it. And with regard to the Preservation of Mast Trees, you will endeavour to procure the best Regulations for that Purpose, consistent with the Charter Rights of the Province. This Letter of Instructions is agreed to by both Houses, to be sent to their respective Agents; between whom it is a further Instruction, that there be a Co-operation of Measures for the Purposes aforesaid. There will be sent to you herewith, a brief State of the Title of this Province, to the Country between the River Kennebeck and St. Croix printed 1762:[1] which you will make such Use of as shall be necessary.

In the Name, and by Order of the House of Representatives; I am Sir your most obedient Servant,

THOMAS CUSHING Speaker

From Ezra Stiles

ALS (draft[2]): Yale University Library

Dear Sir   Newport June 25 1771
This waits on you by Henry Marchant Esqr. Attorney General

9. The Machias grant, which was made first in 1768 and again in identical terms in 1770, was also to be void if not approved within eighteen months. See Maine Hist. Soc., *op. cit.* n. 3, XIV, 80–2, 95–7.

1. The enclosure was an appendix to the *Mass. House Jour.* for the third session of 1762–63; it and the letter reached London while BF was absent on his tour. The similar letter that the Council sent to Bollan elicited a gloomy reply: he and BF had no legal standing and therefore no authority, without which they could not work effectively for the province. 6 Mass. Hist. Soc. *Coll.*, IX, 274–5. Bollan did, however, submit to the Council a proposal of his for resolving the problems of the eastern lands; and he and BF agreed, after the latter's return, to await their constituents' reaction to this plan before taking any further steps. See BF to the Mass. Committee of Correspondence below, Jan. 13, 1772.

2. Stiles's peculiar abbreviations have been silently expanded.

144

of this Colony, and its joynt Agent with Jos. Sherwood Esqr. at the Court of Great Britain. I doubt not you will afford him your friendly Advice and Assistance in the Agency.[3] I need not remind you that he is One of the First Fruits of the College in Philada. which rose up greatly thro' your Patronage. Mr. Marchant certainly does Honor to it. He studied Law under Judge Trowbridge at Cambridge.[4] By Assiduity Application and Success in Business he has risen up to the first Eminence in the Practice of the Law in this Colony. He is a Man of growing Knowledge and enlarging Views; and I doubt not, if it please God he lives a few years, he will not only figure in public Life with Dignity, as indeed he already doth, but will probably become a man of very considerable Erudition in the Law. Indeed he has already made such Acquirements in the Laws of Nature and Nations and in the common and Statute Law of England and the municipal Laws of the Colonies, and also entered so far into the Genius and Principles of the Jus Civilis especially those parts of it which apply to the maritime Courts and have otherwise affected the English Constitution that I should heartly rejoyce to see him honored with a *Doctorate in Laws*. And I the rather take Liberty to mention this to my greatly respected Friend because that, as Mr. Marchant intends to travel into Scotland as well as to the Continent into Holland and to Paris at least, it would be a good opportunity for him to receive that Degree in one of the Scotch Universities. He has received the Degree of *Master of Arts* both at *Philadelphia* and *Harvard* Colleges. And if you should upon a renewed Acquaintance with him have the same Opinion of his promising Abilities that I have, you would excuse my asking your Recommendation of him to this Honor.[5]

3. Marchant and Sherwood are identified above, x, 316 n, 413 n. The latter was Rhode Island's resident agent, 1759–73; Marchant, who was its new attorney general and was coming to London on personal business, had been commissioned to seek reimbursement for the colony's outlay on the Crown Point expedition in 1756. He and BF quickly became friends, and were traveling companions in Scotland.

4. Edmund Trowbridge (1709–93), a judge of the Massachusetts Superior Court and formerly attorney general, had taught a generation of able young lawyers. *DAB*.

5. Stiles had a particular concern with honorary degrees from British universities, and suspected that BF was serving his own ends in sponsoring candidates; see above, XVI, 122–5. The suggestion of Marchant bore fruit, though

If his Business would permit I could wish him an extensive Travel on the Continent, that the actual view of the Manners, Policies, and the system of Government in different Cities and Kingdoms in the present Age, might establish an happy Enlargment of his Understanding, and lay a Foundation of his greater Usefulness in Life. I hope he will preserve the *Religion of Jesus*, and the *Love of his Country*, sacred and inviolate in his own Breast, in every View of Mankind Kingdoms and Empires and thro' all Connexions Communications and Intercourse with those who are too knowing too great and too wise to be instructed by the Light of the World the Light of the Universe. A Man that shines in America may be lost in the Blaze of London, Paris or Rome. A Man that shines even thro' the World itself (as to say it without Flattery, does the Electric Philosopher) may be lost in the Splendor of the celestial world, where they "shew a Newton as we shew an Ape."[6] And yet why should I say *lost?* for everyone that acts his part worthily below, and imitates the sun of Righteousness in Beneficence, shall shine as the Brightness of the Firmament in the Kingdom of Jesus. My Expressions are strong, but not beyond what may possibly be the Truth of any Man, and I am sure not stronger than my Wishes for you Sir, your present Virtue [?] and final participation with all the wise and good of all ages in the Felicty and Glories of the Resurrection state. The Santon *Herewi* in the Time of Turkish Emperor Orchanes could say that he had led victorious armies from Tigris to Nile, governd Provinces and Kingdoms with his Sceptre, been triumphantly adorned with precious stones and glittering Arms, and had made the World tremble at the very mention of his Name. Till he was satiated with human Glory—and having eno' of it, he retired into Deity and took up his portion and that satisfaction in God which the World could not give. Solomon came to the same Conclusion.[7] May you and my

---

it did not ripen: BF offered to recommend him, when the two were together in Edinburgh the following November, for a doctorate from the University; but Marchant declined. Franklin B. Dexter, ed., *The Literary Diary of Ezra Stiles . . .* (3 vols., New York, 1901), I, 304.

6. Alexander Pope, *An Essay on Man*, II, 34.

7. Sultan Orchan or Orkhan, who reigned from 1326 to *c.* 1362, began the Ottoman intrusion into Europe. But his so-called contemporary was fictitious: the Muslim holy man from Herat—the meaning of Santon Herewi—

Friend Marchant make quick Arrival to the same Conclusion
without the dangerous Experiments in Vice made by too many of
the great, whose Folly overtakes them before they arrive at philosophic Conclusions, before they reach the Temple of Wisdom. I
am, Sir, Your most Obliged and devoted humble Servant

EZRA STILES

Dr. Franklin

From the Massachusetts House of Representatives

LS: University of Virginia Library

Sir,　　　　Province of the Massachusetts Bay June 29th, 1771

Your Letter of the 5th. of Febry last has been laid before the
House, the Contents are important, and claim our fixed Attention.
We cannot think the Doctrine of the Right of Parliament to tax us
is given up while an Act remains in Force for that Purpose, and is
daily put in Execution, and the longer it remains the more Danger
there is of the People's becoming so accustomed to arbitrary and
unconstitutional Taxes, as to pay them without Discontent, and
then as you justly observe no Minister will ever think of taking
them off, but will rather be encouraged to add others.[8] If ever the
Provincial Assemblies should be voluntarily silent on the Parliament's taking upon themselves a Power thus to violate their Constitutional and Charter Rights, it might hereafter be considered as
an Approbation of it, or at least a tacit Consent that such a Power
should be exercised at any future Time. It is therefore our Duty
to declare our Rights, and our determinate Resolution at all Events
to maintain them.

The Time we know will come when they must be acknowledged, established and secured to us and our Posterity. We severely
feel the Effects not of a Revenue raised, but a Tribute extorted
without our free Consent, or Controul; Pensioners and Placemen
are daily multiplying, a Fleet and a Standing Army posted in

was either pure legend or had been embellished out of all recognition in whatever work Stiles had read. The Solomon of the opening chapters of Ecclesi-
astes was equally fictitious.

8. The responses to BF, here and later, are all to his letter of Feb. 5 above.
This comment is upon his second paragraph, which was not one of his most
logical.

North America, for no other apparent or real Purpose than to protect new Exactors Collectors of the Tribute, for which they are to be maintained, and many of them in Pomp and Pride, to triumph over, and insult an injured People, and suppress if possible even their Murmurs. And there is Reason to expect that the continual Increase of the Number will lead to proportionable Increase of a Tribute to support them. What will be the Consequence? either on the one Hand an abject Slavery in the People, which is ever to be deprecated, or a determined Resolution to openly assert and maintain their Rights and Liberties and Privileges; the Effect of such Resolution may be for some Time retarded by flattering Hopes and Prospects; and while it is the Duty of all Persons of Influence here unitedly to endeavor to inculcate the Sentiments of Moderation, it will be in our Opinion equally the Wisdom of British Administration to Consider the Danger of forcing a free People by oppressive Measures into a State of Desperation. We have Reason to believe that the American Colonies, however they may have disagreed among themselves in one Mode of Opposition to arbitrary Measures, are still united in the main Principles of constitutional and natural Liberty; and that they will not give up one single Point in Contest of any Importance, tho' they take no violent Measures to obtain them. The taxing their Property without their Consent, and thus appropriating it to the Purposes of their Slavery and Destruction, are justly considered as contrary to, and subversive of their original social Compact, and their Intention in uniting under it. They cannot therefore readily think themselves obliged to renounce those Forms of Government to which alone, for the Advantages implying or resulting, they were willing to submit. We are sensible, as you observe, that the Designs of our Enemies in England, as well as those who reside here, is to render us odious as well as contemptible, and to prevent all Concern for us in the Friends of Liberty in England; and perhaps to detach our Sister Colonies from us, and prevent their Aid and Influence in our Behalf,[9] when the Projects of oppressing us further, and depriving us of our Rights by various violent measures should be carried into Execution. In this however we flatter ourselves they have failed: But should all the

9. The sentence, except for this clause, is partly paraphrase and partly quotation of BF.

other Colonies become weary of their Liberties, after the Example of the Hebrews; this Province, we trust, will never submit to the Authority of an absolute Government.

We are now led to take Notice of another fatal Consequence which we are under strong Apprehensions will follow from these Parliamentary Revenue Laws; and that is making Governors of the Colonies and other Officers independent of the People for their Support. You tell us there is no Doubt of such Intention, and that it will be persisted in if the American Revenue is found sufficient. We are the more inclined to believe it, not only because the Governor of the Province of New York has openly declared it, with regard to himself, to the Assembly there,[1] but also because the present Governor of this Province has repeatedly refused to accept of the usual Grants for his Support, tho' he has not been so explicit as to assign a Reason for it. The Charter of this Province recognizes the natural Right of all men to dispose of their own Property; and the Governor here, like all other Governors, Kings, and Potentates, is to be supported by the free Grants of the Representatives of the People. Every one sees the Necessity of this to preserve the Ballance of Power and the Freedom of any State. A Power without a Check is subversive of all Freedom. If therefore the Governor, who is appointed by the Crown, shall be totally independent of the free Grants of the People for his Support, where is the Check upon his Power? He becomes absolute, and may act as he pleases: He may make Use of his Power, not for the Good of those who are under it, but for his own private seperate Advantage, or any other Purpose to which he may be inclined or instructed by him upon whom alone he depends. Such an Independency threatens the very Being of a free Constitution; and if it takes Effect will produce and firmly establish a Tyranny upon its Ruin. The Act of Parliament of the 7th. Geo. 3, intitled An Act for granting certain Duties in the Colonies &c. declares that it is expedient that a Revenue should be raised in his Majesty's Dominions in America, for making more certain and adequate Provision for defreying the Charge of the Administration of Justice, and the Support of the Civil Government in such Provinces where it shall be found necessary, and towards further defreying the Expences

1. For Lord Dunmore's salary from the crown while he was in New York see above, XVII, 287.

of defending, protecting and securing the said Dominions. These
are the very Purposes for which this Government by the Charter
is empowered to grant Taxes—So that by the Act aforementioned
the Charter is in Effect made void.[2]

Agreable to the Design of that Act, the Governor it seems is first
to be made independent, and in Pursuance of the Plan of Despot-
ism, the Judges of the Land and all other important civil Officers
successively, next follows an independent military Power to compleat the Ruin of our civil Liberties. Let us then consider the
Power the Governor already has, and his Majesty's Representative
on all our Acts, and judge whether the Purposes of Tyranny will
not be amply answered. Can it be expected that any Law will pass
here, but such as will promote the favorite Design; and the Laws
already made, as they will be executed by Officers altogether de-
pendent on the Crown, will undoubtedly be perverted to the worst
Purposes? The Governor of the Province and the principal Fort-
ress in it are probably already thus supported.[3] These are the first
Fruits of the System: If the rest should follow, it would be only in
a greater Degree a Violation of our essential natural Rights. To
what Purpose then will it be to preserve the old Forms, without
the Substance? In such a State and with such Prospects, can Britain expect any thing but a gloomy Discontent in the Colonists?
Let our Fellow Subjects then recollect what would have been
their Fate long ago, if their Ancestors had submitted to the unreasonable and uncharitable Usurpations, Exactions and Impositions of the See of Rome in the Reign of Henry the Eighth. Soon
would they have sunk into a State of abject Slavery to that haughty
Power which exalteth it self above all that is called God: but they
had the true Spirit of Liberty, and by exerting it they saved themselves and their Posterity. The Act of Parliament passed in the
25th. of that Reign is so much to our present Purpose, that we cannot help transcribing a Part of it, and refer you to the Statute at

2. The argument here, except for its appeal to the charter, elaborates that
in the original instructions of the House to BF, *ibid.*, pp. 281–2.

3. The surmise turned out to be correct on both counts. Hutchinson's
instructions, at the time he was promoted from lieutenant governor to governor, forbade him to accept a salary from the General Court and transferred
Castle William from provincial to royal jurisdiction. *Acts Privy Coun., Col.*,
v, 265, 556. For the development of the salary issue see the Mass. House to
BF below, July 15, 1772.

large. In the Preamble it is declared that the Realm of England "hath been, and is free from Subjection to any Man's Laws but only to such as have been devised, made and ordained within the Realm for the Wealth[4] of the same"; and further, "It standeth therefore with natural Equity and good Reason, that in every such Law humane, made within this Realm or induced into this Realm by the said Sufferance, Consent, and Customs,[5] your Royal Majesty, and your Lords Spiritual and temporal, and Commons *representing the whole State of your Realm* in this your Majesty's high Court of Parliament, hath full Power and Authority, not only to dispence but also to authorize some *elect* Person or Persons to dispense with those and all other humane Laws of this your Realm, and with every one of them as the Quality of *the Persons and Matter may require*. And also the said Laws and every one of them to abrogate, annul, amplify or diminish, as it shall seem to your Majesty, and the Nobles and Commons of your Realm present in your Parliament meet and convenient for the Wealth of your Realm. And because that it is now in these Days present seen that the State, Dignity, Superiority, Reputation and Authority of the said imperial Crown of this Realm by the long Sufferance of the said unreasonable and uncharitable usurpations and Exactions is much and sore decayed, and the People of this Realm thereby impoverished."

It is then enacted, "That no Person or Persons of the Realm, or of any other his Majesty's Dominions shall from henceforth pay any Pensions, Censes,[6] Portions, Peter pence, or any other Impositions to the Use of the said Bishop or of the See of Rome, but that all such Pensions &c which the said Bishop or Pope hath heretofore taken &c, shall clearly surcease and never more be levied,

4. In the sense of welfare. The statute is the Dispensations Act of 1534; we have supplied quotation marks, few of which are in the original letter, but have not noted omissions or minor errors. Citing this statute as England's declaration of independence from Rome carried with it an implicit threat of colonial independence. How the threat could have strengthened BF's hand in working for reconciliation, if that was the intent of the House, is difficult to see.

5. An omitted passage in the preamble referred to Papal exactions that had been incorporated, by sufferance, into the law and customs of the land—an obvious analogue with Parliamentary exactions that the colonists had suffered without complaint.

6. Any kind of tribute or tax.

nor paid to any Person or Persons in any manner or wise." Nothing short of the Slavery and Ruin of the Nation would have been the Consequence of their submitting to those Exactions: and the same will be the Fate of America if the present Revenue Laws remain, and the natural Effect of them the making Governors independent takes Place. It is therefore with intire Approbation that we observe your Purpose freely to declare our Rights and to remonstrate against the least Infringment of them. The capital Complaint of all North America hath been, is now, and will be, until relieved, a Subjugation to as arbitrary a Tribute as ever the Romans laid upon the Jews or their other Colonies. The repealing these Duties in part is not considered by this House as a Renunciation of the Measure: It has rather the Appearance of a Design to sooth us into Security in the midst of Danger. Any Species of Tribute unrepealed will stand as a Precedent to be made Use of hereafter as Circumstances and Opportunities will admit: If these Colonies acquiesce in a single Instance, it will in Effect be yielding up the whole Matter in Controversy. We therefore desire that it may be universally understood, that altho' the Tribute is paid, it is not paid freely. It is extorted and torn from us against our Will; We bear the Insult and Injury for the present, Grievous as it is, with great Impatience, hoping that the Wisdom and Prudence of the Nation, will at length dictate Measures consistent with natural Justice and Equity: For what shall happen in future, we are not answerable. Your Observation is just, that it was certainly as bad Policy, when they attempted to heal our Differences by repealing Part of the Duties only, as it is bad Surgery to leave Splinters in a Wound which must prevent its healing, or in time occasion it to open afresh.

The Doctrine that no Agent ought to be received or attended to by Government, who is not appointed by an Act of the General Court, to which the Governor has given his Assent, if established, must be attended with very ill Consequences: For besides the just Remarks you have made upon it, if whatever is to be transacted between the Assemblies of the Colonies and the Government, is to be done by Agents appointed by and under the Direction of the three Branches, it would be utterly impracticable for an Assembly ever to lay before the Sovereign their Complaints of Grievances occasioned by the corrupt and arbitrary Administration of a Governor. This Doctrine, we have Reason to think was first advanced by Governor Bernard, at a Time when he became the principal Agent in involving the Nation and the Colonies in Controversy and Confusion. Very probably it is now become a Subject of Instruction to Governor Hutchinson, who refuses to confirm the Grants of the Assembly to the Agents for the respective Houses. In this he carries the Point beyond Governor Bernard, who assented to Grants made in general Terms, for Services performed, without holding up the name of Agents; but Governor Hutchinson declines his Assent even in that Form.[7] So that we are reduced to a Choice of Difficulties; either to have no Agent at all, but such as shall be under the Influence of the Minister, or to find some other Way to support an Agent than by grants of the General Assembly. But we are fallen into Times, when Governors of Colonies seem to think themselves bound to conform to Instructions, without any Regard to the Civil Constitutions or even the publick Safety. In the Name and by order of the House of Representatives I am with respect your most humble Servant

THOMAS CUSHING Speaker

To Benjamin Franklin Esqr LLD

(Duplicate)

Endorsed: Thos. Cushing, Speaker to B. Franklin, June 29th, 1771

7. This oversimplifies a complex and long-standing issue. Richard Jackson was the last agent duly appointed by the governor and both houses of the legislature. During his term, 1765–67, the House also appointed Dennys DeBerdt as a special agent to work for repeal of the Stamp Act, and subsequently tried to retain and instruct him as agent for the province. The Council reluctantly concurred in paying him, but Governor Bernard refused on the ground that an agent appointed by the House alone was unconstitutional. In 1768 he did agree to reimbursing DeBerdt for services rendered to the province; he consistently withheld consent, however, to paying him *qua* agent. Albert Matthews, ed., "Letters of Dennys DeBerdt, 1757–1770," Colonial Soc. of Mass. *Pub.*, XIII (1910–11), 342, 452; *Mass. House Jour.*, 1st session, May–June, 1767, pp. 60–1, 69; 2nd session, Dec., 1767–March, 1768, pp. 89, 143. In 1769 the Council appointed William Bollan as its agent, while the House continued to retain DeBerdt; neither man's position was recognized by the governor, and neither received any salary. In April, 1771, the House again considered authorizing salaries for both and for BF as well, and actually

To Thomas Percival

Extract printed in *Memoirs of the Literary ana Philosophical Society o Manchester*, II (1785), 110–13.

The following letter marks the beginning, as far as we know, of Franklin's interest in the question of where and how raindrops grow.[8] This question, one of the key ones in modern cloud physics, had been posed two years earlier in a form that threw investigators off the track for years to come: Dr. William Heberden had announced to the Royal Society that rainfall at the top of a tall building was markedly less than at the bottom.[9] Thomas Percival sent Franklin, with his letter above o, May 16, a paper that propounded a theory to account for this phenomenon; and Franklin is here replying. A charged particle in a cloud, Percival argued, is attracted to neighboring particles of opposite charge, with which it coalesces to form drops that grow until they are large enough to fall. Their direction of fall, toward the center of the earth, makes them converge and, drawing in other drops by collision and electrical attraction, become steadily larger as they approach the ground.[1]

Franklin accepted as fact that the amount of rainfall varies with altitude because falling drops increase in size. But he tentatively advanced an explanation that he preferred to Percival's: the increase is due to the drops' acquiring water vapor that condenses on them from the air through which they fall. He pointed out the objection to this theory at the end of the extract, and advised waiting for more evidence. He could not guess that the evidence would eventually demolish the original premise that drops grow *after* leaving the cloud.[2] Neither could he

---

voted money for the first two; BF's name did not come up again that year. Governor Hutchinson followed Bernard's practice and refused to sanction payment of men who in his eyes were pseudo-agents. *Ibid.*, 4th session, April, 1771, pp. 234, 239, 242; Mass. Arch., XXVII, 52–5, 136, 160. The governor's position was indeed confirmed by his instructions, which arrived on July 3. See *Acts Privy Coun.*, *Col.*, V, 264; Hutchinson, *History*, III, 248; Bowdoin to BF below, Nov. 5.

8. As early as 1749 he had speculated about their origin, and as late as 1784 he gave further thought to the precipitation of snow, hail, and rain: above, III, 369–71; Smyth, *Writings*, IX, 215–16.

9. *Phil. Trans.*, LIX (1769), 359–62. For Heberden see above, VIII, 281 n.

1. Percival subsequently published the paper in his *Philosophical, Medical and Experimental Essays . . .* (London, 1776), pp. 109–28.

2. That discovery, oddly enough, was made by BF's great-grandson, Alexander Dallas Bache, who demonstrated that vertical and horizontal wind currents, not height, account for the varying quantities of rain at different altitudes. Bache's work opened the way to the modern conclusion that drops

guess that he and Percival had each identified one of the two factors, condensation and coalescence, that account for the formation of drops in the cloud.

[June ?, 1771[3]]

On my return to London I found your favour, of the sixteenth of May (1771). I wish I could, as you desire, give you a better explanation of the phaenomenon in question, since you seem not quite satisfied with your own; but I think we want more and a greater variety of experiments in different circumstances, to enable us to form a thoroughly satisfactory hypothesis. Not that I make the least doubt of the facts already related, as I know both Lord Charles Cavendish, and Dr. Heberden to be very accurate experimenters: but I wish to know the event of the trials proposed in your six queries; and also, whether in the same place where the lower vessel receives nearly twice the quantity of water that is received by the upper, a third vessel placed at half the height will receive a quantity proportionable.[4] I will however endeavour to explain to you what occurred to me, when I first heard of the fact.

I suppose, it will be generally allowed, on a little consideration of the subject, that scarce any drop of water was, when it began to fall from the clouds, of a magnitude equal to that it has acquired, when it arrives at the earth; the same of the several pieces of hail; because they are often so large and weighty, that we cannot conceive a possibility of their being suspended in the air, and remaining at rest there, for any time, how small soever; nor do we conceive any means of forming them so large, before they set out to fall. It seems then, that each beginning drop, and particle of hail, receives continual addition in its progress downwards. This may be several ways: by the union of numbers in their course, so that what was at first only a descending mist, becomes a shower; or by

form in the cloud and rarely grow larger as they fall. See William E. Knowles Middleton, *A History of the Theories of Rain* . . . (New York, [1966]), pp. 98–9, 168–70.

3. BF returned from the north on or before June 1 (see the résumé of Williams' journal above, under May 28), and we are assuming that he answered Percival's letter during the month.

4. For Cavendish see above, X, 41 n. Percival's paper ended with six queries for further experimentation, and elsewhere in it he mentioned that a measuring vessel, when placed some fifty feet above another, received just twice as much rain: Percival, *op. cit.*, pp. 125–8, 112 n.

each particle in its descent through air that contains a great quantity of dissolved water, striking against, attaching to itself, and carrying down with it, such particles of that dissolved water, as happen to be in its way; or attracting to itself such as do not lie directly in its course, by its different state with regard either to common or electric fire;[5] or by all these causes united.

In the first case, by the uniting of numbers, larger drops might be made, but the quantity falling in the same space would be the same at all heights; unless, as you mention, the whole should be contracted in falling, the lines described by all the drops converging, so that what set out to fall from a cloud of many thousand acres, should reach the earth in perhaps a third of that extent, of which I somewhat doubt. In the other cases we have two experiments.

1. A dry glass bottle, filled with very cold water, in a warm day, will presently collect from the seemingly dry air that surrounds it, a quantity of water that shall cover its surface and run down its sides, which perhaps is done by the power wherewith the cold water attracts the fluid, common fire that had been united with the dissolved water in the air, and drawing that fire through the glass into itself, leaves the water on the outside.

2. An electrified body left in a room for some time, will be more covered with dust than other bodies in the same room not electrified, which dust seems to be attracted from the circumambient air.

Now we know that the rain, even in our hottest days, comes from a very cold region. Its falling sometimes in the form of ice, shews this clearly; and perhaps even the rain is snow or ice when it first moves downwards, though thawed in falling: And we know that the drops of rain are often electrified. But those causes of addition to each drop of water, or piece of hail, one would think could not long continue to produce the same effect; since the air, through which the drops fall, must soon be stript of its previously dissolved water, so as to be no longer capable of augmenting

5. BF had long distinguished between electrical and common "fire," both of which he considered to be fluids; see above, III, 366, 368–70; V, 146–7; VII, 185–9; X, 38–41, 49–50. His common fire, which he conceived of as an imponderable fluid rather than a property of matter, was a forerunner of Lavoisier's later "caloric" fluid. See Abraham Wolf, *A History of Science, Technology and Philosophy in the Eighteenth Century* (2nd ed. revised; 2 vols., New York, [1961]), I, 177–8.

them. Indeed very heavy showers, of either, are never of long continuance; but moderate rains often continue so long as to puzzle this hypothesis: So that upon the whole I think, as I intimated before, that we are yet hardly ripe for making one.

From Alexander Colden[6]   ALS: American Philosophical Society

Dear Sir,   General Post office New York July 2d 1771
The [favour?] of yours of the first May I received by the Duke of Cumberland Packet [torn].

Mr. Foxcroft and his Lady who I have the Pleasure to [have seen] at this time tells me he has wrote to you by this Packet and mentioned that upon his return to this place from visiting the offices to the Eastward the Accounts in the late Comptroller's books will be Stated in such a manner that they may be transmitted home. I have Since the books fell into my hands, used every means in my Power to settle the Accounts in those books, but have found it more difficult than I expected however I have taken Such Steps as will put them in a proper State before Mr. Foxcroft returns.[7]

The Letter Mr. Jesser wrote me Encloseing an Advertisement about Elizabeth Holland, came to hand at a time when I lay dangerously ill and incapable to attend to business.[8] By some means when I recoverd, the letter was mislaid and I have not been able to find it Since or should have inserted the Advertisement as desired. I would have informed Mr. Jesser of this unlucky affair but could not recollect his Name nor how to direct to him. If Mr. Jesser will send me [illegible] Advertisement or if in the mean time [illegible] extract with the letter I will take Care the Advertisement be Inserted in the papers [according to his] desire.

6. The New York postmaster and surveyor of customs, for whom see above, VI, 113 n.

7. The accounts of Comptroller James Parker, who had died in the previous summer, took years to settle.

8. For the missing heiress see above, X, 248–9, 341. Jesser was a London lawyer acting for the London Hospital, which was somehow involved in the legacy; see his letter to BF below, Oct. 7, 1772. The advertisement he sent to Colden was doubtless the same one that appeared in the *Va. Gaz.* (Purdie) on Aug. 30, 1770; it asked that any one having information about Elizabeth Holland get in touch with Colden or with John Dixon, the Williamsburg

My Father who is in in his usual State of health and flow of Spirits, Mr. and Mrs. Nichols, my Brother David and Mrs. Colden[9] Join in hearty and Sincere Compliments to you with Dear Sir Your Very Oblidged and Obedient humble Servant

ALEXR COLDEN

Benjn Franklin Esqr.

To Noble Wimberly Jones

Transcript[1]: Harvard University Library

Sir,   London July 3. 1771.

In mine of May 1. I enclosed a copy of the Petition intended to be presented to the King in Council, in behalf of the possessors of the lands claimed by Sir William Baker's assigns. I am now to acquaint you, that it was presented accordingly, and is referred down to the Board of Trade for their opinion. But as the Board is about to adjourn for some months, we are advised not to press the consideration of it till they meet again, as they have now too little time to attend to it properly. Immediately on their return to business we shall urge for their report.[2]

I see by the Newspapers that your new Assembly is also dis-

---

postmaster. For the next phase of the search see BF to Colden and to Dixon below, Oct. 7, 1772.

9. His father, eighty-three at the time, was Cadwallader Colden, Lieutenant Governor of New York. Richard Nicholls, the former New York postmaster, was Alexander Colden's father-in-law; David Colden, who was much interested in electricity, served as his father's secretary. All have appeared frequently in earlier volumes.

1. It was made for Jared Sparks by Julius T. Ducatel (1796–1849), a professor of natural science at St. John's College and the University of Maryland, who in an accompanying note to Sparks explained that he had given the original to Dr. Joshua Cohen (1801–70), a Baltimore physician and book-collector; it was sold by Stan V. Henkels in 1907, and has since disappeared. The sale catalogue printed a portion of it, from which we have slightly amended that part of the transcript.

2. For the petition see above, XVII, 148–50. The Privy Council had referred it to the Board of Trade in May, 1771: *Acts Privy Coun., Col.,* V, 295–6; *Board of Trade Jour.,* 1768–75, pp. 274–5. The Board seems never to have reported on it.

solved,[3] I am sorry for these Differences, which must be uncomfortable to you and all that wish the Welfare of the Province.

It is now thought that a Peace between the Turks and Russians is likely soon to be concluded,[4] which gives a better Prospect of the continuance of Peace among the other Powers of Europe, for it seldom happens that a War, begun between any two of them, does not extend itself sooner or later till it involves the whole. Spain shew'd a strong inclination to begin with us, but France being not willing or ready to join her, she has smother'd that inclination for the present.[5] With great esteem, I am Sir, Your most obedient humble Servant   B FRANKLIN

Addressed: Noble Wimberley Jones Esq. Savannah-Georgia

To Cadwalader Evans

Reprinted from Samuel Hazard, ed., *Hazard's Register of Pennsylvania,* XVI, no. 5 (August 1, 1835), 92.

Dear Doctor,   London, July 4, 1771.

I acquainted you some time since that I expected soon to obtain satisfactory Answers to your Queries relating to the Specimens of Silk you sent over;[6] but I was disappointed till lately that I had a Meeting with Mr. Patterson, esteemed one of the best judges of that Commodity,[7] who favoured me with the enclos'd Paper, and, in Conversation, with the following particulars.

He thinks that the Water, tho' clear at first, may grow foul with the Impurities of the Cocoons reel'd in it, and therefore should be chang'd as that appears to be the Case.

He gave me a Skain of what is called the best Italian Silk

3. On April 26: Jones to BF below, July 8.
4. The Russo-Turkish war of 1768 had produced a series of Russian victories, and an Austro-Prussian offer of mediation in the spring of 1771 gave rise to the rumor of peace, for which see the *London Chron.,* June 20–22. The war actually lasted until 1774.
5. French counsels were divided during the Falkland Islands crisis, but the advocates of peace prevailed.
6. See BF to Evans above, Feb. 10, which explains some references later in this letter.
7. For the little information available on Patterson or Paterson, an English silk-manufacturer, see *Acts Privy Coun., Col.,* V, 205–6.

imported here, and advised me to send over as a Pattern, for our People to endeavour to imitate, with regard to its Evenness, Cleanness from Nibs[8] and Lustre; and that they might better see the Difference and understand his remarks he wish'd the Skains sent over hither might be returned with it. I send them altogether accordingly.

He says the Silk reel'd from 12 Cocoons fetches nearly as good a Price as that from 6, because it winds well, and there is less *fine Waste*; the Dropping accidentally or through Inattention 3 or 4 of the Cocoons out of 12 not weakening the Thread so much in Proportion as when the same Number are dropt out of 6; nor is the Thread so apt to break in Winding.

I observe that the Italian Silk had a sweet smell as if perfumed. He thinks it is the natural smell of the Silk when prepared in perfection.

He understands that the Piedmontese Reel is esteemed preferable to Mr. Pullein's.[9]

He says we may carry that Produce to what Length we please, it is impossible to overstock the Market, as the Demand is continually increasing, Silk being more and more worn, and daily entering into the composition of more and a greater Variety of Manufactures.

I communicated your Thanks to Mr. Walpole, who was pleased to assure me he should always be ready to afford the Design all the Assistance in his Power, and will endeavour to procure some Eggs for you from Valencia against the next Season.

I am much obliged to you for the Snuff box. The Wood is beautiful. The Manufacturer should be encourag'd.[1]

I hope our People will not be disheartened by a few Accidents, and such Disappointments as are incident to all new Undertakings, but persevere bravely in the silk Business till they have conquer'd all Difficulties. *By Diligence and Patience the Mouse ate in twain the Cable.*[2] It is not two Centuries since it was as much a Novelty in

8. Kinks or lumps of lint.

9. The Rev. Samuel Pullen or Pullein, an Irishman born in 1713, was the author of *The Culture of Silk...* (London, 1758) and other works on the subject.

1. See Evans to BF above, May 4.

2. Used by BF in *Poor Richard Improved...* (for 1758; Philadelphia, [1757]), p. [11].

France as it is now with us in North America, and the People as much unacquainted with it.

My Respects to my good old Friend Mr. Wharton. I hope he is recovered of the Indisposition you mention.[3] With sincere Esteem, I am, Dear Sir, Your affectionate Friend, and humble Servant,   B. FRANKLIN.

Dr. Cadw. Evans.

To Deborah Franklin   ALS: American Philosophical Society

My dear Child   London, July 4.[4] 1771
This is just to let you know that I am well, and that I shall write fully to you per Capt. Sparks or Falconer. My Love to Sally; and Son Bache, and the little Gentleman. I am as ever Your affectionate Husband   B FRANKLIN

Addressed: To / Mrs Franklin / Philadelphia / per favour of / Capt. Gill[5]

To Deborah Franklin   ALS: American Philosophical Society

My dear Child,   London, July 4. 1771.
I received your kind Letters of April 24. I hope that very bad Cold you had is gone off without any ill Consequences. I have found by a good deal of Experience, that three or four Doses of Bark taken on the first Symptoms of a Cold, will generally put it by. It was a terrible Accident indeed which happened to poor Mr. Rogers and his Family.[6] If I were to build again, I would contrive my House so as to be incapable of burning, which I think very possible and practicable.

I pray God that your Grandson, in whom you seem to take so

3. See the letter of May 4.
4. Probably an error for the 3rd; see the next document.
5. Robert Gill, the master of the *Pa. Packet*, left London on July 12 and was in Philadelphia two months later: *Pa. Gaz.*, Sept. 12.
6. Thomas Rogers and an aged woman lost their lives in a fire in his house on the night of April 6; the other occupants escaped with difficulty. *Pa. Gaz.*, April 11, 1771.

much Delight, may be preserv'd as a Comfort to you. By your Accounts (and indeed by all the Accounts I have heard) he must be a charming little Fellow. My Love to him. I send him a small Token of it in a new Hat.

You ask me when I think I shall return? I purpose it firmly after one Winter more here. In answer to your other Questions, Nanny is still with Mrs. Stevenson as a House- and Cook-Maid. She knows not what is become of her Husband. By good Luck she had no Child. Capt. Ourry is abroad, as a travelling Tutor to a Son of Lord Galway. Sir John Peyton we have not seen for some Years. Mrs. Stevenson still has the French Crown you sent him over, as Gloves.[7] Mrs. Clarke went with her Husband, Capt. Clarke in his Ship to Barbadoes, where she remains among his Relations.[8] Mr. and Mrs. Strahan and Family, Mr. and Mrs. West, Mrs. Stevenson, Mr. and Mrs. Hewson, and Sally Franklin, are all well. When I see any of those first named, they enquire of your Welfare, and desire to be remembered to you. Sally presents her Duty.

I send you per Capt. Falconer two plated Canisters and a Sugar Ditto, which I hope will be agreable to you. I brought them lately from Sheffield. You can get a little Chest made for them as well there as it could be done here.

I wrote a few Lines to you yesterday per Packet, and per Capt. Gill,[9] and am as ever, Your affectionate Husband

B FRANKLIN

Mention to me in your next every thing you want and would have me send or bring with me.

Addressed: To / Mrs Franklin / at / Philadelphia

To [Charles Willson] Peale ALS: American Philosophical Society

Sir,   London, July 4. 1771

I received your obliging Letter of April 21 and it gave me great

7. For Ann Hardy, Mrs. Stevenson's servant, and Capt. Louis Ourry see above, XVII, 167; and for Sir John Peyton, DF's friend from Virginia, XIV, 206 n. DF, we presume, had given Peyton a French crown (écu à la couronne) for Mrs. Stevenson, who had converted it into gloves.

8. See Anne Clarke to BF above, May 5.

9. See the preceding document.

Pleasure to hear that you had met with such Encouragement at Philadelphia, and that you succeed so well in your Business in your native Country. If I were to advise you, it should be, by great Industry and Frugality to secure a Competency as early in Life as may be: For as your Profession requires good Eyes, cannot so well be follow'd with Spectacles, and therefore will not probably afford Subsistence so long as some other Employments, you have a Right to claim proportionably larger Rewards while you continue able to exercise it to general Satisfaction.[1]

The Arts have always travelled Westward, and there is no doubt of their flourishing hereafter on our side the Atlantic, as the Number of wealthy Inhabitants shall increase, who may be able and willing suitably to reward them, since from several Instances it appears that our People are not deficient in Genius. You have my best Wishes for your Prosperity and Happiness, being with great Regard, Sir, Your faithful humble Servant   B FRANKLIN

Mr. Peale

To William Smith   ALS: Huntington Library

Reverend Sir,   London, July 4. 1771

I received the Box containing eleven Copies of the Transactions sent me by order of the Society, and have already delivered most of them as directed.[2] There should be more care taken by the Binder in collating the Sheets, particularly of Books sent so far.

1. Peale remembered this advice, and repeated the substance of it in his diary almost fifty years later (Dec. 17, 1818; APS). But he did not follow it: "I have never been so economical as I ought to have been, yet never quite a spend-thrift. But my fancy for getting everything that I have conceived might be convenient or useful I have indulged. . . . My only consolation now is, that I have by my labors always made myself happy, although often in straightened circumstances." We are grateful to Mr. Charles Sellers for furnishing us a transcript of this entry.

2. For the dispatch of the first volume of the APS *Trans.* see Smith to BF above, May 3. Smith eventually sent the missing sheet and more copies for distribution; see his letter to BF below, May 16, 1772. On the title page of a copy in the APS is a note in BF's hand, "Proposed and Set on foot, 1744 by B.F.—dormant some Years: resum'd in 1768—united to a new one 1769." For the revival and reunion see above, XV, 259–61.

The Book for the Society of Arts had one Sheet twice over, and the Duplicate was return'd to me on a Supposition that it might be wanting in some other Volume. This I did not find: But the Book for Dr. Fothergill wanted a Sheet in the Appendix to the Astronomical Papers, from p. 33 to 40 inclusive, and the other Sheet would not supply the Defect. When the other Box arrives, I shall take care to deliver and dispose of the Books agreable to the Intentions of the Society. I am, Sir, Your humble Servant

B FRANKLIN

Dr. Smith, Secry. to Philosl. Society

From Thomas Bond[3]   ALS: American Philosophical Society

Dear Sir.   Philadelp: July 6. 1771.
This will be delivered to You by Mr. Daniel Kheun, the Brother of Doct. Kheun, Professor of Materia Medica and Botany in our Colledge.[4] He is going to Sweeden to study Divinity and proposes returning here with the pastoral Charge of some of the Swedish Congregations. His Brother thinks Doct. Franklin's Patronage will be of particular Service to him in his Designs and both he and I shall think ourselves much obliged for your Civilities to him.

My Second Son Richard is studying Physic and Surgery with such Application his Friends have Expectations of his making a Figure in the different Branches of his Profession, especially the latter. He is to be examined in our Colledge next Year, and is then

3. The Philadelphia physician, BF's old friend and a co-founder with him of the Pennsylvania Hospital. See above, II, 240 n and subsequent volumes.

4. Daniel Kuhn received his B.A. from the College of Philadelphia in 1768 and his M.A. in 1771. He served in various Lutheran churches in Pennsylvania, matriculated at Uppsala in the fall of 1772, returned to Pennsylvania, and died about 1779. University of Pa., *General Alumni Catalogue*... ([Philadelphia], 1917), p. 19; Uppsala University, *Matrikel*, XIII (1928), 173; Frederick L. Weis, *The Colonial Churches and the Colonial Clergy of the Middle and Southern Colonies*... (Lancaster, Mass., 1938), p. 40, and "The Colonial Clergy of the Middle Colonies...," Amer. Antiquarian Soc. *Proc.*, LXVI (1956), 255. Daniel's brother Adam (1714–1817) was a physician and botanist, who also studied at Uppsala, received his medical degree from Edinburgh in 1767, became physician to the Pennsylvania Hospital, and was one of the founders of the Philadelphia College of Physicians. *DAB*.

to finish his Studies in Europe.[5] But where to send him to the greatest Advantage, is with Me a Doubt. Most of our young Men have depended on Edenbourgh and London for their Education. The School of Edingburgh seems at this Time to be better calculated to please the Fancy, than to form the Judgement; and indeed the many extraordinary Novelties inculcated there, would be a Barr to public Confidence in this Part of the World. As far as We can judge from the public Exhibitions, Surgery in London is a mere *mechanic Art*, well executed. The Accademy of Surgery in Paris, aims at uniting Science to their Profession and have done thereby Honour to it. But whether they have men of Eminence in their Hospitals and Theatres of Anatomy I know not. My Friends Astrue, Winslow, Ferin, Huno, and Le Cat are dead. From the Character and Writings of Gaubius there is Reason to Think Physic is scientifically, and usefully, taught in Leyden, and yet it is said that School is neglected. Vanswieten has aimed at a Reform of the medical Institutions in Vienna, and yet the World is annually misled by Absurdities and Falsehoods under his Sanction.[6] Who, that has tryed the Cicuta, can read the Account given of it without a Blush? The Uva Ursi has indeed the Appearance of being a safe and valuable Addition to the Materia medica: this We

5. He is not listed among the graduates of the College of Philadelphia, and did not live to make a figure, but died of consumption at the age of twenty-two: *Pa. Gaz.*, Dec. 23, and *Pa. Packet*, Dec. 28, 1772.

6. Bond's five friends had all been well known, and so were the two living men. Le Cat had taught Bond's brother: above, v, 333 n. Jean Astruc (1684–1766), for a time physician to the King of Poland, taught at Toulouse, Montpellier, and Paris, and wrote many medical works. Jakob Benignus Winslow (1669–1760) and Antoine Ferrein (1693–1769) were two of the most eminent anatomists of their day. Winslow was a Dane who settled in Paris as professor of anatomy at the Jardin du roi, and wrote a classical treatise on the structure of the human body; Ferrein was an army doctor with the French in Italy, and returned to Paris as professor of medicine and surgery at the Collège royal. François-Joseph Hunauld (1701–42) was Winslow's student and subsequently a professor, like him, at the Jardin du roi; he was noted for his study of vertebrate bones. Hieronymus David Gaubius (1705–80), a German, had a considerable reputation as a practitioner and teacher at Leyden. Gerhard van Swieten graduated from Leyden and went to Austria, where he reorganized medical instruction; he was an authority on the treatment of syphilis. For Gaubius see the *Nieuw Nederlandsch Biografisch Woordenboek* (10 vols., Leyden, 1911–37), and for all the others the *Biographisches Lexikon der Hervorragenden Ärtze...* (5 vols., Berlin and Vienna, 1929–34).

will give them Credit for.[7] Thus, my dear Friend, You see the Difficulties I am under, in an Affair I have much at Heart, and which it is in your Power to remove. Every Man who is acquainted with the Writings of Sir John Pringle, must wish to see Physic cultivated on his Principles, and would be much pleased with his Advice in a medical Education. If therefore You could, at some Liesure Hour, collect his Sentiment on this Occasion, and communicate it to me, it would be the highest Satisfaction. Oh! what Pleasure it would give Me to have the Portrait of that medical Sage at your right Hand.

Good Mrs. Franklin has presented Me with a new Picture of You which has been much visited, and much admired, it is generally agreed there is in it a remarkable sensible meaning, added to a most stricking Likeness. I most sincerely thank you for this additional Instance of your Friendship.[8]

On the 28th: of June We had a Commencement in the Colledge the Farce was prettily played off. I have sent You one of the medical Dissertations Dedicated to Yourself and the Governour: the Author is really a Man of Merit.[9] There is another on a Dropsy, which mentions the extraordinary Success of my Method in the Cure of Dropsies in the Pennsylvania Hospital, which I would Gladly have Sent to Sir John, but the Facts are there so badly chosen, and the Principles so much mistaken, that I cannot patronise it.[10] This will lay me under the disagreable Necessity of revising my Notes on that Subject.

7. Cicuta, or hemlock, has poisonous roots, but poultices of the leaves and even the powdered roots were thought to be useful for inflammations and tumors; see BF's reprint of Thomas Short, *Medicina Britannica*... (Philadelphia, 1751), pp. 136–7. The dried leaves of *Arctostaphylos uva-ursi*, or bearberry, were a diuretic and astringent used for inflammations of the urinary tract.

8. See BF to DF below, Aug. 14.

9. He was Jonathan Elmer (1745–1817), whose work was *Dissertatio medica, inauguralis, de sitis in febribus causis et remediis*... (Philadelphia, 1771). For Elmer's subsequent career as physician, legislator, and jurist see the *DAB*.

10. The object of Bond's ire was *Dissertatio medica, inauguralis [de Hydrope]*... (Philadelphia, 1771) by James Tilton (1745–1822), who may have been mistaken in medical principles but turned out to be sound in practice. He made a name for himself as an army doctor and hospital reformer during the War of Independence, and in 1813 became surgeon general of the army. *DAB*.

Our Philosophical Society continues, tho' few Papers have been sent to it since the Publication; a Correspondence with the learned Societies in Europe would be useful and reputable, and probably a Spur to Us. This I hope you will keep in View, whereby You will greatly oblige all the Members, and particularly Dear Sir Your most affectionate humble Servant   TH BOND

From Noble Wimberly Jones

ALS: American Philosophical Society

Dear Sir   Savannah July 8, 1771
I received on the first instant yours of 5th March and first of May,[1] am very glad the Bills to reimburse the Money you kindly advanced for the province are paid. I am kindly obliged to you for intresting yourself in favour of Mr. Winter. It amazes me to hear that his regard for, or connections with, Mr. Whitefield, a gentleman to whom the utmost Mallice could scarce charge with anything blame worthy, should be an objection of Ordination to him, especially by a Society whose profession and duty it is to encourage Religion (impartially) by every means in their power, and even supposing he has been Educated in another sphere I think if he is now quallified it is rather an acquisition to the Church than an objection to him, for if a parent &c put's a Child to a profession or trade he does not like when capable of judging for himself, is he tho' ever so disagreable to him still obliged to continue in it? Surely no; I trust however that by your interposition Mr. Winters Ordination may still be effected. My sentiments of Mr. Whitefield intirely coincide with yours and I greatly lament the little prospect of any to near equal his Integrity and Indefatagable Zeal for the good of Mankind. With respect to what you mention from Mr. Maudit relative to the Dissenters,[2] am realy at a loss how to act and therefore have not said anything to Frink as yet fearing (on our present footing) it may give offence but as I am thoroughly convinced of the necessity of as general an union as posible in America, if I can think of any mode, will very readily and heartily

1. Much of what follows is explained above in the annotation of the first of these letters; the second has not been found.
2. See the following document.

do all in my power to settle the difference. If we should have an Assembly suffered to again sit to do business they may probably do something therein, when if the entreaties of my neighbours should over rule my private intrest and inclinations I then may do more than I choose to do in a private capacity as I think my right there to speak frely on any subject that occurs: but whether shall serve again can't yet determine. It would give me pleasure to see the people better supplied. The Laws of the province you ought certainly to be furnished with. The reasons for Dissolving the first Assembly must what ever he may say, have been the committing the deputy Secretary which I imagine the King himself would not have done in such a case as that was.[3] It could not be the other reason, as the Governor Acknowledged having answers to his first Letter's (I think in September) which must be what the Board of Trade referred to.[4] Why therefore he would not construe it in that light I cant conceive, however he received what he deemed sufficient a day or two before the Dissolution and therefore time enough to prevent it if so disposed and that the cause;[5] but to shew the Man and his disposition, because I would not rest silent under a false imputation as in his Harangue to the Council, tho' I only in the most modest manner denied what I never heard him say or understood he meant, for he could have no other reason, he carried his resentment to that hight that when I was chose Speaker of the next Assembly, he disapproved the Choice, which the Assembly by a great majority (indeed every disintrested person) looking on as what he had no right to either by Law or reason, tho' they did to prevent delaying the business of the province

3. The King, he means, would not have dissolved the Assembly.
4. The "other reason," and the real one, was the Assembly's refusal to pass a tax bill; see Jones to BF above, March 4. Jones must have been mistaken about the Governor's letters. In July, 1770, Wright sent to London the Assembly's demand for representation of the southern parishes, and in October raised the question again; but he did not have his answer until February, 1771. William W. Abbot, *The Royal Governors of Georgia, 1754–1775* (Chapel Hill, [1959]), pp. 153–5; Candler, ed., *Ga. Col. Recs.*, XI, 255–6. BF doubtless mentioned, in his missing letter of May 1, that he had inquired about the matter at the Board of Trade and learned that it had been settled months before.
5. Jones is saying that the Governor could have satisfied the House instead of dissolving it. This distorts the facts, for which see the annotation of Jones' letter just cited.

make choice of another Member as Speaker, yet thought proper
to shew they deemed it a breach of their privilledges and therefore
came to a Resolution accordingly which you have no doubt seen
in the public papers as from the Journals of the House of the
25. April &c[6] (The Parliament would not give up the point as in the
case of Sir Edwd. Seymour in King Charles the 2ds. Reign[7] vide
Parliamentary debates) and for which Resolution as he says no
other mode would serve him but to dissolve that Assembly also
notwithstanding the rumours of Wars the want of several very
necessary Laws and of Taxes for the support of the provincial
Government &c and is now leaving the province without one.
His Creatures[8] in reference to an Agent tells us the Governor will
have no Coadjutor. Your Sollicitations in behalf of the Negro Law
&c, am certain will be greatfully acknowledged by every well
wisher to the province. As the Election Act was offered for the
Assent, as early as the Negro Law, I can't conceive after the pro-
fessions he made what could be the cause it did not go with that
to the Board of Trade.[9] I hope all difficulties may be got over respecting Sir William Bakers claim as the property of many depends

6. Ever since the Stamp Act agitation, and particularly after Jones' election
as speaker in 1768, the government had distrusted him as a radical. Wright
had apparently inveighed against him in the Council, but the harangue was
not included in its minutes. After the dissolution the new House, meeting in
April, again elected Jones as speaker; and the Governor vetoed the choice.
This action produced two resolutions, one endorsing Jones and the other
branding the veto as a breach of privilege that subverted the people's rights.
Candler, ed., *Ga. Col. Recs.*, XV, 311–12. Both resolutions were published in
the *London Chron.*, June 25–27. For the constitutional issue raised by the controversy see BF's reply to this letter below, April 2, 1772.

7. A poor example. When Charles II removed Seymour from the speaker-
ship in 1669, the House of Commons failed to make good its objections; the
King managed to have another speaker elected.

8. Presumably his supporters, who were referring to the Governor's
grudging acceptance of BF as agent.

9. In 1770 the Governor had assented to the Negro Act, which had the
usual suspending clause until approved by the crown, and had withheld assent to the Election Act until approved. The first was allowed in the following
spring. The second was considered and forwarded by the Board of Trade
in November; no action was taken upon it, however, because its provisions
lay within the sphere of the prerogative. Candler, *op. cit.*, XI, 255; XVII,
590, 592–6; *Board of Trade Jour.*, 1768–75, pp. 206–7, 212–14, 237; *Acts
Privy Coun., Col.*, V, 578; above, XVII, 137–8, 145–7.

on their land being some way or other confirmed to them and Law being very expensive, must in behalf of many concerned wish your utmost endeavours in that matter as soon as the obsticles you mention are removed. The Governor will scarce afford you any assistance in that tho he probably will be present, for he as I have heard received a Fee in Carolina when Attorney general there from Sir Williams Attorneys and has always seemed to favour that claim, so has Mr. Habersham.[1] I mention this that you may be on your gard. I wish you had (as you intended by yours of 5. March) wrote to the Committee of Corrispondence relative to public matters they were not dissolved with the House as you imagined, if you'l observe they continue during the continuance of the Ordinance which did not expire untill the first June last,[2] but they might certainly have received at any time till others were appointed, an Account of transactions that hapened to that very day. Your Letters containing some matters of a private nature or what the Committee had nothing to do with, did not choose to send the Letters to them, and some of the Committee being those that assisted the Governor in using me Ill (and belying me) could not well in person communicate them, when I might omit such parts as were unecessary, or improper. However that you may have no more trouble about it will contrive some Method to acquaint them with what they have a right to know. I now beg leave to conclude with best wishes for your health, prosperity and continuance to represent the Commons of Georgia. With the utmost Esteem I am Dear Sir Your Most Obedient and Very Humble Servant   N W JONES

From John J. Zubly   ALS: American Philosophical Society

Sir   Savanah July 9. 1771.
  By a Letter lately received of Mr. Jasper Mauduit I find that Gentleman (whom I have not the Pleasure to know) has applied

  1. For the land claimed for Sir William Baker's estate see *ibid.*, pp. 148–50. The Governor, a South Carolinian by birth, had been attorney general of that province, 1739–57; see *S.C. Hist. Mag.*, LIX (1958), 60. He sailed for England about when Jones was writing, and his office devolved upon the president of the Council, James Habersham, for whom see above, III, 72 n.
  2. See above, XVII, 139–40.

for your kind assistance to remove Some Greivances imposd in this place on protestant dissenters. I am very happy to learn that Mr. Jones Speaker of our late assembly has accordingly recievd a Letter from You on the Subject.[3] From Your known Regard to the civil and religious Rights of Mankind I should not have expected less tho I was loath the litle disputes between our Rector and myself should ever be known beyond this place and never offerd the Letter publishd on the occasion any where for Sale but in our little Comunity. I am still in Doubt whether it ever reachd England and beg Leave to inclose a Copy merely to put you in full Posession of the Case and should be happy in any Gentlemans animadversions that may think I should have treated this Subject in a gentler manner. Give me Leave Sir to offer you my humblest thanks for thus far interfering in our Cause, if to remove Impositions and establish or confirm a friendly Cariage among Members of the same Community, should, as I hope, be the Consequence, I know You will feel an ample Reward for Your trouble in Your own Bosom.

This demand is still kept up, but now under another Name that [?] of Sextons fees for attendance. We can have no objection to pay the Parish Sexton at the same Rate with the other Parishioners when his attendance is required and I have on that footing only last week allowed him two shillings for attending a funeral, but I conceive a material Difference between allowing him some thing of my own accord and being obliged to pay him whether he is employed and performing any duty or no. Small attempts of this kind have at times been attended with very great Consequences. It is easier to preserve a Right then to recover it and what dissenters may expect, in part may be judged from the Tenor of the Bill sent by the upper house to the lower, in which a Rate is fixd on all dissenters to be paid to the Rector tho his attendance is not required nor any Duty performed. This Bill indeed had not a single Vote in its favour in the lower house, where I had a hearing on the Subject, but it very sufficiently indicates the disposition of the upper, so very Tenacious [?] and of such narrow principles as to refuse a Second reading to a Bill passed in the lower to lay out a Burying Ground for protestant dissenters in the Commons of this place, in which as freeholders we have an undoubted [?] property. It is not

3. See BF to Jones above, March 5, where Zubly is identified and the quarrel about which he is writing is explained.

impossible but a Bill in favour of the Jews for the same purpose met with the same fate for being in bad Company. Our Slaves however, who I suppose are no more in the Establishment than Jews or dissenters bury in that Commons unmolested by any.

It happens hence that unlucky thus in political as well as religious Matters, I am a Dissenter from Governor and Council. The principles of the humble Enquiry are diametricaly opposed to those who saw people with halters on their Neck for complaining of and opposing the Stamp act. This thriving Country is nevertheless in a very Strange Situation and for a very just [?] Cause have been exposd to a Doubt whether it may claim the Benefit of some Laws the Want of which would endanger its very Existence. I beg Leave respectfully to subscribe my self Sir Your most obliged humble Servant   J J ZUBLY

From Samuel Cooper   ALS (draft): British Museum

Dear Sir,   Boston N.E. 10th July. 1771

I should sooner have acknowledg'd the Receit of your Favors of Decemr 30. and Feby 5. had not the State of my Health call'd me out of Town, and oblig'd me to be sparing in Writing. My Thanks are due to you for writing me with so much Freedom and I endeavor to make the best Use of what you communicate to me. Your Interposition in Favor of the Charter was kind, and must endear you to ev'ry true Friend of the Province. But what shall we say of those who were capable of forming or promoting such a Design? Can we suppose them possess'd of such Ideas and Principles as entitle them to influence the Council of a great Nation?[4] I could not but regard with a revengeful Pleasure the Figure which the Secretary made in his Conversation with my Friend. He must have been uneasy, not only from an Apprehension of loosing his Place, but from feeling also his own Littleness; and his Self sufficiency, for a Moment at least, must have been suspended amidst all the Pomp and Parade of his Office. His Measures respecting this Province, exactly answer the Picture you have given of him,

4. For the supposed threat to the Massachusetts charter see above, XVII, 282, 302, 308, 311.

and while we have in the American Department a Man of a Size and Temper to be a Tool to St Francis, His Majesty's Service here will be perpetually embarrassed.[5] The Project for making Governors independent for their Salaries upon the Grants of the People they govern gives great Uneasiness to the most considerate Friends of the Constitution. The reasons you mention against it, are I think unanswerable.[6] It was taken for granted when the Charter was receiv'd here, that the Governor was to be supported by the free Gift of the Province, and this was doubtless one Reason for acquiescing in a Compact that gave so great a Pow'r and Influence to the Crown; and accordingly this has been the Manner in which the Representatives of the Crown have constantly been supported. It is a strong Connection between the Ruler and the People, tending in ev'ry View to promote the great End of Government, and the Want of which no Expedient can supply. The Civil List is the free Grant of a British Parliament, and is augmented from Time to Time at their Pleasure; but the American Revenue is not the Gift of the American Assembly, it is extorted from them by meer Pow'r contrary to their just Remonstrances, and humble Petitions, and tho the Assembly may make a Grant to a good Governor at the Close of his Administration, yet it is in the Pow'r of the Crown to cut off from the People this very small Resource of Influence, by obliging it's Representative not to accept such a Grant; while by it's absolute Appointment of Him, it is absolute Master of his Conduct. Nor can there be any Pretence for this threatning Innovation, from the Conduct of our Provincial Assembly upon this Point. For even in the highest Political Contests with St Francis B. so sensible were the House of the importance of supporting the King's Governor while He remain'd in Office, that they never once propos'd to diminish or delay, much less to deny his Salary—and surely it is to be hoped that the Assembly will never meet with a stronger Provocation to such a

5. In the letter to Cooper of Feb. 5 BF had enclosed his account of the meeting with Hillsborough on Jan. 16. Cooper may have written "Sr Francis," but we think not. Bostonians, angered by Bernard's elevation to a baronetcy, occasionally referred to him as St. Francis. They suspected him of being the *éminence grise* behind the American Secretary, see Cushing, *Writings of Samuel Adams*, II, 233.

6. See the letter from the House to BF above, June 29. For BF's views see above, XVII, 312–13, and BF to Cushing, Feb. 5, 1771.

Measure than they did in Him. I cannot forbear to add, tho writing to one who has a much more thoro Comprehension of the Subject than my self, that this propos'd and (I am afraid) determin'd Independance, is impolitic on the Part of the Crown, and tends to prejudice it's Interest, even consider'd seperate from that of the People, as it will prove a strong Temptation to Governors to hold a Conduct that will greatly lessen their Esteem and Influence in the Province, and consequently their Pow'r to promote the Service of the King. Caution and Watchfulness in Governors, and some Regard to the Interest, and even the Inclinations and Humors of the People, must I think be a Security to the Prerogative; But Independance will take off this Guard, and lead them to be inattentive to, if not directly to encourage and promote such Things as will still further weaken the Political Connection between the Parent Country and the Colonies. So that the Ministry, I hope, upon cool Consideration, may be induc'd to lay aside this Measure, as they wish the Continuance of the Constitutional Pow'r of the Crown, and that it may long retain the peaceful and happy Government of America. I doubt not of your exerting your Abilities and Influence for so good a Purpose, and should you succed you will do a most important and obliging Service to the Province. But what are we to expect, when the Means of Self-Defence upon such great Points are to be taken from us, and no public Monies are allow'd for the Support of an Agent, unless He be under the Controll of the Chair?[7]

You will no doubt be particularly inform'd of a new Point, that has alarm'd us as much as any Thing, and is regarded almost universally, as an undisguis'd Violation of a fundamental Principle of the Charter—I mean the Governor's refusing to sign the Supply Bill, because the Commissioners were not exempted by it from Taxes.[8] The Crown grants by Charter that the General Assembly shall have *full Pow'r* and Authority to impose Rates and Taxes upon all and ev'ry the Proprietors and *Inhabitants* of the Province

7. The Governor, presumably because he was chairman of the Council in its executive capacity. The House had claimed the sole right to appoint its own agent as a measure of self-defense: *Mass. House Jour.*, 1st session, May–July, 1771, p. 112. See also above, BF's interview with Hillsborough, Jan. 16, and Mass. House to BF, June 29; Bowdoin to BF below, Nov. 5.
8. See the Committee of the House to BF below, July 13.

—no Persons, however related to the Crown are excepted. The King now says by his Instructions, no Supply Bill shall be pass'd, unless the Commissioners are exempted. Is not this to claim a Right, to rescind by Instruction what was solemnly ceded by Charter and Compact? The Governor may indeed refuse His Assent to a Supply Bill. But can He do it upon a declar'd Principle subversive of the Capital Privilege of the Charter, and only because they exercise the Pow'r and Authority granted them in it? If the Crown can exempt five Persons, it may with equal Right five hundred—not only the Commissioners but all Judges, Justices, Clerks of Courts, Constables, and all Friends to Government, as Men of slavish Principles affect to be called, and have the whole Burden of Taxes upon those who wish well to the Rights of their Country. In this Manner People reason here. But out of the Eater cometh forth Meat.[9] Good may arise from this. It is bold and open, and strikes ev'ry Size of Men. It is not a Point confined to Trade. It regards, in itself, and much more in it's Tendency, the Pocket of the Farmer, and the Farmer will regard his Pocket. It shews the Disposition of the Commissioners, who for such a Trifle, as the Tax they pay, and which perhaps affects their Pride much more than their Purse, have started a new and important Subject of Contention, and how fit they are for that Influence in Governmental Measures which they have so long and so mysteriously possess'd.

I long to see your Treatise, shewing that ev'ry Lady of Genoa is not Queen of Corsica.[1] I doubt not you will be able to prove your Point. But tho I believe you capable of confuting a whole Island of Queens, I fear whether you could perswade them silently to renounce their Crowns and Sceptres. I am Sir with the greatest Esteem, and Attachment Your Obedient &c   S. COOPER

Dr Franklin.

To Samuel Franklin   ALS: New-York Historical Society

Loving Cousin,   London, July 12. 1771
I received your kind Letter of May 17. and rejoice to hear that you and your good Family are well. My Love to them.

9. The riddle that Samson put to the Philistines. Judges 14: 14.
1. For the metaphor and treatise see above, XVII, 311.

With this I send you the Print you desire for Mr. Bowen.[2] He does me Honour in accepting it.

Sally Franklin presents her Duty to you and Mrs. Franklin.

Yesterday a very odd Accident happened, which I must mention to you as it relates to your Grandfather. A Person that deals in old Books, of whom I sometimes buy, acquainted me that he had a curious Collection of Pamphlets bound in 8 Vols. Folio, and 24 Vols 4to. and 8vo. which he thought from the Subjects I might like to have, and that he would sell them cheap. I desired to see them, and he brought them to me. On examining, I found that they contain'd all the principal Pamphlets and Papers on Publick Affairs that had been printed here from the Restoration down to 1715. In one of the blank Leaves at the Beginning of each Volume the Collector had written the Titles of the Pieces contain'd in it, the Prices they cost him, &c. also Notes in the Margin of many of the Pieces. And this Collector I find, from the Hand-Writing and various other Circumstances, was your Grandfather, my Uncle Benjamin. Wherefore I the more readily agreed to buy them. I suppose he parted with them when he left England and came to Boston soon after your Father, which was about the Year 1716 or 17, now more than 50 Years since.[3] In whose Hands they have been all this time I know not. The Oddity is, that the Bookseller, who could suspect nothing of any Relation between me and the Collector, should happen to make me the Offer of them. My Love to your good Wife and Children, concludes from, Your affectionate Cousin   B FRANKLIN

Saml [?] Franklin

2. See Franklin to BF above, May 17, and Penuel Bowen to BF below, Nov. 6.

3. BF's Uncle Benjamin (A.5.2.7) emigrated from London to Boston in 1715; see above, I, 3–4. The pamphlets were presumably the 51-vol. collection that BF acquired in August, 1771, from Thomas Martin for six guineas (Jour., p. 37), and that the Library Company purchased at the sale of his books in 1801. The handwriting in the volumes, however, is not Uncle Benjamin's: Edwin Wolf, II, "The Reconstruction of Benjamin Franklin's Library...," Bibliographical Soc. of America Papers, LVI (1962), 9–10.

From Miss Todd[4]

AL: American Philosophical Society

⟨Friday, July 12, 1771; a note in the third person. Will call on Franklin at noon tomorrow and accompany him to Walthamstow, and will bring him safe to town on Monday morning.⟩

From Jonathan Williams, Sr.

ALS: American Philosophical Society

Honoured sir   Boston July 12th 1771
   Cap. Lloyd was to Sail yesterday; I inclos'd a Bill for £100 and put it in the Bag a few oures afterward I Received another Bill for one thousand Gilders £90 Sterling Which I now inclose to you. Please to Credit me for the Net Proceeds. Mr. Foxcroft and Lady Came to town the night before last Well.[5] I am your Dutyfull Nephew and much Oblig'd Humble Servant   JONA WILLIAMS

Addressed: To / Benjamin Franklin Esqr / at Mrs Stevensons in Cravinstreet / London / per Lloyd

From a Committee of the Massachusetts House of Representatives

LS: University of Virginia Library

For many years the Massachusetts General Court had passed annual legislation that taxed the income of all royal officials residing in and paid by the province.[6] In 1768 the customs commissioners, created by one of the Townshend Acts, were also assessed as resident officials. Although they argued that their salaries were exempt as coming from the crown, not the province, they said that they paid under threat of prosecution by local tax collectors. In 1769, however, they requested Lieutenant Governor Hutchinson to secure them exemption in future. He considered their grievance valid and was inclined to agree in

   4. In all likelihood a sister of Anthony Todd. The hand is that of an adult and his only surviving daughter, Eleanor, was about nine at the time.
   5. Williams' next letter (below, Aug. 5) makes clear that he is repaying BF's loans to his sons, for which see BF to Williams above, March 5. The Foxcrofts were John and Judith.
   6. For recent examples of these bills, 1768–70, see *Mass. Acts and Resolves,* IV, 959–73; V, 5–20, 89–106.

principle; yet he saw no possibility, as he wrote Hillsborough, of convincing the House. The matter was submitted to the law officers of the crown, who reported early in 1770 that all royal officials, whatever the source of their salaries, were subject to any tax levied on them by the province in which they resided. This opinion was forwarded to Hutchinson, and by him to the commissioners.

There the matter rested until February, 1771, when the government suddenly overrode the earlier legal opinion and that of Richard Jackson, counsel to the Board of Trade.[7] Hutchinson had been promoted to governor, and his instructions were being prepared; in them was inserted an article forbidding him to assent to any tax bill that did not exempt salaries of royal officials paid by the crown.[8] The Governor was taken aback by this article; Whitehall's reversing itself to support the commissioners, he believed, created a needless political crisis and was a disservice to government.[9] But he had no choice. In early July he vetoed the tax bills for that year, and notified the House that he had done so on instruction. In its angry response the House asserted some startling constitutional views: it denied the right of Parliament to create the customs commissioners or to collect any revenue in America, claimed that the provincial charter empowered the House to tax as it pleased, and stigmatized the Governor's act as an abrogation of the charter.[1] These assertions rested upon bold premises. If the commissioners had no legal standing, Parliament had no power to regulate colonial trade. If the Governor violated the charter by obeying his instructions about a tax bill, as about moving the General Court or refusing a salary from it,[2] the royal prerogative was circumscribed by whatever interpretations the colonial legislatures might put upon their charters. The position of the Massachusetts House, in short, was a significant logical advance along the road toward independence.[3]

7. For the developing controversy over the commissioners see *ibid.*, v, 53–5. The documents printed there give no explanation of the government's volte-face.

8. *Board of Trade Jour.*, 1768–75, pp. 169–70; *Acts Privy Coun., Col.*, v, 264–5.

9. Hutchinson, *History*, III, 247.

1. *Mass. House Jour.*, 1st session, May–July, 1771, pp. 107–9, 111; see also Gipson, *British Empire*, XII, 44–5. The argument ignored the King's right under the charter to veto any legislation of the General Court, as Hutchinson subsequently pointed out: *History*, III, 248.

2. See above, BF to Cushing, June 10, n. 1, and the House to BF, June 29.

3. The squabble in which the House took its position precluded any tax bills in 1771–72. A surplus in the treasury met the operating expenses of

Sir,   Boston July 13th. 1771.

We take this Opportunity just to acquaint you that our Governor has received a late Instruction by which he is expressly forbid for the future upon any Pretence whatever to give his Consent to any Law or Laws whereby the Commissioners, or any Person employed in the King's Service whose Offices have no peculiar Relation to this Province shall be liable to pay Taxes during his Residence here, for such Salaries or Allowances as do not issue out of any Monies granted by the Legislature of this Province. This Instruction was communicated to the House the last Day but one of the late Session and threw the House into great Consternation, as it was looked upon to be as arbitrary a Measure as any that has yet [been] taken by Administration. You will see the Message of the Governor to the House in Consequence of this Instruction and their Answer, in the inclosed Paper. This is indeed a natural Effect of the Right assumed by Parliament to tax America; for if the Property of the Colonists is at the Disposal of the Mother Country, to be taxed by Parliament at Pleasure, it infers a Right in them to exempt such Persons as they please from any Share of the Burthen. The People of every Class in Town and Country, except the Crown Officers, are greatly alarmed, and think it would, if conceded to, be a Precedent, for the future Exemption of all who will fall into and support the oppressive Measures, which will have a Tendency to increase the Number of their Dependents, and consequently to give them an Influence which must be to the greatest Degree dangerous. We have not Time to enlarge at present, but shall write you more fully by the next Opportunity. In the mean Time we inclose you an Account of the Taxes the Commissioners have paid, under the Hands of the Assessors,[4] which appear to have been so light, that we can hardly think their Complaint of them can arise from any other

the province, although taxes were still collected under a supply bill of 1770 for retiring the provincial debt. Whether the commissioners' salaries were actually taxed for this purpose we do not know; the available evidence suggests merely that the whole controversy petered out. See Hutchinson, *History*, III, 251, and his letters in Mass. Arch., XXVII, 190–5, 301–2, 353, 485; "State of the Proceedings Respecting the Commissioners of the Customs' Complaint of Being Taxed by the Boston Assessors," William Salt Library, Stafford.

4. The enclosure was actually in Cushing to BF below, July 20.

Principle but a haughty Disposition to be independent of the Government of this Province, which they have heretofore treated with an insufferable Insolence: We are with respect Your most humble Servants   THOMAS CUSHING   JAMES OTIS
                    SAML ADAMS
                    Committee of the House of Representatives

Benjamin Franklin Esqr

Endorsed: Thos. Cushing, Jas. Otis, and Saml Adams Com. Ho. of Reps of Mass to Benjn Franklin July 13th 1771.

To John Bartram   ALS: Yale University Library

My good and dear old Friend,   London, July 17. 1771

I received your kind Letter of April 29. wherein you complain of your Friends here not writing to you. I had written a Letter to you on the 20th. of the same Month per Osborne, which I hope is long since got to hand; but I confess I ought to have written sooner, to acknowledge the Receipt of the Box of Seeds, whereby I was much obliged.

As to your Pension, there is not, I believe, the least Reason for you to apprehend its being stopped. I know not who receives it for you here, or I should quicken them in writing to you. But there is no Instance in this King's Reign of taking away a Pension once granted, unless for some great Offence. Young is in no Esteem here as far as I can learn.

I wish your Daughter Success with her Silkworms. I am persuaded nothing is wanting in our Country for the Produce of Silk, but Skill; which will be obtain'd by persevering till we are instructed by Experience.

You take Notice of the Failing of your Eyesight.[5] Perhaps you have not Spectacles that suit you, and it is not easy there to provide one's self. People, too, when they go to a Shop for Glasses, seldom give themselves time to chuse with Care, and if their Eyes are not rightly suited, they are injured. Therefore I send you a compleat Set, from No. 1. to 13. that you may try them at your

5. The matters BF is discussing are explained in Bartram's two letters above, XVII, 290–1; April 29, 1771.

Ease; and having pitch'd on such as suit you best at present, reserve those of higher Numbers for future Use as your Eyes grow still older; and with the lower Numbers, which are for younger People, you may oblige some other Friends. My Love to good Mrs. Bartram and your Children. I am, as ever, Your faithful Friend and Servant   B FRANKLIN

P.S. July 30. On Enquiry I find your Pension continues, and will be regularly paid as it becomes due to the Person you empower to receive it for you.

Mr Bartram

Endorsed: B. Franklin to John Bartram Dated London July 17. 1771.

To Ebenezer Kinnersley   ALS: University of Pennsylvania Library

Dear Sir,   London, July 17. 1771

I was much oblig'd by your Account of the Effect of the Lightning on Mr. Holder's[6] House. It will be in the Transactions here. I wonder it is not to be found in yours.

Those here who aimed at obtaining a very great Electric Force, have been much discouraged by the Breaking of the Bottles that compos'd their Batteries. A Gentleman of my Acquaintance lost 8 out of 20 at one Stroke; another 12 out of 40.[7] Having heard that Pere Beccaria had lined the Inside of a great Iron Kettle with Cement, and then coated a Part of the Cement with Tinfoil, from whence he could discharge a great Stroke; and if any Crack

6. A misspelling of Moulder; see above, XVII, 249.

7. Experimenters, partly in the hope of simulating the effects of lightning, were trying to build the largest possible charges in their batteries, which were commonly made by connecting a number of Leyden jars; see above, IV, 202. Breaking of the jars was a widespread problem, to which Edward Nairne and Giambatista Beccaria eventually published solutions: *Phil. Trans.*, LXIV (1774), 87; Beccaria, *A Treatise upon Artificial Electricity...* (London, 1776), pp. 118–21. Either of these men may have been one of the acquaintances to whom BF refers. The other was unquestionably Priestley; BF and Canton were with him in June, 1771, when several of his jars exploded. Priestley, *History*, II, 242–6, and *Experiments and Observations Relating to Various Branches of Natural Philosophy* (3 vols., London, 1779–86), II, 286–7.

happen'd to his Cement, he mended it again with a hot Iron; I recommended trying to make Batteries of Paper, by straining the Sheets on Frames, drying them hot before the Fire, then impregnating them with melted Wax, and afterwards coating them with Tinfoil.[8] This another ingenious Friend has try'd, and as he writes me it succeeds.

The same (Mr. Henley) has invented an Electrometer which seems useful. I send you a Draft of it.[9] It shows in what degree a Bottle is charg'd, that is, whether half, three quarters, &c. So that knowing the Force of a full Charge of any Bottle or Battery, you may by this, while charging, know the Proportion you have of such Force.

Your Experiment showing that a Stroke with black Lead on Paper would conduct a Shock, was new to me. I mention'd it to some who since tell me that they also find the solid Black Lead in a Pencil conducts as well as Wire; Which indeed, (the other being true) is not to be wonder'd at. It is however the only Property of Metal Black Lead possesses, as far as we yet know it.[1]

Mr. Canton melts Silver and Gold Wire by Electricity, not only into fine bright little Globules, but also into Spherules of Glass, some of which he has shown me by his Microscope. They were transparent, the Light passing thro' them, and appearing in a Focus on the Paper.[2]

Mr. Henley has several Times melted Iron Wire lying at the Bottom of a White Stone Plate filled with Water. The Iron was destroy'd, and mark'd the Plate with an indelible black Stroke.

8. BF presumably heard of Beccaria's innovation from Priestley, who was also experimenting with cement (*ibid.*, pp. 287–91); how the Italian could have mended cement with a hot iron we do not venture to guess. BF's suggestion of paper for batteries was a development of the glass sheets, covered with thin lead, that he had used many years before: above, III, 357–8.

9. For another drawing and a description of Henly's electrometer see above, XVII, 259–61.

1. Black lead or graphite is a form of carbon which, unlike the diamond, is an excellent conductor. Priestley was experimenting with another conductive form, charcoal: *History*, II, 193–200.

2. Gold and silver, like other metals, disintegrate when exposed to a sufficient charge, and form small particles that reflect brilliantly. Although the gold in fact remains gold and the silver silver, the metals were widely thought to be changed—as if by alchemy in reverse—into some kind of glass-like material. See *ibid.*, p. 292.

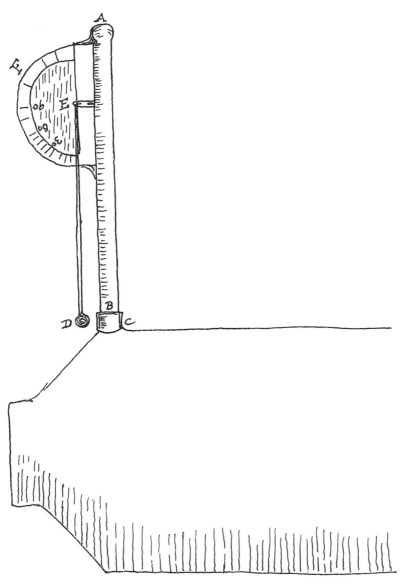

A B   An Ivory Rod, round with a Knob at the Top, 6 Inches high
  C   A short Tin Socket, fix'd to the Primo Conductor, to receive the End of the Ivory Rod.
  D   a Cork or Pith Ball, at the End of a small Ivory Arm, turning on an Axis at E
  F   a semicurcular Plane of Ivory graduated at the Edge, to mark the Rise of the Ball, by the small Arm passing over the Graduation

Sparks flew from it out thro' the Water, and fell red hot on the Table.[3]

I wish I had any thing of more Importance to communicate. Business, during the Winter, takes up my time, so that I make no Experiments myself, but what I hear of I shall continue to send you. Being, with sincere Esteem, Dear Sir, Your most obedient humble Servant   B FRANKLIN

P.S. I cannot find the Draft I promised, so must attempt a Sketch.

[*The drawing and legend on p. 183 follow here in MS. The drawing is based on the original, which is too faint to reproduce.*]

Mr Kinnersley

Endorsed: To Dr Ebenezer Kinnersley. From Dr. Benjamin Franklin

To Jane Mecom   ALS: American Philosophical Society

Dear Sister,   London, July 17. 1771

I have received your kind Letter of May 10. You seem so sensible of your Error in so hastily suspecting me, that I am now in my turn sorry I took Notice of it.[4] Let us then suppose that Accompt ballanced and settled, and think no more of it.

In some former Letter I believe I mention'd the Price of the Books, which I have now forgotten: But I think it was 3*s*. each.[5] To be sure there are Objections to the Doctrine of Pre-existence: But it seems to have been invented with a good Intention, to save the Honour of the Deity, which was thought to be injured by the Supposition of his bringing Creatures into the World to be miserable, without any previous misbehaviour of theirs to deserve it.

3. Henly, we conjecture, was trying to improve the construction of lightning rods. Priestley was conducting experiments along similar lines, from which he concluded that an electrical discharge affected wet metals more than dry. *Ibid.*, p. 271; see also pp. 251–2, 263–4.

4. Both Jane's letter and BF's earlier one to her are missing; the misunderstanding may have been over the rent that Jane was receiving, for which see Williams to BF above, Jan. 19, and BF's reply on March 5.

5. The books were the religious tracts that BF had sent her in December; this and the following paragraph amplify what he had written her then. Above, XVII, 315–16.

This, however, is perhaps an officious Supporting of the Ark, without being call'd to such Service. Where he has thought fit to draw a Veil, our Attempting to remove it may be deem'd at least an offensive Impertinence. And we shall probably succeed little better in such an Adventure to gain forbidden Knowledge, than our first Parents did when they ate the Apple.

I meant no more by saying Mankind were Devils to one another than that being in general superior to the Malice of the other Creatures, they were not so much tormented by them as by themselves. Upon the whole I am much disposed to like the World as I find it, and to doubt my own Judgment as to what would mend it. I see so much Wisdom in what I understand of its Creation and Government, that I suspect equal Wisdom may be in what I do not understand. And thence have perhaps as much Trust in God as the most pious Christian.

I am very happy that a good Understanding continues between you and the Philadelphia Folks.[6] Our Father, who was a very wise man, us'd to say, nothing was more common than for those who lov'd one another at a distance, to find many Causes of Dislike when they came together; and therefore he did not approve of Visits to Relations in distant Places, which could not well be short enough for them to part good Friends. I saw a Proof of it, in the Disgusts between him and his Brother Benjamin; and tho' I was a Child I still remember how affectionate their Correspondence was while they were separated, and the Disputes and Misunderstandings they had when they came to live some time together in the same House. But you have been more prudent, and restrain'd that "Aptness" you say you have "to interfere in other People's oeconomical Affairs by putting in a Word now and then unasked." And so all's well that ends well.

I thought you had mentioned in one of your Letters a Desire to have Spectacles of some sort sent you; but I cannot now find such a Letter. However I send you a Pair of every Size of Glasses from 1 to 13. To suit yourself, take out a Pair at a time, and hold one of the Glasses first against one Eye, and then against the other, looking on some small Print. If the first Pair suits neither Eye, put them up again before you open a second. Thus you will keep them

6. BF had been afraid of a misunderstanding at the time of Jane's visit to DF: *ibid.*, pp. 284, 316.

from mixing. By trying and comparing at your Leisure, you may find those that are best for you, which you cannot well do in a Shop, where for want of Time and Care, People often take such as strain their Eyes and hurt them. I advise your trying each of your Eyes separately, because few Peoples Eyes are Fellows, and almost every body in reading or working uses one Eye principally, the other being dimmer or perhaps fitter for distant Objects; and thence it happens that the Spectacles whose Glasses are Fellows suit sometimes that Eye which before was not used tho' they do not suit the other. When you have suited your self, keep the higher Numbers for future Use as your Eyes may grow older; and oblige your Friends with the others.

I was lately at Sheffield and Birmingham,[7] where I bought a few plated Things which I send you as Tokens, viz. A Pair of Sauce-boats, a Pair of flat Candlesticks, and a Saucepan, lined with Silver. Please to accept of them. I have had one of the latter in constant Use 12 Years, and the Silver still holds. But Tinning is soon gone.

Mrs. Stevenson and Mrs. Hewson present their Compliments, the latter has a fine Son. Sally Franklin sends her Duty to you. I wonder you have not heard of her till lately. She has lived with me these 5 Years, a very good Girl, now near 16. She is Great Grandaughter of our Father's Brother John, who was a Dyer at Banbury in Oxfordshire, where our Father learnt that Trade of him, and where our Grandfather Thomas lies buried: I saw his Gravestone. Sally's Father, John's Grandson, is now living at Lutterworth in Leicestershire, where he follows the same Business, his Father too being bred a Dyer, as was our Uncle Benjamin. He is a Widower, and Sally his only Child. These two are the only Descendants of our Grandfather Thomas now remaining in England that retain that Name of *Franklin*. The Walkers are descended of John by a Daughter that I have seen, lately deceased. Sally and Cousin Williams's Children, and Henry Walker who now attends Josiah are Relations in the same degree to one another and to your and my Grandchildren, viz[8]

7. See the résumé of Williams' journal of the trip above, May 28.
8. For a more detailed genealogy see above, i, l–lxv. In setting down his own generation BF's pen slipped: he called his cousin, Anne Franklin Farrow, "Anne W."

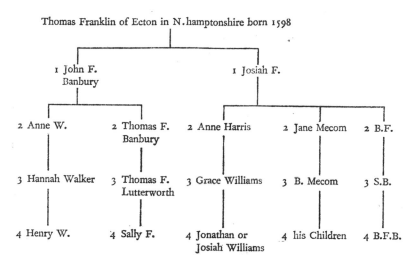

Thomas Franklin of Ecton in N. hamptonshire born 1598

1 John F. Banbury		1 Josiah F.		
2 Anne W.	2 Thomas F. Banbury	2 Anne Harris	2 Jane Mecom	2 B.F.
3 Hannah Walker	3 Thomas F. Lutterworth	3 Grace Williams	3 B. Mecom	3 S.B.
4 Henry W.	4 Sally F.	4 Jonathan or Josiah Williams	4 his Children	4 B.F.B.

What is this Relation called? Is it third Cousins? Having mentioned so many Dyers in our Family, I will now it's in my Mind request of you a full and particular Receipt for Dying Worsted of that beautiful Red, which you learnt of our Mother. And also a Receipt for making Crown Soap. Let it be very exact in the smallest Particulars.[9] Enclos'd I send you a Receipt for making soft Soap in the Sun.

I have never seen any young Men from America that acquir'd by their Behaviour here more general Esteem than those you recommended to me. Josiah has stuck close to his musical Studies, and still continues them. Jonathan has been diligent in Business for his Friends as well as himself, obliging to every body, tender of his Brother, not fond of the expensive Amusements of the Place, regular in his Hours, and spending what Leisure Hours he had in the Study of Mathematics. He goes home to settle in Business, and I think there is great Probability of his doing well. With best Wishes for you and all yours, I am ever, Your affectionate Brother   B FRANKLIN

I have mislaid the Soap Receipt but will send it when I find it.

9. Jane sent the recipes, which BF acknowledged in his letter to her below, Jan. 13, 1772. That for crown soap is printed in Van Doren, *Franklin–Mecom*, pp. 129–32; see also above, I, 348 n.

To Cadwalader Evans

Reprinted from Samuel Hazard, ed., *Hazard's Register of Pennsylvania*, XVI, No. 5 (August 1, 1835), 92–3.

Dear Doctor,   London, July 18, 1771.

I wrote to you of the 4th instant per Gill, and sent you a Paper of Observations on your Specimens of Silk drawn up by Mr. Patterson, who is noted here in that Trade, with a Specimen of Italian Silk as a copy for our People to imitate. But they must not be discouraged if they should not come up to the Lustre of it, that being the very finest, and from a particular District in Italy, none other being equal to it from any other District or any other Country.

The European Silk I understand is all yellow, and most of the India Silk. What comes from China is white. In Ogilby's Account of that Country, I find that in the Province of Chekiang "they prune their Mulberry Trees once a year as we do our Vines in Europe, and suffer them not to grow up to high Trees, because thro' long Experience they have learn'd that the leaves of the smallest and youngest Trees make the best Silk, and know thereby how to distinguish the first Spinning of the Threads from the second, viz. the first is that which comes from the young Leaves that are gather'd in March, with which they feed their Silkworms; and the second is of the old Summer Leaves. And it is only the Change of Food, as the young and old Leaves which makes the Difference in the Silk. The Prices of the first and second Spinning differs among the Chinese. The best Silk is that of March, the coarsest of June, yet both in one year." I have copied this passage[1] to shew that in Chekiang they keep the Mulberry Trees low; but I suppose the Reason to be, the greater Facility of gathering the Leaves. It appears too by this passage, that they raise two Crops a year in that Province, which may account for the great Plenty of Silk there. But perhaps this would not answer with us, since it is not practis'd in Italy, tho' it might be try'd. Chekiang is from 27 to

---

1. He did not copy it; he was averse, as mentioned before, to quoting even himself precisely. In this case he paraphrased with so much freedom that he introduced one point not in the original: the superiority of young trees as well as young leaves. The passage is in John Ogilby's translation of Johan Nieuhof, *An Embassy from the East India Company of the United Provinces, to the Grand Tartar Chan, Emperour of China* (London, 1669), p. 254.

31 Degrees in North Latitude. Duhalde has a good deal on the Chinese Management of the Silk Business.[2]

Dr. Pullein is an Acquaintance of mine. I will forward any Letters you may send him. He lives in Ireland, but often comes to London.[3]

As you did not write to Dr. Fothergill, I communicated to him what you wrote in favour of Mr. Parke who is to wait on him tomorrow. I shall be glad to render the young Man any Service here.[4]

We had a cold backward Spring here, and it is since the Solstice that we have had what may be called a warm Day. But the Country now looks well with the Prospect of great Plenty. It is however the general Opinion that Britain will not for some years export much Corn, great Part of the arable Land being now enclosed and turn'd to Grass, to nourish the immense Number of Horses raised for Exportation, there being a Rage in France and other parts of Europe for English Horses, that seems increasing every year.

I hope our Friend Galloway will not decline the Public Service in Assembly with his private Business. Both may be too much for his Health:[5] But the first alone will be little more than an Amusement: And I do not see that he can be spared from that Station without great Detriment to our Affairs and to the general Welfare of America. I am with sincere esteem Your affectionate friend and humble Servant.   B. FRANKLIN.

Dr. Cadw. Evans.

P.S. The enclosed Notes were given me by Mr. Small a Leading Member of the Society of Arts,[6] with a Desire that I would send them over to some Member of your Philosophical Society; supposing the Herb may be of some use.

2. Jean Baptiste du Halde, *A Description of the Empire of China and Chinese Tartary...* (2 vols., London, 1738–41).

3. See BF to Evans above, July 4.

4. For Thomas Parke, Evans' former student and protégé, see Evans to BF above, May 4.

5. Evans had spoken of Galloway's ill health two years earlier, and Galloway had mentioned in the previous September his discontent with politics (XVI, 156–7; XVII, 228–9); but BF may well be responding to some comment in a more recent letter from Evans that has disappeared.

6. William Small, the erstwhile professor of natural history at William and Mary, now living in Birmingham. See above, XI, 480 n.

From Thomas Cushing   ALS: American Philosophical Society

Sir   Boston July 20: 1771
   At the desire of the Committee of the House of Representatives
I now transmitt you a Copy of the Commissioners Taxes in the
Towns of Dorchester, Roxbury, and Brooklyn for the years they
respectively resided in those towns certified by the Assessors of
the Several Towns aforementioned.[7] I am with respect Your most
humble Servant   T Cushing

Benjamin Franklyn Esqr

To Jonathan Shipley   AL (draft): American Philosophical Society

                                                     July 25. 1771
I should have been happy in accompanying your Lordship on that
agreable Party, or in being at Twyford instead of this dusty Town;
but Business kept me here longer than I expected. I now purpose
to set out on Tuesday next,[8] if nothing at present unforeseen does
not happen to prevent me. I hope to find the good Family well,
which will add greatly to the Pleasure I promise my self in that
sweet Retreat. With the greatest Respect, I am, Your Lordship's
most obedient humble Servant

Ld. Bishop of St. Asaph

From John Whitehurst[9]   ALS: American Philosophical Society

Dear Sir   Clumber Park July 25 1771
   I sent the two Clocks on Tuesday last by Clark; to the Bell in
Wood Street, Directed for you in Craven Street, the Strand.[1]
   I hope they will please and Come Safe to hand. I have been So
much out, I could not Engrave the Plates, and therefore Chose to

7. See the House Committee to BF above, July 13.
8. July 30.
9. The Derby clock- and instrument-maker; see above, IX, 42 n; X, 70 n.
1. For BF's interest in clock design see above, VIII, 216–19, and Whitehurst's second letter below, Aug. 1. BF must have ordered these clocks, perhaps as presents, when he was in Derby in May; they were probably sent by
John Clark, a linen draper of Wood Street, Cheapside: *Kent's Directory*...
(London, 1770).

Send them in the State they are In rather than keep them longer. Mr. Tompson Engraver in red lyon Street Clerken well,[2] will do them in a day or two at any time, giving him proper Directions. Please to give him a line when you Chuse he Should wait on you. I am Sir your Most Obedient Servant   JOHN WHITEHURST

Addressed: To / Docr. Benjn: Franklin / Craven Street the Strand / London

Endorsed: J. Whitehurst Clocks

From Richard Jackson   ALS: American Philosophical Society

Dear Sir   Hedly[3] Saturday Night [July 27?,[4] 1771]

Does it suit you to go to Ireland with me in a week, a fortnight, or three weeks?[5] I am sorry you leave London so soon, fearing as I do I may chance to miss seeing you. I wish much to hear from you a few of the Particulars you have heard of the Voyage of the Endeavour and of the Observations of the Passengers. I will try to see you before you leave London, but as I may chance not to be able to come to Town till Wednesday, I should take it as a great favor to receive a Word on the Subject in writing in a Letter to Southampton Buildings. I am Dear Sir yours sincerely

RD JACKSON

Addressed: To / Benjn Franklin Esq / at Mrs Stephensons / Craven Street / Strand / London / from R Jackson

2. John Thompson, of that address, was a clock- and watch-maker: *ibid.*

3. Presumably either Headley, Surrey, or Headley, Hants.

4. The approximate time of year is established by the *Endeavour*'s return on July 16 from her voyage around the world. BF planned to leave for Twyford on Tuesday the 30th; see his letter to Shipley above, July 25. Jackson, doubtless because he knew of the plan, expected to miss him in town on Wednesday, and hence was probably writing on the previous Saturday night. In that case BF answered immediately: an item in a loose bill among his papers is for a letter sent to Jackson on the 28th.

5. The answer turned out to be a month: the two left for their Irish tour on Aug. 25.

Complaints of William Hunter against William
Hewson   AD (in Franklin's hand): American Philosophical Society

In the autumn of 1762 William Hewson, Polly Stevenson's husband-
to-be, entered into partnership with Dr. William Hunter, the famous
anatomist, to give lectures and demonstrations to medical students. In
1769 Hunter finished building a new house in Great Windmill Street,
where Hewson had a small apartment; the two now shared equally in
the profits of the course. Hewson and Polly were married on July 10,
1770, and soon afterward moved into a house near Hunter's. But in the
spring of 1771 Hunter announced that the partnership would be dissolved the following winter because Hewson's family responsibilities
were preventing him from giving enough time to his work.[6] Both men
took their trouble to Franklin. He was well acquainted with Hunter
and, through his long friendship with Polly, was involved in Hewson's
affairs. He made at least two memoranda of his discussions with Hunter,
this one of the anatomist's complaints against his young partner, and
another of his stipulations for the remaining months of the partnership.
The second Franklin dated.[7] The first he did not, but internal evidence
suggests that it preceded the stipulations by at least a few weeks; we
are therefore assigning it to July.[8]

[July?, 1771]
Complaints
    That he gave Leave to go to Blenheim once, but not repeatedly,
not for an Absence of 10 Days from Business, which was the more
inconvenient as Dr. H. was then indisposed with a Lax.[9]
    That Dr. H. has not only suffer'd this Loss of Mr. H's Time and
Assistance but by his Management has lost a Friend, Mr. B.
    That Mr. H. would have used a Body of Dr. Hunter's Purchas-
ing to make a Skeleton, who it could not be expected should purchase Bodies for him for such purposes.
    That he had employ'd a Man to pick Bones out of the Tubs and

6. Thomas J. Pettigrew, *Memoirs of the Life and Writings of the Late John
Coakley Lettsom...* (3 vols., London, 1817), I, 140–3 of second pagination.
    7. See the extract from it below, Aug. 23.
    8. The article in which it was first printed discusses the Hunter–Hewson
quarrel with extensive references: Lloyd G. Stevenson, "William Hewson,
the Hunters, and Benjamin Franklin," *Jour. of the History of Medicine and
Allied Sciences*, VIII (1953), 324–8.
    9. Diarrhea.

William Hewson

fit up a Skeleton for him, without Leave of Dr. H. which ought not to have been done till the Lectures were over.

That Mr. H's Behaviour to Dr. H. was extreamly rude, and that he had said, *he was a Fool to expect that Dr. H. would act like a Gentleman.*

That for this Reason he Dr. H. must now come to a dead Stand, and insist on a specific and exact Compliance with the Articles; that Mr. H. should expect nothing from him for the future but what those intitled him to; that however this Resolution should have no retrospect. That he had endeavoured to serve Mr. H. who had turn'd that Endeavour to his Prejudice. He could therefore no longer be his Friend, tho' he should not be his Enemy.

That he had taken a Guinea of two Dissecting Pupils who had not been attended for Dr. H. contrary to his express Declaration that he would have nothing.

That Mr. H. complain'd of being prevented giving half the Lectures. But Dr. H. knowing his Dislike to giving such as required much Speaking, had given those to favour Mr. H. That he had offered to leave it to the free Choice of the Pupils, which Mr. H. had declined. That he had refused to give one which Dr. H. had requested him to give. That Dr. H. should not have given so many, but that he had been inform'd the Pupils were not so well satisfied with Mr. H.'s Lecturing, at least on some Points.

Dr. H. began by saying I had got into an unpleasant Situation that of hearing the Complaints of two Persons who could not agree; that he was sorry to give me the Trouble of hearing his, but it was in some degree necessary as he suppos'd I heard the others. At the Conclusion I told him, I should think it no Trouble to hear their Complaints if I could be of the least Use in accommodating their Differences; but since that was not likely, I could only wish as I had a Regard for both, that they would go on to the End of their Term as quietly as possible, since that would be most to the Credit of both. That I had given and should give this Advice to Mr. H. which I hoped he would follow.

Some other Particulars of Complaint were mention'd, such as Mr. H's calling the House his, and threatning to break into it. Proposing to *make Preparations* of two Fetus Heads which Dr. H. had *already prepar'd.*

The Lectures were of little importance now to Dr. H. But he had built a House for them, and must either continue them or lose the Expence, unless he let the House. I thought he was about to intimate, that if Mr. H. had behav'd well, he might have let it to him, but he did not go so far.

To James Read[1]   Extract[2]: Historical Society of Pennsylvania

[Before August 1, 1771[3]]
The most friendly Advice I can give you, is, to begin paying the Debt immediately, tho' in ever so small Sums.[4] This will show an honest Disposition, and may in time compleat the whole. If you would stand fair in the Opinion of your Friends, and cannot pay the Principal, pay at least the Interest as it arises.

From John Whitehurst[5]   ALS: American Philosophical Society

Dear Sir   Derby 1 Augt. 1771
I received your favour, and have sent the Account of the Clocks underneath. The other Clock which you was so kind to order is in hand and will soon be compleated.

I found it necessary to depart from Mr. Fergusons Plans, for the sake of greater simplicity. The moons southing, and time of high water, ought to be as visible as the time pointed out by the Indixes. I believe you will agree with me in this alteration. I consulted Mr. Ferguson before I alterd his Designs.[6] I wish you much

1. BF's old friend and neighbor, who before he embarked on a legal career had been a bookseller. See above, III, 39 n.
2. Read quoted the extract in a letter to an unknown correspondent, probably Thomas Wharton, of Sept. 10, 1771.
3. Read remarked in his letter that he had already answered BF, and he could scarcely have had time to do so unless BF had written him in July or earlier.
4. The by now notorious debt to William Strahan, which Read had acquired in 1748 and never did repay. See above, III, 316 and later references; J. Bennett Nolan, *Printer Strahan's Book Account: a Colonial Controversy* (Reading, Pa., 1939).
5. See his letter to BF above, July 25.
6. For James Ferguson (1710–76), portrait-painter, astronomer, teacher, and inventor of scientific instruments, see the *DNB*. Just as Whitehurst changed his design for the clocks, so Ferguson, years before, had changed BF's design; see above, VIII, 216–19. The description of a clock similar to White-

pleasure in your Excursion,[7] and am Sir, your most Obedient
Servant JOHN WHITEHURST

To two small Clocks at 30s. each	£3 os. od.
Box	1s. 6d.
	£3 1s. 6d.

Addressed: To / Doctr Benj. Franklin / Craven Street the Strand /
London

From William Franklin ALS: American Philosophical Society

Honoured Father Burlington Augst. 3d. 1771
I am just return'd from Philadelphia, where I have been for
some Days with Betsy, in order to see her Brother Downes and
his Wife and Daughter who arrived there last Sunday from Barbados. He is in a very bad State of Health, and we have brought
him Home with us that he might be out of the Heat of Philada.[8]
On my Return I found your Letter of the 5th. of June, which gave
me the Pleasure to hear you were return'd safe from your Tour
through the manufactoring Towns. As the last Post which has any
Chance of reaching the Packet has pass'd by, I send this by the
Stage to New York just to let you know that we are well, and that
Sally tells me she is resolved, if her Husband will consent to take
her, to accompany him to England this Fall, where he is going on
Business.[9] I could wish, if she should, that my Mother had some
clever Body to take care of her in Sally's Absence; as her Memory
has failed her much, and she becomes every Day more and more
unfit to be left alone. Besides I think the Expence of such a Voyage,
especially if they stay the Winter in London, will be more than
will suit with Mr. B's present Circumstances, or be consistent with
Justice to his Creditors.

---

hurst's appeared in Ferguson's *Select Mechanical Exercises...* (2nd ed.,
London, 1778), pp. 11–19.
7. To Ireland and Scotland. The trip began on Aug. 25.
8. The Rev. Jonathan Downes, former fellow of St. John's College, Cambridge, and rector of St. Peter's Church, Barbados, was at death's door; he
lived only until Oct. 14. *Pa. Chron.*, Oct. 28–Nov. 4, 1771. For further light
on the Downes family see Vernon O. Stumpf, "Who Was Elizabeth Downes
Franklin?," *PMHB*, XCIV (1970), 533–4.
9. He apparently did not consent, for Sally stayed in Philadelphia.

Enclosed is a Piece just published (and said to be written) by Goddard, with a View of prejudicing Mr. Galloway at the next Election.[1] Betsy joins in Duty with Your ever dutiful Son

WM: FRANKLIN

Addressed: To / Benjamin Franklin, Esqr., / Depy. Postmaster General of N. America / Craven Street / London / Via New York per Packet / On His Majesty's Service

From Jonathan Williams, Sr.

ALS: American Philosophical Society

Honoured Sir   Boston augt 5th. 1771
I now enclose you the first per Exchange for one Hundred Pounds Sterling Drawn by Thos. Symmes on Messrs. Gardoqué & Sons merchants in Bilboa, payable in London, I Remitted you two hundred and Ninty Pounds before this in the Whole £390 to Reimburse the money you Were So Good to advance my Sons.[2] I Shall allways Retain a greatfull Sence of your Generosity and kindness to them.

We are all well, Aunt Mecom Dined With us a few Days ago With a Large Company Mr. Foxcroft and his Lady &c. We are uncertain Whether our Sons and Brother are in England, Soposing Jona. to be Gon to the East Indies and Josiah and his Uncle Imbarkd for Boston[3] if thay Should be Still in England We Desire to

1. In 1769 William Goddard had broken with Galloway, his former patron, over the management and policy of the *Pa. Chron.*, and had attacked him in print. A second attack came on July 29, 1771, in *A True and Faithful Narrative...* (Philadelphia, 1771), which was WF's enclosure. A third attack in September led the Assembly to censure Goddard, who was already in jail for debt. Ward L. Miner, *William Goddard, Newspaperman* (Durham, N.C., 1962), pp. 96–103; Benjamin H. Newcomb, *Franklin and Galloway: a Political Partnership* (New Haven and London, 1972), pp. 214–20. BF glanced at the *Narrative* and then lighted the fire with it: to WF below, Jan. 30, 1772.

2. For BF's loans and the earlier payment see BF to Williams above, March 5, and the latter's reply on July 12. Thomas Symmes was a Boston merchant; for the Gardoquis, who later furnished valuable financial aid to America during the War of Independence, see Samuel Flagg Bemis, *The Diplomacy of the American Revolution* (New York, [1935]), p. 91.

3. He could not have been more mistaken. Jonathan had embarked for Boston; Josiah stayed until the following spring, and their uncle John for much longer.

be kindly Rememberd to them, our Compliments to Mrs. Stevenson &c. My Wife and Children Joine in Love and Duty With your Dutyfull Nephew and Humble Servant   JONA WILLIAMS
NB The enclosd Letter of advice Please to forward. J.
Addressed: To / Doctr Benjamin Franklin / at Mrs Stivensons in Cravin Street / London / per Capt Cauzeno

From Alexander Colden   ALS: American Philosophical Society

Dear Sir   General Post Office New York Augt 6th 1771
The 2d of last Month I wrote you by the Packet in Answer to yours of the first of May. I have since made strict search for Mr. Jessers letter but can't find it.[4]
By order of Mr. Foxcroft Inclosed I send you the second set o those Bills, he sent last Packet. Mr. Foxcroft and Lady are both at Boston and in good health the last Letter [*torn:* I had from?] him.
By the Papers you will [*torn:* see that our?] New Governor Mr. Tryon is Arrived and taken the Administration of the Government upon him. His Aimable Disposition leaves no room to doubt we will be happy in having so worthy a Gentleman for our Governor. Lord Dunmore has sent his servants and Baggage to Virginia. When he goes to that Government not known.[5] His Lordship at present is on a Tour to Lake Champlain.
The Lt. Governor Mrs. Colden and Familly [*torn:* join?] in Sincere Compliments with Dear Sir Your Very Obedient Most humble Servant   ALEXR COLDEN

From W[illiam] Small[6]   ALS: Library of Congress

Dear Sir,   Birmingham 10. Aug. 1771
The reason of your having no sooner received the Quotation

4. See Colden's earlier letter of July 2.
5. Governors were being shifted in bewildering fashion, one from New York to Virginia and the other from North Carolina to New York. In his former governorship Tryon had just suppressed the Regulators; in his new one he was about to confront the Green Mountain Boys. See Drage to BF above, March 2; *N.Y. Col. Docs.*, VIII, 252, 272–7.
6. The Birmingham scientist, for whom see above, XI, 480 n.

from Celsus is, that I wished to employ my very first leisure in looking in several other ancient books for passages to the same purpose, and to send you all together. But Mr. Keir[7] having told me of your desire to see that immediately, you have it almost alone.

In the article de Tabe in his third book, treating of the cure He says "cavendae *destillationes,* ne, si quid cura levarit, exasperent; *ob idem vitanda cruditas,* simulque et Sol, et frigus." Here indigestion seems to be reckoned the principal cause. If you have not attended to that particular before, you may be surprized to find Sunshine among the causes of colds, but such is the doctrine of all the Ancients. A passage about the instruments of cure in coughs may perhaps amuse you "Utilis etiam in omni tussi est peregrinatio, navigatio longa, loca maritima, *natationes.*"[8]

From several things in Zenophon and in Plato, the prevailing opinion in their time seems to have been that what we now commonly call colds and catarrhs arose almost solely from excess and indolence. On this account Zenophon says that in Persia in the days of Cyrus, to spit or to blow a nose was infamous. Plato often commends simple spare diet, but in one place, he says it prevents all catarrhs. Whether he means precisely what we call catarrhs however, in that passage, may be doubted.

I do not recollect any absolutely express testimony in your favor from Hippocrates. Mucus (of the Nose) and Saliva he judges to be signs of repletion, and he maintains that persons who drink and eat sparingly are free from diseases occasioned by moisture. Abundance may be found in Galen to your purpose. A modern author, who ought to have understood this subject, for he has written so great a book about catarrhs that you had better have 20 colds than read it, is entirely of your opinion. Illa, illa, inquam cibi potusque abundanter citat catarrhos. Eosdem abigat frugalitas et

7. In all likelihood James Keir (1735–1820), a former army officer who was becoming a distinguished chemist. *DNB*. Although no correspondence between him and BF is extant, the two had a mutual acquaintance in Matthew Boulton, and may well have met during BF's recent visit to Birmingham.

8. Aulus Cornelius Celsus wrote his influential treatise on medicine in the reign of Tiberius. The most convenient modern edition is in the Loeb Classical Library: *Celsus De Medicina with an English Translation by W. G. Spencer* (3 vols., Cambridge, Mass., and London, 1935–38), where the two passages that Small quotes are I, 328 and 390 respectively.

labor. ... Ut ex luxu et otio nascuntur catarrhi, ita horum mede-
cina est in sobrietate, in continentia, in exercitationibus corporis,
in mentis tranquillitate. Quotusquisque vero haec praecepta, has
leges vivendi custodit? Homo frugi est rara avis, &c. *Hinc* nemo
mortalium fere est sine catarrhis.[9]

Mr. Boulton will soon present you with one of the boxes with
invisible Hinges. He has astonished our rural philosophers exceedingly by calming the waves a la Franklin.[1]

I am trying some experiments in relation to the improvement of
telescopes. Should they answer you shall hear of them.

I beg you will make my most respectful Compliments to the
fellow travellers who were with you here,[2] and believe me to be
with the highest regard Dear Sir Your much obliged and most
obedient Servant   W. SMALL

Endorsed: From Dr Small on Catching Cold

To Anna Mordaunt Shipley[3]   ALS: Yale University Library

It has been well said of this letter that "nothing in all Franklin's writings
better reveals why he was always such a favorite with young people."[4]

Dear Madam,   London, Aug. 12. [*i.e.*, 13[5]] 1771

This is just to let you know that we arriv'd safe and well in Marl-
borough Street about Six, where I deliver'd up my Charge.[6]

9. BF has here added a note: "the book upon the Catarhs is probably that of
Schneiderus consisting of 4 volumes in quarto." He was referring to Conrad
Victor Schneider, *Liber primus (-quintus) de catarrhis...* (6 pts., Wittenberg,
1660–62). We should, for our part, prefer to have twenty colds than to try to
locate the quotation.

1. For Matthew Boulton see above, p. 116 n. He presumably calmed the
waves with oil, repeating the experiment that BF had described to Pringle
above, x, 158–60.

2. John Canton, Dr. Ingenhousz, and Jonathan Williams, Jr.

3. The Bishop's wife; see the headnote on BF to Shipley above, June 24.

4. Leonard W. Labaree and Whitfield J. Bell, Jr., eds., *Mr. Franklin: a
Selection from His Personal Letters* (New Haven and London, 1956), p. 22.

5. BF clearly misdated his letter. Mrs. Shipley had insisted on his staying at
Twyford through the 12th, because that was his grandson's birthday; see BF
to DF below, Aug. 14.

6. Catherine (Kitty) Shipley, who was about eleven at the time and was returning to school in London; see the note on her below.

The above seems too short for a Letter; so I will lengthen it by
a little Account of our Journey. The first Stage we were rather
pensive. I tried several Topics of Conversation, but none of them
would hold. But after Breakfast, we began to recover Spirits, and
had a good deal of Chat. Will you hear some of it? We talk'd of
her Brother, and she wish'd he was married.[7] And don't you wish
your Sisters married too? Yes. All but Emily; I would not have her
married. Why? Because I can't spare her, I can't part with her.[8]
The rest may marry as soon as they please, so they do but get good
Husbands. We then took upon us to consider for 'em what sort of
Husbands would be fittest for every one of them. We began with
Georgiana.[9] She thought a Country Gentleman, that lov'd Travelling and would take her with him, that lov'd Books and would
hear her read to him; I added, that had a good Estate and was a
Member of Parliament and lov'd to see an Experiment now and
then. This she agreed to; so we set him down for Georgiana, and
went on to Betsy. Betsy, says I, seems of a sweet mild Temper, and
if we should give her a Country Squire, and he should happen to
be of a rough, passionate Turn, and be angry now and then, it
might break her Heart. O, none of 'em must be so; for then they
would not be good Husbands. To make sure of this Point, however, for Betsey, shall we give her a Bishop? O no, that won't do.
They all declare against the Church, and against the Army; not
one of them will marry either a Clergyman or an Officer; that they
are resolv'd upon. What can be their reason for that? Why you
know, that when a Clergyman or an Officer dies, the Income goes
with 'em; and then what is there to maintain the Family? there's

7. For William D. Shipley (1745–1826), who had just taken his M.A. at
Oxford, and who did not marry until 1777, see the *DNB*.
8. She was soon forced to. Amelia or Emily (1750–1800) was the first to
marry, in 1774; for her husband, William Sloper, a retired army officer who
later became an M.P., see Namier and Brooke, *House of Commons*, III, 445–6.
9. Georgiana (1756–1806), named after her cousin the Duchess of Devonshire, grew up to be the most colorful member of the family. She was both a
beauty and an excellent conversationalist, versed in modern languages and
the classics, and she studied painting under Sir Joshua Reynolds. Her husband, whom she married in 1784 much against her father's will, was a far cry
from the one Kitty and BF had imagined for her. Francis Hare-Naylor, an
impecunious author, belonged to the Duchess's circle; she provided him with
an annuity, on which the couple spent most of the rest of their lives abroad.
DNB under Hare-Naylor.

the Point. Then suppose we give her a good, honest, sensible City Merchant, who will love her dearly and is very rich? I don't know but that may do.[1] We proceeded to Emily, her dear Emily, I was afraid we should hardly find any thing good enough for Emily; but at last, after first settling that, if she did marry, Kitty was to live a good deal with her; we agreed that as Emily was very handsome we might expect an Earl for her: So having fix'd her, as I thought, a Countess, we went on to Anna-Maria. She, says Kitty, should have a rich Man that has a large Family and a great many things to take care of; for she is very good at managing, helps my Mama very much, can look over Bills, and order all sorts of Family Business. Very well; and as there is a Grace and Dignity in her Manner that would become the Station, what do you think of giving her a Duke? O no! I'll have the Duke for Emily. You may give the Earl to Anna-Maria if you please: But Emily shall have the Duke. I contested this Matter some time; but at length was forc'd to give up the point, leave Emily in Possession of the Duke, and content myself with the Earl for Anna Maria.[2] And now what shall we do for Kitty? We have forgot her, all this Time. Well, and what will you do for her? I suppose that tho' the rest have resolv'd against the Army, she may not yet have made so rash a Resolution. Yes, but she has: Unless, now, an old one, an old General that has done fighting, and is rich, such a one as General Rufane; I like him a good deal; You must know I like an old Man, indeed I do: And some how or other all the old Men take to me, all that come to our House like me better than my other Sisters: I go to 'em and ask 'em how they do, and they like it mightily; and the Maids take notice of it, and say when they see an old Man come, there's a Friend of yours, Miss Kitty. But then as you like an old

1. Betsy (1754–96) was even more fastidious than they were for her: she died a spinster. *Gent. Mag.*, LXVI (1796), 85.

2. Emily settled for a retired army officer, as already mentioned; she "has done much better for herself," Kitty wrote BF years later, "than if she had married the Duke we allotted to her on our journey." Sept. 30, 1785 (APS). Anna Maria (1748–1829) found a husband in 1783 who became more famous than most earls. William Jones (1746–94), a member of the Duchess of Devonshire's circle like Hare-Naylor, was both a lawyer and one of the most brilliant linguists and scholars of his day. Just before his marriage he was knighted and named a judge of the high court in Calcutta, where he rendered enormous service in codifying and explaining the Indian legal system. *DNB.*

General, hadn't you better take him while he's a young Officer, and let him grow old upon your Hands, because then, you'll like him better and better every Year as he grows older and older. No, that won't do. He must be an old Man of 70 or 80, and take me when I am about 30: And then you know I may be a rich young Widow.[3] We din'd at Staines, she was Mrs. Shipley, cut up the Chicken pretty handily (with a little Direction) and help'd me in a very womanly Manner. Now, says she, when I commended her, my Father never likes to see me or Georgiana carve, because we do it, he says, so badly: But how should we learn if we never try? We drank good Papa and Mama's Health, and the Health's of the Dutchess, the Countess, the Merchant's Lady, the Country Gentlewoman, and our Welsh Brother. This brought their Affairs again under Consideration. I doubt, says she, we have not done right for Betsey. I don't think a Merchant will do for her. She is much inclin'd to be a fine Gentlewoman; and is indeed already more of the fine Gentlewoman, I think, than any of my other Sisters; and therefore she shall be a Vice Countess.

Thus we chatted on, and she was very entertaining quite to Town.

I have now made my Letter as much too long as it was at first too short. The Bishop would think it too trifling, therefore don't show it him. I am afraid too that you will think it so, and have a good mind not to send it. Only it tells you Kitty is well at School, and for that I let it go. My Love to the whole amiable Family, best Respects to the Bishop, and 1000 Thanks for all your Kindnesses, and for the happy Days I enjoy'd at Twyford. With the greatest Esteem and Respect, I am, Madam, Your most obedient humble Servant   B FRANKLIN

3. Lieut. Gen. Rufane, Colonel of the Sixth Regiment of Foot, failed Kitty by not living long enough; he died in 1773. John W. Fortescue, ed., *The Correspondence of King George the Third*. . . (6 vols., London, 1927–28), II, 454. Kitty's badinage recalls the father in *The Beggars' Opera* who tells his newly-wed daughter that "the comfortable state of widowhood is the only hope that keeps up a wife's spirits." But Kitty was never a wife, let alone a widow: born in 1759, she lived unmarried to the ripe age of eighty-one. *Gent. Mag.*, new ser., XIII (1840), 551. She and Georgiana continued to correspond with BF. For further references to the family see Norman Tucker, "Bodrhyddan and the Families of Conwy, Shipley-Conwy and Rowley-Conwy...," Flintshire Hist. Soc. *Jour.*, XX (1962), 8–18, 24–5; Garland Cannon, ed., *Letters of Sir William Jones* (2 vols., Oxford, 1970), *passim*.

From Jonathan Shipley

ALS: American Philosophical Society

Dear Sir   Twyford Aug: 13th [1771]

I have sent You my Letters to the Primate and Mr. Jackson,[4] which I will beg the favour of You to get conveyd to them even if You should not have an opportunity of calling upon them. Mrs. Shipley and her Daughters join with me in much more than Compliments, and in most sincerely regretting the Loss of You. We join too in wishing that after your Return it may not be inconvenient either to spend some leisure Days at Twyford, or to retire thither to carry on some work of closer Application. It concerns the publick Interest that your Treatise on Colds should not be deferr'd too long.[5]

We return our thanks for taking the Charge of your Fellow Traveller, which must have been no small Exercise of your Care and Patience. If her Spirits were not dampd by the melancholy Idea of returning to School, I may presume You did not want Conversation. I have learnt from her Sister Georgiana that having overheard something of a haunted House at Hinton She had the Sauciness to conceive a Plot of fishing out the whole Secret from You by pretending to know it. How did She succeed?[6] I am, Dear Sir, Your obligd and affectionate humble Servant   J. St. Asaph

4. The first letter was addressed to Richard Robinson (1709–94), Archbishop of Armagh and Primate of Ireland, for whom see the *DNB*. Jackson we cannot identify. He might have been Charles Jackson, who was then Dean of Christ Church, Dublin, and Bishop of Kildare, except that Shipley here, and BF in other letters, refer to him always as "Mr."

5. BF was perhaps considering a revision of his early essay on colds (above, I, 252–4); his interest had certainly revived, for the subject often appears in his correspondence with Rush, LeRoy, and Barbeu-Dubourg in the next two years. But the most he ever did, apparently, was to compile lengthy notes on ways of catching cold and avoiding it. Smyth assigns the notes to 1773 (*Writings*, VI, 62–77); they may have been written earlier, but scarcely during this first visit to Twyford, when BF was composing the first part of his *Autobiography*.

6. BF's description in the preceding document of his trip to London with young Kitty Shipley does not mention her curiosity about the house at Hinton Ampner, near Twyford; it had an evil reputation for ghosts. *Cassell's Gazetteer of Great Britain and Ireland* (6 vols., London, 1893–98), III, 256.

To Deborah Franklin

AL (incomplete): American Philosophical Society

My dear Child,   London, Augt. 14. 1771

I received yours of June 29. per Packet. I am glad to hear of all your Welfares, and that the Pictures, &c. were safe arrived.[7] You do not tell me who mounted the great one, nor where you have hung it up. Let me know whether Dr. Bond likes the new one better than the old one; if so, the old one is to be return'd hither to Mr. Wilson, the Painter.[8] You may keep the Frame, as it may be wanted for some other Picture there.

I wrote to you the Beginning of last Month to go per Capt. Falconer, and have since been in the Country, am just come to town, and find him still here, and the Letters not gone. He goes however next Saturday. I had written to many of my Friends by him. I spent three Weeks in Hampshire at my Friend the Bishop of St. Asaph's.[9] The Bishop's Lady knows what Children and Grandchildren I have, their Ages, &c. So when I was to come away on Monday the 12th. in the Morning, she insisted on my staying that one Day longer that we might together keep my Grandson's Birthday. At Dinner, among other nice Things, we had a Floating Island, which they always particularly have on the Birth Days of any of their own Six Children; who were all but one at Table, where there was also a Clergyman's Widow now above 100 Years old. The chief Toast of the Day was Master Benjamin Bache, which the venerable old Lady began in a Bumper of Mountain.[1] The Bishop's Lady politely added, *and that he may be* as good *a Man as his Grand-*

7. Probably the pictures that BF mentioned but did not describe in his letter to WF above, April 20.

8. He had evidently not yet received Bond's letter above, July 6. The old portrait, the second of two by Benjamin Wilson, was a replica of one that BF had ordered for himself in 1759. It displeased him when he saw it on his return to Philadelphia, because of a crackle in the paint, and when he was back in London he said as much to the artist. Wilson agreed to do another gratis if the old one was returned to him. Bond received this new portrait in the summer of 1771; BF had some difficulty in getting the other back, but eventually succeeded. See Charles C. Sellers, *Benjamin Franklin in Portraiture* (New Haven and London, 1962), pp. 410–11.

9. In two visits, one in late June and the other in early August; during the second he began to write his *Autobiography*.

1. The widow was possibly the Mrs. Rickets mentioned in BF to Shipley below, Aug. 15. Mountain is a Malaga wine made of white grapes.

father. I said I hop'd he would be *much better*. The Bishop, still more complaisant than his Lady, said, We will compound the Matter; and be contented if he should not prove *quite so good*. This Chitchat is to yourself only, in return for some of yours about your Grandson, and must only be read to Sally, and not spoken of to any body else; for you know how People add and alter silly Stories that they hear, and make them appear ten times more silly. Just while I am writing the Post brings me the enclos'd from the good Bishop, with some Letters of Recommendation for Ireland,[2] to see which Country I am to set out next Week with my old Friend and Fellow-Traveller Counsellor Jackson.[3] We expect to be absent a Month or Six Weeks. The Bishop's youngest Daughter, mention'd in his Letter is about 11 Years of Age, and came up with me in the Post Chaise to go to her School.[4] Capt. Osborne is not yet arrived here, but is every day expected.[5] I hope he will come before I set out, that I may hear from you by him. I desire you will push the Enquiry after the Lancaster Dutchman, and not let [it] sleep and be forgotten.[6] I send you per Capt. Falconer a Box of Looking Glasses for the Closet Doors. [*The final paragraph is torn vertically; the few remaining words of each line give no clue to the subject.*]

To John Canton   ALS: the Royal Society

Dear Sir,   Augt. 15. 71
    I have just received the enclos'd from Dr. Priestly. And as it contains an Account of a new Discovery of his, which is very curious, and, if it holds, will open a new Field of Knowledge, I send it to you immediately.[7] Please to communicate it to Dr. Price

2. See the preceding document.

3. See Richard Jackson's note above, under July 27, suggesting that BF join him on the trip.

4. See BF to Mrs. Shipley above, Aug. 13.

5. The arrival of Peter Osborne, master of the *Pa. Packet*, was noted in *Lloyd's Evening Post*, Aug. 19–21.

6. Possibly a debt, mentioned in DF's missing letter of June 29, left over from the complicated affairs of Samuel Holland, BF's former journeyman and printer for a time of the *Lancastersche Zeitung*, who had owed him £25 in 1756. See above, IV, 506–8; V, 198–9. But we cannot guess why this old obligation should have come to life after so many years.

7. The enclosure, which has not survived, was Priestley's account of his experiments on restoring air that had been breathed or otherwise rendered

when he returns. I am just about taking a Trip for a few Weeks to Ireland. I hope I shall find you well at my Return. I am, with great Esteem, Dear Sir, Your most obedient humble Servant

B FRANKLIN

Addressed: To / Mr Canton / at the Academy / Spital Square / Bps. Gate Street

To Jonathan Shipley[8]   ALS: Yale University Library

My dear Lord,   London, Augt. 15. 1771

Many Thanks for your Letters to the Primate and Mr. Jackson; which I shall take care to forward if I should happen not to have an Opportunity of delivering them personally.

Your repeated kind Invitations are extreamly obliging. The Enjoyment of your Lordship's Conversation, good Mrs. Shipley's kind Care of me sick and well, and the ever-pleasing Countenances of the whole amiable Family towards me, make me always very happy when I am with you. But I must not abuse so much Goodness, by engrossing it. You have many other Friends, and I ought to be contented with my Turn.

I own that I do flatter my self that my Pamphlet upon Colds may be of some Use. If I can persuade People not to be afraid of their real Friend *Fresh Air*, and can put them more upon their guard against those insidious Enemies, *full Living* and *Indolence*, I imagine they may be somewhat happier and more healthy.

You guess'd rightly, that after my Fellow-Traveller had recover'd her Spirits, we did not want Conversation. The Story of the Noises at Hinton she did introduce, by intimating that having by Accident heard a Part, it had been thought proper to tell her

noxious with carbon dioxide, experiments that began his investigation of the photosynthetic process. See Schofield, *Scientific Autobiography*, pp. 86–7, and the headnote on BF to Priestley below, under the end of July, 1772. The account became part of Priestley's "Observations on Different Kinds of Air," *Phil. Trans.*, LXII (1772), 147–264, which finally won him the Royal Society's Copley Medal in 1773. See Douglas McKie, "Joseph Priestley and the Copley Medal," *Ambix*, IX (1961), 1–22; Henry Guerlac, "Joseph Priestley's First Papers on Gases and Their Reception in France," *Jour. of the History of Medicine and Allied Sciences*, XII (1957), 1–12.

8. BF is replying to Shipley's letter above, Aug. 13, which explains almost everything mentioned in this letter.

the whole; "but, says she, I do not believe any such thing, not a word of it; and I wonder that so sensible a Woman as Mrs. Rickets can be in the least uneasy about it." I had not the smallest Suspicion of any Plot to draw the Story from me; and this Declaration, of her not at all believing any such things, was very proper to put me off my Guard, and induce me to talk freely on any of the Circumstances; so that I might have fallen into the Trap, if her *knowing the whole already* had not made me think it useless to mention any of them. I assure you she gave me no kind of Trouble on the Journey, behav'd in the most agreable womanly Manner all the Way, and was very entertaining.

I purpose to set out on Tuesday next for Ireland.[9] I wish all kinds of Happiness to you all, being with the sincerest Esteem and Veneration for your Lordship, and much *Affection* (if that Word is permissible) for Mrs. Shipley, Your most obliged humble Servant

B FRANKLIN

Bishop of St. Asaph

To Deborah Franklin   ALS: American Philosophical Society

My dear Child,   London, Aug. 17. 1771
I wrote to you some time since to go by Capt. Falconer, but he is still here. I have since written to you per Packet. And now write this Line to let you know I continue pretty well, but find more Exercise necessary to preserve my Health, and therefore am about to make the Tour of Ireland with my old Friend Mr. Jackson,[1] purposing to return thro' Scotland, and to be in London [once?] again, God willing, before the Parliament meets, that is, in about Six Weeks.

I have received your kind Letters of June the 29th. and July 6. I would not have you send me the Receipts for the Money you pay, as they can be of no Use here, and may possibly be lost. But it would be agreable to me to see from time to time an Account of the considerable Sums.[2]

9. *I.e.*, Aug. 20. BF and Jackson did not actually leave until the 25th.
1. See BF to DF above, Aug. 14.
2. The disappearance of DF's two letters is particularly unfortunate, because in one or both she appears to have responded to BF's strictures on her extravagance in his letter above, May 1.

I am glad the little Fellow continues well, and that Sally is so careful to be with him out of Town during the Hot Weather. I consider her as nursing him for me, and shall pay her handsomely for her Trouble when I return.

I receiv'd the enclos'd Letters lately from our Relations by Marriage still remaining at Birmingham. Mr. Tyler who is mention'd in them brought them to me. He has concluded to go over and settle in Philadelphia, and I have given him a Letter of Introduction to you.[3]

I have been three Weeks at my Friend the Bishop's,[4] and he has made me promise to spend the Christmas Holidays with him; which I shall do if I live and am well. My Love to all enquiring Friends, from Your affectionate Husband   B FRANKLIN

Addressed: To / Mrs Franklin / at / Philadelphia / per favour of / Mr Foxcroft.

To Jonathan Shipley   ALS: Yale University Library

My Lord,   London, Augt. 19. 1771.
By the Southampton Coach, I have sent your Lordship the Book of State Trials, which would have been sent sooner but that I hoped to send the Northumberland Book with it. I have search'd and enquir'd among my Friends for that Book, and cannot find it.[5] I suppose I have lent it, and do not yet recollect to whom.

3. For DF's many relatives in Birmingham and elsewhere see above, VIII, 138–46. The Tyler, or Tiler, children are not named there; the one who brought the letters to BF was John, who spelled the name Tyler. He won BF's approval, moved to Philadelphia, became an iron-manufacturer, and supplied arms to American troops during the War of Independence. See BF to DF below, Jan. 28, 1772; Tyler to BF, June 6, 1787 (APS); Smyth, *Writings,* IX, 549.

4. See BF to DF above, Aug. 14.

5. No one-volume collection of state trials is recorded before 1771, but BF may have sent either a single volume of any of a number of multi-volume collections, or a pamphlet from the lot he had recently bought (see BF to Samuel Franklin above, July 12); Mr. Edwin Wolf, II, informs us that one of the pamphlets contained accounts of treason trials. The "Northumberland Book" was doubtless a volume of John Wallis, *The Natural History and Antiquities of Northumberland. . .* (2 vols., London, 1769).

I din'd on Sunday last at Sir John Pringle's with Messrs. Banks and Solander, and learnt some farther particulars. The People of Otahitee (Georges Island) are civilized in a great degree, and live under a regular feudal Government, a supreme Lord or King, Barons holding Districts under him, but with Power of making War on each other: Farmholders under the Barons; and an Order of Working People Servants to the Farmholders.[6] They believe a supreme God, and inferior Gods, all Spirits, with a celestial Government similar to their own. They have some Ceremonies of Adoration, but seldom used. They erect Temples for their Gods; but they are small and stuck up on a Pole in the Fields, partly to honour the Gods, and partly for their Convenience to lodge in when they happen to come down among Men: a little Temple being, they say, as commodious for a Spirit as a large one. Their Morals are very imperfect, as they do not reckon Chastity among the Virtues, nor Theft among the Vices.[7] They have Honours and Distinctions belonging to different Ranks, but these are paid to a Father no longer when he has a Son born, they are afterwards paid only to that Son; and this keeps some from marrying who are unwilling to lose their Rank, and occasions others to kill their Children that they may resume it. They had no Idea of Kissing with the Lips, it was quite a Novelty to them, tho' they lik'd it when they were taught it. Their affectionate and respectful Salutation is bringing their Noses near each other's Mouths and snuffing up one another's Breath. Their Account of the Creation is, that the Great Spirit first begot the Waters, then he begot the Earth and threw it, a great Mass, into the Waters; then not liking to see it all in one place, and a great Part of the Waters without any of it, he fastned a strong Cord to it, and drew it so swiftly through the

6. For Sir Joseph Banks (1743–1820), naturalist and president of the Royal Society, and Daniel Solander (1732–82), Swedish-born botanist, see the *DNB*. Both men had been with James Cook on the *Endeavour*; they had observed the transit of Venus from Tahiti (Otahitee or Georges Island), had explored the coasts of Australia and New Zealand, and had reached home only a month before. London was agog with news of their discoveries.

7. These characteristics are amply borne out in Cook's description of the natives, for which see John C. Beaglehole, ed., *The Journals of Captain James Cook on His Voyages of Discovery* (3 vols. in 4, Cambridge, 1955–67), I, 74–139.

Waters that many of the loose Parts broke off from it and remain in the Sea, being the Islands they are acquainted with. They believe the great Mass is still in being somewhere, tho' they know not where; and they ask'd our People if they did not come from it. They have a considerable Knowledge of the Stars, sail by them, and make Voyages of three Months westward among the Islands. Notwithstanding all the Advantages our People could show we had from our Arts, &c. they were of Opinion after much Consideration that their Condition was preferable to ours.

The Inhabitants of New Zealand were found to be a brave and sensible People, and seem'd to have a fine Country.[8] The Inhabitants of New Holland[9] seem'd to our People a stupid Race, for they would accept none of our Presents. Whatever we gave them, they would look at a while, then lay it down and walk away. Finding 4 Children in a Hut on one Part of the Coast, and seeing some People at a distance who were shy and would not be spoke with, we adorn'd the Children with Ribbands and Beads, and left with them a Number of little Trinkets and some useful Things; then retiring to a Distance, gave Opportunity to the People to fetch away their Children, supposing the Gifts might conciliate them: But coming afterwards to the Hut, we found all we had left, the Finery we had put upon the Children among the Rest. We call this Stupidity. But if we were dispos'd to compliment them, we might say, Behold a Nation of Philosophers! such as him whom we celebrate for saying as he went thro' a Fair, *How many things there are in the World that I don't want!*[1]

Please to present my best Respects to good Mrs. Shipley. Her kind Letter has reliev'd me from an Uneasiness I was under lest by some *Sottise* or other in my long hasty scrawl I might have given Offence. My Love to all the young Ladies accompanies the sincere and great Esteem and Respect with which I am, My Lord,

8. The returning explorers seem to have been more deeply impressed by the virtues of the New Zealanders than of any other people they encountered. A movement began, perhaps inspired by this dinner party at Sir John's, to bring the islanders the benefits of British civilization; and BF was involved in appealing to the public for funds. See below, Aug. 29.

9. The name that the Dutch had given to Australia during their explorations a century before.

1. A saying attributed to Socrates. Cook said much the same thing about the natives in more humdrum words: Beaglehole, *op. cit.*, I, 399.

Your Lordship's most obedient and most humble Servant

B FRANKLIN

Our Journey is postpon'd to Saturday next.

William Hunter's Stipulations in Regard to William Hewson[2]

AD: extract from Franklin to William Hunter, October 30, 1772, Royal College of Surgeons

[Aug. 23, 1771[3]]

Dr. Hunter expects Mr. Hewson should go on with his Business as usual during the Remainder of the Term they are to continue together; and during that time should make Preparations, at Dr. Hunter's Expence, such as the Dr. should direct to be made, and others, so that those directed are not neglected or omitted: That all the Preparations are to be the Doctor's sole Property, and at his absolute Disposal, so that if he afterwards should give any of them to any Person (which he would not be understood to promise) such Gift is to be considered as the sole Effect of his Good-will.[4]

From Samuel Cooper

ALS (draft): British Museum

Dear Sir,   Boston 23. Aug—71

Tho I wrote you not long since by Mr. Lane,[5] yet Commodore

2. See Hunter's complaints against Hewson above, under the end of July.

3. So dated in the letter from which the extract is taken. The extract itself is from a memorandum, now lost, that BF made of an interview with Hunter.

4. This provision led to misunderstanding. Hewson thought he would be permitted to keep the anatomical preparations that he was making for his own course of lectures, and was chagrined when Hunter refused the permission. See Polly's sketch of the episode in her memoir of her husband: Thomas J. Pettigrew, *Memoirs of the Life and Writings of the Late John Coakley Lettsom*... (3 vols., London, 1817), I, 143–4 of second pagination. Hunter subsequently relented to the point of giving some preparations to BF, who immediately passed them on to Hewson. BF to Hunter below, Oct. 30, 1772.

5. Probably John Lane, the "Son" of Lane, Son and Fraser, London merchants trading with Boston. See Wroth and Zobel, *John Adams Legal Papers*, II, 373 n, 390 n.

Gambier telling me He shall take Pleasure in bringing you a Letter; I cannot forbear mentioning the Obligations we are under to this Gentleman in his Department as Commander of the Ships station'd here. Ever attentive to the Kings Service He has enterd into no Parties; He has treated with great Humanity and Politeness all who have had any Business to transact with him; He has oblig'd the Trade in ev'ry Point consistent with his Duty as a Commander: and the Order and Tranquility He has preservd in the Squadron and the Town have been truly remarkable; I have heard the most judicious and experienc'd Gentlemen among us, and those capable of the longest Recollection, particularly our Friend Mr. Erving,[6] (who desires this may be mention'd to you) affirm, they never knew, all Circumstances consider'd, an equal Instance. Upon these Accounts his early and unexpected Departure is regretted, and He leaves Sentiments of Respect and Gratitude in the Breasts of all Parties.[7]

The Merchants have given him a public Testimony of such Sentiments in their Address, and the Town would have done the same, had not some few tho't, not rightly in my opinion, that the Services not be seperated from the Man, and that such a Step must imply some Kind of Acquiescence in the Measure of stationing a Fleet in this Port.[8] This Measure is indeed greatly and generally dis-

6. Capt. John Erving (1728–1816) was one of Boston's richest merchants and a member of the Massachusetts Council, in which he strongly opposed governmental policy: *Sibley's Harvard Graduates*, XII, 152–4.

7. Commodore Gambier, who commanded for only a year on the North American station before being replaced by Admiral Montagu, had arrived with a warm recommendation from Thomas Pownall, which made him welcome; he also had sage advice from his uncle, Samuel Mead, on how to handle the Bostonians, and in his brief stay became as much attached to them as they to him. See BF to Cooper below, Jan. 13, 1772; 6 Mass. Hist. Soc. *Coll.*, IX (1897), 208–10, 285–6, 431–2. Gambier lived long enough to become a vice-admiral, but his personal success in Boston was never matched by professional success. "I have seldom heard any seaman speak of Gambier as a good naval officer," Lord North wrote of him in 1778, "or as one who deserved to be trusted with any important command." George R. Barnes and John H. Owen, eds., *The Private Papers of John, Earl of Sandwich* . . . Navy Record Soc. *Pub.*, LXXI, 39. For BF's relations with Gambier's relatives see above, XVII, 197 n.

8. Samuel Adams, writing under a pseudonym, had complained in the press of the squadron's presence and of those who approved of it. Cushing, *Writings of Samuel Adams*, II, 203. The merchants thanked Gambier for pro-

agreable to us in a Civil and Commercial View, but no Man could have rendered such a Service more easy than Mr. Gambier. I should be glad you would upon his Arrival let it be known by the public Papers how much this Gentleman's Conduct here deserves the public Esteem; and the rather because that after putting himself to great Trouble and Expence in providing for this Station He has not been allow'd to remain upon it above one Third of the usual Time. You will excuse this Freedom upon Account of a Gentleman who has taken ev'ry Opportunity to mention you with particular Regard.

Our General Court, contrary to the particular Desire of the House in a Message is prorogu'd to Novr. and may be to a further Time.[9] I suspect among other Things a Design that the Period for which you are chosen Agent may elapse. If this should be the Case we all hope you will continue your Exertions for us as usual. There is no Doubt I think of your being rechosen the first Opportunity. Speaker Cushing shew'd me this Morning an anonymous Letter directed to him as from London in a feigned Hand, representing you as a Tool of L. H—h. Whether it originated on this or your Side the Water is uncertain.[1] It will make no Impression to your Disadvantage, but rather confirm the Opinion of your Importance, while it shews the Baseness of it's Author. I am with the greatest Regard Your obedient humble Servant   S. C.

To Dr Franklin.

To Jonathan Williams, Sr.

Reprinted from Jared Sparks, ed., *A Collection of the Familiar Letters and Miscellaneous Papers of Benjamin Franklin...* (Boston, 1833), p. 142.

Dear Cousin,   London, 25 August, 1771.
    I have received yours of July 8th and 12th, with the bills, which

tecting their property; their address and his reply appeared in the *Boston Evening-Post*, Aug. 26.

9. During the first short session of the new General Court, the House of Representatives quarreled with the Governor on a number of issues, and was prorogued in early July until the following spring.

1. Cushing received, we are convinced, a Bostonian copy of the extract from Arthur Lee's letter to Samuel Adams above, June 10.

are carried to your credit. I hope your son Jonathan may be with you by this time. Josiah is well, and sticks close to his business.[2]

I have not time to add more, being this minute setting out on a short trip to Ireland, to visit some American friends, or rather friends to America, and take that portion of exercise and fresh air, which is every year necessary to my health. My love to your spouse and children. I am sincerely Your affectionate uncle,

B. FRANKLIN

Introduction to a Plan for Benefiting the New Zealanders

Printed in [Alexander Dalrymple, *Scheme of a Voyage by Subscription to Convey the Conveniences of Life . . . to Those Remote Regions, Which Are Destitute of Them . . .* London, 1771[3]].

In July, 1771, James Cook and the crew of the *Endeavour* returned from a three-year voyage around the world. They had spent six months on the coasts of New Zealand, and had carefully examined the islands for the first time; the inhabitants, they reported, were "a brave and generous race, who are destitute of Corn, Fowls, and all Quadrupeds except Dogs."[4] A group of men, including Franklin and Alexander Dalrymple,[5] discussed this report; and the suggestion was made that the British

2. It was studying music under John Stanley; see above, XVII, 212–13. His brother Jonathan, after less than a year in England, had returned to Boston to set himself up in business.

3. The title appears in the middle of the pamphlet; the APS microfilm copy, on which our text is based, is catalogued as "[Scheme to convey the conveniences of life to New Zealand. London, 1771]." Whether the pamphlet was actually published in 1771 is not clear. It was almost immediately translated into French, and appeared in the *Ephémérides du citoyen . . .* VI, tome 2 (1772), pp. [213–]27; but BF might have sent it in MS to Barbeu-Dubourg. When Benjamin Vaughan included the English version in his *Political, Miscellaneous, and Philosophical Pieces . . .* (London, 1779), he remarked in a note (p. 37) that it had been printed and circulated "some two or three years ago." If its appearance in English was in fact delayed until the war years, public indifference to the scheme is understandable.

4. This and the following quotation, as well as the factual material in the headnote, are drawn from the pamphlet.

5. Dalrymple began his career with the East India Company and developed into an explorer and hydrographer of note. He was proposed for the command that Cook eventually received, but lost the opportunity by insisting

had a duty to bring the amenities of their civilization to the newly discovered people. Franklin took up the suggestion, and said that "He would with all his heart subscribe to a voyage intended to communicate *in general*, those benefits which we enjoy to Countries destitute of them, in the remote parts of the Globe." The company warmly agreed. Dalrymple consented to take command of such an expedition, and to draw up a prospectus in the hope of eliciting subscriptions. The purpose of the scheme he sketched was to carry out livestock, corn, iron, etc., and to bring back whatever flora could be advantageously grown in England; the estimated cost of a 350-ton ship and a crew of sixty, and of wages for three years, was £15,000. When the prospectus was printed for circulation, Franklin contributed the foreword below.[6] It was not enough to arouse public enthusiasm,[7] for the expedition never took place.

August 29, 1771.[8]

Britain is said to have produced originally nothing but *Sloes*. What vast advantages have been communicated to her by the Fruits, Seeds, Roots, Herbage, Animals, and Arts of other Countries! We are by their means become a wealthy and a mighty Nation, abounding in all good Things. Does not some *Duty* hence arise from us towards other Countries still remaining in our former State?

Britain is now the first Maritime Power in the world. Her Ships are innumerable, capable by their Form, Size, and Strength, of

---

on a naval commission, which the Admiralty refused. For his subsequent career see the *DNB* and Howard T. Fry, *Alexander Dalrymple (1737–1808) and the Expansion of British Trade...* (London, 1970).

6. But possibly not in the precise form in which it appears. The pamphlet says of the foreword that BF "communicated his sentiments by way of introduction, to the following effect," which might mean that his ideas were considerably edited. The style in places is unlike his, and one of the two Latin quotations seems too esoteric to belong in his collection. But the appearance of the pamphlet in the *Ephémérides*, and again in Vaughan's *Miscellaneous Pieces*, clearly indicates that BF accepted authorship of his part of it.

7. In fact the only response we have encountered was a touching offer, more than a year later, of four ducats from an impoverished Dutch nobleman who had read of the scheme in the *Ephémérides*; see Baron Westerholt to BF below, Nov. 12, 1772.

8. We conjecture that the date, which is Dalrymple's, was when BF's draft was put into final form by some one else. BF is most unlikely to have written anything on the 29th, for he was then on his way to Holyhead to embark for Ireland; see the preceding document.

sailing all Seas. Her Seamen are equally bold, skilful, and hardy; dexterous in exploring the remotest regions, and ready to engage in Voyages to unknown Countries, tho' attended with the greatest dangers. The Inhabitants of those Countries, our *Fellow-Men,* have Canoes only; not knowing Iron, they cannot build Ships: They have little Astronomy, and no knowledge of the Compass to guide them; they cannot therefore come to us, or obtain any of our advantages. From these circumstances, does not some duty seem to arise from us to them? Does not Providence, by these distinguishing Favours, seem to call on us, to do something ourselves for the common Interests of Humanity?

Those who think it their Duty to ask Bread and other Blessings daily from Heaven, should they not think it equally a duty to communicate of those blessings when they have received them; and show their Gratitude to their Great Benefactor, by the only means in their power, promoting the happiness of his other Children?

Ceres is said to have made a Journey thro' many Countries, to teach the use of Corn, and the art of raising it. For this single benefit, the grateful Nations deified her. How much more may Englishmen deserve such Honour, by communicating the knowledge and use, not of Corn only, but of all the other enjoyments Earth can produce, and which they are now in possession of. *Communiter bona profundere, Deum est.*[9]

Many Voyages have been undertaken with views of profit or of plunder, or to gratify resentment; to procure some advantage to ourselves, or do some mischief to others: but a voyage is now proposed, to visit a distant people on the other side the Globe; not to cheat them, not to rob them, not to seize their lands, or enslave their persons; but merely to do them good, and enable them as far as in our power lies, to live as comfortably as ourselves.

It seems a laudable wish, that all the Nations of the Earth were connected by a knowledge of each other, and a mutual exchange of benefits: But a Commercial Nation particularly should wish for a general Civilization of Mankind, since Trade is always carried on to much greater extent with People who have the Arts and Conveniencies of Life, than it can be with naked Savages. We may therefore hope, in this undertaking, to be of some service to

9. The quotation is almost certainly post-classical, but a long search has failed to locate it.

our Country, as well as to those poor people, who, however distant from us, are in truth related to us, and whose Interests do, in some degree, concern every one who can say, *Homo sum*, &c.[1]

From William Franklin

ALS (incomplete): American Philosophical Society

[September 3?,[2] 1771]

[*Beginning lost:*] Allen and Turner procured any Information to be given me, that the People would rise and destroy all their Iron Works in New-Jersey; that Mr. Turner had mentioned the Matter to him, and that upon his telling Turner that it was a Machine not within the Law, he laugh'd, and said that he knew very well what it was, and that if it was not strictly within the Letter, yet it certainly was within the Meaning, and that it was a poor Evasion, &c. Mr. Ogden added, that if it should even appear to be actually such an One as the Law prohibited, yet I could not cause it to be abated till it should be judg'd so by a legal Process, in which case the Owners would be subject to a Penalty of £200 Sterling, besides having their Work destroyed.[3]

I have acquainted you with these Particulars that you may be enabled to represent the Matter in its true Light, should you hear

1. "Homo sum: humani nil a me alienum puto." Terence.
2. On Jan. 30, 1772, BF acknowledged receipt of four letters from WF, of July 3, Aug. 3, Sept. 3, and Nov. 5, 1771; and only that of Aug. 3 has survived entire. With the letter of which this is a fragment WF enclosed an extract of Hillsborough's letter to him of June 21, which he could not have received by July 3; the fragment must be of his letter of Sept. 3 or Nov. 5, and in accordance with our policy we have opted for the earlier date.
3. In this incomplete paragraph WF was, we believe, recounting what Ogden had told him. Joseph Turner of Philadelphia and his partner, Chief Justice William Allen of Pennsylvania, owned extensive ironworks in New Jersey. Charles S. Boyer, *Early Forges & Furnaces in New Jersey* (Philadelphia, 1931), pp. 233–43. Turner accused Ogden of owning a slitting mill, it seems, in violation of the Iron Act of 1750; and Ogden denied that his mill was covered by that statute. David Ogden, with his son Samuel and son-in-law Nicholas Hoffman, operated a slitting mill at Old Boonton on the Rockaway; it was disguised as a grain mill, the story goes, and when WF paid it a surprise visit he was deceived by the disguise, and beguiled by Ogden's charm, into concluding that the report of illegal operations was groundless. *Ibid.*, pp. 42–3.

any thing further concerning it. I think to inform the Ministry of all that I know of the Affair by the next Pacquet, as I doubt not it will be convey'd to them by Allen or Penn in some Way or other.[4] My Opinion of the Act in Question is much the same with yours,[5] but I think that all Laws until they are repealed ought to be obeyed and that it is the Duty of those who are entrusted with the executive Part of Government to see that they are so. The Americans ought at least before they attempt to evade it, use all their Endeavors to obtain a Repeal, and I believe it would be for the Interest of both Countries that all partial Acts of that Nature were abolished.

I am glad that you preferr'd the short Letter,[6] as his L.P. seems to be coming about, and inclined to be a little more complaisant, which you will perceive by his last Letter (No. 31) a Copy of which is enclosed. I likewise send you an Extract of a Letter from him and the Board of Trade dated June 21, respecting the Agency, which seems well calculated to lead me into another Squabble with the Assembly, for it is a Point they will never give up, and if I refuse to pass the Support Act with the Words objected to in it, I, and all the other Officers of Government must go without our Salaries.[7] This brings to my Mind, that your Friends Mr. Read and Mr. Smith desired me lately to mention to you that it would be proper for you to empower some Person here as your Attorney to receive the Warrants for your Salary, and the Money of the Treasurer, (as was done by all the former Agents) in which Case your Warrants would be drawn every Quarter for your Salary with those of the other Officers of Government. The Money remitted

4. Chief Justice Allen was the father-in-law of Lieut. Gov. John Penn, who had returned to England the previous May.

5. For BF's opinion of the Iron Act see above, XV, 10–11.

6. WF's letters to Hillsborough were often submitted to BF to amend if he thought fit; see above, XVI, 36 n. The shorter version that BF selected is presumably that printed in 1 N.J. Arch., X, 230–2.

7. The New Jersey Assembly claimed, on the basis of long usage, the sole right of appointing an agent for the colony, and had asserted its right in the support bill that provided BF's salary. Hillsborough was intent on re-establishing the practice of appointment by the governor and both houses, and the Board of Trade had instructed WF to veto any support bill that asserted the Assembly's claim. 1 N.J. Arch., X, 301; see also the headnote on BF's interview with Hillsborough above, Jan. 16. The sequel is in the resolution of the N.J. House and Council below, Dec. 11–20.

to you by the Committee of Correspondence was not, it seems, intended to be appropriated to your Salary, but to defray such Expences in Soliciting, &c. as might be from Time to Time incurr'd. I think it would be best if you were to write to Mr. Joseph Smith, one of the Committee, to receive it for you; a Letter will be a sufficient Power.[8] Betsy sends her Duty. I am as ever, Honoured Sir, Your ever dutiful Son   WM: FRANKLIN

P.S. I have begun a Letter to you on the Subject of our Account, which I shall finish so as to send by the next Opportunity.

From Jonathan Williams, Sr.

ALS: American Philosophical Society

Honoured Sir   Boston September 19 1771
    Your favour of the 10th of June I duly received note the Contents. When I wrote you of receiving the Money of Hall in august I thought I might depend upon it as I not only had his Promise, but a mighty good Character of him from some Gentlemen Who Were aquainted With him. I have Since inquir'd into the Circomstances of the Bondsman Edward Thurston Junior. Mr. Mumford the Post tels me that he is Safe, tho' at present I Cant think but Hall is good for the Sum, and I Will make a point of Settleing it as Soon as Possible.[9] Circomstances and your Letters Convince me that my Zeal in favour of a Person of Real Merit has carred me

8. For Charles Read, a member of the Council, and Joseph Smith, an Assemblyman who acted as secretary of its committee of correspondence, see above, respectively, X, 313 n, and XVI, 256 n. BF followed WF's suggestion and empowered Smith to receive the money; see BF to Smith below, Feb. 6, 1772. The salary was only £100 a year. Smith kept it for him, except for one £200 draft in 1774: Smith to BF, Oct. 1, 1772, May 13, 1774 (APS). At the end of 1774 BF recorded that he was owed £400, and the debt was discharged when he returned to America. Jour., p. 57; Ledger, p. 41.

9. Samuel Hall, BF's nephew by marriage, had been indebted to him for years, and BF now wanted the money for Jane Mecom; see above, X, 358 n; Williams to BF, Jan. 19, 1771; and BF to Williams below, Jan. 13, 1772. Hall had moved to Salem from Newport; his bondsman may well have been the Edward Thurston whom Ezra Stiles subsequently mentioned several times as a Newport Loyalist: Franklin B. Dexter, ed., The Literary Diary of Ezra Stiles . . . (3 vols., New York, 1901), II, 132, etc. Benjamin Mumford was the post-rider between Newport and Boston: ibid., I, 507 n.

(prehaps) beyond the Bounds of prudence tho' I hope the honesty of my intentions will Plead my excuse.

We most hartly thank you for determining our Sons India Voyage as his usefullness to himself our Famley and Friends for 7 or ten years to Come in our Opinion is off more Value then the Chance of an East India fourtune.

I likewise receiv'd your kind favour by our Son Who through the goodness of God is ariv'd Safe and Well, is now Entering into Business with the utmost Diligence Care and Industary and With the Blessing of Heaven We Doubt not but he Will Rise in Life With Honour to himself Justice to his Creditors and a Credit to his Connections and Friends, to facilitate Which nothing in my Power Shall be Wanting.[1] We are Very happy to find you advise our Son Josiah (God Bless him) Stay untill he has accomplished himself as We know with your advice he Will be easeey and Happy.

As to the indorsment on your Bond of £22 10s. Sterling Received by John Cooke Who (as I am inform'd) Was Impowered by Mr. Howard to Receive the money and it apears to me Mr. Howard is the Person that ought to be accounted for he Could not With any manner of Propriety Receive the Bond of Mr. Cook Without at the Same time Receiving the Money or some Obligation for it, as the Receipt on the Bond Cant be a Voucher to Soport a demand against Cook When the Bond is Discharg'd so that I conceive Mr. Howard is under a necessity of either paying the Money or Producing the Obligation to Clear himself and then it may appear Whether Cook acted for himself or you for the Words *Attorney for Mr. Benjamin Franklin* Dose not appear to be Wrote by Cook. You have a Copy of the Receipt as it Stands on the Bond as follows Viz

Boston 22 June 1768

Receiv'd twenty two pounds ten Shillings Sterling Money of Great Britain in part of the Within Bond.

JNO. COOKE *attorney for Mr Benjm Franklin*[2]

1. On Sept. 9, 1771, the *Boston Gaz.* reported young Jonathan's return. For the rumor of his voyage to India see his father to BF above, Aug. 5.

2. This problem, as complicated as Williams' syntax, appears to have grown out of the effort to collect Samuel Hall's debt. In 1764 Martin Howard, Jr., a Newport attorney, had offered help in getting money from Hall for BF, but during the Stamp Act disturbances had had to flee from Rhode Island.

The Balance of your Account was £282 11s. 10½d. Sterling after Giveing me Credit for the first Bill of Nathl. Wheatley for £100. Since I have Sent you another Bill for £100 of Nathl Wheatley, more one of Thomas Symmes, for £100 and Abram. Lemmers Draft for 1000 Gilders and I now Inclose you two more Due Bills they are 3d Bills the first and Second not Come to hand yet, one of them is for 975 Gilders and the other 779 Boath 1754 is £160 16s. 0d.[3] in the Whole Since the Balance you have

	£459	16s.	8 d.
Deduct the Balance	282	11s.	10½d.
	£177	4s.	9½d.

All our Friends are Well in perticular my much Esteem'd Aunt Mecom and her Daughter. Please our Best Respects to good Mr. Stanley Love to Josiah and Brother our most Respectfull Compliments to good Mrs. Stivenson &c. My Wife Joines in Duty to you With my Children. I am With the Greatest Esteem Your Dutyfull Nephew and Humble Servant   JONA WILLIAMS

NB You have Inclosd Likewise N Wheatley 2d and Thos Symmes 2d Bills and Abrm Limmers 2d a Duch Bill for 100 Gilders the first of thease I have Inclos'd to you before.

Questions about Ireland   AD: American Philosophical Society

These questions reveal Franklin as the thoughtful tourist. He had long been interested in Ireland, but primarily in its relationship with the

---

Above, XI, 459 n, 461. He had left his papers, and doubtless a power of attorney, with an agent in Newport, John Cooke, who had collected but not sent him some money due BF; instead Cooke added it to his debt to Howard. Howard to BF, Aug. 12, 1775 (APS). We assume that this money was the £22 10s., and that it came from Hall in partial repayment of what he owed BF—who clearly had not seen a penny of it. The question was from whom to try to recover. Williams was arguing that Howard was liable, because he had received either the cash or a promissory note (the "obligation") from Cooke. The affair dragged on for another four years and was probably never settled.
   3. The bills from Wheatley, a Booton merchant, have not appeared before; for the others see Williams to BF above, July 12, Aug. 5. BF recorded the Wheatley bills in August, and entered the 1,754 guilders as £162 11s. 6d.: Jour., pp. 36–7.

empire;[4] on his first visit he clearly intended to examine its internal economy, which he viewed from a physiocratic, anti-mercantilist standpoint.[5] His memorandum seems to be guidelines for his curiosity. The fact that he began it as questions relating to, and endorsed it as queries in, Ireland strengthens our belief that he had it with him on his travels, and hence that he wrote it shortly before or after he reached the island in September.[6] We are assigning it, tentatively and perhaps arbitrarily, to that month.

[September?, 1771]

Questions relating to Ireland

Can the Farmers find a Ready Money Market and a good Living Price for the Produce of their Lands?

Or do they raise less than they might do, if the Demand was greater and the Price better?

If their Rents were lower would or could they improve their Lands to a greater degree and so produce more from them?

Does the Increase of Manufacturers occasion a greater Consumption of Corn within the Kingdom?

Is Ireland much in Debt to England or any Foreign Country for Goods or Merchandize consum'd in it?

Is any other Country much indebted to Ireland for its Produce or Manufactures?

Are the Sums remitted to Absentees transacted in real Money, or done by Bills, founded on the Produce and Manufactures of Ireland sold in other Countries?

Is Ireland in general in a State of progressive Improvement, or the contrary?

Are all Rents paid in Ready money? or are some paid in kind?

Is it easy or difficult in Ireland to borrow Money at legal Interest, on good Land Security?

4. For an example in 1729 see above, I, 162.

5. The questions have, we believe, a real if indirect relationship with the views he expressed in 1769 (above, XVI, 107–9, 314–15) and in his "Remarks on Agriculture and Manufacturing" at the end of this volume. For his conversion to physiocratic doctrine see Lewis J. Carey, *Franklin's Economic Views* (New York, 1928), pp. 140–55.

6. If it had been written later, we should expect it to have given some indication of how deeply shocked BF was by the condition of the people, as he made clear in his letters to Babcock, Cushing, and Galloway below, Jan. 13, Feb. 6, 1772.

Is it easy or difficult to find a Purchaser who will pay ready Money and a reasonable Price for a Landed Estate to be sold?

If the Ballance be on the whole, yearly against Ireland, how is it accounted for that any Money remains in it?

Would not more Money remain if there were no Paper passing as Money?

Is there any great Quantity of Goods such as Woollens or Wool smuggled out of the Kingdom, so that no Account can be taken of it among the Customhouse Accounts?

Endorsed: Queries in Ireland[7]

From Thomas Cushing   ALS: American Philosophical Society

Boston, Octr. 2. 1771

This will be handed you by William Storey Esqr. who will deliver you the Votes of the last sessions of the General Court.[8] He goes home to sollicit for releif from the Difficulty under which he at present labours; Natha. Wheelwright Esqr. during Mr. Storeys being Deputy Register in the Court of Admiralty had a Vessell and Cargo Seized and Condemned in said Court from which judgement he appealed; However the Vessell and Cargo were Sold at Public Auction at which Mr. Wheelwright was a Considerable

7. In a blank space at the end of the MS BF listed people to whom he was writing (and to many of whom he did write in August, 1772), and made some simple—and often incorrect—calculations in British currency. These jottings were set down, we believe, long after he wrote the memorandum.

8. Little is known about Story, although he was the grandfather of the famous Justice Story. In 1763, according to John Adams, he had been a member of the radical Boston Caucus. Butterfield, ed., *John Adams Diary*, I, 238. But he had also been deputy Register of the Vice-Admiralty Court, an office prominent enough to make him, as mentioned below, a victim of the mob during the Stamp Act disturbances. His position enabled him for a time to play both sides of the street: he left for England with letters of introduction from Gov. Hutchinson to Hillsborough and Bernard, with this letter from Cushing, and with another from Samuel Adams to Arthur Lee. When Adams heard of the Governor's letters, however, he quickly wrote Lee again to warn him to treat Story cautiously. Hutchinson to Hillsborough, Oct. 2, 1771, Mass. Arch., XXVII, 238–9; Cushing, ed., *Writings of Samuel Adams*, II, 237, 245–6. Story returned to Boston in 1772; see the annotation of Williams to BF below, June 13, 1772.

purchaser. Mr. Temple the surveyer General, with a View of favouring Mr. Wheelwright as much as possible directed Mr. Storey, as he Informs me, to take Mr. Wheelwrights note of hand, in lieu of the Money, p[er?] amount of such goods as he purchased payable [as] soon as the affair of the appeal was fully determined. After some Time Mr. Wheelwright failed and has never been able to Discharge his Note.[1] The Kings Advocate has sued Mr. Storey for the Money. Mr. Storey thinks [*torn:* it would be unreaso?]nable and unjust to oblidge him to pay it, [*torn:* when he?] Acted in Consequence of orders received from the Surveyer General. He has applied to the Commissioners of the Customs here, but as it was a Matter transacted before their appointment they can do nothing about it, he therefore has undertaken this Voyage in order to apply for releif to the Commissioners at home. Any assistance you may afford him by your Advise or thro your Influence with those before whom this matter may lie I shall esteem as a favor. I would just mention that Mr. Storey was a Considerable Sufferer in the time of the Stamp Act by having his House and Furniture much Damaged by the Mob, who distroyed most of his Books and Papers amoung which there were some relative to the Seizure above mentioned, and for want of which he is fearfull he shall be a great Sufferer. He had some Compensation made him by our General Court but as all the rest of the Sufferers at that time excepting Mr. Storey, have been Consider'd and in some way or another Compensated by the Government at home he hopes he shall have the more favourable hearing relative to this Matter.[2] I conclude with great respect your most obedient humble Servant

T CUSHING

To Benjamin Franklin Esqr

1. For John Temple see above, x, 389 n; xvi, 207 n. He had been Surveyor General of the Customs at the time of Nathaniel Wheelwright's bankruptcy in 1765; Wheelwright had fled town, and died in Guadeloupe the next year. Anne R. Cunningham, ed., *Letters and Diary of John Rowe*... (Boston, 1902), pp. 55, 74, 99.

2. For the attack on Story's house in 1765 see Edmund S. and Helen M. Morgan, *The Stamp Act Crisis*... (Chapel Hill, [1953]), pp. 126–7, 183. Story had asked the General Court for £136 in compensation but had received only £97. Mass. Arch., xliv, 604–11. For his fortunes in England see the end of bf to Cushing below, Jan. 13, 1772.

224

From John Holt[3]

ALS: American Philosophical Society

Dear Sir   New York 2nd. October 1771

An unhappy Difference has taken place between my Neighbour Mr. Hugh Hughs (a Man I greatly esteem from my Experience of the real Goodness of his Character) and his Brother John, and as I am perfectly acquainted with the whole Cause and Process of that Difference, and know that my Neighbour is desirous you should have a right Knowledge of it, as he highly regards your Opinion of him, I thought it my Duty as a Neighbour, who has on sundry Occasions, received good Offices from him, to give you an Account of what I know to be true concerning the Difference between the two Brothers.[4]

When the News of the Stamp Act had spread a general Alarm all over the British colonies, Mr. Hugh Hughs was one who from the first, warmly interested himself against it. There had till then subsisted the greatest Cordiality between the two Brothers, of which I was a Witness, as I was shewn many of the Letters that passed between them. And it was with the greatest Concern that my Neighbour Hugh informed me of the Report he had heard, that his Brother was a Promoter of the Stamp Act. Several Letters passed between them on that Occasion, which on one Side proceeded from an affectionate Concern for the Rectitude of his Brothers Conduct, and on the other from a much less commendable Motive. On one Side the Letters were argumentative, persuasive and affectionate; on the other, much in the dictatorial Stile, destitute of Argument, mixt with Reproach, and tinctured with that overbearing Haughtiness, assumed by fancied Superiority, not only of Fortune, but Intellects, over those in less happy Circumstances; but with an inflexible Obstinacy of Perseverance, that would admit of no Expostulation. This Intercourse ended in a Breach between them, that seems to be irreperable. Before this, soon after Mr. Hughs had acquainted me with the Report concerning his Brother in Philadelphia, I had written him a Letter,

3. Printer of the *N.-Y. Jour.*, for whom see above, V, 441 n. The late James Parker's attempts to collect outstanding debts from Holt, both for the post office and himself, have appeared frequently in these volumes.

4. For Hugh and John Hughes see above, respectively, X, 290 n; VI, 284 n; and for their disagreement XIII, 14 n.

tho' I had but little personal acquaintance with him. My Reasons for writing I mention'd, which were, not only my Friendship for his Brother, who I knew would be deeply affected by the part he should Act, but on Account of the Cause itself. I mention'd a few of the most striking Arguments against the Act. The Importance of uniting the american Interest in Opposition [to it.] The Certainty of Success in Case of such Union, which had a[lready] so far taken place, that there was no Probability that the Act [could] ever be carried into Execution. I therefore earnestly advised [him] for his own Sake, for his Brother's Sake, and for the Sake of his [Coun]try that he would not favour, but join in Opposition to this most [hat]ed Act, calculated to enslave his Country, and which would certainly produce nothing but Misfortune, Uneasiness of Mind [and] everlasting Imfamy to all concerned in its Contrivance or Pro[curement?].

Such was the Substance of what I wrote and sent away without the Privity or Knowledge of Mr. Hughs, or any other Person—or the least intimation to any One, of my having such a Design. Nor did I know at that Time, that any Letters upon the Subject, had passed between the Brothers. It unluckily happen'd, that I sent my Letter by Mr. Bradford,[5] who was here, just setting out for Philadelphia. And he, it seems, tho' I then knew nothing of the Matter, was one of a Party in Philadelphia, who had warmly opposed Mr. Hughs. My Letter being directed by the Hands of Mr. Bradford, Mr. Hughs concluded, that his Brother in New York, and Mr. Bradford, were Privy to the Contents of my Letter, and that it was written in Consequence of a concerted Plan of the Party who opposed him: My Letter therefore had an Effect quite contrary to what I intended; and not only irritated Mr. Hughs against his Brother in New York, but against me also, whom he considered as the Tool of a Party, with whom I had not the least Correspondence or Acquaintance. I received no Answer to my Letter—but I find he has bestow'd on me a good deal of unmeritted Abuse, in his Letters to his Brother, and to other People, which having been communicated to me, I should before now have made a Proper Return to, if I had not been engaged in Matters of more Consequence.

5. Either William Bradford (1722–91) or his son Thomas (1745–1838), printers of the *Pa. Jour.* Both had opposed the Stamp Act and attacked John Hughes in print. See above, XII, 263 n.

I believe you know something of the unhappy Situation of Mr. Hugh Hughs's Affairs. By being Security he became insolvent; and tho' the Principal, has found Means to get discharged, yet Mr. Hughs remains still liable as Security, without Possibility of recovering of the Principal[6] And to avoid an Arrest, has, for many years past, made himself a voluntary Prisoner in his own House, where he has supported a numerous Family of Children, by teaching School, given his Children a very good Education, and greatly improved his own Knowledge; his, being much the best, as well as most considerable English School in Town. Yet his Income is but a bare Sufficiency for the Support of so large a Family, and a Life so sedentary for so long a Time, has greatly impaired his Health and Constitution: So that he seems at Present, with some Anxiety, to be looking out for the Means of extricating himself, or of falling into some other Course of Life for a Support. But I cannot find he has any probable Prospect of either—and if you could advise or assist him, it would be conferring a Benefit upon a Man very worthy to receive it.

His Brother had often intimated his Intention of doing something to relieve and assist him, which Design, after the Difference before mention'd, seem'd for sometime to be suspended. But at last, by a [line?] in the same imperious Stile he had lately adopted, he signified his Willingness, notwithstanding the Difference, to give the Assistance before proposed; but mention'd such Terms, and in such a Manner that the Acceptance was immediately declined, and I think with the greatest Reason. I do not now recollect Particulars, but I remember they were such, that I believe no Man of Spirit or Sense could accept. I remember the Method proposed was such as implied distrust of his Brother's Honesty and Integrity, was I believe impracticable, was vague and uncertain with Regard to himself, and so humiliating to his Brother that any Assistance he should receive, would have been at the Price of his Freedom and Independency. I did not hear of the Proposal til after Mr. Hughs had declined the Acceptance, but I heartily approved his Refusal. If I remember right, it was proposed that he should deliver an exact Account on Oath, of all his Debts and Effects, and then his lordly Brother, *would consider what could be done for him,*

6. For Hughes' financial straits see above, XII, 232, 260 n, 355 n; XIII, 13–14, 342; XIV, 240 n.

and what he should think proper to do, would be done purely on his own self Motion, uninfluenced by any other Person. Here again he mention'd me, in Terms of disrespect. All which shows him to be a haughty imperious Man, sour'd in his Temper, hasty and often unjust in his Conclusions, positive in his Purpose as well in the wrong as right, and such a person as no Man of Sense and Spirit would choose to be dependant upon, if he could live, or die without it.

I have written this Epistle purely to give you this Information, the Truth of which I will answer to the Face of the Man of whom I write, and am Dear Sir your well wisher and Humble Servant
JOHN HOLT.

Addressed: To | Doctr. Benjamin Franklin | In | London

From Jonathan Williams, Sr.

ALS: American Philosophical Society

⟨Boston, October 3, 1771. Wrote a few days ago to enclose the third set of bills for 1,754 guilders.[7]⟩

From Ann Clay[8]

ALS: American Philosophical Society

Honoured sir   Newcastle Octobr: 4 1771
    This comes with a letter from my son.[9] I hope you will pardon the liberty I take in recommending his request to your notice; And shou'd he succeed I have no doubt of his good behavior, as the partiality of a parent wou'd not induce me to say that he is a sober discreet young Man did he not really merit it.

7. See Williams to BF above, Sept. 19.
8. Ann Curtis Clay (1723–89) was the daughter of Judge Jehu Curtis and the widow of Slator Clay, both of whom are briefly identified above, respectively, IV, 456 n and VI, 426 n.
9. She had, as she mentions below, eleven children. Which one this was is impossible to say, but a likely candidate is Robert (1749–1831), who was starting his career as a Philadelphia merchant; he was subsequently ordained and served as rector of Immanuel Church in his native town of New Castle, Del. William B. Sprague, *Annals of the American Pulpit*... (9 vols., New York, 1857–69), V, 357.

I have now been a widow four years and am in such circumstance as Ager prayed for when he says give me neither poverty nor riches,[1] wisely judging that state the most likely to produce happiness. I have eleven Children and have as yet thank God reason to look upon that as an addition to my happiness.

He has beged the favor of you if there shou'd be a necessity for it to advance 200 guineas, for the payment of which I will be his security.

I have nothing more to add but wishing you a great deal of happiness, I conclude sir, your sincere friend and very humble servant ANN CLAY

Addressed: To | Benjamin Franklin Esquire

From [William Henly]

AD (incomplete): American Philosophical Society; remainder printed in the Royal Society, *Philosophical Transactions...*, LXIV (1774), 402-3[2]

The experiment described below was part of a series that Henly undertook in 1771–72 to test Franklin's theory about the path of the lightning discharge. The theory was under attack from Benjamin Wilson, who held that the discharge, given several alternative routes to ground, takes a single one, that which has the fewest surfaces to break through, is the shortest, and in which the property of the material provides the greatest conducting power.[3] Franklin, on the other hand, seems to have held that any available conductor receives some part of the charge, although conducting power is a major factor in determining how much.[4] Years earlier he had suggested that that factor varies in conductors,[5]

1. The prayer of Agur, son of Jakeh. Proverbs 30: 8.
2. The fragmentary AD is in Henly's hand and dated, and was part of a longer account, which he presumably sent to BF; Henly later revised the account slightly when he included the experiment in a series described in his paper in the *Phil. Trans.*, where the illustration is on p. 388. We print the fragment from his MS, noting any significant changes he made in the finished paper, and the remainder from the printed text.
3. For Wilson's theory see above, VIII, 239–63. For a later phase of the argument between Wilson and BF see the report on the Purfleet magazine below, Aug. 21, 1772.
4. Above, V, 76–7; XIV, 262. We say "seems" because one or two of BF's other statements are open to a different interpretation.
5. Above, V, 523.

and he had recently proposed to Priestley and others that they determine the variation by exposing wires of the same thickness and different
metals to equal and increasing charges until each wire was visibly
affected.[6] Henly developed the suggestion, and the experiment below
enabled him to disprove Wilson's hypothesis. This line of experimentation was a prelude, we believe, to the later theory of resistance.

Octr: 7. 1771.

I made the following experiment, having placed a very large Jar
in contact with my prime conductor, I fixed to the outer coating
of it an Iron Chain 10 or 12 Inches long which I also connected
with a plate of Metal on which I intended to make the discharge,
with my discharging Rod. This done I hooked another chain much
longer and of Brass to the[7] side of the Jar, and brought the end of
it within $8\frac{1}{2}$ Inches of the Metal plate. In contact with this end I
laid a small Oak-stick 8 Inches long which I cover'd with Sawdust of Fir wood. On making the discharge upon the plate, both
the chains[8] were luminous through their whole lengths, as was
also the sawdust which was cover'd by a streak of Light near an
Inch diameter making a very pleasing appearance. I repeated the
experiment several times. Perhaps if I had used a Bar of Iron instead of the Chain (first spoken of,) there might have been no
appearance of light in the second Chain or upon the sawdust; especially as the electricity had full $\frac{1}{2}$ Inch of air to pass through,
before it reached the point of the stick. But from this experiment
may I think be inferred the necessity of making the Conductors
erected as a security to Buildings from the damage of Lightning,
both of the best materials, and of a very sufficient substance;[9] and,
for this purpose, perhaps nothing will be found so proper as *lead*,
which will remain in the earth many centuries without any con-

6. Priestley, *History*, II, 368–71. Equal charges could be determined with
Henly's electrometer.
7. The printed text here adds "opposite."
8. The printed text italicizes "both the chains," and for good reason: their
luminosity disproved Wilson's theory. Brass was known to have less conducting power than iron, the brass chain was longer, and a charge passing by
that route, via the oak and sawdust, had more surfaces to break through. If
electricity behaved as Wilson thought, therefore, it would pass only through
the iron.
9. The MS fragment ends here.

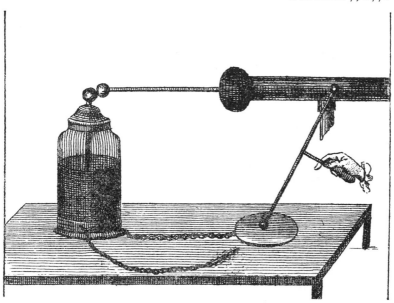

siderable decay; and the tops of chimneys being covered with it,[1] and furnished with a long, sharp-pointed rod of copper, or iron pointed with copper, which I think should extend at least five, or six feet, above the top of the chimney, or highest part of the building; a communication should be made from it by plates of lead, eight, or ten inches broad, with the lead, on the ridges, and gutters, and with the pipes which carry down the rain-water; which pipes should be continued to the bottom of the building, and there made to communicate, by means of other leaden pipe, or a plate of it, as before-mentioned, with the water in a well, the moist earth, or the main pipe which serves the house with water.

1. [*Author's note:*] I mention covering the tops of chimneys with lead as a protection to the upper courses of bricks, from the effects of wind; and not as being of any essential service to the conductor, any farther than as it may assist in fixing the pointed rod, which is to be elevated above it, more securely.

From Joseph Galloway

Dear Friend   Trevose Bucks Octr. 12. 1771

By an Express from Philada. I hear that Sparks sails To Morrow, and being unwilling to let slip this Opportunity as I have done too many this Summer by being in the Country, I take up my Pen to inform you that I have your Certificate for £500 Sterling your Salary, and wo'd have remitted you the Money, had any Provision been made for the Payment of it. There being no Governor at the last Meeting of the House this cou'd not be done.[2] In January I imagine Provision will be made for the Public Debts, when I shall remit it.

The Express waiting I have only Time to assure you that you shall hear fully from me in a few Days and that I am unalterably your very Sincere and Affectionate Friend   J. GALLOWAY

From the Pennsylvania Assembly Committee of Correspondence

LS: Library of Congress

Sir   Philada: Octr: 16th. 1771.

By Order of the House we inclose their Resolves appointing us their Committee of Correspondence, and you their Agent to transact the Affairs of this Province in Great Britain for the ensuing Year.[3]

The House have Nothing to add to the Instructions sent by former Assemblies except that as they observe from your Letter to the Speaker of the 29th of July, that there is a Disposition in Government to promote, at the next Session of Parliament, such Measures as may tend to conciliate the unhappy Differences subsisting between the Mother Country and her Colonies, They desire that you will be attentive and Exert your utmost Endeavours

2. The Pennsylvania Assembly, unlike the Massachusetts House, acted with the governor in paying its agent, and could do nothing in an interregnum. Lieut. Gov. John Penn had left for home in May; his brother Richard did not arrive to succeed him until Oct. 16: *Pa. Col. Recs.*, IX, 780.

3. The new Assembly had convened two days before, unanimously chosen Galloway as speaker, reappointed BF as agent, and elected a new Committee of Correspondence. 8 *Pa. Arch.*, VIII, 6723–6.

in Opposition to whatever may affect the general Liberties of America and the rights of this Province, particularly to any Plan that may be proposed for an American Representation in Parliament.⁴ We are Your assured Friends

Jos. GALLOWAY Speaker
Jos. Fox
SAML RHOADS
ABEL JAMES
WM. RODMAN
ISA. PEARSON⁵

Addressed: To / Benjamin Franklin Esqr. / Agent for the Province of Pennsylvania / at / London / per Favr. / Capt. Sparks

From Peter Timothy⁶ ALS: American Philosophical Society

Dear Sir, Charles Town October 20th, 1771.

I wrote you on the 28th past, but the Pilot having neglected to put my Letter on board the last Packet-Boat, it accompanies this.

The Assembly have continued sitting longer than I thought they would have done. Last Week all the *Patriots* and *principal Speakers*, made themselves sure of carrying the £1500 into the Estimate, under the *Expedient* of including the same in the Treasurer's Accounts: But were surprized, in putting the Question, to see all the young Members rise against it, and vote for the other, "that it should be inserted in the Schedule in the very Words it had formerly stood." It was then generally apprehended an immediate Dissolution would take Place; but that not happening, this Week the Members for the *Expedient* have (after a good deal of private Conference with the Members in Opposition) proved that the Vote was irregular, and carried the Question their own Way. Now the

4. The rumor of such a scheme was going the rounds in London, oddly enough, as this letter was being written. "The plan for a new American representation has been adopted by a noble Earl," *Lloyd's Evening Post* reported on Oct. 18–21, "and will be laid before an august Assembly at their first meeting."

5. All the signers have been identified in previous volumes; Abel James, the newcomer on the committee, had been in contact with BF in London the year before.

6. See above, xv, 199.

Bill is to go before the Council. If they scrutinize too narrowly, they must reject it: if they do not, the Governor will not (I believe) withhold his Assent—and thus public Credit may be restored, and universal Harmony revive.[7]

I am very sorry to tell you, that I believe you will not hear from your Friend Mr. Hughes by this Packet. I assure you, my good Friend, I begin to be under very serious Apprehensions about his doing well. Within this Fortnight his Cough has encreased, his Strength and Spirits failed, and he is scarce at any Time now without a Fever. He is sensible of his dangerous Situation, yet flatters himself that the Winter will restore him but he appears to me to be too far gone. I should not be among those who would regret him the least, for I should lose a most agreeable, sensible and engaging Companion, I think I may add Friend. If he holds out till the be-

7. In this paragraph Timothy is describing one small battle in the political war that raged in South Carolina for six years before the Revolution. In December, 1769, the Commons House of Assembly ordered the provincial treasurer to pay £1500 to the Society of the Gentlemen Supporters of the Bill of Rights in London, an organization formed to defend John Wilkes and pay his sizable debts; and the treasurer did so. For many years the House had been in the habit of ordering such grants for routine domestic purposes in the colony, and then reimbursing the treasury in the next tax bill; but the purpose this time was neither routine nor domestic. The Privy Council ruled that the House alone could not legally order any expenditure, even for local services, without the consent of the Governor and Council; and Lieut. Gov. Bull was instructed to assent to no money bill that did not specify how the funds were to be used within the colony. The House defied the ruling, asserted its right to vote money for whatever purpose it saw fit, and included in its tax bill for 1770 a repayment to the treasury for the £1500. Bull and his Council turned down the bill, and the Assembly was prorogued. When it met again in September, 1771, it faced the Governor, Lord Charles Greville Montagu (1741–84), back from a two-year leave in England. The House tried to get around him by the expedient to which Timothy refers: a provision in the tax bill to repay the estate of the late treasurer the money he had advanced for enumerated and "other" services, the latter being the gift to Wilkes. The "young Members" scorned this subterfuge, but failed to have the gift named in the bill ("the schedule") as it had been the year before. Timothy, who had consistently supported the House in his *S.-C. Gaz.*, hoped that the Governor and Council would ignore the obvious, that the evasive clause in the measure flouted the government's intention. But the bill was rejected, and the war went on. See Jack P. Greene, "Bridge to Revolution: the Wilkes Fund Controversy in South Carolina, 1769–1775," *The Jour. of Southern History*, XXIX (1963), 19–34.

ginning of December, I shall then have Hopes that changing his Climate in the Spring may prolong his Days—but really he appears far gone.[8]

We have had Abundance of Rain for this Week past, which I believe has done some Damage to late Crops, yet we may calculate the Rice made this Season at 100 Thousand Tierces, and Indigo at about 400 Thousand Weight.[9]

I hope you enjoy perfect Health, wish you its Continuance, and every Thing desirable, and am, with the greatest Regard Dear Sir Your most affectionate obliged and obedient humble Servant

PET. TIMOTHY.

P.S. Doct. Haly having surrendered him self his Trial will come on Tuesday or Wednesday. I never knew a Man have so many potent Friends start up to him as he has; and I suppose he will be found guilty of Manslaughter. If ever a Man was compelled to fight contrary to his Inclination he was;[1] if I had Time to relate Particulars, you would be of that Opinion.

8. For BF's successful effort to get John Hughes, his old friend, transferred from the customs post in Portsmouth, N.H., to that in Charleston see above, XVII, 157 n. Hughes did hold out through December, but died the following month. *S.-C. and Amer. General Gaz.*, Jan. 29–Feb. 6, 1772.

9. A tierce is larger than a barrel and smaller than a hogshead. Another contemporary estimate was that Charleston exported 130,601 barrels of rice between Nov. 1, 1770, and Oct. 10, 1771, and in the year 1771 produced 655,133 pounds of indigo. Leila Sellers, *Charleston Business on the Eve of the American Revolution* (Chapel Hill, N.C., 1934), pp. 157, 166.

1. In the previous August Peter De Lancey, a relative of the New York De Lanceys and an ardent Anglophile, got into a bitter argument with John Haley, a Charleston physician, who challenged him and killed him. Haley's prosecution for murder had political overtones because of the victim's British sympathies; the Doctor was defended by the best young talent of the Charleston bar and convicted, as Timothy prophesied, only of manslaughter. See *S.-C. Gaz.*, Aug. 22, 1771; Maurice A. Crouse, ed., "The Letterbook of Peter Manigault, 1763–1773," *S.C. Hist. Mag.*, LXX (1969), 189–90; Joseph Johnson, *Traditions and Reminiscences, Chiefly of the American Revolution in the South . . .* (Charleston, S.C., 1851), pp. 45–7. Timothy, as a champion of colonial rights, was naturally on the side of the defense.

To William Strahan   ALS: Princeton University Library

Dear Friend,   Edinburgh, Oct. 27. 1771
    Thro' Storms and Floods I arrived here on Saturday night, late,
and was lodg'd miserably at an Inn: But that excellent Christian
David Hume, agreable to the Precepts of the Gospel, has *received
the Stranger,* and I now live with him at his House in the new Town
most happily.[2] I purpose staying about a Fortnight, and shall
be glad to hear from you. I congratulate you on certain political
Events that I know give you Pleasure. Let me know how it is with
you and yours, how my Wife[3] does, and Sir John Pringle, and our
other Friends. With sincerest Esteem I am, my dear Friend, Yours
most affectionately   B FRANKLIN
Addressed: To | William Strahan Esqr | Newstreet | Shoe Lane |
London | B Free FRANKLIN

From Mary Hewson   ALS: American Philosophical Society

                                  Broad Street Oct. 31. 1771
Welcome! my dear and honour'd Friend! Welcome once more to
our Island! The Wind may blow now without making our Hearts
ake. You were constantly in our Thoughts during the late stormy
Weather. I have pray'd for you at Midnight when I have been
suckling my little Boy and heard the Window Sashes rattle.[4] I
thank God you are safe. The same merciful Being has preserv'd
us all in Health and Happiness. Mr. Hewson says "don't forget to
mention the little Boy[,] Molly." An Insinuation that I could not
write without saying a great deal about him. But I shall not tell
you what a fine Child he is grown, I hope you will see him soon.

    2. BF got over from Ireland, David Hume reported to Strahan, in a brief
interval between two hurricanes. Nolan, *Franklin in Scotland and Ireland*, pp.
172–3. Hume, like the Biblical reference, requires no annotation. He and BF
had been friends for more than a decade, and Strahan had probably brought
them together. See above, IX, 228 n.
    3. Margaret or Peggy, Strahan's youngest daughter, was about twenty at
the time. BF had been using this nickname for her since at least 1762.
    4. William Hewson, Jr., was then six months old. The stormy weather was
the product of two hurricanes; see the preceding document.

My Mother receiv'd both your Letters Yesterday. She says there is a deal of Reading for you when you come Home; so much that you must shut yourself up for a fortnight and be *invisible*. A packet arriv'd this Week from our worthy Friend Jonathan, which my Mother, knowing the Seal, took the Liberty to open. It containd Letters to Josiah, therefore she was glad she did open it. He is well and all his Friends.

Mr. Bache is at Preston, where he will wait with the pleasing Expectation of seeing you in your Return. We are all very much pleas'd with him.[5]

My Mother is much oblig'd to you for your kind Services. I hope her honest Trade will be successful.

Lady Barwell desires her best Respects to you:[6] She and my Mother have been chattering all the Time I have been writing.

I omitted telling you that two of your Packets are directed to be forwarded to you from the first Port.

I really cannot write any more; and I believe I have nothing material to add. So with the Love of this Family, offer'd with respectful Sincerity, I conclude my Letter. I am Dear Sir your faithful   MARY HEWSON

My Mother says, "You have not sent my Love." I told her I consider'd her as the Head of this Family. But she is not satisfied with hers being in the same Lump, therefore I make up this separate Parcel.

Addressed: To / Dr Franklin / at / Edinburgh

5. Jonathan Williams, Jr., had returned to Boston the previous summer while his brother Josiah remained in London; see BF to Jane Mecom above, July 17. Richard Bache, before going north to see his family, had apparently stayed with the Stevensons while BF was absent on his tour; but Bache's itinerary is uncertain. See his letter to DF below, Dec. 3.

6. For our conjecture about Mrs. Stevenson's "honest Trade" see Polly's note below of Nov. 2, and for Mary Barwell see above, XVII, 194 n.

From M[ary] H[ewson] ALS: American Philosophical Society

My dear Sir   Friday Night [late October, 1771?[7]]
   My Mother desires me to tell you that there are two Letters
from New York and one from Philadelphia and three Packets of
News Papers but she is afraid to send them as you have not receiv'd that Mr. Hewson sent you. I write in great Haste. We are
all well. Yours affectionately   M H

From Mary Hewson ALS: American Philosophical Society

My dear Sir   Broad Street Novr. 2. 1771
   My Mother orders me to set down to answer all your *Hows*.
The Hewsons young and old are well and thank you for your kind
Enquiry. Your Dolly is well. I had a Letter from her to day from
Bromley. Lady Barwell is well. Josiah when we heard of him, and
Sally, and Mr. and Mrs. Jackson, I met them last Week at Bar-
well's. All well.[8] My Mother herself is grown quite young, and
continues her Regimen. She can make no Enquiry about her Mer-
chandize, not knowing the Name of the Vessel it was sent in.[9]

   7. The note might at first glance be dated at any time when BF was away
from London between Polly's marriage in 1770 and his departure for America
in 1775. But internal evidence shows that on this occasion his absence was a
long one, and suggests that his itinerary was uncertain: he must have been
informed by letter that mail had been forwarded to him, and replied by letter
that he had not received it, all before Polly wrote; and her mother was still
not sure of reaching him on his travels. These circumstances fit only one trip,
his tour of Ireland and Scotland from the end of August to the end of November. We have tried to narrow the dating within those three months, but can
only offer a flimsy guess that Polly was writing in the last weeks of October.
Although the mail waiting for BF is unidentifiable, a packet arriving at that
time might well have brought it: the *Earl of Halifax* sailed on Sept. 9, and
arrived in mid-October. *N.Y. Gaz.; and the Weekly Mercury*, Sept. 16; *London Chron.*, Oct. 12–15. The disappearance of mail forwarded earlier increases
the likelihood, to our mind, that Polly was writing while BF was in Ireland.
   8. Most of the people mentioned in this paragraph have appeared frequently
in the preceding volumes. The Jacksons were Charles, the Post Office official,
and his wife; Richard Jackson was a lifelong bachelor.
   9. The merchandise was presumably intended for the "honest Trade" to
which Polly had referred in her note above of Oct. 31. Irish linen encouraged
honesty because it was not dutiable; BF had called Mrs. Stevenson a "Smug-
gler upon Principle." Above, XVI, 208; see also pp. 191, 193.

238

I have read the foregoing to my Mother who finds great Fault, in the first Place she reprov'd me for not telling you about Lady Barwell's Negociation, now, really I can tell you nothing but that she continues to negociate.[1] Then she cast her Eye over my Paper and discover'd the Blot and bade me write all over again upon a fresh Sheet; I could not obey, because I have no more than this. My Husband knows I was given to scribbling before I married, and thinking that Scribblers do not make good Housewives he wisely locks up the Paper. Perhaps if I ask'd him he would trust me with the Key upon my telling him to whom I was writing, but he was busy in the Kitchen with Paint and Grease.[2] My Mother insisted upon my making this Apology.

We all wish for you in London. I want you to see my little Boy. He resembles you in many particulars. He is generally serious, no great Talker, but sometimes laughs very hearty; he is very fond of being in his *Birthday Suit*, and has not the least apprehension of *catching cold* in it; he is never troubled with the *Airophobia*, but always seems delighted with fresh Air. The good Mrs. Wakefield gave us some American Biscuits to feed him with, and we tried them two days, but we found he was not so well as when he liv'd entirely upon Milk, so we return'd to our old Method and he continues well and has cut three Teeth. A fine long Paragraph he has furnished! I hope you will not *seriously* think it too long; you are welcome to laugh at it and your affectionate MARY HEWSON

My Mother sends Love. Sally her Duty. Mr. and Miss Hewson respectful Compliments.[3] Mr. Bache is at Preston; I had a Letter from him to day in which he tells me that one I enclos'd to him was from his dear Sally of 2d of Sepr. All well at Philadelphia.

Addressed: To / Dr Franklin / at / Edinburgh

1. Perhaps something to do with her brother's affairs. See above, XVII, 194 n.
2. He was probably working on flexible models for his and Dr. Hunter's anatomy course. See the headnote on Hunter's complaints against him above, end of July.
3. Sally Franklin (A.5.2.3.1.1.1.) often stayed in Craven Street and has frequently appeared before. Little is known about William Hewson's siblings, but a few years earlier he had had three sisters living.

From John Balfour[4]

ALS: American Philosophical Society

Dear Sir   Edinr: Novr: 5th 1771

The friendship you showd me in transacting the Debt that was due to me by Benjamin Mecom (for which I reckon myself much oblidgd to you) embol[dens me] to ask the favour, that with your Convenience you will also tr[ansact the] debt due to me, by Mr. James Parker of New York lately deceasd.[5] [*Torn.*] I send you the Accompt, by which there is a ballance due to [*torn*] 14s. 8d. also three of his Letters to me, wherein he homologates[6] [the Accompt?] but complains of great losses he sustain by a Friend of [*torn*] afterwards by one Mr. Holt.[7] I dare say this is very true, but I apprehend that I am not liable for any of his transactions without my knowledge, with any other person. In one of his Letters to me he takes notice that he receivd the Books as sent upon your Recommendation, in this he is mistaken, for it was upon Mr. Strahans, unless perhaps he means that it was you, that recommended him to Mr. Strahan.

As I am very much persuaded that Mr. Parker was a very honest man, and really hurt by the persons mentiond above, I shoud be very well pleasd to compromise the matter upon easy terms, and if you will be so good as take this trouble for me, I shall be greatly oblidgd to you, and give you full power to act as you shall see proper, and to do every thing, as if the debt were intirely your own, and I shall be perfectly well satisfied with whatever you, being perfectly assurd that you will do the best for my Interest. If it is necessary to get the Account sworn to before a Magistrate, let me know, and it shall be done. You will see by his letters, that he seems to acknowledge, that in strict Law he is liable for the Accompt, but setting this aside, I woud have the matter transacted intirely upon the footing of equity, and as you shall see circumstances consider[?]. Whatever you may [effect I will?] look upon my self as entirely oblidgd to you for it. I am with [the great]est

4. The Edinburgh bookseller, for whom see above, ix, 295 n.
5. For Mecom's and Parker's debts to Balfour see above, xii, 251–2, 383; xiii, 10–14; xiv, 186; xv, 59, 144, 289.
6. In Scots law, to validate.
7. For the tangled financial relationship between Parker and Holt see in particular above, xiii, 300–7.

Esteem and Respect Dear Sir [your] most Obedient Servant
                                                    JOHN BALFOUR
P S Besides the 3 letters of Mr. Parker [*torn*] I have also sent you another of his, dated March 4th. 1769.
Addressed: To / Dr Benjamin Franklin / Edinburgh

From James Bowdoin ALS (draft): Massachusetts Historical Society

Dear Sir   Boston Novr. 5 1771
    I thank you for the Copy of the Instructions from the Committee of Plantations to Mr. Randolph inclosed in the last Letter [dated Feby. 5. 1771][8] with which you honoured me. His Answer to the Enquiries he was directed to make (if to be had) and compared with the present State of this Province, would probably shew in the Articles enumerated the Increase since that time. In the present Year, pursuant to a late Act of the Genl. Court for enquiring into the rateable Estate of the Province, Lists of the Poles and other Rateables have been taken in each Town, which at the next Session of the Court will be laid before the House of Representatives in order to the setling the Proportion each Town is to bear of future Province Taxes.[9] As this may be a matter of curiosity to you, and may serve (compared with prior Lists) to confirm your conjecture with regard to the Increase of the Colonists, I will endeavour to procure the sums total of the rateables and send to you but when this can be done is quite uncertain, as it is uncertain when the Genl. Ct. will meet: the meeting of which, at least till the next May (which is the Charter) Session, seems to depend on Instructions not known to be yet received.[1] With regard to Instructions, it is obvious from such as have been lately operated

    8. Brackets in the original. For the enclosure see the annotation of BF's letter.
    9. See *Mass. Acts and Resolves*, V, 156–9, 209–11.
    1. The first session of the General Court had been prorogued on July 5; the second did not meet until April 8, 1772. *Ibid.*, V, 181. The charter required the governor to convene the Court at least once a year, on the last Wednesday in May, and permitted him to summon it at such other times as he thought necessary. *Ibid.*, I, 11. Hutchinson received no instruction that altered this procedure.

that there's a plan for annihilating the Charter by them in a silent piecemeal manner: which if persisted in will be as effectual for that Purpose as if done by Act of Parliament, as was lately intended by the ministry.[2] Through the same influence the Grants that have been made to you and Mr. Bollan by the two Houses failed: and 'tis not expected that any future Grants will pass till the Agents in their appointment are subjected to the Influence of Instructions.[3] I have understood that in several of the Colonies particularly in Virginia the Two Houses have each a seperate Agent, independent of the Governor who without any difficulty pases the Grants that from time to time are made them; and that those Agents are acknowledged as such by the Ministry. But in this matter I have not been able to come at certainty.[4]

I heartily join with you in hoping that "in time Harmony will be restored between the two Countries, by leaving us in the full possession of our Rights."

I am much obliged to you for your kind expressions with regard to my son: to whom I have recommended it to put himself under the Instruction of Dr. Priestly at Warrington on the plan pointed out in his Essay on Education for Civil and active life.[5] I think this will be no unsuitable introduction to the study of the Law: the Profession of which he prefers to any other. As I understand you are well acquainted with Dr. Priestly, I shall be much obliged if

2. For the recent design of amending the provincial charter see above, XVII, 279 n, 282, 302–3, 308, 311; Cooper to BF, July 10, 1771.

3. For the background of the dispute over the agents see above, p. 153 n. In July the House voted money for DeBerdt's estate and again for Bollan, but BF's salary was not mentioned. Hutchinson, reinforced by his newly arrived instructions, once more refused assent. *Mass. House Jour.*, 1st session, May–July, 1771, pp. 93, 100–1, 105, 107, 111–13, 117. The issue continued to come up intermittently until 1773; for the next reference to it see Cushing to BF below, July 15, 1772. BF never did receive a salary while he was in England. After he returned to America in 1775 he was paid for four years at £400 per annum: Ledger and Jour., both p. 57.

4. Neither have we. Considerable evidence suggests that Bowdoin was right; see Jack M. Sosin, *Agents and Merchants* ... (Lincoln, Neb., 1965), pp. 15–16; Kammen, *Rope of Sand*, p. 134. But for William Bollan's quite different account of Virginia practice see Mass. Arch., XXII, 585–6.

5. For young Bowdoin's journey to England see his father to BF above, Jan. 2. Priestley had left Warrington more than four years before for Mill Hill Chapel, Leeds; his plan was set forth in *An Essay on a Course of Liberal Education for Civil and Active Life*... (London, 1765).

you'll favor him with a few lines to the Doctor: I purpose he should return to N England in about 12 Months with his Uncle Mr. George Erving, who does me the favour to be the Bearer of this Letter. I beg to recommend Mr. Erving to you as a sensible worthy Gentleman who will be able to give you full information with regard to the affairs and Transactions in this Country.[6]

I have repeatedly had great pleasure from the Perusal of the last Edition of the Excellent Letters which you did me the honour to send me. I have already thanked you for the Book and now thank you for that pleasure. I wish it was in my power to execute in this Instance the Lex Talionis: in which case you should receive as high a degree of pleasure as you have communicated: and if all the Readers of your Book could carry the same law into execution, you would be the happiest man existing. I wish the few letters which bear my Signature in the same Volume were more worthy the honour you have done them.[7] I am with the Sincerest Esteem, in which Mrs. B joins me Dear Sir your most obedient humble Servant.   JAMES BOWDOIN

To Benja. Franklin Esq.

From John Foxcroft   ALS: American Philosophical Society

Dear Sir   Philada. Novr. 5th. 1771
I was favour'd by my Brother with a few Lines from you,[8] just Acquainting me with your Intentions of taking a Trip to Ireland. I hope this will find you safe return'd and in Good health.

I expect two Casks of Flour up every tide Manufactured by the same Man who I had the other two off,[9] if they get up by Friday they will come in Falconer if not it will be too late, and they will

6. George Erving (1738–1806), Mrs. Bowdoin's brother, was a Whig merchant who later became a Loyalist; for his career see *Sibley's Harvard Graduates*, XI, 515; XIV, 151–7; Sabine, *Loyalists*, I, 406–7.

7. The volume was the fourth edition of *Exper. and Obser.* (London, 1769). The *Lex talionis*, or law of retribution, was the exaction of an eye for an eye and a tooth for a tooth.

8. Thomas Foxcroft, the Philadelphia postmaster, had returned from a visit to London.

9. For the earlier shipment see BF to Todd above, June 15.

come by the next Vessel. Mrs. F joins me in best Compliments to your self Mrs. Stevenson and Family. I am &c.

JOHN FOXCROFT

Addressed: To / Benjamin Franklin Esqr. / at Mrs. Stevensons / in Craven Street Strand / London / J. Free FOXCROFT

From Penuel Bowen[1]   ALS: American Philosophical Society

Sir   Boston 6th Novr 1771

The honor you have done me, by the present I lately receivd thro' the hands of Mr. Saml. Franklin of this Town, emboldens me to give you this trouble.

Please to accept Sir, my most sincere and hearty thanks for your high favor.

I account myself and my house signally honor'd by the picture of a gentleman, whom I have always hear'd spoken of, and for whom I have conceiv'd the highest opinion—As the distinguish'd genius of America, the Patron of Philosophy and Literature, a friend to his Country and of mankind. May heaven long preserve a life in various great stations, of the first importance; And eminently so to England and the British Colonies.

Sir I esteem it a singular happiness to have this opportunity of letting you know, with what high sentiments of honor and gratitude, In common with my Countrymen, I am Much respected Sir Your greatly obliged Friend And most Obedient Humble Servant

PENUEL BOWEN

Doct: Franklin

Addressed: For / Benja Franklin Esqr. / L.L.D. F.R.S. / In London.

1. Bowen (1742–88) graduated from Harvard in 1762, and four years later became the minister of the Congregational New South Church in Boston. In 1772 he resigned; he subsequently went to South Carolina and became an Episcopalian. See *Sibley's Harvard Graduates*, XV, 196–200. In this letter he is acknowledging the receipt, through Samuel Franklin, of a mezzotint portrait of BF; see Franklin to BF above, May 17.

From Samuel Franklin[2]   ALS: American Philosophical Society

Dear kinsman   Boston 8th November 1771.

With pleasure I Embrace this oppertunity of informing you that I and my wife and my four Daughters thro Gods goodness are all well and Desire kindly to be remember'd to you hopeing that these may find you and Coz Sally in the Same good health. I am Sir much oblidged to you upon my own part for the prints you sent me for Mr. Bowen. I had it Neatly fram'd, and Guilt and Sent it to him. Who return'd for answer that it did honour to him and to his house and that he was greatly oblidged to you for the present—he has enclosed in mine a few Lines.[3] I am verry Glad that them books of my Grandfathers fell into your hands and Should be verry Glad to have a sight of one of them at Least when you Can Spare it. I and my family Shall be glad to have you Come once more amongst us and still Continue hopeing that it Will not be Long first. Your sister and all frends here are well. I Remain after my kind Love to you your Loving kinsman

SAMUEL FRANKLIN

PS My kind Love to Coz. Sally
Addressed: To Dr / Benjamin Franklin / In London

From the Managers of the Philadelphia Silk Filature to Franklin and John Fothergill

LS: American Philosophical Society

Gentlemen,   Philadelphia 8th. November 1771.

The Subscribers Managers of the Contributions for promoting the Culture of silk in Pennsylvania, having purchased in the course of the last Season and procured to be reeled at the Filature erected here such a quantity of Cocoons as have produced about 155 lbs. of raw Silk proper for Exportation, are encouraged from your

---

2. For the writer, and the matters mentioned in this letter, see his letter to BF above, May 17, and BF's reply, July 12.

3. They may possibly have been the preceding document, but that has its own address—the same vague one as Franklin's—and is on much larger paper; Franklin would have had trouble enclosing it.

known Partiality to the productions of this Province, and Disposition to promote whatever may advance its Interest or Reputation to commit this first Adventure to your Care and Disposal, requesting that the undermentioned Parcels may be presented as directed in such respectful manner as your good Understanding shall point out, and that the remainder be sold at either public or private Sale as you may think most conducive to the Benefit of the Institution.[4] Inclosed is the Certificate required by Act of Parliament for obtaining the Bounty.

From the want of more Experience in this new Manufacture, we are not competent Judges of the Quality or Value; but upon comparing our own with the Samples of Silk we have received from other Parts of the World we apprehend some of it is not much inferior to them. If Persons of more skill with you should be of the same Opinion, we have little Doubt that the raising of Silk will soon become an Object of general Attention in this Province, and probably in time a considerable Remittance to our Mother Country; an Event in which we should have great pleasure; as a mutual Advantage to both.

We flatter ourselves that it is unnecessary to apologize for giving you this Trouble when we consider that benevolent Minds are never more agreeably exercised than in the Promotion of Public Good. We are, Gentlemen, with the highest Esteem, Your assured Friends and very humble Servants,[5]

EDWD: PENINGTON	FRA: ALISON
CHAS. MOORE	C: EVANS
ISAAC BARTRAM	THO CLIFFORD
WM SMITH Broker	R STRETTELL JONES
ABEL JAMES	JOS: PEMBERTON
BENJN. MORGAN	

4. For the "institution" and the promoting of silk culture in Pennsylvania see the correspondence above between BF and Cadwalader Evans: Feb. 10, May 4, July 4 and 18. The receipt for two trunks of raw silk shipped to BF and Fothergill is in Franklin's papers in the APS.

5. The signers, managers of the silk filature, were for the most part prominent residents of Philadelphia. All but three, Bartram, Morgan, and Pemberton, have been identified in previous volumes; and not much is known about those three. Isaac Bartram (c. 1725–1801) was John's second son by his first marriage: Hinshaw, *Amer. Quaker Genealogy*, II, 335. Frequent minor references to Benjamin Morgan may be found in the cumulative index (1954) of

No. 1 6 lbs. for the Queen
  2 4 „   „   Lady Juliana Penn
  3 4 „   the Relict of the late Honble
                 Richd. Penn Esqr. deceased
  4 4 „   the Lady of the Honble. John Penn Esqr.[6]

Drs Franklin and Fothergill

From Samuel Noble ALS: American Philosophical Society

An old friend of Franklin rarely makes his appearance so late in these volumes. But Samuel Noble was clearly such a friend; he has not hitherto come into the correspondence and, as far as we now know, reappears only once.[7] The information about him is almost nonexistent. The connections that he speaks of in Burlington indicate that he was the son of Joseph and Mary Noble of that town, where Joseph died in 1773.[8] He himself was clearly a Philadelphian. But this single letter, and the leather soles that went with it, are all that has transpired about his relationship with Franklin.

Philada. 11th of the 11 mo. 1771

Well Esteemed Friend Benjamin Franklin
   Thou, being my Neighbour in my Infancy and Acquaintance, and Fellow Citizen, I make Free to write a Little to thee, and Herewith Present thee with a pair of Soles of Leather of my Own Tanning to Keep thy feet warm, as American Produce. It is Tan'd in a Mode of my own Invention, I think Never Practiced on this Side the Water to my Knowledge. The Steer of Whicth Hide Was

---

the *PMHB*; they indicate merely that he held a number of public positions. Joseph Pemberton (born 1745) was the son of the well known Quaker merchant, Israel Pemberton.

6. The three Penn ladies, in the order of their listing, were Lady Julia Fermor Penn (1729–1804), the wife of Thomas; Hannah Lardner Penn, Richard's widow and the daughter of Dr. John Lardner of London; and Ann Allen Penn, John's second wife and the daughter of Chief Justice William Allen.

7. He may or may not have been the Samuel Noble who contributed to the Pa. Hospital (v, 329). He reappears only in BF's belated reply in 1774, which tells nothing more about him than is obvious from this letter: Smyth, *Writings*, x, 277–8.

8. Hinshaw, *Amer. Quaker Genealogy*, ii, 245, 400; Amelia M. Gummere, "Friends in Burlington," *PMHB*, vii (1884), 8–9, 10 n; *The Friend*, xxxv (1862), 284.

Fatted at Carpenters Island,[9] and Killed for our markett. The Hide, in the hair, weighed 140 lbs. and was 21[?] months in Tanning, and when Dry Leather weighed Near 70 lbs. on Proof of this Kind and Manner, Some of Our Best Shoemakers Say, Hammers Well. I Just Lett thee Know, that We as Tanners are Endeavoring to Excell Eacth Other in Doing our Best in this Manufactory and I think may be Justly Said the Trade is Improveing, I think we have Some as Good Hides in our Parts as in England, although not So General, Nor Yett So heavy.[1]

I take this Little Pleasure to Converse with thee, Well Knowing thou art a Friend to America, and Townsman of mine. I, Haveing Some Connections at Burlington, Was there Lately and See Governor Franklin, Who was Well. Thus Conclude with mucth Love, thy affectionate Friend   SAMUEL NOBLE

Addressed: To / Benjamin Franklin Esqr / in, / London / per favor of / Capt Falconer

From Isaac Hunt[2]   ALS: American Philosophical Society

Honored Sir,   Philadelphia November 12th: 1771

As the Letter I wrote to you by the Packet might not get safe to Hand, I take the Liberty, by this opportunity, to acquaint you, that the Attorney General of Bermudas[3] is dead; and to sollicit your good offices to procure me, if possible, that Law-Department.

The great Number of our Profession at present in Philadelphia, and the Scarcity of Business, arising from the Non-Importation Agreement, make my Application for an Appointment to that Station absolutely necessary at this Time; and as I am sensible you delight in Acts of Beneficence, I entertain the pleasing Hopes of being favored in this Business with your Interest and Patronage.

9. In the Delaware River near the confluence of the Schuylkill.

1. BF's experience bore out this remark. He had the soles incorporated in shoes, wore them for two years, and found them firmer and more durable than his London shoes. See his reply cited above.

2. For this old acquaintance of BF see above, XIII, 279 n.

3. John Slater, who had held the office since 1756. See Henry C. Wilkinson, *Bermuda in the Old Empire...* (London, New York, Toronto, 1950), p. 441.

Mrs. Hunt[4] joins me in Respects to you, and I am, as I have ever been, since I had the Honor of knowing you, With Esteem Your real and obliged Friend   ISAAC HUNT.

Addressed: To / Benja. Franklin Esqr. LLD. FRS / London / per favor of / Capt. Falconer

From a Committee of Philadelphia Tradesmen
LS: American Philosophical Society

Sir   Philadelphia Novr 13th 1771

We received your Favour of July 29th with a Copy of Yours dated Augst 28th 1770 as also the Pamphlet, by the Hands of our faithful Friend Capt. Falconer. We still regret the Loss of the Original of August 28th in due Time; for notwithstanding the Honest and sincere Endeavours of the Tradesmen &c. could not possibly withstand the Torrent of Corruption, and self Interest then Predominant; we really believe your just and spirited Sentiments communicated to us, would have been a means of inspiring Us, and some of our Noble and Patriotic Friends amongst the Merchants with fresh Courage, to have held out (at least) a few Months longer; which possibly might have had the desired Effect. We are happy however in reflecting that our Attempts though unsuccessful, have met with your Approbation: and though the Mechanic's are Censured and Despised for attempting to judge or intermeddle in any Public Affairs; Yet we are determined to pursue One steady Plan, of embracing every Opportunity of doing real Service, to our most Gracious Sovereign, and our fellow Subjects; and with [all the] Prudence and Moderation we are capable off, to [resist ev]ery Attempt made to Oppress us, or Violate our [rights and liber]ties. We are much Obliged to You for the [*torn:* service you?] have done Us in Writing your Sentiments so [candidly? We as]sure You that we shall be always ready to [*torn*] and that no part of your Letters shall [be allowed out?] of our Hands.

The Pamphlet you have been pleased to favour us with is much esteemed and we have taken the Liberty of committing it to the Press here without giving the Printer the least hint from whom it came being convinc'd it will be of infinite Service in the American

4. For Mary Shewell Hunt see above, XVII, 251.

Colonies.[5] We pray that you may long live the Illustrious Patriot of America and that your Strenuous Endeavours for the Service of Your Country may be Crowned with immortal Success. We remain Sir Your most Respectful and faithful Friends and Well Wishers   THE COMMITTEE OF TRADESMEN &c
Sign'd by Order of the Committee JOSEPH [STILES[6]]

P.S Wm. Masters being indispos'd Capt. Jos Stiles Plac'd in the Chair   WILLM THORNE Secy[7]

Addressed: To / Doctor Benjamin Franklin Esqr / London / per Favour of / Capt Falkner.

To William Strahan   ALS: American Philosophical Society

Dear Sir,   Edinburgh, Nov. 17. 1771
    I have been at Blair Drummond on a Visit to my Friend Lord Kaims, thence I went to Glasgow, thence to the Carron Works, viewing the Canal by the Way.[8] Extream bad Weather detain'd

5. We have been unable to identify the pamphlet, which was apparently not sent to a newspaper but printed separately.

6. Stiles was born in Berkshire and came to Philadelphia as a young man. He served on a privateer during King George's War, for which he was censured by the Philadelphia Meeting, and was subsequently a merchant captain. Hinshaw, *Amer. Quaker Genealogy*, II, 660; Geneal. Soc. of Pa. *Pub.*, IX (1926), 168; *PMHB*, XXIV (1900), 505; XXV (1901), 130. For references to his career after 1771 see *Pa. Col. Recs.*, XI–XVI, *passim*; 1 *Pa. Arch.*, XI, 202–3; Henry D. Biddle, "Owen Biddle," *PMHB*, XVI (1892), 315.

7. The meeting must have been private, for it was not mentioned in the *Pa. Chron.*, *Pa. Gaz.*, or *Pa. Jour.* The group that met was presumably the organization of tradesmen, artificers, and mechanics that Charles Thomson had been instrumental in forming eighteen months earlier, for which see Crane, *Letters to the Press*, pp. 210–11. For William Masters see above, XVI, 275 n. For meager references to William Thorne, an accountant and writer of a school copybook, see 1 *Pa. Arch.*, V, 143–4; *PMHB*, XXVIII (1904), 101.

8. For Lord Kames and Blair-Drummond see above, IX, 5 n; XIII, 478 n. The Carron ironworks, among the most famous in Britain, produced the cannon named after them, carronades. The canal was the Forth and Clyde, the work of BF's old acquaintance John Smeaton; it had been begun in 1768 and was not completed until 1790. For this part of BF's journey see Nolan, *Franklin in Scotland and Ireland*, pp. 182–7, 189–97.

me in several Places some Days longer than I intended: But on Tuesday I purpose setting out on my Return,[9] and hope for the Pleasure of seeing you by the Tuesday following. I thank you for your kind Congratulations on the News you have heard. I like immortal Friendships, but not immortal Enmities; and therefore kill the latter whenever I have a good Opportunity, thinking it no Murder.[1] I am but just come back hither, and write this Line just to let you know I am well and again under the hospitable Roof of the good Samaritan.[2] As to News, which you seem to expect from me, I protest I know of none, and I am too dull for Invention. My Love to Mrs. Strahan and your Children, and believe me ever, my dear Friend, Yours most affectionately   B FRANKLIN

Addressed: To / William Strahan, Esqr /King's Printer / London / B Free FRANKLIN

From Agatha Drummond[3] AL: Historical Society of Pennsylvania

Cannongate eight o Clock. [November 19,[4] 1771]
Most respectfull complements from Mrs. Drummond to Doctor Frankland. She could not get an oportunety to Day, to beg he would allow her to send him to London Mr. Pens Pickture which the Doctor will remember to see at Kames.[5] She will take it out

9. He actually left on Thursday, Nov. 21. *Ibid.*, p. 199.
1. The news in all likelihood was about Hillsborough, and may have been a rumor that he was on his way out. The Earl, to BF's surprise, had cordially received and entertained him in Ireland: *ibid.*, pp. 162–5; BF to WF below, Jan. 30, 1772. But the enmity between the two had been scotched, not killed; a few months later it was thriving again.
2. BF's host, David Hume.
3. Lord Kames's wife (1711–95) was often called Lady Kames by BF and others; see above, IX, 6, 9; XIII, 478. But she followed Scottish usage by reverting to her maiden name as Mrs. Drummond, and BF learned to follow her lead; see his reply to this note below, Jan. 11, 1772.
4. BF and Marchant dined with the Kameses on the 19th, and apparently did not see them again before leaving Edinburgh on the 21st. Nolan, *op. cit.*, p. 201. Hence the reference to "to Day" presumably means the 19th.
5. BF had become interested in this painting, ostensibly of William Penn, on his visit to the Kameses in 1759, and had asked to have it sent him so that he could arrange for a copy: above, IX, 7–9. His request had apparently been forgotten until his hosts were reminded of it on his return visit more than a decade later.

of a Clumsay Frame and have it very easily and well packd. Has again the pleasure to wish him a safe journey, and begs to be rememberd to Mr. Marchent.

To Mary Hewson with a Postscript to Dorothea Blunt
ALS: American Philosophical Society

Dear Friend,   Preston, Nov. 25. 1771.

I came to this Place on Saturday night right well and untir'd with a 70 miles Journey that day. I met with your and my Dolly's joint Letter which would have refresh'd me with its Kindness if I had been ever so weary. The Account you give of a certain Lady's having entertain'd a new Gallant in my Absence, did not surprize me:[6] For I have been us'd to Rivals; and scarce ever had a Friend or a Mistress in my whole Life that other People did not like as well as myself. And therefore I did not wonder when I read in the Newspapers some Weeks since, that "the Duke of C." (that general Lover) "had made many Visits of late to an old Lady not many Miles from Craven Street."[7] I only wonder'd, considering the Dislike she us'd to have for the Family, that she would receive his Visits: But as I saw soon after, that Prince Charles had left Rome and was gone a long Journey nobody knew whither, I made no doubt but the News Writers had mistaken the Person, and that it was he who had taken the Opportunity of my Absence to solace himself with his old Friend.[8] I thank you for your Intelligence

6. In the absence of Polly's and Dolly's letter this nonsense can be explained only by conjecture. Ours is that the lady was Mrs. Stevenson and the gallant was BF's host in Preston, Richard Bache, who had been cordially received in Craven Street during BF's absence on his tour.

7. BF of course amended the quotation but probably did not invent it. On Oct. 2 the Duke of Cumberland (1745–90), the King's brother, had married in secret Anne Luttrell Horton at her home in Mayfair; the marriage was not reported for a month: *London Chron.*, Nov. 5–7; *Lloyd's Evening Post*, Nov. 8–11. See also Wilmarth S. Lewis and A. Dayle Wallace, eds., *Horace Walpole's Correspondence with the Countess of Upper Ossory* (3 vols., New Haven, 1965), I, 64; Wilmarth S. Lewis and Warren H. Smith, eds., *Horace Walpole's Correspondence with Sir Horace Mann* (11 vols., New Haven, 1954–71), VII, 344.

8. Charles Edward, the Young Pretender, was living in Italy. In August, 1771, he turned up in Paris, where negotiations were begun that eventuated

about my Godson. I believe you are sincere when you say you think him as fine a Child as you wish to see. He had cut two Teeth, and three in another Letter make five; for I know you never write Tautologies. If I have over reckon'd, the Number will be right by this time. His being like me in so many Particulars pleases me prodigiously; and I am persuaded there is another which you have omitted tho' it must have occurr'd to you while you were putting them down. Pray let him have every thing he likes; I think it of great Consequence while the Features of the Countenance are forming. It gives them a pleasant Air, and that being once become natural, and fix'd by Habit, the Face is ever after the handsomer for it, and on that much of a Person's good Fortune and Success in Life may depend. Had I been cross'd as much in my Infant Likings and Inclinations as you know I have been of late Years, I should have been, I was going to say not near so handsome, but as the Vanity of that Expression would offend other Folks Vanity, I change it out of Regard to them, and say, a great deal more homely. I rejoice that your good Mother's new Regimen succeeds so well with her.[9] We are to set out, my Son and I, tomorrow for London, where I hope to be by the End of the Week, and to find her and you and all yours, well and happy. My Love to them all. They tell me Dinner is coming in, and I have yet said nothing to Dolly, but must nevertheless conclude, my dear Friend, Yours ever most affectionately   B FRANKLIN

I am very happy here in the pleasant Family of Mr. Bache's Mother and Sisters.

Mrs Hewson.

Dear Dolly

I love you more than you can imagine. Yours most sincerely,
                                                        B FRANKLIN

To Miss Dorothea Blunt.

---

in his marriage the following year. Winifred Duke, *In the Steps of Bonnie Prince Charlie* (London, New York, etc., [1953]), pp. 267–9. BF embroidered his nonsense by bringing the Prince to London and making him an old friend of Mrs. Stevenson.

9. See Mary Hewson to BF above. Nov. 2.

From Humphry Marshall ALS: American Philosophical Society

West Bradford Chester County Pensilvania
the 27th. of the 11th. mo 1771

Esteemd Friend

I recieved thy favour of the 22d of the 4th mo. Last in Which thou Wart Pleased to favour me With an account that the Coppies of thy Letters Sent Back Was not much to thy Predejuce Which Was Pleasing to hear. Our Collonies is Gone into the Importation of Goods by accounts more Largely than Ever. However I hope their remains Such a Sprerit to promote Industry and frugallity among the ablest of the farmers that they Will Purchase But as few of their Goods and they Can Well avoid. Our China Manefactury I hope will Improve and the Making of Derible[?] flint Glass Seems to make noise among us.[1] The Culture of Silk Seems in a fair Way at present to be Improved in our Country there is Numbers of people that raises Silk reels it them Selves and mixes it With Worsted Which makes Good Sort of Crape Which Some of our people have made themselves Cloathes of already and before this reaches thee, I Expect thoul hear how much reel'd Silks our people have Sent over to London.[2] But the people have met With Considerable Discorougement this Last Season by their Worms Sickening and Dying Just When the wares[3] ready to Spin.

I acknowledge thy kindness in Sending over to me Some of the Naked Barly, I Shall Endeavour to Improve it to See if their is any Differrence Bettween that as thou Sent and Some I had by the Way of Carolina about 5 Years Since Which I have Supplyed

---

1. For Marshall's interest in the manufacture of china see BF's letter to him above, XVII, 109. Gousse Bonin and George Morris had established a new factory in Philadelphia, but the competition of cheap English china forced it out of business before the end of 1772. *Pa. Chron.*, Dec. 25–Jan. 1, 1769–70; Harrold E. Gillingham, "Pottery, China, and Glass Making in Philadelphia," *PMHB*, LIV (1930), 115–17. Glass had apparently been manufactured in Philadelphia since 1691; a new glasshouse was started in 1771, and that of Henry William Stiegel at Manheim was undergoing great expansion: *ibid.*, pp. 123, 125–8; George S. and Helen McKearin, *American Glass* (New York, [1941]), pp. 81–4. All this activity was what made "noise among us."

2. For silk culture in Pennsylvania see above, XVI, 179, 201–2; XVII, 151, 211.

3. Unquestionably what Marshall wrote; he must have meant to write "they were."

254

Several of my Neighbours With, and Some bushell of it have been raised amongst us.[4]

I have sent thee my observations for twelve month and a few Days that I have made in the Sun's Disk respecting the Spots that appear thereon, having Drew a circle With a pencil to represent the Suns Circumferrence and then with my Pencil Dilineated the Spots both in Magnitude and Position as near the truth as I Could as they Pas'd, in appearance from East to West. I have not time to Give thee my thoughts respecting them at present. I have Likewise given Some account of the Weather for Some of the time as also Some of the Emmersions of Jupitars Sattelites by my Clock having Set it by a meridian Line as near as I could having no other means.

I have also Sent thee a small Box of Seeds that I had Left after packing a few for Dr. Fothergill but I was in So much hast that I omitted Drawing a list of them. They are Chiefly Lapt up in paper and the Name wrote on With my pencil. My Book of observation on the Sun is Like Wise in the Box. And as thou Signifies it Would be some Pleasure to thee to Serve me in Some Small matters I Should take it kind of thee and as a favour if itt Should lay in thy Way to promote a corrispon[dence] between me and Some of the Seeds men or Nursery men in and about London or any Country Gentlemen that is Curious in Making Collections of our American Vegetables or Simples as I am Pretty Well acquainted With the most Sorts that Grows in our Parts of the Country having been in the practice of Collecting a few Seeds for this many years for my Cousin John Bartram, and Within this four or five Years have Sent Some Boxes of plants and Seeds to Dr. Fothergill; I think I Could afford to Collect Boxes of Young plants of the most of our Common trees and Shrubs as Well as Seeds at a little Lower rate than they are Commonly Done for, if thou Should meet With any Such Gentlemen that Should have a mind to try me for a season or two, and they Would Please to Send their orders, I Should Endeavour to Comply With them.

Be Pleased to favour me So much after thou hast opened and perused My book of observations to present them to the royall

4. Marshall and his cousin, John Bartram, presumably shared BF's present of naked barley, and both also obtained it from Carolina. See above, XVI, 111.

Society in My Name⁵ and I Shall acknowledge the favour perhaps it may find Exceptance With Some of the Members. From thy real Friend and Welwisher   HUMPHRY MARSHALL

P.S. Thou may Shew my observations to my Friend Jno. Fothergill if thou think them Worthy of his Notice.

Addressed: To / Dr. Benjamin Franklin / at / London / Via Bristol / per Capt Spain and With a Small Box of Lancelot Cowper Merchant.⁶ [*In Cowper's hand:*] forwarded per your humble Servant [L. C]owper as well the box when landed.

From Mary Bache⁷   ALS: American Philosophical Society

Preston Decr: 3 [1771]
What extreme pleasure did my Dear Brothers letter give Me and Mine, to hear you had so greeable a Journey and that our Dear Sons Leg was so little worse for his Confinement in the Chaise, we shall all rejoice to hear it is quite recover'd.⁸ I was no little happy that My Dear Daughter, your good Lady and our Dear little Boy was well when you heard from philedelphia, pray God grant a continuence of it.

We are Much please'd at the hopes you give us of injoying your good and agreeable Company again at my house, you likewise Make us happy by Nameing a Longer Stay. I hope Nothing will

5. Marshall kept records of sun spots for some years, and sent them to both the APS and BF. The former did not publish them, but BF eventually arranged to have later observations accepted by the Royal Society. APS, *Early Proceedings...* (Philadelphia, 1884), p. 69; Brooke Hindle, *The Pursuit of Science in Revolutionary America, 1735–1788* (Chapel Hill, [1956]), p. 173; *Phil. Trans.*, LXIV (1774), 194–5.

6. Lancelot Cowper was a Bristol merchant trading with (and at the moment clearly returning from) America; his address was 48 Queen Square: *Sketchley's Bristol Directory...* (Bristol, 1775), p. 21. He sent the box as promised, but it was delayed in arrival. See below, BF to Cowper, March 13, and to Marshall, March 20, 1772; BF to Marshall, Feb. 14, 1773, Yale University Library.

7. Richard Bache's mother.

8. BF had spent two days in Preston. For his first meeting with his son-in-law, Bache's leg injury, and their trip to London together see the following document and Nolan, *Franklin in Scotland and Ireland*, pp. 203, 206–7.

intervene to prevent us that Much Wish'd for happyness. Our best respects to good Mrs. Stevenson tell her we are Much oblige'd to her for Nursing my Dear Sons Leg tis' kind indeed we being at so great a distance. Dear Sally would thank her too did she know it but tis well she is ignorant of it.

The day after you left us we was agreeabley Surpris'd by two Gentlemen that Comes from North America the one your fellow traveller,[9] they spent the Evening with us we strove to be as Cheerfull as we Could after the loss we Sustain'd.

I can assure my Dear Brother I am no little happy in having it in my power to style my self your affectionate Sister and humble Servant   MARY BACHE

Addressed: To / Benjamin Franklin Esqr: / at Mrs. Stevensons / Craven Street Strand / London

Richard Bache to Deborah Franklin

Transcript[1]: Yale University Library

Dear and honored Madam,   London, 3d December, 1771.
This is a pleasure I have not done myself, since my arrival in England;[2] I have waited for an event, which, I know, as it is

9. Henry Marchant, who had been with BF on part of his Scottish tour, and Marchant's friend and companion Edward Church, the brother of Dr. Benjamin Church. *Ibid.*, pp. 174–5.

1. It appears to be in the handwriting of William J. Duane, Sally Bache's son-in-law and the son of BF's editor. Some one else has corrected in the margin a few obvious errors in transcription, and we have silently incorporated these alterations.

2. How Bache got to England and where he went after his arrival are not entirely clear. He was in Jamaica in early March; he then returned briefly to Philadelphia, for Sally tried and failed to get him to take her with him to England. Bache to DF, March 6 (APS); WF to BF above, Aug. 3. Bache must have reached London by early October, for he spent some time there en route to the north, as the end of this letter makes clear, and was in Preston before the month was out. Polly Hewson to BF above, Oct. 31. According to one account, BF received in Edinburgh a note from Bache that made him cut short his Scottish tour and hurry to Preston to meet his son-in-law, whom he found suffering from a leg injury incurred during the voyage from America to Liverpool. Nolan, *Franklin in Scotland and Ireland*, pp. 198–9, 206. The author gives no evidence, and we can corroborate none of his story except that BF stayed at Preston and that Bache had somehow hurt his leg; see the preceding document.

interesting to me is so to you—I mean the reception I should meet
with from my father. I can now, with great satisfaction tell you,
that he received me with open arms, and with a degree of affection
that I did not expect to be made sensible of at our first meeting.[3]
We met at Preston, and I thought this a lucky circumstance, as it
was amongst my friends and relations. He stayed two days at my
mother's house, and from thence we came up to London together.
We were made happy upon our arrival here, by letters from you
and Sally, informing us you were all well the 16th October. I am
under many obligations to good Mrs. Stevenson and Mrs. Hewson
her daughter, for the favourable impressions they have endeavoured
to make on him in my behalf by their several letters to him, during
the time he was in Ireland and Scotland. Besides, I shall ever
honor and esteem the good old Lady for the kind and friendly reception she gave me on my coming first to England: had I been
her son, she could not have received me with more cordiality, or
treated me with more kindness. I must now say something to you
about her grandson, who is a great favorite with us all;[4] I often
nurse him, and entertain him as I used to entertain Ben; and I
really think the lower part of his face something like Ben's: It is
not difficult, when I have him on my knee, to imagine I have got
Ben, for he is a fine, lusty, lively fellow, and seems very fond of
me. At Preston one of my sisters took my profile, which was hung
up in the parlour: several of my friends coming in were asked
whom they thought it like, one and all agreed it was like my father,
and was generally thought to be intended for his:[5] this circumstance confirms your opinion of my being like him, and is not a
little pleasing to me, for I should be glad to be like him in any
respect.

3. This was a momentous occasion. BF had disapproved of Richard's and
Sally's marrying when they did, in October, 1767; in the four intervening
years he had corresponded little with his son-in-law, who was understandably
nervous about meeting him. Sally shared the nervousness. "I trust you met
with an agreable reception from Papa," she wrote him the day before his
letter to DF. "I am indeed anxious to hear, if it should not be as cordial as I
could wish at first yet I know when you consider it is my Father, your goodness to, and afection for me, will make you try a little to gain his esteem and
Friendship, but I need not tell my dearest Lad how much happier I should
be to hear he had receiv'd you with afection." APS.
4. William Hewson, born the preceding April.
5. Bache clearly means BF, not his own father.

258

My mother and sisters desire to be affectionately remembered to you; they really love you as does, dear Madam, your dutiful and affectionate son and very humble servant   RICHD BACHE.

Addressed: To Mrs. Franklin / Philadelphia.

From Sir John Pringle   AL: American Philosophical Society

⟨Friday, December 6, [1771⁶], a note in the third person. Requests Franklin's company at dinner next Sunday to meet Mlle. Biheron and Dr. Ingenhousz before the latter's departure.⟩

From William Bollan   AL: American Philosophical Society

Southamptn. street Saturday, Dec. 7th. [1771⁷]
Mr. Bollan presents his compliments to Dr. Franklin, and desires to see him this afternoon about five, if convenient, upon a matter which chiefly relates to himself, and will not admit of much delay.⁸

Addressed: For / Dr. Franklin

From Jonathan Shipley   ALS: American Philosophical Society

Dear Sir   Twyford Dec: 10th. [1771⁹]
Taking it for granted, that You are at last returnd from your Travels and settled in Craven Street, I can not help reminding

6. During BF's second mission Dec. 6 fell on a Friday in 1765 and 1771, and the latter was almost certainly the year. BF's papers first refer to Mlle. Biheron and Ingenhousz in 1767–68 (above, XIV, 4; XV, 115); she was in town at some time during 1771, he was there on Nov. 28, and BF expected to be back from the north by Nov. 30. Barbeu-Dubourg to BF below, May 31, 1772; Sir Archibald Geikie, *Annals of the Royal Society Club...* (London, 1917), p. 112; BF to Mary Hewson above, Nov. 25.

7. Dec. 7 was a Saturday in 1771, and not again during BF's mission. Bollan moved to Southampton St. in that year; see his letters in 6 Mass. Hist. *Coll.*, IX, 269, 274.

8. Bollan wanted to see BF, we conjecture, to discuss whether they could still do anything as agents for Massachusetts, a point on which Bollan had been extremely pessimistic a few weeks before; see Mass. House to BF above, June 25, n. 1.

9. The letter speaks of BF's return from his travels, and of the Shipleys' impending visit to Mr. Wilmot from "next" Friday to the following Tues-

You in the name of Mrs. Shipley and my Girls, as well as my own, of the Hopes You flatter'd us with; that You would spend your Christmas at Twyford. I can promise You the same Ease and Liberty, the same hearty Welcome, and every thing but the same fine Weather, which You met here before. We should have made interest with You before now for a little more of your Company, which all of Us I assure You, know how to value, if We had not been almost constantly engagd in Parties abroad, or with Company at home. Next Friday We go to Mr. Wilmot's at Farnborough Place and return the Tuesday following.[10] His House stands close by the Road, six Miles on this side Bagshot, and is well known to the Postillions. If You could set out for Twyford on that day, We should have the pleasure of accompanying You the greatest part of your Journey. If You write on Wednesday I shall recieve your Letter here on Thursday; if afterwards I beg You will direct to me at H. Wilmots Esq. at Farnborough Place near Bagshot Surry. I have nothing to add but the kind Compliments of the Family and our hearty Wishes that no Philosophical or American Business may oblige You to write that You can not come. I am, Dear Sir, with the greatest Esteem, Your obligd and affectionate humble Servant   J. St. Asaph

Action of the New Jersey House, Council, and Governor Appointing Benjamin Franklin as Agent

Copies: American Philosophical Society

Hillsborough, as mentioned before, was insisting that colonial agents be appointed by the governor and both houses of the legislature. On this basis he had denied Franklin's credentials from Massachusetts in

day, presumably Dec. 13–17. In 1771 BF got home from his Irish and Scottish tour in late November. He had been invited to Twyford for Christmas (to DF above, Aug. 17), and on Dec. 14, below, he wrote the Bishop that press of business left him no hope of accepting, and sent his respects to Mr. Wilmot. The answer was oddly casual, if it was to this specific invitation; but we believe that it was.

10. Henry Wilmot was the solicitor for Thomas Penn and BF's predecessor as agent for New Jersey: above, XIV, 176 n; Kammen, *Rope of Sand*, p. 326. Wilmot mentioned his country estate, Farnborough Place near Aldershot, in a letter to Thomas Penn, July 24, 1771, Hist. Soc. of Pa.

January, and in June had forbidden the Governor of New Jersey to assent to any support bill that asserted the Assembly's sole right to appoint an agent.[11] William Franklin privately deplored this challenge, which would jeopardize the salaries of all public officials by plunging him into a squabble with the Assembly.[1] Publicly he promised to do his best, but pointed out that the lower house had long exercised the right of appointment in New Jersey and most of the other colonies.[2] Assemblymen assured him that he had no chance of persuading them to delete the offending clause; yet somehow, by working behind the scenes, he managed to do it. In December he reported his success to Whitehall in a tone of some surprise: a support bill had been passed in acceptable form.[3] All that remained was to appoint an agent in the same form, which was done in the resolutions below. In his agency for New Jersey, Benjamin Franklin's position was now above reproach.

New Jersey. House of Representatives, Wednesday Dec. 11th. 1771.

Resolved That Doctor Benjamin Franklin be, and he is hereby appointed, Agent of this Colony.

A true Extract from the Votes,

RICHD. SMITH[4] Clerk of Assembly.

New Jersey Council Chamber, Wednesday December 11th. 1771.

The House taking into Consideration the Necessity of having an Agent for this Colony in Great Britain,

Resolved That Doctor Benjamin Franklin be, and he is hereby appointed Agent for transacting the Affairs of this Colony in Great Britain.

A true Extract from the Votes.

CHA. PETTIT,[5] D Clk of the Council

New Jersey At a Council held at Burlington on Friday December 20th. 1771.

11. See the Hillsborough interview above, Jan. 16; 1 *N.J. Arch.*, x, 301.
1. WF to BF above, under Sept. 3.
2. 1 *N.J. Arch.*, x, 317.
3. *Ibid.*, pp. 320, 323.
4. For Smith (1735–1803), the brother of Samuel Smith, the historian, and the uncle of Joseph Smith, see the *DAB*.
5. Pettit (1736–1806), a merchant of Trenton and Philadelphia, had recently succeeded his brother-in-law, Joseph Reed, as deputy secretary of New Jersey and as clerk of the Council and of the Supreme Court; *ibid.*

Present[6]

His Excellency the Governor	JAMES PARKER Esqr.
CHARLES READ Esqr.	STEPHEN SKINNER Esqr.
JOHN STEVENS Esqr.	DANIEL COXE Esqr.
SAMUEL SMITH Esqr.	JOHN LAWRENCE Esqr.

The Resolves of the Council, and House of Assembly of the 11th. Instant, appointing Doctr. Benjamin Franklin Agent for this Colony, being laid before the Board, His Excellency, with the Advice of the Council, was pleased to give his Concurrence to the said Resolves.

A true Copy from the Minutes of the Privy Council.

CHA. PETTIT D Clk of the Council

Deed to Benjamin Franklin from Samuel and Hannah Parker[7]

Transcript: Department of Records, Recorder of Deeds, City of Philadelphia

⟨December 13, 1771. In 1741 Christopher and Mary Thompson deeded to Franklin a lot, with the reservation of an annual ground rent of £3 17s.[8] In 1759 Thompson bequeathed his real property to his daughter Sarah, wife of Alexander Parker, and upon her death to her four children in equal shares. In January, 1771, the

6. Three of the Council members in attendance have been identified above, as follows: Read, x, 313 n; Smith, iv, 209 n; Coxe, xiv, 300 n. John Stevens (c. 1715–92) was a prominent New York merchant and landowner in Hunterdon Co., N.J., and brother-in-law of William Alexander, who called himself Lord Stirling. James Parker (1725–97) was mayor of Perth Amboy, and Stephen Skinner was a former treasurer of the East Jersey Proprietors. John Lawrence, one of several of the name in the province, had been an assemblyman from Burlington. See 1 N.J. Arch., ix, 335 n, 446 n; x, 37 n, 302 n.

7. Not much seems to be known about them. Samuel Parker was a Quaker, who was censured by the Philadelphia Meeting in 1764 for taking arms to defend the city against the Paxton Boys. In 1765 he married Hannah George, who was apparently not a Quaker, for their marriage brought him again into trouble with the Meeting. He was a brass-founder of considerable reputation in Philadelphia. Geneal. Soc. of Pa. Pub., xiii (1941), 32, 212; 2 Pa. Arch., ii, 191; PMHB, xxii (1898), 259; xlvi (1922), 256; Henry J. Kauffman, American Copper & Brass [Camden, N.J., 1968], pp. 210–11.

8. See above, ii, 311.

four divided the real estate among themselves by quadripartite indenture, whereby the ground rent on the Franklin lot came to Samuel Parker, brass-founder. He and his wife Hannah, in return for a payment from Franklin of £64 3s. 4d. in Pennsylvania money, now discharge him and his heirs and assigns from all future ground rent. Signed by Samuel and Hannah Parker and witnessed by Matthew[9] and Mary Clarkson. Followed by Samuel Parker's receipt for the payment from Franklin, and separate acknowledgments of the deed by him and his wife before Matthew Clarkson, justice of the peace. Recorded March 10, 1812.⟩

From Grace Williams   ALS: American Philosophical Society

Honered and Dear Sir   Boston Decer 13 1771

I had the Pleasuer of your favor with my son Blesed be God we Recved him in good Helth and I hope Uncurrupted in his Morrals. In this my Prayers is answerd. I am obligd to his Frinds that advisd his Return tho he mant never Git a East India fortune he may do verry well and In my oppnion Great Richees never made the Poeseser a greater Wiser nor Haper man he Seams to Enter into Bussiness with the Gratest Dilegence and Cherfulness tho the town is ful of goods he hath no reason as yet to be discouragd. I Shall take Pleasure in asisting him all in my Power and I doubt not with Gods Blesing but he will be abele to do justes to his Crideters.[1]

Sir knowing you was allways fond of Fish I have Sent you by Capt. Acworth two half Barrells of Cod Sounds and Toungs[2] wich I beg your acceptance as a Small token of my Grattitude for the Great kindness you were Pleast to treat my Sons. I must Still beg you to Continue your Perternal care of that helpless Unfortunate youth my Dear Son Josiah I know it was best for him to Stay til he had accomplished the Design of his going but knowen his help-

9. Matthew Clarkson was a merchant connected with Baynton, Wharton & Morgan, and an early member of the APS; he later became mayor of Philadelphia. He had been associated with BF in 1765 in land speculation in Nova Scotia. William O. Sawtelle, "Acadia: the Pre-Loyalist Migration and the Philadelphia Plantation," *PMHB*, LI (1927), 273–4 n.

1. For young Jonathan's dream of an East India fortune and his return to Boston see his father to BF above, Aug. 5, Sept. 19.

2. The sound, or air bladder, of the cod was considered a great delicacy.

less Situation I cannot but be thoughtful and concernd for him tho I know he is in the Care of Such worthy Frinds wich will do all in thear Power for him.

I am very Hapey to hear that his Boy is of the Franklins lyne, I flatter my Self he will be teacheable and Honeast and fathful to his Master if So he will never want a frind at least while I live.[3] The Toyngs and Sounds must be Seockt [soaked] in warm water about one Houre then Peal of the black Skin Shift the water and Boyl them abought as Long as tha Wold Boyl an Egg Eat them with Melted Buter. I have the Honer to Subcrib my Self your Duteful Neas   G WILLIAMS

Aunt Mecm was hear yesterday and Sends her love to you and Mrs. Stvenson.

Benjaman Frnklin Esqr

Addressed: To | Doctr Benjamin Franklin | at Mrs Stevenson Cravenstreet | London

From Jonathan Williams, Sr.

ALS: American Philosophical Society

Honoured Sir,   Boston Decemr 13th 1771
The Inclos'd Letter from Mr. Thurston Will give Some Idea of the Situation of your money if Hall finely fails. Mr. Thurston Circumstances I am told are good tho it dose not appear Probable that the money will be Soon paid.[4] I am anxious for my Son Josiah Whose helpless Situation will we fear Render him too Troblesom to you and your Friends; as he is verry apt to grow Melancholy

3. The boy was Henry Walker (A.5.2.3.3.1.2), who by this time had just turned fifteen. He crossed the ocean with Josiah the following spring, and was apprenticed in Boston; Mrs. Williams, to his mother's relief, did keep her eye on him. Hannah Walker to BF, June 20, 1773, APS.

4. For Samuel Hall's debt, and his bondsman Edward Thurston, see Williams to BF above, Sept. 19. Thurston had recently tried to allay Williams' suspicions that Hall was on the verge of bankruptcy, had promised to try to collect £60 of the debt, and had begged for patience with the remainder. Thurston to Williams, Nov. 28, 1771, APS.

but musick and good Company must Divert him. The Bearer of this is Mr. John Maliquet Who was an Officer in the 29 But is now Left the Regiment and marred [married] our Neighbour and Friend Daughter; Speaker Cushing Neice,⁵ any Civilities Shall be greatfuly acknoledgd By your Dutyfull Nephew and most Oblig'd Humble Servant   JONA WILLIAMS

Aunt Mecom Dined with us this Day Desires me to Remember her Love to you &c. Our Love to our Son and Brother and Compliments to all Friends.

Addressed: To / Doctr Benjamin Franklin / at Mrs Stevensons Cravin Street / London / per favr of Mr Maliquet

From Jonathan Williams, Jr.

ALS: American Philosophical Society

Dear and honoured Sir   [December 13?, 1771⁶]
   The Bearer hereof Mr. John Milliquet, is my esteemed Friend and Intimate, and being particularly acquainted with Josiah, he will be happy to see him in London. Therefore hope you will pardon the Liberty I take of introducing him to You.
   Any Civilities shewn him will be esteemed a great Addition to the Obligation I am already under. I am Your dutifull and Affectionate Kinsman   J WILLIAMS JUNR

To Benja Franklin Esq

Addressed: To / Doct Benja Franklin / London

   5. Josiah was studying music with John Stanley, the organist and composer—the blind teaching the blind. John Melliquette had been commissioned as an ensign in the 29th in 1762, and had recently married Hannah Newman, the daughter of Henry and Margaret Fletcher Newman; Hannah's maternal aunt, Deborah, was Cushing's wife. See Worthington C. Ford, comp., *British Officers Serving in America, 1754–1774* (Boston, 1894), p. 71; *The Manifesto Church: Records of the Church in Brattle Square, Boston . . . 1699–1872* (Boston, 1902), pp. 144, 149, 172, 246–7; Thomas B. Peck, *The Bellows Genealogy . . .* (Keene, N.H., 1898), p. 188.
   6. So dated because of the preceding document, in which the bearer of this note is identified.

To Jonathan Shipley ALS: Yale University Library

London, Dec. 14. 1771.

Hearing that your Lordship had called in Cravenstreet during my Absence, I went next Day to your House[7] hoping to find the Family there, but was mortified with the Information of your being still at Twyford. I should have thank'd you before for your kind Letters in my favour to the Primate and Mr. Jackson.[8] The Primate was at Armagh, and did not come to Dublin 'till just as I was leaving it. He was however exceedingly polite, and condescended to honour me with his particular Notice in the House of Lords and at the Lord Lieutenant's;[9] but I could not accept his hospitable Invitations, being fully engag'd for the little time I had to stay, and my Fellow-traveller impatient to be gone on Account of pressing Business. In my Life I never saw People more earnestly desirous of obliging a Stranger, or more anxiously intent on showing Respect to a Recommendation, than the Jacksons and their Brother (a worthy Man) Mr. Philips. Yet I could but once afford myself the Pleasure of Dining with that agreable Family, being entangled with numerous Engagements in Town, and they live in the Country about 7 Miles from Dublin.[10] It is a handsome Seat, the Gardens and Fields belonging to the House very beautiful, as well as the surrounding Prospects. The House is well built, copied, one would think, from yours at Twyford, so similar is the Disposition of the Rooms, Stairs, Chimneys, &c. I will tell you more Particulars when I am happy in being with you, which is not likely to happen so soon as I wish'd and you kindly

7. His town house in Jermyn Street; see his note to BF below, under Jan. 25, 1772.

8. See Shipley to BF above, Aug. 13.

9. Viscount Townshend (1724–1807), Lord Lieutenant since 1767, had invited BF and Richard Jackson to dinner with a number of Irish dignitaries. This is BF's only mention of visiting the Irish House of Lords; for his reception by the House of Commons see his letters below to Cushing, Jan. 13, and to WF, Jan. 30, 1772.

10. We cannot positively identify Jackson; see Shipley to BF above, Aug. 13. If he was the Dean of Christ Church, Dublin, the others mentioned were presumably his wife and her brother; and the family might naturally have been living at Tallagh, the Archbishop's country seat six miles from town, for which see [Philip Luckombe], *A Tour through Ireland* . . . (London, 1780), pp. 47–8.

propose;[1] for having been absent twice as long as I intended, I find
my Business so accumulated, and such Heaps of Letters to answer,
that it will be scarce possible for me, with the greatest Diligence to
get through before the Meeting of Parliament. Be so good as to
accept my best Wishes of every kind of Felicity to you *and yours*,
and believe me ever, with the greatest Respect and Esteem, My
Lord, Your Lordship's most obliged humble Servant, B FRANKLIN

I had the Pleasure of hearing an exceeding good Character of
your Lordship Mrs. Shipley, and the younger Ladies, from an
old Man and Woman that keep your House at St. Asaph.[2]

Please to present my Respects to Mr. Wilmot.

Lord Bp. of St. Asaph.

From Sir John Pringle   AL: American Philosophical Society

⟨December 16, [1771], a note in the third person. Requests the
company of Franklin and Mr. "Beech"[3] at dinner next Wednesday at half past three.⟩

Agreement between Benjamin Franklin and Joseph Massie[4]   ADS: American Philosophical Society

⟨December 18, 1771, in Massie's hand. On December 22, 1770,
Franklin had received from him a collection of manuscripts,

1. See Shipley to BF above, Dec. 10. This reply was sent, we believe, to
Farnborough Place, where the Shipleys were visiting the Mr. Wilmot mentioned in the postscript.
2. The Bishop, according to the *DNB*, spent only a month of each year in
his diocese. BF and Jackson had sailed from Holyhead on Sept. 4, and had
obviously taken the northern route through Wales; St. Asaph is midway
between Denbigh and the sea.
3. Richard Bache had returned to London with BF from Preston.
4. Massie (*d.* 1784) had amassed by 1764 a collection of some fifteen hundred economic treatises, printed during the past two centuries. He had drawn
on these for his own prolific writings, which ranged in subject from taxes and
interest rates to sailors' wages and foundling hospitals; he was unusual among
economists of the day in his emphasis on the importance of agriculture and in
his compilation and use of statistics. *DNB*; William Cunningham, *The*

papers, and printed books on certain conditions, and had paid him sixty guineas therefor on certain conditions, enumerated in the receipts that were then exchanged.⁵ The present agreement is to extend the time for either or both parties to perform the conditions until June 24, 1772.⟩

From the New Jersey Assembly Committee of Correspondence

ls: American Philosophical Society

Sir   Burlington Decemr. 21st. 1771.

Your Letter of the 12th Feby has been received and laid before the House of Assembly who were of Opinion it would be proper not to push the farther Consideration of the Septennial Act until you see a favourable Opportunity to get it allowed.⁶ Respecting this Law as well as others that may hereafter come under Consideration of his Majestys Ministers we must Confide entirely in you as to the time most proper to sollicit a Confirmation of them, and make no doubt of your Exerting your Abilities and influence to bring them to a favourable determination and as Speedily as may be.

Growth of English Industry and Commerce ... (2 vols., Cambridge, 1890–92), II, 384–90, 426–7. In March, 1772, BF subscribed £3 3s. for Massie's "Charts of Commerce" and in August, 1773, paid him £5 5s. for "Military Papers"; in between he lent or paid him £23 2s.; Jour., pp. 40–1, 43, 50. In April and May, 1774 (p. 54), he charged Massachusetts £36 19s. 11d. for pamphlets, some of which Massie had written. Worthington Ford assumed that this agreement concerned the pamphlets: Mass. Hist. Soc. *Proc.*, LVI (1922–23), 97–9. We differ, because of the other payments and because, as late as 1778, BF inquired about MSS that he thought Massie still had: Matthew Ridley to BF, Nov. 24, 1778, APS.

5. BF's entry of the payment (Jour., p. 27) mentions only books. His receipt has been lost, and with it the conditions; but one of them might well have been delivery of the MSS and papers.

6. BF apparently never saw his opportunity, and the act was never confirmed. It provided, as its name implies, for elections to the Assembly every seven years. It had been passed in 1768, and the Committee of Correspondence had inquired rather casually about it in 1769. But the Board of Trade believed that the act merely provided for what had long been customary, and tabled it in July, 1770. *Votes, N.J.*, April–May, 1768, p. 13; 1 *N.J. Arch.*, x, 142–3; XVII, 478, 497–8; *Board of Trade Jour.*, 1768–75, p. 203; above, XVI, 254.

His Majesty having thought proper to Disallow the Act to erect Courts for the trial of Causes of Ten pounds and under, the Prosecution of Suits for the recovery of Debts were become so various that it necessarially became an Object of the attention of the Legislature; and when it was considered, that to Six pounds the mode of recovery was before Single Magistrates, from that Sum to Ten pounds a tedious and Expensive Mode by the Practice of Common Law from ten pounds to Fifty another Mode, and from thence by the Old and usual manner of recovery. The Assembly endeavour'd to remidy this, by bringing the determination of Causes, from Six to Ten pounds before the Justices in the County Court in a Short speedy and less expensive way which They hope will have the Effect designd, and be a Plan of making a Law more consonant to the Constitution upon the Expiration of the Six pounds Law than perhaps that or the Fifty pound Law are. By this Law the house apprehend that the Objections made against the late £10 Law, will be removed as they all rested on the first objection—To wit, *The Erecting New Courts which by being Vested in a single Magistrate with power to hold them as often as he thought proper, was Dangerous as well as unconstitutional.* And thereupon[?] most of the Objections Assigned by Mr. Jackson were founded. This Induced the House to fall upon a mode by which His and every reasonable Objection might be removed. Providing therefore against the first, by bringing Causes of Six pounds and under Ten, before known and Constitutional Courts, only, Rendering the Practice simple Cheap and Expeditious, they hope will obviate his first Objection, and every other drawn from it, and Induce his Majestys Ministers to approve of their Conduct and Advise the Confirmation of a Law so Salutary and necessary, or Permit it to Continue during its Limitation. When you consider the Objections made by Mr. Jackson the Expensive manner of recovering such small Debts, which this Law provides against; as well as the Intentions of the Legislature in passing it, your better Judgement will suggest to you Every argument in support of the Intentions and wishes of the House, and hope Mr. Jackson will, when he has this Law under his Consideration, be induced to give it a favourable report.[7]

7. The acts in question were parts of a legislative program to lower fees in the collection of debts, a matter that had been before the legislature for the past two years and more; see *ibid.* The act of 1769, pertaining to cases of £10

The Law to enable persons not Naturalized to hold Lands &c. we dont find has met with his Majestys Approbation, and as you are Silent about it we beg you will use your endeavours to have it passed. It is similar to One of New York to which the Royal Assent has been given, and Therefore we hope that the Royal favour will be extended also to those of his Subjects in this Colony that are in the same situation; many of them in the reign of Queen Ann settled in this Country during the War with France from the Palatine and being Ignorant of the Laws of England neglected to procure a Naturalization, and having acquired Estates: the same have descended to their Children, and have been Sold to Denizens who having never enquired wether such foreigners were Naturalized are in danger of loosing their Purchases. These reasons Induced the Assembly to pass the Law and they hope his Majesty will approve whenever the Equitable motives of the Legislature are Laid before him.[8] We desire you will endeavour it and enforce your Application by Every Argument your good Judgment will suggest. As to the Fifty pounds Law we are of Opinion that if his Majestys Ministers do not take it up, it will be best not to push it, but let it sleep in peace if possible.

We with pleasure inform you that the differences that have some time Subsisted between the House and Government touching the Subsistance of the Troops lately Quartered in the Colony, have been at this Session happily Settled. The Assembly have paid the Quartering of the Troops and as they are removed we hope all occasion of dispute on this Head will be removed for the future.[9]

and under, was disallowed in June, 1771. The new act replacing it was passed on the day this letter was written, and meanwhile the "Fifty Pound Law" had been passed in the spring of 1770. Both were limited in duration to five years, and both were allowed. See Samuel Allinson, ed., *Acts of the General Assembly of the Province of New-Jersey from 1702...to...1776* (Burlington, N.J., 1776), pp. 338–9, 366; *Board of Trade Jour.*, 1768–75, pp. 219–20; *Acts Privy Coun., Col.*, v, 309–11.

8. These acts in New Jersey and New York had been passed in 1770; their purpose was to abolish the requirement that naturalization should precede the legal purchase or inheritance of land. The New Jersey law, unlike the New York, contained no suspending clause; it was disallowed when the other was confirmed. See 1 *N.J. Arch.*, XVIII, 282–3; *Laws of New-York, from the Year 1691, to 1773 Inclusive* (2 vols., New York, 1774), II, 561; *Board of Trade Jour.*, 1768–75, pp. 237, 261; *Acts Privy Coun., Col.*, v, 320–1.

9. WF had had a long battle with the Assembly over the expenses of quar-

At the same time that we apologize for not writing to you for so long a time occasion'd by our distance from one another we are directed to return you the thanks of the House as well for your attention to the Concerns of the Colony as for your present to the House of the Senators Remembrancer.[1] We are, Sir with respect and Esteem Your most humble Servants

CORTD: SKINNER
AARON LEAMING
ABRM. HEWLINGS

Be pleased to Direct to C. Skinner or Jos. Smith. Thy Respectful Friend Jos SMITH[2]

As soon as the Votes and Laws are printed they shall be duly forwarded.

Doctr. Franklin

To John Canton

AL: The Royal Society

[December, 1771?[3]]

⟨An undated note in the third person. Business prevents Franklin from visiting him that afternoon as expected; Mr. Collinson,[4] who was to have come with him, is out of town. They will call instead next week.⟩

---

tering troops; the lower house had refused to pay as long as the crown refused to permit bills of credit or a loan office in the colony. After Gage, acting on Hillsborough's suggestion, withdrew the troops in the autumn, the Assembly agreed to pay the arrears due for quartering. See 1 *N.J. Arch.*, x, 321–3; John Shy, "Quartering His Majesty's Forces in New Jersey," N.J. Hist. Soc. *Proc.*, LXXVIII (1960), 91, 94; Edgar J. Fisher, *New Jersey as a Royal Province, 1738 to 1776* (New York, 1911), pp. 438–9.

1. For this odd work see Katherine French to BF above, Feb. 18.

2. The postscript is in Smith's hand. For him and the signers see above, XVI, 256 n. Skinner was no longer Speaker; he had vacated the position for reasons of health, and Stephen Crane had succeeded him. 1 *N.J. Arch.*, XVIII, 37, 186.

3. In the volume of Canton's papers this note follows BF's letter to him above, Aug. 15; its placing warrants a guess that it was written after that date, and it was obviously written before Canton's death the following March. From Aug. 25 until the end of November BF was absent on his tour of Ireland and Scotland; hence we are assigning the note to December as the earliest probable date.

4. Peter Collinson's only son, Michael.

To Mary Hewson

AL (incomplete?): American Philosophical Society

[Late 1771?5]

Voltaire in his *Questions sur l'Encyclopedie*, which I have been reading this Morning, gives Translations of several Greek Epigrams into French, to show that the latter Language was as capable of Correctness as the former. I had a mind to try if [I could] not render them more concisely in English, [but have] not succeeded; but you (or some of our *bouts-rimés*6) may, if you please to try; for I am confi[dent that the]English Language is denser than the French, else wh[at shall we make?] of Rosscommon's Assertion,

> The Weighty Bullion of one Sterling Line
> Drawn to French Wire would through whole Pages shine?7

So I send them for your Amusement at Bro[mley. You may] communicate them to Dolly if you write to h[er. Living in the?] Country she may want Amusement if you don't.

Addressed: Mrs Hewson8

5. The article BF had been reading is in *Questions sur l'Encyclopédie par des amateurs*... (9 vols., [Geneva], 1770–72), V, 220–5. The publication of the fifth volume in 1771 fixes the earliest date when this note could have been written. The MS is badly torn; we have conjecturally supplied BF's missing words, and have silently completed the quotation from the original.

6. Rhymed word endings of lines, from which a versifier fills in the rest of the lines; hence by extension the versifier himself.

7. Wentworth Dillon, Earl of Roscommon, "An Essay on Translated Verse," in *Poems by the Earl of Roscomon*... (London, 1717), p. 9.

8. Above the address BF has penciled another quotation:

> Venus take my votive Glass.
> Since I am not what I was,
> What I from this Day shall be,
> Venus, let me never see.

This is a slight amendment of Matthew Prior, *Poems on Several Occasions* (London, 1766), p. 75.

Remarks on Agriculture and Manufacturing

AD: Yale University Library[9]

These comments, although they have been assigned to an earlier date,[1] were in fact upon a chapter in the anonymous *Considerations on the Policy, Commerce and Circumstances of the Kingdom* (London, 1771).[2] In that chapter the author argues that agriculture and the trade in provisions to which it gives rise have never materially enriched a country and never will. This was orthodox mercantilist doctrine, which favored industry and commerce over the produce of the soil. But it conflicted with Franklin's developing conviction, that agriculture, like the earth for Antaeus, was the fundamental source of America's economic strength.[3]

[Late 1771?]
Remark on Chap XI. of the Considerations on Policy, Trade, &c.

Suppose Husbandry well understood and thoroughly practised in a Country, and all the Lands fully cultivated:

Those employ'd in the Cultivation will then raise more Corn and other Provisions than they can consume.

But they will want Manufactures.

Suppose Each Family may make all that is necessary for itself.

Then the Overplus Corn must be sold and exported.

Farms near the Sea or navigable Rivers may do this easily. But those distant will find it difficult. From some the Expence of Carriage will exceed the Value of the Commodity. Therefore if Some other Means of making an Advantage of it are not discovered, the Cultivator will abate of his Labour and raise no more than he can consume in his Family.

But tho' his Corn may not bear the Expence of Carriage to Market, nor his Flax nor his Wooll, yet possibly Linnen and Woollen Cloth may bear it. Therefore if he can draw around him working

---

9. Interleaved in a bound volume of BF's correspondence with Bishop Shipley, which began in 1771.

1. By Lewis J. Carey in *Franklin's Economic Views* (Garden City, N.Y., 1928), p. 144; he believed that the comments were among BF's earliest expressions of the physiocratic views that he had imbibed from his French acquaintances.

2. We are deeply grateful to Professor Joseph Dorfman, of Columbia University, for drawing our attention to this work.

3. See for example above, XVI, 107–9.

People who have no Lands on which to subsist, and who will for the Corn and other Subsistence he can furnish them with, work up his Flax and Wooll into Cloth, then is his Corn also turn'd into Cloth, and with his Flax and Wooll render'd portable, so that it may easily be carry'd to Market, and the Value brought home in Money. This seems the chief Advantage of Manufactures.

For, Those working People seldom receive more than a bare Subsistence for their Labour; and the very Reason why Six penny Worth of Flax is worth perhaps twenty Shillings after they have wrought it into Cloth, is, that they have during the Operation consum'd nineteen Shillings and sixpence worth of Provision.

So that the Value of Manufactures arises out of the Earth, and is not the Creation of Labour as commonly supposed.4

When a Grain of Corn is put into the Ground it may produce ten Grains: After defraying the Expence, here is a real Increase of Wealth. Above we see that Manufactures make no Addition to it, they only change its Form. So Trade, or the Exchange of Manufactures, makes no Increase of Wealth among Mankind in general; no more than the Game of Commerce at Cards makes any Increase of Money among the Company, tho' particular Persons may be Gainers while others are Losers. But the clear Produce of Agriculture is clear additional Wealth.

From Johann Reinhold Forster5

ALS: American Philosophical Society

Sir   No 2. Sommerset house Stable Yard [late 1771?6]

Having lately translated Prof: Kalm's travels through North America, Bossu's travels through Louisiana, and published a Catalogue of North-American Animals, with another of American

4. BF is here responding to a specific passage, pp. 95–6: "Six-pennyworth of ore, from a mine, may be wrought into curious manufactures to the value of twenty guineas, and of course furnish, from skill and labour, what will support a numerous...family for the better part of a year. The same may be said in a greater degree with regard to flax."

5. For Forster see above, xv, 147–8.

6. Or possibly January, 1772. All the books mentioned in it were published in 1771, and early the next February BF forwarded this letter to the APS: BF to Bond below, Feb. 5, 1772.

plants, and a Centuria of new Insects, not described by Dr. Linnaeus, many of which are Americans; and flattering myself that these publications contain materials not altogether unworthy of the Attention of the learned and curious in America: I take the liberty by Your means, to present the Society for promoting useful knowledge established at Philadelphia in Pensilvania with a Set of the abovementioned works;[7] hoping the Society will be pleased to consider them as a small token of the esteem and due regard with which I am Sir Your most obedient humble Servant

JOHN REINHOLD FORSTER.

Addressed: To Benjamin Franklin Esqr. / President of the Philosophical / Society for promoting useful / knowledge established in / Pensylvania / in *Craven-Street* / *Strand*

Endorsed: John Reinhold Forster

Donations Transn. Kalms Travels N A Do Bossu's—Do Louisiana American Plants Centuria of Insects no

From [Jonathan Shipley]   AL: American Philosophical Society

[1771–75[8]]
⟨Jermyn Street, Wednesday morning, in the third person. Invites Franklin to dinner next Monday.⟩

7. The works that the APS received were Peter Kalm, *Travels into North America...* (3 vols., Warrington and London, 1770–71); Jean Bernard Bossu, *Travels through That Part of North America Formerly Called Louisiana...* (2 vols., London, 1771); and Forster's *A Catalogue of the Animals of North America...* (London, 1771), *Flora Americae Septentrionalis; or a Catalogue of the Plants of North America...* (London, 1771), and *Novae species insectorum: Centuria I...* (London, 1771).

8. BF's friendship with the Shipleys appears to have begun in 1771, and we are therefore printing the invitation under the earliest likely date.

Index

Compiled by Mary L. Hart and Joy G. Sylvester

Customs commissioners, taxation of, in Mass., xxvi, 174–5, 177–9, 190

Dalrymple, Capt., I. Garrigues ships with, 21

Dalrymple, Alexander: identified, 214 n; BF's introduction to pamphlet by, 214–17

Dan River, N.C., mentioned, 40

Dartmouth, Lord: and alleged BF-Lee conspiracy, 120 n

Deane, Gen. William, sends greetings, 37; promoted, 37 n

Deane, Mrs. William: on *Poor Richard*, 37; letter from, 37

DeBerdt, Dennys: and efforts to repeal Stamp Act, 10; Mass. House agent, 10, 11, 13, 27, 153 n; Mass. salary, 242 n

DeBerdt, Dennys, Jr., mentioned, 27

Debts: BF on payment of, 194; N.J. acts on collection of (1769, 1770), 269, 270 n

Defoe, Daniel, *A Tour through...Great Britain*, 67

De Lancey, Peter, killed in S.C. duel, 235 n

Delaware River, mentioned, 248 n

Denny, Gov. William, Pa. Assembly rewards, 124 n

Derbyshire, Eng., BF and party visit, 114, 116, 190 n

Description of the Empire of China... (du Halde), mentioned, 189 n

Dessin, Pierre, Hotel d'Angleterre proprietor, 107 n

Devil's Arse, 114

Devonshire, Duchess of, mentioned, 200 n

Diderot, Denis, *Encyclopédie...*, 17, 69, 117–18

Dispensations Act (1534), quoted, 150–2

Dissenters: in Rowan Co., N.C., 41, 46; and election of Anglican vestry (N.C.), 42 n; and N.C. Regulators, 48; and N.C. tax, 49; and Anglican support of dissenting clergy, 54; in London, 54; bill on burial of, in Savannah, 172. *See also* Presbyterians

Dissertatio...[de Hydrope] (Tilton), Bond on, 166 n

Dissertatio...de sitis in febribus... (Elmer), dedicated to BF, 166 n

Dissertation on the Use of the Negative Sign in Algebra (Maseres), for Harvard Lib., 30

Dixon, John, and search for Elia. Holland, 157 n

Dobbs, Gov. Arthur: and Scotch Irish settlers in N.C., 40; mentioned, 41

Doctrina particularum linguae graecae (Hoogeveen), for Harvard Lib., 30, 138

Dog Tavern (London), mentioned, 59

Dorchester, Mass., taxes customs commissioners, 190

Downes, Jonathan, illness of, 195

Drage, Theodorus Swaine: ordination of, 38; N.C. Anglican mission, 38–9; death, 39; Tryon supports, 40 n; recommends Rintleman, Layerly, 49–50; and N.C. Lutherans, 50 n; *The Great Probability of a Northwest Passage*, 75 n; letter from, 38–50

Dropsy, Bond's treatment of, 166

Drummond, Agatha. *See* Kames, Agatha Drummond

Dublin, BF visits, 85. *See also* Ireland

Du Halde, Jean Baptiste, *A Description of the Empire of China...*, 189 n

Duke of Cumberland (ship), mentioned, 157

Dumas, Charles-Guillaume-Frédéric: book for Lib. Co., 61; teaches Dutch students, 61; translates Anderson work on commerce, 61; wants *Pa. Gaz.*, 62; letter from, 61–2

Dunbar, David, and eastern Maine land grants, 141

Dunkers. *See* Ephrata Community

Dunmore, Lord: and Va. objections to Walpole Co., 75 n; salary as N.Y. governor, 149; Va. governor, 197; tours Lake Champlain, 197

Du Pont de Nemours, Pierre Samuel, edits *Ephémérides*, 111 n

Durrach, David, mentioned, 98

Dutens, L., translates d'Esprie work, 34 n

Dye, BF wants recipe for, 187

Earl of Halifax (ship), 238 n

Edinburgh: "Society of Gentlemen" in, 62–3 n; BF visits, 236, 239, 241

Edinburgh, University of: and degree for Marchant, 146 n; medical studies at, 165

Education, of Negroes, 53 n

Edward I, mentioned, 114

Edward, Duke of Kent, mentioned, 118 n

Egerton, Francis. *See* Bridgewater, Duke of

Elastic gum: for BF, 110; for J. Williams, Jr., 110 n

Eleanor, Queen of England, Northampton memorial to, 114

Electricity, experiments and theories on: BF's, 19, 110, 229–30; Henly's, 19–20, 182, 183; Beccaria's, 110; Priestley's, 181 n, 230; Canton's, 182; Kinnersley's, 182; graphite in, 182; gold, silver, and iron in, 182. *See also* Conductors; Electrometer; Leyden jar; Lightning

Electrometer, Henly's, 19, 182, 230 n

Stevens, John, on N.J. Council, 262
Stevenson, Margaret: birth of grandson of, 91; gloves for, 162; sends greetings, 162, 186, 237, 239; "honest trade" of, 237, 238 n; R. Bache visits, 237 n, 252 n, 257, 258; "regimen" of, 238, 253; mentioned, 16, 100, 105, 197, 221, 244, 257, 264
Stewart, Duncan: trip to England, 5; recommended to BF, 5
Stewart, John, *The Senator's Remembrancer*, 36, 38
Stiegel, Henry William, Mannheim glass factory of, 254 n
Stiles, Ezra: recommends Marchant, 145; on Marchant's character, 145–6; and honorary degrees, 145 n; letter from, 144–7
Stiles, Joseph, signs Tradesmen's letter, 250
Stirling, Lord, mentioned, 262 n
Stirling, Capt. Walter, N. Biddle recommended to, 84 n
Story, William: and N. Wheelwright bankruptcy, 223–4; recommended: to BF, 223–4, to Hillsborough, Bernard, A. Lee, 223 n; losses of, in Boston stamp riot compensated, 224
Strahan, Margaret (Peggy), mentioned, 236
Strahan, Mrs. Margaret Penelope, mentioned, 162, 251
Strahan, William: warns WF on BF-ministerial relations, 65; prints Robertson book, 67; and Walpole Co. petition, 75 n; and books for Lib. Co., 117; on BF's inactivity, 119; J. Read's debt to, 194; and BF-Hume friendship, 236 n; and books for Parker, 240; letters to, 236, 250–1; mentioned, 12, 162
Stucco, 33
Suffren, Baillie de, mentioned, 88 n
Sugar, tax on, 26 n
Sun spots: seen from London, 31; Marshall's observations on, sent to BF, 255
Susquehannah River, proposed canal to Schuylkill from, 94
Sutton Coldfield, Eng., BF and party visit, 116
Swietan, Dr. Gerhard van, and Vienna medical reform, 165
Symmes, Thomas, bill of exchange by, 196, 221

Tabulae motuum solis et lunae... (Mayer), for Winthrop, 30
Tahiti: government, religion, customs of, 209–10; Venus transit observed from, 209 n
Tallagh, Ireland, mentioned, 266 n

Taxation, colonial: of customs commissioners and other royal officials in Mass., xxvi, 174–5, 177–9, 190; assemblies' right of, 27; and N.C. Regulators, 45 n; in N.J., 135; in Mass. charter, 150, 174–5, 178–9; of rateable estates in Mass. towns, 241
Taxation, Parliamentary: views on right of, 26–7, 122, 147, 148, 152, 173, 178, 179; of sugar, molasses, tea, 26 n, 29, 147, 152; and colonial assemblies, 27; as possible cause of future colonial independence, 102–3; and salaries of colonial officials, 125. *See also* Townshend Acts
Taxation without representation, colonial views on, 147
Tea: nonimportation of, 3 n; tax retained on, 26 n, 29, 66, 147, 152
Telescope: Galilean and achromatic, for Harvard, 30; Small's experiments on, 199
Telfair, Edward, mentioned, 52
Temple, John, and N. Wheelwright debt, 224
Tenants, Pa. act on distraining (1770), 79
Terence, quoted, 215 n
Terrick, Robert, Bishop of London: aids N.C. Lutherans, 50 n; and C. Winter's ordination, 53
Thompson, Christopher and Mary, deed to BF, 262
Thompson, John, and clocks for BF, 191
Thomson, Charles: and organization of tradesmen, 250 n; mentioned, 17, 129 n
Thorne, William, secretary of Tradesmen's Committee, Phila., 250
Thurston, Edward, and S. Hall debt, 219, 264
Tickell, Mrs. Mary, mentioned, 100
Tiles, for flooring, 33 n
Tilton, James, *Dissertatio*... [*de Hydrope*], 166 n
Timothy, Peter: on S.C. dispute over Wilkes' fund, 233–4; letter from, 233–5
Todd, Miss: and BF trip to Walthamstow, 177; letter from, 177
Todd, Anthony: and rumors about J. Foxcroft, 8; invites BF and others to visit, 66, 133, 177 n; in Walpole Co., 66 n; flour for, 132–3; country home, 132 n; letter from, 66; letter to, 132–3
Todd, Eleanor, mentioned, 177 n
Tour through...Great Britain (Defoe): Rivington prints, 67; type for, 67
Townshend, Viscount, BF dines with, 266 n
Townshend Acts: partial repeal of, xxv, 26 n, 29, 66, 147, 152; efforts to repeal, 9, 129; Mass. circular letter against (1768), 51 n; amount of duty collected